Education and Society 1500–1800

Themes in British Social History

edited by Dr J. Stevenson

* The Gentry: the Rise and Fall of a Ruling Class   *G. Mingay*
  The English Family 1450–1700
  The Englishman's Health: Disease and Nutrition 1500–1700
* A social History of Medicine   *F. Cartwright*
* Education and Society 1500–1800; the Social Foundations of
    Education in Early Modern Britain   *R. O'Day*
  Religion and Society in Tudor and Stuart England
  Poverty and English Society 1500–1660
  Crime in Early Modern England 1550–1750
  The Labouring Classes in Early Industrial England
* The Press and Society from Caxton to Northcliffe   *G. A.*
    Cranfield
* Popular Disturbances in England 1700–1870   *J. Stevenson*
  Population and Society 1750–1940
* Religion and Society in Industrial England   *A. D. Gilbert*
* Before the Welfare State: Social Administration in Early
    Industrial Britain 1780–1850   *U. Henriques*
* The Army and Society 1815–1914   *E. M. Spiers*
* Leisure and Society 1830–1950   *J. Walvin*
* Sex, Politics and Society: the Regulation of Sexuality since 1800
    J. Weeks
  Crime and Criminal Policy in England 1878–1978
  The Press and Society in Britain since Northcliffe

* already published

Education and Society 1500–1800

The social foundations of education in early modern Britain

Rosemary O'Day

Longman
London and New York

Longman Group Limited
Longman House
Burnt Mill, Harlow, Essex, UK

*Published in the United States of America
by Longman Inc., New York*

First published 1982

British Library Cataloguing in Publication Data

O'Day, Rosemary
  Education and society 1500–1800. – (Themes in
  British social history)
  1. Education – England – History
  I. Title   II. Series
  370′.942   LA631

  ISBN 0-582-48917-2
  ISBN 0-582-48918-0 Pbk

Library of Congress Cataloging in Publication Data

O'Day, Rosemary.
  Education and society, 1500–1800.

  (Themes in British social history)
  Bibliography: p.
  Includes index.
  1. Educational sociology – Great Britain – History.
I. Title.   II. Series.
LC189.03   370.19′0941   81-17150
ISBN 0-582-48917-2   AACR2
ISBN 0-582-48918-0 (pbk.)

Printed in Singapore by
The Print House (Pte) Ltd.

To Alan and Andrew with love

Contents

List of Abbreviations

Arch. J.	*Archaeological Journal*
Agr. H. Rev.	*Agricultural History Review*
A.U.R.	*Aberdeen University Review*
B.I.H.R.	*Bulletin of the Institute of Historical Research*
B.J.E.S.	British Journal of Educational Studies
B.L.	British Library
C.J.	*Commons Journals*
C.U.L.	Cambridge University Library
D.N.B.	*Dictionary of National Biography*
E.D.R.	Ely Diocesan Records
E.E.T.S.	Early English Text Society
E.H.R.	*English Historical Review*
G.C.L.	Gloucester City Library
G.D.R.	Gloucester Diocesan Records
G.L.M.S.	Guildhall Library MSS
H.C.Q.	*History of Childhood Quarterly*
H.J.	*Historical Journal*
H.L.Q.	*History of Law Quarterly*
J.B.S.	*Journal of British Studies*
J.E.H.	*Journal of Ecclesiastical History*
J.H.I.	*Journal of the History of Ideas*
L.J.R.O.	Lichfield Joint Record Office
N.L.W.	National Library of Wales
N.R.O.	Northampton Record Office
P.R.O.	Public Record Office
P. & P.	*Past and Present*
Q.S.R.	Quarter Sessions Rolls
S.R.	*Statutes of the Realm*
S.R.O.	Staffordshire County Record Office.
T.B.G.A.S.	*Transactions of the Bristol and Gloucester Archaeological Society*
T.R.H.S.	*Transactions of the Royal Historical Society*
U.B.H.J.	*University of Birmingham Historical Journal*
V.C.H.	*Victoria County History*
V.E.	*Valor Ecclesiasticus*
W.S.L.	William Salt Library, Stafford
W.P.P.C.C.	Will proved, Prerogative Court of Canterbury

Glossary

Act	Ceremony conferring degrees in the University of Oxford.
Barristers	Members of the Inns of Court who were admitted to their Inn's Bar, and thereby also allowed to practise in the central courts of Westminster. Sometimes also referred to as utter barristers or apprentices.
Commencement	Ceremony conferring degrees in the University of Cambridge.
Determination	Final stage of a student's university disputation in which the moderator or determiner decided the question and apportioned praise or blame.
Diocese	District under pastoral and administrative care of a bishop.
Disputation	Organised, formal debate which all undergraduates were expected to perform before graduation.
Exercises	General term covering the activities which students were required to perform before graduation by the universities. The chief of these exercises were the disputations which were required of the student at various points in his academic career.
Induction and institution	Admission of cleric to the temporalities and spiritualities of an ecclesiastical living.
Inner barrister	A student at the Inns of Court who sat outside the bar of that court.
Reader or bencher	Rank in internal hierarchy of Inns of Court to which utter barristers aspired. Admission was, until the reign of Charles II, regulated according to seniority and the delivery of Lenten and August Readings. From the bench of the Inn were selected Serjeants-at-Law and Judges.

Acknowledgements

In writing this book my chief debt has been to my students in the Honors Program of the University of Maryland, College Park, who for two semesters studied the nature of the relationship between education and specific societies. They helped me to clarify my own thoughts on this issue and forced me to present the material more clearly.

Research for the book was greatly facilitated by the generosity of the Woodrow Wilson International Center for Scholars, Washington, DC. During the academic year 1978–79 I took up a fellowship therein to study the origins of the professions and their professionalisation in early modern England and Virginia. Part of the results of my research in this area appears in this study in the form of three chapters which treat the clergy, the barristers and the teachers of sixteenth- and seventeenth century England.

My debts to other historians are numerous – too numerous to be mentioned individually. I thank the following scholars in particular: Professor Elizabeth Eisenstein of the University of Michigan, Ann Arbor; Professor Hilda Smith of the University of Maryland, College Park; Professor Jo Ann Moran of Georgetown University, Washington, DC; Professor David Cressy of Pitzer College, Claremont, California; Professor Esther Cope of the University of Nebraska, Lincoln; and Professor Daniel Hirschberg of the University of Pennsylvania, Philadelphia. The staffs of libraries and record offices in both England and the United States have offered me considerable and welcome assistance. I thank especially the staff of the Folger Shakespeare Library, Washington, DC. I wish also to express my gratitude to Dr Ann Hughes of the University of Manchester for her help on various points.

The editor of this series, Dr John Stevenson, has given me much help and encouragement in preparing the book for publication and for this I thank him.

My parents, the Rev. and Mrs T. H. Brookes, have always supported me, encouraged me and shown an interest in my research and writing. I am especially sad at this time that my father did not live to see this book published. I thank him and my mother for all that they have done for me.

My husband, Dr Alan O'Day, has been constantly helpful. He has read the typescript several times and has subjected it to severe criticism of a very constructive nature. The faults which remain in the book certainly are not attributable to him, but he should take credit for such virtues as it may possess. Andrew, our son, helped considerably with the preparation of the typescript, by reading and checking that the footnotes were in correct sequence. Both Alan and Andrew have tolerated the inconveniences which accompany preoccupation with a book manuscript – a model of tidiness has not been presented to our son! I thank them both again and dedicate this book to them.

This publication was prepared under a grant from the Woodrow Wilson International Center for Scholars, Washington, DC. The statements are those of the author and are not necessarily those of the Wilson Center.

Introduction

The history of the sixteenth and seventeenth centuries in Britain, as it has been written in the years since the Second World War, seems to be preoccupied with the idea of the watershed. According to one writer, for example, the sixteenth century witnessed a revolution in government – the beginning of the modern, centralised and bureaucratic state. For others the period is primarily notable as that of an economic revolution – a commercial revolution; the coming of capitalist society. For still others, it is important as the period in which the laity came to assert their dominance in the life of the Christian Church – constituting a religious revolution of no small dimension. Not surprisingly, this concept of the early modern period as an age of radical change and, incidentally, of preparation for the modern world, simply begged for an educational revolution. If there was a revolution in government, for example, then surely there must have been radical changes in educational provision to accommodate this development and alterations in curriculum to ensure that the lay bureaucracy was adequately manned.

The required revolution was provided in 1964 by Lawrence Stone, who wrote a seminal article, published in *Past and Present*, entitled quite simply 'The Educational Revolution'. In this article the author charted a numerical revolution in both elementary and higher education. More youths partook in institutionalised higher education in the early part of the seventeenth century than at any time until the late nineteenth century. The upper and middle classes in society encouraged the spread of schooling and opened up its benefits to the classes below them. They had faith that education, controlled by an élite, would bring about a betterment of society. The popularity of such a view was enhanced by the conviction among Protestants that all people should be able to read the Word of God, whatever their social station. Disillusionment came only with the civil wars and the ensuing troubles, which made it clear that a little learning was socially disruptive and did not bring harmony to the commonwealth. In constructing his thesis, Lawrence Stone drew considerably upon the work of J. H. Hexter on the English aristocracy's attitude to education and on Mark Curtis's study of the universities of Oxford and Cambridge during the reigns of the Tudors and the Early Stuarts. Later writings, notably Wilfrid Prest's thorough study of the Inns of Court, Louis Knafla's article on the matriculation revolution, and Joan Simon's work both on Tudor education in general and on the social composition of the Cambridge student body in particular, have sometimes taken issue with Stone on matters of detail but have contributed to his general thesis that the years 1540 to 1640 witnessed an educational revolution of magnitude.

During the 1970s, however, some historians began to urge that the early modern period was as much an era of continuity as of change. And the educational revolution itself was questioned. Notable among the attacks have been the works of David Cressy and of Elizabeth Russell.

In this book I have endeavoured not to become bogged down by this question of 'revolution' as such but, none the less, to examine the case for regarding education as a force for change or for stability in early modern society.

In the past historians of education have often subconsciously approached their task from the perspective of the present, for students of education have always sought to find in history the origins of modern educational theory and practice. While such an approach has its virtues, many other more important historical questions are neglected by preoccupation with this line of inquiry. One historian argued that 'after Locke, the education of the child increasingly' became 'social rather than religious', 'its aim was social, to equip the child with accomplishments that would secure for it gainful employment'. In other words, in the eighteenth century 'education for society became paramount'. But this assessment is indeed misleading. Education was always conceived of as a social tool. To take the view that 'education for society' was an eighteenth-century concept would be to engage in historical myopia, born of a conviction that 'society' does not exist until it is freed from the pervasion of religious views. As we shall see, sixteenth- and seventeenth-century attitudes towards education were no less utilitarian in their way than those of the eighteenth century. What seems to have differed is the definition of *what* is useful. The real issue is surely whether education was thought of as functioning as a conservative agent within society or as a force for radical change at any given moment in time.

The historian of education must examine the relationship between education and society at a number of different levels. It is not enough to describe official attitudes towards education; to give the views of educational theorists; to count the number of schools or even the number of pupils. The general issue of the function of education in society raises myriad sub-questions. Clearly it is important to gauge the impact of theory upon practice; to assess the balance between conservative and advanced views of the educational process; to estimate the absorption of contemporaries with formal channels of education; and to suggest the social effects of particular educational developments. But more than this is necessary. Social, economic, political, religious and cultural developments shape a society's thinking about educational provision and curriculum. They act upon education; they are acted upon by education. To study the history of education without seeing it in this broader context of interaction is to lay the way open for gross misunderstanding of the subject.

In my attempt to discuss the interaction between education and society I have adopted a topical layout. The reader will find here chapters discussing the place of children and youth in family and society; literacy; curriculum and method; the universities of Oxford and Cambridge; certain of the learned professions; education after the Restoration; education in Scotland; the education of girls; the treatment of the poor; and the extent to which the system adapted itself to the needs of a new commercial society.

But this is not intended as a general textbook. In selecting the subjects touched on I have attempted as wide a coverage as possible but, first and foremost, all the chapters serve the main aim of the book. In some way, each chapter contributes to our understanding of the function of education within society and of the manner in which contemporaries regarded that function. While it has not been possible to mention all educational theories of the period or to list examples of every type of school or every teaching method, I have tried by this approach to indicate that education was viewed in different ways by particular groups and individuals. We should avoid the temptation of stamping all sixteenth-century Englishmen as optimistic or all seventeenth-century men as pessimistic in their attitude to education and its potential. There are dangers, of course, in stressing the infinite variety of human experience at any one point in time. Every attempt has been made to guard against such dangers by trying where possible to assess the balance and to estimate the numerical or class strength of a particular viewpoint or practice.

My preoccupation with the central issue of the role of education in society dictated the choice of some topics rather than others. To achieve the purpose of the book, it was essential that each topic be treated in considerable depth. This meant that some important subjects were given scant attention or totally neglected. I am painfully aware, for example, that the book does not do justice to the proud educational tradition of Scotland. Lack of space meant that I could not treat the subject adequately in its own right and I chose to use Scotland as a complementary study of the relationship between education and social change in a society very different from that of England. Similarly, I have not discussed the development of scientific or mathematical education other than in the context of the emerging commercial society of the eighteenth century. And the absence of a chapter on the medical profession is regrettable. A painful decision was made to exclude consideration of the attorneys from the chapter on the education of lawyers, despite a burgeoning literature on the subject.

My interest in the methodological problems involved in identifying periods of historical change will also become evident in the first chapters of the book. It is, for example, only too easy to see the later sixteenth century as a period of educational revolution if we totally ignore the educational history of the later Middle Ages. In those chapters which deal with the sixteenth and early seventeenth centuries I have tried to bring together some of the evidence which suggests points of continuity with the recent past and to indicate alternative interpretations for the so-called educational revolution of the period 1560–1640.

Finally, I hope that the present book will perform a useful function in bringing together the disciplines of the history of education and social history by making it abundantly clear that the one is comprehended by the other. For those today who see education as a dispensable trimming on the tree of civilised society, it may help a little to demonstrate the function of education in society and to underline the intricacy of the interaction between the two. The history of education must be brought in from the cold.

Chapter 1

Children and childhood

The commonplace belief in historical circles that the sixteenth and seventeenth centuries saw a deep-rooted educational revolution seems to demand a parallel belief in a revolution in attitudes to childhood. The debate which rages concerning the existence of a clearly marked history of childhood is usefully seen as a part of that wider debate between those who see the pre-industrial past as similar to the present in many respects and readily comprehensible to the modern mind, and those who see it as truly a world which we have lost, which we have to struggle to recapture and understand and which was revolutionised into a recognisably modern world sometime during the period 1450 to 1800.

On the one hand, one might feel that childhood and adolescence are unchanging characteristics of the human condition – that parents have always had similar relationships with and attitudes towards their children and that their role within the family has remained constant. Human emotion is an unchanging factor in history.

Yet, if there is social change, the implication is that the attitudes and behaviour of individuals have also altered, however subtly and gradually. Where we can detect changes in education we should be able to discern changes in attitudes towards the place of children in the family and in society as a whole.

Concepts of childhood and youth

Philippe Ariès has argued that there was no concept of childhood as a separate and distinctive phase in the life of man in the Middle Ages and that it developed gradually and unevenly. Medieval culture was a young culture and, by implication, an unsophisticated one. Similarly, the economy was a relatively simple one. People of all ages shared in the same games and pastimes. And, after the age of infancy, every able person was expected to contribute to the economic well-being of the household. There was relatively little emphasis upon the rights of any individual. There was little or no privacy.[1]

There is at least a case for arguing that changes in attitude to the needs of children and youth were a feature of accelerated change in the western economies. The unmistakable trend towards specialisation in the English economy during the period 1450–1800 meant that parents and masters were not always able to prepare youth for the work which was required of them. Some system was required which would be *in loco parentis* in this respect. In the late fifteenth and sixteenth centuries, also, members of the English upper and upper middle classes become convinced that their ability to fulfil a God-given role in society was in part dependent upon a theoretical preparation for life, acquired through the pursuit of a very specific curriculum of study in the classics and religion which would be accomplished early in life. Out of increasing economic specialisation and English Renaissance social theory grew a heavier reliance upon pre-existing forms of apprenticeship and schooling.

Parents and children were exposed to the idea that, while God might call each man to his vocation, that vocation was to be discovered in man's natural aptitude as well as his social position. Theorists such as William Perkins were in the 1590s meeting directly the potential conflict posed by vocational 'choice' in adulthood and the need for educational preparation in adolescence. While the vocational options open to boys from specific social groups were much more limited than is today the case, parents who had before them the problem of providing for a number of sons and daughters were eager to guarantee the future with an appropriate education for each child. The decision was an economic one in more senses than one.[2]

Simultaneously the life style of the English household was undergoing certain changes. There was a marked drift toward town living during the period 1500 to 1800. Whereas in 1600 some 7.9 per cent of the total English population lived in towns of over 5,000 people, by 1700 the percentage had risen to 16.2. The total number of people living in anything which might be termed 'a town' was probably in the region of 22 per cent by 1700. In the environment of even a small town, the medieval kinship group or clan had less place. The disintegrative effect of urban life upon such medieval forms seems clear, even if we accept that the town could be a force for integration in other ways. The architecture of the urban house changed as a response to the demands of work and society. Townspeople actually lived in their houses and spent money on furnishing them with luxuries. Housekeeping became a reality. The town house accommodated the need for increased individual privacy and for a sharper distinction between living and work space. These were not new features but their importance was heightened by the drift to the towns. The household was also, after the Reformation, thrown back upon itself culturally to an increasing degree. Individual reading and family activities tended to replace those based on the whole community,

the church and the guilds. The father's responsibility for the religious education of his family underlined this emphasis on the life of
the individual household.[3]

In English society as a whole, the emphasis of the Tudor and
Stuart state upon the family unit as an agency was also important
although the position was never simple.[4]

Differing patterns of childhood

Conditions were ripe, therefore, for the development of childhood
and youth as distinct phases in the life of man or woman. We must
beware, however, of either assuming that such phases were recognised and precisely defined immediately or that a homogeneous pattern emerged throughout England and Wales. For example, it seems
clear that a concept of girlhood did not develop as fast as a concept
of boyhood. And childhood scarcely began for the son of a landless
labourer before it was curtailed by the need to work, whereas the
son of a prosperous yeoman might prolong his age of irresponsibility
until he was eighteen or older.[5]

The institutions in which the young were educated developed and
defined the concept of childhood and adolescence. Schools and universities took children and youth and planted them not in other
households but in groups which were to some extent age-identified.
The child developed an institutional identity as well as a family-
membership identity. The boy (and it was almost invariably a boy)
was no longer simply son: he was child. The school child was totally
dependent. He was being brought up by others – a 'passive' victim.
He was not participating in the economy. For many boys the sixteenth and seventeenth centuries witnessed an extension of this
period of dependence which had traditionally ended early, at the
age of seven. Medieval children had achieved a semi-independent
condition much earlier than did the Tudor or Stuart schoolboy.
Educational theorists saw this extended period of dependence as a
necessary prelude to economic independence. A period of adolescence emerged as children were kept within the family home and
school for a longer period of time and were more carefully supervised.

But schooling was by no means universal even among the better
off sections of society. Even when a child did attend school or have
a tutor at home, it might be for a short period or a chronically interrupted period. The burgeoning concepts of extended childhood and
adolescence came into sharp conflict with the persistent traditions of
the medieval economy. As William Stout wistfully recalled of his
childhood in the 1670s:

'As we attained to the age of ten or twelve years, we were very much taken
off the school, especially in the spring and summer season, plough time, turf

time, hay time and harvest, in looking after the sheep, helping at the plough, going to the moss with carts, making hay and shearing in harvest . . . so that we made small progress in Latin, for what we got in winter we forgot in summer, and the writing master coming to Bolton mostly in winter, we got what writing we had in winter.'

And Stout was, in fact, among the better educated of the yeomanry, whose parents eventually educated him for apprenticeship.[6]

Many boys and girls were prepared for their adult life via a period of apprenticeship or indentured servitude away from the parental home. Economic and demographic realities made age-identification of apprentices and servants inevitable. The outstanding example is that of the London apprentices but it is probable that apprentices in Bristol, York, Norwich, Southampton, Exeter and Canterbury exhibited similar tendencies to combine if on a smaller and less politicised scale. Thousands of boys from throughout England were apprentices yearly in London, their ages ranging between 14 and 24, in accordance with the rules for admission to the London companies at a minimum age of 24. The fact of their age, removal from home and semi-dependence on a master provided the one unifying aspect of their existence, for the London apprentices were drawn from all social classes and all parts of the land. Popular literature of the time, however, recognised that they exhibited the characteristics of an age-group which was organised and cohesive. Group consciousness inspired religious and political activities but was also reinforced by them. At the same time, contemporaries were also conscious of the apprentices' dependence – a dominant distinction in early modern life.[7]

Studies of English communities help to demonstrate the impact of apprenticeship and servitude upon middle- and lower-class English homes. A study of Ealing in 1599 indicates that it was especially boys within the 15 to 24 age-group and girls within the 15 to 19 age-range who lived away from home. A study of Kirkby Lonsdale in 1695 supports this contention. Here it was the 'farmers' of the community who most commonly sent their children away but even among the gentry/yeomanry classes and the poor, more families sent their children away for an extended period during adolescence than kept them at home. For these absentees the object of their removal was more normally apprenticeship and servitude than schooling. The age of apprenticeship had changed little if at all since the Middle Ages although it is just possible that the age of servitude was pushed up in the early modern period by more prolonged formal schooling.[8]

It is tempting to suggest that three distinct periods of dependence were age-identified by seventeenth-century society: childhood, adolescence (in school) and youth (in apprenticeship or service) – and that every child experienced these passages. Yet we know that the pattern was heterogeneous – sex, class and other variables diffe-

rentiated the upbringing of young people as did their chosen vocation in life.

Treatment of children

Certain historians have argued that early modern children were
emotionally deprived. Some have even urged that children in the
sixteenth and seventeenth centuries were habitually abused. It is
common in such schools of thought to argue that the situation improved gradually but markedly over time.[9]

In fact, a careful examination of the evidence which survives of
early modern school and family life (and it is sadly deficient) suggests that this picture is considerably overdrawn. There were in fact
a multitude of patterns of child rearing in sixteenth-, seventeenth-
and eighteenth-century England, just as there are today. For every
example of child beating we might easily cite a parallel one of love
and affection or of 'cockering' (the term for spoiling or cosseting).
For every example of 'distance' between parents and offspring we
might provide one of intimacy and caring.

It is true of course that there were fashions in child rearing, as in
the modern world. Sometimes these fashions are difficult to interpret in our different world. For example, swaddling has been condemned, in the light of modern medical and psychological knowledge,
as a cruel and restrictive practice. Yet the people of that time did
not have our medical knowledge (which may itself be incorrect) and
swaddling seemed an excellent way of offering a very young child
security and warmth and keeping it out of harm's way. Moreover, in
England children were rarely swaddled for more than the first three
months of life from the seventeenth century onwards. The practice
of baptising very young and sickly infants has also been attacked as
a cruel, barbarian practice. Yet, for the sixteenth- and seventeenth-
century parent, the child's immortal soul was as important as his
mortal life and it was vital to ensure that the baby, for whom hope
on this earth was lost, should retain the hope of eternal life. One
simply must not assess fashions in child rearing in the light of contemporary beliefs and conditions. It is misguided, for instance, to interpret the instances of children in the same family bearing the same
Christian name as evidence that children were not recognised as
having individual identities and personalities by their parents and
that fathers and mothers did not grieve over dead children. Commonly, the naming of a child was in the hands of the godparents (or
gossips) before the later seventeenth century. Even Lord and Lady
Willoughby were in 1586 unsure of the correct name of their new
daughter because the chief godmother, the Countess of Huntington,
had insisted on the name Sophia while the remaining godparents
and the clergyman had called it Katherin, in respect of Lord Wil-

loughby's wishes. The solution seems to have been to call the child Sophia Katherin! Simonds D'Ewes' father was given the name Paul because he had been born on St Paul's day, despite the fact that he had an elder brother with the same name. When the naming of the new child came more firmly into the province of the natural parents, duplication of names fell into disuse. It is interesting to note that the custom of giving more than one name persisted.[10]

Vocation

It would be possible, of course, to list numerous examples of the love and care which the majority of early modern parents felt for their children. I refer the reader instead to the passage in the Diary of Ralph Josselin where the Diarist describes his reactions to the death of his ten-day-old son, Ralph, which is full of poignancy, and to the writings of other contemporaries, such as Adam Martindale, Henry Newcome, John Shaw, William Stout and Simonds D'Ewes.

It seems more relevant to dwell for a while on the extent to which boys and girls were allowed some say in their choice of vocation. In discussing this question one must be aware of the considerable limitations of the available evidence. What we examine is either of a prescriptive nature – occurring in the writings of leading preachers – or it is descriptive, often in ambiguous terms, of the practice in puritan or, at least, religious environments which were, presumably, most open to this sort of prescriptive literature. We may, therefore, be in danger of extending to the whole community the practice of a very restricted and perhaps totally untypical section of it if we generalise from such sources as sermons, tracts and diaries and autobiographies. Nevertheless, we cannot ignore such evidence as we have and, moreover, in discussing such documentation we are presented with sufficient variety of practice to make it possible to urge that there was no single prevalent attitude.

William Perkins, one of the most widely read and influential late Elizabethan preachers, had much to say on the subject of vocation or calling, some of it in respect of the ministerial calling and some with regard to all callings. From our perspective, his most pertinent advice was the following:[11]

Now touching children, it is the duty of parents to make choice of fit callings for them, before they apply them to any particular condition of life. And that they may the better judge aright, for what callings their children are fit, they must observe two things in them: first, their inclination, secondly, their natural gifts.

He added his short list of clues to the correct calling for each child and warned, parents cannot do greater wrong to their children, and the society of men, than to apply them unto unfit callings: as when a child is fit for learning, to apply him to a trade, or other bodily service; contrariwise to apply him to learning, when he is fittest for a trade.

The advice was that, while parents must for practical reasons (and because this is the duty of a good parent to provide for a child's future economic independence) arrange the training of the child and, therefore, determine his or her eventual vocation, this must not be done in defiance either of the child's wishes or of the child's gifts, within the realm of the economically possible.

Contemporary diarists and autobiographers have a good deal to say, in passing, about practice within their own households, which may well suggest the different interpretations put on such advice. Adam Martindale's father wanted Adam to follow him in his trade but permitted the boy to follow his own inclination when he saw that this was what he wanted. Ralph Josselin was more concerned that his wayward son, John, should become economically independent and responsible than that he should be obedient to his parents' slightest wish. William Stout's father appears to have been influenced by a combination of awareness of William's aptitude for arithmetic and the difficulties attending the provision of a farmstead for William when he decided 'to get me constantly to school to get learning in order to be placed to some trade or other employment'. The same father purchased a small farm for his son Leonard 'who very early appeared inclined and active about husbandry and cattle and following the plough'. Rather earlier, John Shaw's parents struggled with their natural desire to have their only son remain with them and his contrary inclination to go to Cambridge:

My parents having no other child but me, and some competent estate to leave me, were very loath to have me depart from them; but desired that I would take up some calling, which I might follow in that country near to them; but they observing my eager desire (when so young) after knowledge and learning, my good God so overruled their hearts as to incline them (at my desire, and seeing me to have no genius to anything but learning) to send me to Cambridge . . .

Significantly, John's desire won the day.[12]

Children from humbler backgrounds were often not so fortunate. Thomas Tryon, son of the village tiler and plasterer in Bibury, Oxfordshire, is a case in point. He described his father as 'an honest sober man of good reputation; but having many children, was forced to bring them all to work betimes'. But there is no evidence here that Tryon's father would have ignored his son's inclinations towards another way of life had such been economically feasible. Thomas Carleton, son of a husbandman, seems to imply that it was his father's wish which combined his sporadic schooling with farming duties. The conclusion is inescapable that it was within the means of the prosperous yeomanry and gentry to allow their offspring a variety of occupational options which those lower down the social and economic scale may well have wished to give but were unable to.[13]

The decisions made by parents and guardians regarding the education of the child were crucial because they determined the employment opportunities of the child but they were not irreversible as the case of Edward Johnson in 1692 makes clear. William Stout, executor of the boy's father's will, sent him to school on a tabling out basis to learn 'Latin, writing and arithmetic till he was about 15 years of age, and then designed him for some shop trade. But he was inclined to nothing but to sea, and was put apprentice in the ship employment.'[14]

It seems evident that, in caring homes, by the seventeenth century boys (and to a limited extent girls) were permitted a degree of choice respecting their immediate education and their eventual occupation. This was, however, a choice restricted by the social and economic position of the family.

Conclusions

From the perspective of the history of education the increasing institutionalisation of childhood and youth is of considerably more significance than changes in the fashions of child-rearing. It would be incorrect to maintain that England and Wales became a schooled society overnight. It would be equally misleading to suggest that all children in the early modern period had identical childhood experiences. This was a heterogeneous society. The state had in no sense imposed a uniform childhood and youth training. While there were differences between sexes and between classes there were also differences within sexes and within classes.

There is a strong case for arguing that the increasing emphasis upon formal schooling for children and adolescents had its roots in growing economic complexity and in the need for both the ruling classes and the professions to find justifications for their changing roles within that society.

Chapter 2

Literacy

What literacy meant in the medieval and early modern periods

It has been suggested that the sixteenth and seventeenth centuries saw the sudden emergence of mass lay literacy in England, against a background of Protestant and humanist encouragement. By implication this spread of lay literacy was in sharp contrast to the situation in the later Middle Ages, when literacy was a clerkly attribute. Recently, however, some work has been produced which indicates that this contrast has been overdrawn: that the clergy (in the modern sense of that word) were not the sole possessors of literacy in the Middle Ages; that literacy was not as widespread among laymen in the early modern period as had been supposed.

Quite clearly, the question of the extent of literacy in pre-industrial society is extremely important for our purposes. It is one important indicator of the success of schooling at the elementary level. Massive swings in literacy levels might reflect equally massive changes in educational provision or, at the very least, determination on the part of parents or sponsors that children should be introduced to reading and writing. Moreover a discussion of the place of literacy in society may help us to a greater understanding of the motivation behind the establishment of schools and the design of their curricula in the early modern period.

Before discussing the evidence for the extent of lay literacy during the period 1400 to 1750, it is valuable to spend a moment considering the complexity of the concept of literacy. What do *we* mean by literacy? Are those who can simply sign their names and read a Ladybird Easy-Reading book literate in today's world? Literacy is a relative concept – judged by the expectations of a given society, class or occupation. What we regard today as functional literacy is far in advance of what was perceived as useful literacy in the late nineteenth century. What then constituted adequate literacy in late medieval and early modern Britain?

Even the modern child, porter or agricultural worker may have both more need and more opportunity to read complex material in a single working day than did the fifteenth-, sixteenth- or seventeenth-century counterpart in the working month or even year. Written material was much less readily available and accessible. This was in part a result of technical problems – it was not possible to reproduce books cheaply and quickly before the advent of the printing press. But it was also partly a consequence of the lack of perceived need for written material among the population as a whole. To some extent, technological advance created this perceived need. But this was not the whole story. Religion, politics and economics all played their part in encouraging the growth of literacy in the sixteenth and seventeenth centuries.

What, then, was useful literacy in the period 1400–1750? The word changed its meaning even within this time. The word 'litteratus' was used in the Middle Ages to denote those who were latinate. It described the level of literacy required of the cleric, who must be able to read and understand the latin services; to write and witness various types of document (including wills); and, as was the case with a particular group of clerics, to copy manuscripts and documents and to perform administrative tasks which required latinity. Until the fourteenth century, Latin was the language used in both courts and church. Commonly, the members of the clerical estate (as opposed to men in major orders alone) were the only members of society who could be expected, *en bloc*, to read and write in the 'literate vernacular'.

Historians, unaccustomed to a society divided not only into horizontal classes but also into vertical estates, have struggled for years with the idea that literacy in the Middle Ages was confined to clerks. Some have argued that there were always literate laymen and that the state's bureaucracy itself was staffed by such laymen. Peter Heath, for example, has maintained that men in minor orders were laymen – and so they were from a modern perspective. But if we look at them from the medieval point of view, can we be so convinced that such clerks were laymen? Because clerics were celibate, the clerical estate was a creation not of birth but of election: boys passed from the lay estate into which they were born into the clerical estate, for which they were educated. In theory, if not in practice, youths had to receive a given education before becoming full members of the clerical estate. When a boy received the first tonsure he was declaring himself a candidate for that estate and, thereby, for that education. This does not mean that the bridge between the lay and clerical estates was always fully crossed. Neither does it mean that all those who received the first tonsure intended to complete the crossing.[1]

Certainly there were many reasons why entry into minor orders would appear attractive in the later fourteenth and fifteenth centuries. Attrition rates among the clergy were high in the late fourteenth century due to epidemics of plague. The bishops appear to have

made a concerted effort to recoup the losses in the form of new recruits. The fifteenth century, also, with the boom in the foundation
of chantries, seemed to provide a happy hunting-ground for men in
both major and minor orders. At least some of the men who remained in minor orders were deflected into administrative careers
by the sudden drying up of career opportunities within the pastoral
ministry, when the Church overcompensated for a past shortfall in
recruits.[2]

It may well be, therefore, that the emergence of an increasingly
large class of literate or latinate laymen can best be explained in
terms of the Church's improved recruitment situation at given points
in the fifteenth century.

If literacy for the 'clerk' meant latinity, it did not mean this for all
classes of society within the lay estate. Literacy had become an important and accepted attribute of both kings and aristocracy by the
late fifteenth century. These classes were impelled towards literacy
by the need to supervise the management of their personal affairs
but, having acquired it, they had the means to turn to reading for
pleasure and information and the private exercise of religious
devotion.[3]

The same economic drive towards literacy is detected among the
merchants, craftsmen and artisans. Until the fourteenth century the
chief need was to be able to read in French; after this, knowledge of
both English and French was demanded until, by the sixteenth century, English had become the sole vernacular. Members of many of
the London guilds were expected to be able to read and write in the
vernacular when they became apprenticed. It was already common
in the fifteenth century for a child to learn to read in English only
and some of the guilds had to accept this fact. In 1422 the Craft of
Brewers decided to keep its records in English because so few of its
members knew either Latin or French. But, for a few, a knowledge
of Latin was essential for just as long as the language remained that
of record and, especially, that of ecclesiastical record. This was true
of the Scriveners, whose company ordered in 1498 that its apprentices should undergo a full education in Latin grammar.

Clearly some crafts which have been associated with a higher rate
of literacy than others – such as the goldsmiths – did not demand
latinity of their members in the late fifteenth century but rather
assumed active vernacular literacy. Often reading and writing were
not an integral part of the occupation as practised but the literacy
test was used as a way of restricting recruitment in particular economic circumstances or as a means of raising the status of the membership.

There was a clearly demarcated hierarchy of literacy in the urban
community. By the late sixteenth century only 3 per cent of goldsmiths were not actively literate whereas 46 per cent of brewers
were illiterate.

Men who worked in the administration or the law had an obvious need for literacy. Over the years 1300–1700 the type of literacy required changed radically. Initially, Latin was the language of record in Chancery, in the Exchequer and the Royal Household, in Parliament and in the Privy Seal (until 1300). During the fourteenth century some 'departments' began instead to use French – the Privy Seal until 1420, for example, and Parliament throughout the fourteenth century. After 1300 Latin had considerably reduced importance in the work of the common lawyers. French was used increasingly in the thirteenth-century courts; even the Yearbooks were in French, and both the fourteenth-century statutes and the later law treatises were penned in the French tongue. French was still used in the law courts until the eighteenth century. English penetrated this world much more slowly. It was beginning to be used in the Chancellor's Equity Court in the late fourteenth century and some parliamentary petitions were also in English by that date. Parliamentary statutes were not recorded in English until 1484, however. Yet in the world of private administration and business English was becoming increasingly important from the fourteenth century on. In the mid-fifteenth century it had become the second language of business.[4]

For the free and the unfree of rural England there was little need to be literate simply to fulfil one's social role. The impetus to literacy for those in bondage came either from the lord (who might sponsor the education of the more evidently able of his serfs to provide potential administrators for the manor) or from the desire of the villein to escape serfdom. This impetus would be directed to latinity. One is faced with the anomaly of the members of the most unprivileged section of society (and presumably the least literate) being that least likely, if educated at all, to stop at mere vernacular competence and the most likely to achieve latinity. With the removal of restrictions on the availability of schooling (by the terms of the Statute of Labourers, 1405/6) and the subsequent slackening of lord – serf ties, there may have been less incentive for the unfree to seek an advanced education.

Literacy in the later Middle Ages, as now, meant many different things to many different people. There was a distinction between practical literacy (functional) and mere literacy. The information which we have about the organisation of late medieval society and economy suggests the degree of literacy which we might expect within any section of society if a strict correlation operated between socio-economic need and the acquisition of active literacy. Unfortunately, no one has yet established that such a correlation was operative. This type of data cannot be used to measure the degree of literacy prevalent in fourteenth- and fifteenth-century England with any precision.

The relevance of the modern definition of literacy

We must beware of labelling the later medieval world as a deficient society because active literacy was not widespread throughout it. Only gradually did people explore the possibilities of communicating via the written word. This was a society which relied upon word of mouth; the method of instruction was oral also. Reading was very much an oral and shared activity. The ear was much more attuned than the eye was focused. People learned by listening to others and by memorising what they heard. When books were involved, it was considered normal for people to listen while the book was read aloud – to many this seemed much more natural than acquiring the skill of reading for oneself. Both reading and writing were regarded in much the same light as cobbling, tanning or thatching – they were specialist skills specific to certain occupations. Even were we to prove that actual literacy levels were low, this would not imply necessarily that the population was 'uneducated'. Rather, it would demonstrate that reading and writing were not considered essential skills required in the transmission of culture or opinion or in the business of daily life.[5]

Nevertheless, it was in the later Middle Ages that the stage began to be set for reliance on these skills. This depended a good deal on the ready availability of cheap texts. When English began to emerge as the language of the upper classes and of written record, the way was cleared for the spread of vernacular literacy.[6] With the advent of the printing press and eventually of relatively cheap printed matter in English, literacy became a practical proposition for those with no clerical aspirations or scholarly aptitude.[7] The adoption of English as the language of devotion in the period of the Reformation and the attitude of the Reformers to the power of the printed word, ensured that vernacular literacy would be encouraged yet further in the sixteenth century. The Reformers were only able to advocate popular literacy against this context of the mass production of literature in English. Now it may well be that some have overestimated the success of this encouragement of mass literacy or at least the speed at which it spread. It is true that many contemporaries feared the outcome of the introduction of the lower classes to print and tried to restrict the movement towards popular literacy. Yet literacy became more certainly the key to cultural life in the sixteenth and seventeenth centuries.

The extent of literacy during the later Middle Ages: 1370–1530

Various attempts have been made to assess the exact extent of literacy in the later Middle Ages, spurred on, no doubt, by the claim of Sir Thomas More that between 50 and 60 per cent of Englishmen were literate in the early sixteenth century. One modern work posited that 30 per cent of the population could read in the fifteenth century, and about 40 per cent in 1530. A study of the London merchant community suggested that 50 per cent of London laymen could read by the 1470s.[8]

On the face of it, wills and their signatures appear a tempting source for a survey of popular literacy. Unfortunately, the class and sex distribution of wills is skewed in favour of men with property. Moreover, wills were normally made during terminal illness and people in failing health and old age may have found themselves incapable of signing despite a usual ability to write.

An alternative source of evidence has been exploited by Jo Ann Moran. After 1460 laypeople appeared regularly in York wills both as witnesses and scribes. Between 23 per cent and 30 per cent of wills (1460–1530) seemed to her to indicate lay literacy on the basis of lay witnessing. Unfortunately, it is altogether unclear whether we can safely assume that witnesses to wills could read what they witnessed.[9]

She also examined the evidence contained in wills of the existence of schools. They revealed the existence of large numbers of song and reading schools and a slower expansion in the number of Latin or grammar schools. From this source she concluded that some 15 per cent of the population of York diocese attended a school in the later fifteenth century as compared with perhaps 9 per cent in the early fifteenth century and some 4.7 per cent in the late fourteenth century. But it may be suspected that these figures err considerably on the generous side. Dr Moran based these estimates on calculations which assumed a regular and constant size for the schools concerned. Later evidence suggests that consistency in this respect was not a feature of early schools.

The significance of Dr Moran's work lies not so much in the precise statistics which it offers as in the exploitation of new forms of evidence; the recognition that the distribution and type of educational facilities available may be a reflection of the state of popular literacy and its importance to a given culture, and her underlining of the presence of lay literacy in late medieval society. Indeed, her calculations suggest that the take-off into lay literacy had begun prior to the Reformation. Scholars have often assumed that lay literacy appeared suddenly and dramatically in English society in the late sixteenth century. Dr Moran's work indicates that lay literacy had a history.

If there was a take-off into lay literacy during the later fifteenth and early sixteenth centuries, what was its cause? The impact of lollardy may have been responsible for the earlier spread of literacy. In Coventry, for example, there is evidence that the group of fifteenth- and early sixteenth-century lollards held fast to their tradition of vernacular Bible reading. Probably Protestantism built upon a pre-existent interest in Bible reading. Nevertheless, lollardy was active only in certain areas of the country.[10]

Book ownership has also often been used to imply literacy and a general religious motivation for its acquisition. For example, in 1500 a foreigner commented that English people heard mass daily and read aloud from their own *Offices of Our Lady* while in Church. Townspeople's wills have indicated quite high levels of lay book ownership of this type in certain areas. But there are two major objections to assuming a close correlation between the ownership of a religious book and the ability to read it. Religious books were common bequests. As such they might have a value as a memento quite distinct from their content. The book might also have a status conferring value, because of its binding or relative scarcity. And for many a Bible or devotional manual had a superstitious use. It was believed, for example, that a key placed between the leaves of a Bible could be used to discover the identity of a thief or other criminal if the names of the suspects were stuffed into the barrel of the key. There were many reasons, therefore, why a Bible might have a treasured place in a late medieval household which depended not at all upon the ability of the purchaser or recipient to read. Secondly, literacy probably varied tremendously between parish and parish. It was particularly high in the sixteenth and seventeenth centuries in some London parishes. Observations such as that of the foreigner in 1500 were probably based upon impressions gleaned in London and from the church-going public. It is dangerous to extrapolate from such selective evidence to the entire population. The ownership of religious books, therefore, is not a reliable indication of the success of religious motivation towards literacy either before or after the Reformation.[11]

It has been common to claim that parents taught their children to read so that they could claim benefit of clergy and escape the gallows if convicted of certain crimes. Certainly it was so common for non-clerks to claim this privilege by the reign of Henry VIII that the monarchy began to restrict its application. During the reign of Elizabeth 32 per cent of capital felons in Middlesex successfully pleaded clergy – a percentage which rose to 39 per cent in the following reign. But a caveat should be entered. Youths may have been taught to memorise and recite the first verse of the fifty-first psalm for just this contingency. The expense of formal schooling to a high level would seem to be a high price to pay to safeguard one's offspring against such an eventuality.[12]

More important by far as an incentive towards basic literacy must have been the attraction of a career in the Church or in associated work. Boys were needed as choristers, as chantry priests, as secular clergy, as regular clergy, as clerks, as scriveners and so forth. If a career in the Church did not materialise, a youth could still use his basic literacy to advantage, still more his Latin skills. The elementary school was used in the later Middle Ages as it was in the early modern period – as a sieve which discriminated between those who were capable of proceeding to a full education in grammar and a clerical career and those who were not. In one sense, then, for members of the lower classes education represented the route to upwards social mobility, not because literacy itself was valued but because it was a prerequisite for clergy. Those who did not proceed to a clerical vocation used their skills in fringe occupations – teaching, administration, law, writing and account keeping. The hope of employment in the Church was an important impetus to the spread of literacy among the laity even before the Protestant Reformation.

In the later Middle Ages there was no coherent movement in favour of teaching the 'people' to read and write. The age of the use of basic education as a positive means of social control or as an agent of propaganda had yet to come. But the scene does appear to have been set for this later use of education by State and Church. By the time of the English Reformation, there were already sufficient numbers of literate laity, especially in the populous towns and among the commercial classes, to make use of the press as a missionary agent feasible.[13]

The impact of lay literacy in the later medieval period is difficult to gauge. Book ownership seems to reveal the conservative, religious interests of the literate laity. Some of the more vital agents of the transmission of popular culture were not books at all but mystery and miracle plays; festivals of the saints; pomp and ceremony within the Church, from candles to stained glass windows to rood screens to Easter tabernacles. Civic ceremonies paralleled these high points of the Church's calendar in urban environments such as that of Coventry. At the Reformation most of these conservative forces were dealt a deathblow. The laity could no longer donate money to support chantries; often they re-channelled their giving to support education. Perhaps even more important, the laity could no longer participate in communal ceremony in the traditional way. The Reformation, in wiping out public ceremony as a major means of transmitting knowledge and values within the community, forced the population in upon itself in a novel way. Public popular culture increasingly became private popular culture, in which the printed word played a prominent role. State and Church now had to discover new ways of controlling the populace. The printing press proved a useful tool.[14]

This argument should not be overstressed. There was still a lively oral culture throughout the period. Printed vehicles of communication such as the newspaper were but poorly developed until the eighteenth century and certainly before the civil wars. The sermon to some extent replaced the traditional ceremonial of the medieval Church as a means of communication, an agent of control and a focus for communal life. There is some evidence to indicate that it was possible to reach only the leaders of society via the printed word prior to the Restoration of 1660. An estimated 300,000 books (on average) came off the London printing presses each year between 1576 and 1640. It has been proposed that this number was sufficient only to supply the members of gentle, clerical and professional households with up to ten books or pamphlets a year. Clearly, some members of other social groups also bought books but the point is sound enough – an extremely large literate population was not assumed by the market. The real explosion in print occurred in the later seventeenth century. Of course, this is not to say that the power to influence opinion in certain sections of the community was insignificant – indeed this simply built upon the age-old pattern of controlling the people as a whole via established and trusted intermediaries.[15]

The spread of literacy in the sixteenth and seventeenth centuries

Some historians have tried to argue that the inflated numbers of laymen in the Tudor and Stuart universities reflected the distribution of basic literacy in the country as a whole. Certainly a substantial proportion of university students came from lower down on the social scale than the gentry. The Reformation and post-Reformation Church was actively encouraging recruitment for the ordinary pastoral ministry via the universities rather than via the grammar schools. But no historian has been able to demonstrate that significant numbers of lower-class boys at the university entered occupations other than the church (or teaching – traditionally the occupation of clerical 'drop-outs'). The universities were drawing from an already select pool of the sons of husbandmen, yeomen and artisans who had already had a relatively rigorous and advanced education. The number of boys from the lower and middling groups of society cannot be used safely as an indicator of the spread of basic literacy within those classes as a whole.[16]

By far the most rigorous and thought-provoking study of early modern literacy has been that published by David Cressy. While agreeing that the signature is a less than perfect key to active literacy (that is, the ability to read and write) he yet maintained that it is the only source available to us which permits comparison between differing groups within society over time and which also possesses a fair degree of accuracy. According to his analysis literacy was hitched firmly to social and economic function, which varied among different social, occupational and gender groups.

In an early study of the East London suburbs of Stepney and Whitechapel, 1580–1639, Cressy discovered that 52 per cent of the population were illiterate (48 per cent actively literate), whereas at the same date the level of illiteracy in the City of London itself among the same groups of artisans and traders was but 24 per cent (76 per cent were actively literate). Even within one broad social spectrum in a large urban area, then, there were great differences in the distribution of literacy which were related to economic need. In this case members of the printing and other skilled trades of the city had a much more obvious use for literacy than had watermen in the suburbs.[17]

His comparison of active literacy levels between social and occupational groupings is also illuminating. Illiteracy was highest among husbandmen and labourers (urban and rural) and among women (whatever their rank). The clergy and other professionals (lawyers, attorneys, solicitors, doctors) and most of the gentry were literate. The yeomanry stood somewhere between these extremes. Probably yeomen learned to read and write in their search for upward social mobility and because they could afford to acquire such skills. Tradesmen and craftsmen were not significantly less literate as a group than yeomen but the composite figure disguised a marked hierarchy of trades. Artisans and outside workmen were more often illiterate whereas shopkeepers and merchants were normally able to sign their names. Some trades boasted 100 per cent literacy, because of the nature of the occupation.[18]

When Lawrence Stone examined the signatures appended to the Protestation Oath of Loyalty to Parliament of 1642 he concluded that there was an average male literacy rate of 30 per cent over the country as a whole. But, he argued, the figures demonstrated much higher levels of literacy in the towns than in the countryside; in the south than in the north. Literacy rates, he claimed, ranged from 15–20 per cent in the rural north to 40 per cent in the home counties and to 60 per cent in some southern towns. Rural signatures were much more clumsily written than urban – indicating more practical experience in writing in town communities.[19]

Cressy's analysis, however, shows that there was in fact high illiteracy in some areas which were very close to London: for example, Herfordshire was 74 per cent illiterate and Berkshire also 74 per cent. Some counties in the lowland zone had illiteracy rates every bit as high as the highland zones which Stone identified as backward. In fact, there was remarkable consistency as between one county and another (with most counties falling within five points on either side of the mean), with the real differences being between parish and parish within any given area. For example, Middlesex and Essex were among the more literate counties but had parish scores ranging from 41 per cent to 77 per cent and 36 per cent to 85 per cent illiteracy respectively. Most literate parishes were either themselves market towns or close to a market town.[20]

This work has called into question the entrenched assumption that literacy was constantly rising between 1530 and 1730. Enthusiasm for education was not a constant but a variable, dependent upon interpretations of the social utility of education. Thus in the sixteenth century education was seen as a cure for social problems, whereas in the seventeenth century there was a 'realization that it also caused them'. According to this view, the enthusiasts for mass education were always more interested in its potential as a means of social control than in its revolutionary effects, despite the fact that one of its chief aims would be the inculcation of Protestant beliefs and values. Not a single one of the educational reformers of the period was *primarily* concerned with providing opportunities for social mobility. Comenius, renowned for his enlightened views, took care to stress that in putting forward a scheme for mass education he was seeking moral and religious change and not an undermining of the social and economic order. In practice, contemporaries backed away from the implications of expanded educational opportunities – attempts to give priority in schooling to poor boys (as laid down by the founders of many schools and colleges) were often resisted or circumvented. Even the Free Schools, which technically offered free tuition to certain specified groups of children – sons of the freemen of the borough, relatives of the founder, poor boys – were often inaccessible to the poor because of the cost of board, books, additional subjects and so on. In addition, the parents who could afford to pay bribed the teachers to ensure places and preferential treatment for their children in school. One might add that the most vociferous defenders of admission according to merit rather than birth tended to be those who were obsessed with the Church's recruitment problems rather than with the desirability of educational provision for the poor *per se*.[21]

A strong argument emerges, therefore, for the actual contraction of educational opportunity for the masses in the seventeenth century, after a period of expansion during the reign of Elizabeth. In the late sixteenth century the yeomen, husbandmen and tradesmen all improved their levels of active literacy but the yeomen were to remain at the level achieved by 1590 until the end of James I's reign, only to improve again in the 1630s. During James's reign illiteracy rates among husbandmen and tradesmen actually fell, although not dramatically, but the 1630s saw a rising number of illiterates in both groups. By the beginning of the Civil War, husbandmen and tradesmen were as likely to be illiterate as they had been at Elizabeth's death. Improvements in the 1660s were noticeable for all three groups but the husbandmen lost ground enormously in the reigns of Charles II and James II.

In short, after a promising increase in active literacy among the middling people under Elizabeth, this promise was not fulfilled in the seventeenth century. Fewer people from these groups were receiving basic education in reading and writing at the very time when we are told that there was an explosion in numbers in higher education.[22]

Several distinct phases can be identified in the overall history of literacy. Between 1530 and 1550 there was marked progress; the years 1550 to 1560 saw a setback; the first twenty years of Elizabeth's reign witnessed rapid overall improvement in literacy rates; but the years 1580 to 1610 were years of setback. Between 1610 and 1640 there was again improvement but the years between 1640 and 1660 saw a decline in literacy; the period between 1660 and 1680 again saw overall improvement. These changes reflected social attitudes towards the wisdom of educating the lower and middling classes. On occasion, as during the civil wars, they were a response to civic turmoil.

Cressy's evidence makes it difficult to assume an active literacy rate of over 30 per cent overall in seventeenth-century England. The statistics drawn from the Protestation Returns in 1641–44 indicate that, outside London and Suffolk, no county had an overall literacy rate higher than 38 per cent of the male population or lower than 27 per cent. The literacy rate in London was exceptionally high: 78 per cent. It is, however, entirely possible that London had an illiterate underworld which simply never reveals itself in the sources which historians use as the basis of such calculations. Nevertheless, it is clear that the metropolis drew large numbers of literates from the provinces (professionals, merchants, gentry) and provided a wealth of educational facilities. The sample of Returns for Suffolk was so small that the margin of error is probably very high.[23]

Overall literacy rates in England, 1370–1710

In the light of this research, suggestions of a 30 per cent active literacy rate in the late fifteenth century and a 40 per cent rate in the 1630s seem wildly optimistic. In total, the recent work on literacy points to the conclusion that literacy was less widespread outside London even in the seventeenth century than has often been assumed; that where it existed it was socially circumscribed; and that the 'take-off' into lay literacy was not as dramatic as had been posited. There were undoubtedly points of continuity with the medieval past. Dr Moran believed that 15 per cent of the total population of York diocese had undergone basic schooling by 1530. Dr Cressy, more cautious, indicates an overall literacy rate at that date of 10 per cent. Progress was made in the ensuing period so that literacy rates rose in a definite fashion but rarely above the 30 per cent mark. This progress was, however, often interrupted and socially differentiated. The upper and professional classes were always much more highly literate than the middle and lower classes.

Any suggestion that the 'educational revolution' penetrated the labouring class should be viewed with suspicion. To the extent that there was a dramatic rise in literacy rates, this was confined to the gentle and professional élites.[24]

Literacy and social mobility

The supposed relationship between the acquisition of literacy and social mobility must be questioned as a result of these findings. Literacy was necessary for some occupations but it was quite possible to live comfortably and even prosperously in the seventeenth century without being able to read and write. Many people used the services of professional or semi-professional literates to perform those tasks which required literacy. Roger Lowe, for example, whose prime means of livelihood was retailing, nevertheless earned additional income from writing letters and other documents for his neighbours in the 1660s. For a man such as Lowe, literacy brought economic advantages simply because it was uncommon, but no close correlation appears to have existed between economic prosperity and literacy levels in early modern England. Yeomen probably sought literacy because they wished to enter the clergy, not because they wished to make more money. There is little indication that literacy was particularly respected in commercial or trade circles during the period in question.[25]

Any assessment of the role of literacy in social mobility must be very tentative, therefore. The sole agent of such mobility which has been easily located and examined by historians has been the Church. Certainly the Church had always played its part in 'upward social mobility' via education, although the importance of education to the parish clergy had increased manyfold during the later sixteenth and early seventeenth centuries. A clerical recruit from the yeomanry was now apt to be highly educated and to have acquired a degree. One might well ask, however, whether he was bound to climb further up the Church's career ladder because of his education than had his fifteenth-century counterpart. With the abolition of minor orders, there was now less competition for benefices and fewer clerical recruits from the lower orders were condemned to a life of fringe employment. Yet such studies as have been made of clerical career patterns indicate that relatively few of the underprivileged (*vis-à-vis* other social groups) reached high positions in the Church. When they did so, it was because they had obtained a college fellowship more often than not. What the Church offered the average husbandman's or yeoman's able son was the opportunity to acquire an education and to take on the mantle of gentility.

Decisions about the bringing up of children (whether in school, apprenticeship or service) appear to have been made at an early stage in the child's life. The decision regarding literacy was for most made in tandem with the one regarding vocation. Of course, there were some who acquired literacy late in life by their own efforts, but for most children opportunities to learn such skills opened up at the age of five or six and closed again when they reached the age of about fifteen. The ABC or petty school was often used by parents, who believed that their child was able, to discover whether a career in the Church or a literate occupation was possible. Because of this sieving out process, as we have said earlier, the pool of literates was always going to be larger than the number of people entering such occupations. The boy who attended grammar school and university could, it is true, waver between one or other of the professions but, beyond this, the choice before every individual for reassessment of his personal route remained strictly limited.

It is becoming clear from work on what might be regarded as emerging professions, for example, the attorneys, that other avenues of social advancement were opening up for the well educated youth who did not attend university. Nevertheless, although social mobility was not impossible in the early modern context it was certainly not facilitated. The obstacles to the rise of the lower and middle classes were many. Few thought it desirable to make the obstacle course less severe. For this reason, recruits into the professions from the classes below the gentry generally hailed from the families of prosperous husbandmen and yeomen.[26]

Literacy and disease in the Commonwealth

So far in this chapter we have assumed that the true measure of individual literacy was the ability to both read and write. Certainly active literacy today implies the possession of both of these skills. But an acquaintanceship with sixteenth-century and seventeenth-century religious and educational thought makes one wonder whether estimates of literacy in England which are based on the study of signatures do not ignore a large reading public, made up of people who were unable to write.

We know, for example, that the government of both Church and State had a vested interest in educating the people in this most fundamental skill of the reception of knowledge and ideas. Used properly, reading could instil in the minds of the people the correct values and beliefs. During the Reformation concerted efforts were made to use print in the service of the Protestant political cause. The committed hoped to influence the opinions and behaviour of the natural leaders of society, above all. The Protestant use of printed propaganda presupposed the ability to read among the social and professional élites. At the same time, Protestant Reformers were anxious to open the Scriptures to the people.

It was not long, however, before a good many Englishmen recoiled from the implications of widespread Bible reading. The monarchy and the Church hierarchy soon appreciated that the positive advantages of presenting the Word to the people might be outweighed by the disadvantages contained in the independence of interpretation which reading encouraged. The attack by laymen on the prerogatives of various classes of professional – cleric, doctor and lawyer alike – owed not a little to the ability of these same laymen to obtain access to hitherto forbidden knowledge via the printed page. This was a predicament which the Protestant clergy found bewildering – their religious convictions bid them open up the Scriptures; their vested interests bade them close them or, as many charged, obscure them. For many among the upper classes, literacy may well have been equated with the devil – it certainly seemed to find deplorable work for idle hands to do. Church and State co-operated to censor the products of the press and to control its growth as part of a determined effort to extinguish dissent and bring about a compliant conformity. Speculation within safe bounds might appear appropriate to the gentleman – who needed no work for his hands – but it was certainly inappropriate for the manual worker – whose hands must be busy and his thoughts still.

The more radical continued, however, to advocate the spread of literacy. For such writers, from Perkins to Baxter, literacy brought with it the possibility of virtue for 'how can they know God's will that cannot read it?' Those ministers and laymen who defended mass literacy and mass Bible reading most vociferously tended to the view that the reading of Scripture did not entail interpretation – the truth was self-evident to all men.

The attempts to render reading a purely passive skill – as a receiver to a State/Church controlled radio station – failed miserably. Dissent mounted throughout the period and made itself felt in a barrage of printed works.

It may be said with a degree of confidence that the ruling classes of England never envisaged employing education as a vehicle of social change, although at times elements among them thought that it might be used to correct some social injustices. For many of the élite, education was important because it offered a justification for continued existence and power in the newly centralised State, as the feudal past receded. In so far as education was seen as relevant to the needs of other classes, it was as a strictly utilitarian tool. Education would prepare men to do the work for which their birth and vocation (often inseparable) had suited them. Education might also be necessary to introduce the people to the values of the State and the Church.

The precise functions of education within society, however, diverged markedly from this vision. In a state in which the idea of innovation was anathema and in which original actions were masked by appeals to a fictitious history, education yet laid the foundations for creativity and originality. Those men and women who objected to the form of the Church of England and who later, perhaps, became dissenters or emigrated to the New World out of protest, asked not for liberty or toleration but for the triumph of their own ideas. Nevertheless, the emerging importance of 'consumer choice' in the world of the mind had revolutionary implications for the future. Some men and women were thinking beyond the boundaries marked for them by society. Some very few wished to abolish boundaries altogether. Most wished to erect new ones. Each one now had the right to choose his own traditions, irrespective of state control and through the exercise of his or her own mental powers. Literacy was not essential for independence of mind but the ready availability of literature pleading every side of a cause must have had a profound influence on the rejection of conformity. One would not conclude that literacy caused dissent, but that it fed dissent. It may not have brought upward mobility but it often brought discontent.

It is apparent that the State and Church hierarchy feared the consequences of teaching the people to read, not the results of teaching them to write. To regard reading as a passive skill is grossly misleading. Reading encouraged habits of mind which were disturbingly active and which caused disease in the commonwealth. Moreover, while it may be true that in the modern world there is a close correlation between those who can write and those who can read, as well as a very low number of persons who can read but not write, what we know of the teaching of reading and writing in early modern England and of the preoccupation of contemporaries with the art of reading suggests that reading without writing was more common then than now. There is a strong case for arguing that writing was a much more socially and occupationally specific skill than reading. A child had to remain in school longer in order to learn to write; he had to pay extra for such tuition. Reading, on the other hand, was the first skill taught and it had a general use.

While it may be possible to measure the extent of active literacy in the modern sense of the ability to read and write, we are far from being able to measure the spread of the ability to read among the early modern English population. Statistics have led us perhaps to a greater understanding of the place of full literacy in early modern society but an understanding of the place of reading in that society is also required. This understanding must be reached through qualitative rather than quantitative analysis.

Chapter 3

A schooled society?

The schooling of society

Sixteenth- and seventeenth-century England and Wales were not a schooled society such as our own. The bringing up of children was still firmly rooted in the family, the Church and the workshop. For centuries academic learning had been the preserve of the clergy and potential clergy because only the clergy needed advanced literacy for their work. Institutionalised, academic education was reserved for members of the clerical estate, which included not only secular and regular clergy but also many of what we would call 'civil servants' and lawyers. To the extent that other groups within society needed book learning, their needs could be satisfied by the father, the master, the churchman. Vernacular literacy was spreading in late medieval society through these agencies and also because the Church could not provide employment for the large numbers of boys who wished to enter the clerical estate.

There did, however, emerge a movement for the schooling of society. Renaissance scholars saw in education on classical lines a way to improve society. John Colet and others were convinced that virtue could be restored to civic and religious life through the medium of a progressive Christian, classical curriculum. In 1509 Colet founded St Paul's Grammar School in London: it became the model for the many sixteenth- and seventeenth-century grammar schools endowed by philanthropists who shared his hopes – for example, Merchant Taylors' School, established in 1560. The idea of the social humanists that the school was a necessary vehicle for social control was part of the heritage of the English ruling classes and of those men who were educated alongside them in the classical tradition – chiefly the clergy and the grammar schoolmasters, who were drawn from a lower social class into a new milieu. Again and again in the literature of the period we read that the school has within it the power to counteract the evil influences of family and society upon the child.[1]

There is a persuasive case for the development of an educational theory rooted in millennial eschatology. For a group of Puritans who grew to manhood in the years before the Civil Wars, 'The New Jerusalem was not conceived in terms of minor religious changes but as a dramatic leap forward which would achieve not only totally successful religious concord, but also social amelioration and intellectual renewal.' Education would prepare men for the millennium. During the 1640s and 50s a number of reformers agitated for universal education, often of a vocational nature. While these reformers attacked the traditions of 'humanist scholasticism', they none the less believed schooling to be important as the instrument of social and intellectual change and actively solicited state aid for their programmes. In 1653, for example, Samuel Hartlib and John Dury, both heavily influenced by the writings of Comenius, presented to the Committee for the Advancement of Learning a plan for a national educational system which proposed the establishment of common and mechanical schools to meet the educational requirements of the poor. Another reformer, William Petty, recommended the establishment of literary workhouses in which manual as well as literary skills would be stressed. Samuel Hartlib also planned workhouses which would provide vocational education as well as strictly utilitarian academic education. These men were not democrats but they were proposing universal schooling which would have guaranteed large-scale male literacy (in some cases, equal education was proposed for women) and the training of all to perform their social roles efficiently.[2]

Contemporary social reformers, therefore, often advocated the extension of schooling as an instrument of change. But what happened in practice? Most important of all, there was no educational 'system' such as we know today in modern societies. It is all too easy to look at the Tudor-Stuart educational scene and equate the ABC and Petty schools with the primary schools of today, and the grammar schools with the present-day secondary schools. Such was not the case.

A number of differing traditions were at work on the early modern educational scene. Among these that which urged institutionalised highly academic schooling for boys was but one, even if it is the one which has received most attention. Family, church and workshop were still important. There was still a strong tradition of academic education for the Church and for affiliated careers. Many town grammar schools were little influenced by the ideas of Renaissance scholars, continuing to emphasise the training of potential clergymen on the one hand and of tradesmen on the other. For this reason, it appears to have been common enough for a town school to combine a classical side with a vernacular side. Certainly a town school often possessed a relatively large Petties department which catered for the demand for basic vernacular literacy. And everywhere there were private schools and freelance school teachers who provided the type of education which the market demanded.

In the next chapter we shall be looking more closely at what was taught in the various types of school and how it was taught; here we shall concentrate on the numbers and distribution of different types of school.

The provision of schools in the Diocese of Lichfield and Coventry

Geographical distribution

The ephemeral schools run by freelance schoolmasters and mistresses are, of course, the most difficult to trace. The historian is forced to use diocesan archives for research into the development of such schools, but can such ecclesiastical records be expected to provide full and accurate information concerning the number, distribution and type of schools in an area? What are the limitations of our available evidence? In post-Reformation England the links between the schools and the Church were as marked as ever. Schoolmasters in the endowed grammar schools were ecclesiastical officers, often in orders, and held responsible in some sense to the Church authorities. Curates in the parishes were held responsible for the catechising of children – they often taught them to read simultaneously. Freelance schoolmasters and mistresses were obliged to obtain a licence to teach from the ordinary (bishop) of the diocese for a fee, just as were their counterparts in established schools. But how concerned were the ecclesiastical authorities to record accurate information about educational provision or to maintain control over teachers?[3]

In theory no one might exercise the office of teacher without prior admission and licensing by the bishop or his surrogates. This rule applied throughout the reigns of Elizabeth, James I and Charles I. It was feared that unlicensed schoolmasters might spread Catholic or Puritan religious views and thus prove dangerous. Dread of nonconformity rather than interest in education for its own sake seems to have been at the root of ecclesiastical concern to control teaching personnel. Schoolmasters after 1562 were made to subscribe to the Thirty-nine Articles of Religion and to the royal supremacy. This system of licensing was theoretically a perfect vehicle for episcopal control over education within the dioceses. In practice it was deficient in several respects. Even assuming the initial interest of the bishop in controlling education, the regulations were difficult to enforce. The dioceses were large in area. Bishops and even archdeacons did not exercise an immediate control over them. It was easy to evade the eye of the authorities and teach without a licence, particularly in the more remote parishes. Bishops had the machinery of the triennial episcopal visitation of all parishes at their command, but returns of unlicensed schoolteachers were still both spasmodic and unreliable because the decision to present a school-teacher to the authorities rested with the parishioners, who might not wish to lose their schoolteacher. Diocesan *libri cleri* (lists of ecclesiastical officers who presented their licences for inspection at the visitation) are no more satisfactory as a source. It cost 10 shillings to buy a licence and 3d. or more to exhibit one; it was expensive to travel to exhibit the licence or to hire a proxy to exhibit on one's behalf. Finally, it is clear that the authorities were primarily interested in exercising a close control over the grammar schools of the land and displayed only spasmodic interest in the control of freelance teachers and private schools. More often than not, such interest seems to have been stimulated from above – the Privy Council or the Archbishop.

Any estimate of the number, size, and type of schools within a given area which is based on the use of ecclesiastical records must be regarded, therefore, as a base figure rather than as an accurate representation of the growth and spread of schools within an area. This is not to say that we cannot glean a good deal about the distribution and type of schools from diocesan records.

Research into unendowed schools and freelance private school-masters has been thin on the ground, understandably. Nevertheless some detailed work has been done, and that on the Midland diocese of Coventry and Lichfield is of interest. This diocese spanned the counties of Staffordshire and Derbyshire and archdeaconries within the counties of Warwickshire and Shrewsbury. It contained approximately 420 to 500 units (depending upon whether or not chapelries are counted and peculiar jurisdictions included). The diocese possessed, for the most part, a rural population involved in agriculture. There were, however, pockets of urban growth and incipient industrial activity. The prosperous medieval city of Coventry was situated within the boundaries of the diocese and formed the focus of population in the Archdeaconry of Coventry, despite its own decline. Towns such as Derby, Shrewsbury and Birmingham were increasing in size and importance throughout the seventeenth century. Small market towns of only local importance, however, dominated the local economy.

I have tried to provide a minimum estimate of the school provision within this area between 1584 and 1639 based upon a thorough survey of the surviving diocesan records. This is a low figure not only because of the deficiencies in the enforcement of licensing by ecclesiastical officials but also because of the patchy survival rate of the documents. The documents at Lichfield do not cover all the four archdeaconries in equal depth – the county of Derby is especially poorly covered while Stafford archdeaconry is exceptionally well represented. In view then of the generally incomplete nature of the documentation it is the more significant that they reveal that at least 200 of the parishes in the diocese were at some time during the period of 1584 to 1642 served by at least one schoolmaster. In view of the regional bias of the visitation information available, one might expect that the impression of the relative distribution of educational facilities between the archdeaconries is distorted. Certainly the overly heavy representation of Stafford and the low documentation for Derby in the visitation books seems to be reflected in the regional breakdown of these 200 parishes: Stafford (70 [in 104 parishes and free chapelries]); Derby (47 [in 110]); Coventry (38 [in 109]); and Salop (45 [in 65]). Also difficult to explain is the low number of Archdeaconry of Coventry parishes apparently served by a schoolteacher during the period. Once one accepts that established grammar and town schools generally appear in the visitation presentments at some point during the time covered, it becomes clear that it is the private schools and schoolteachers which are in some areas either lacking or evading the record. The figures available for such schools are much more likely to be distorted than those for the endowed schools, for which, ironically enough, we often have other evidence in any case.

Within the diocese many parishes had 'schools' which depended for their very existence upon the services of an individual. When this schoolteacher either left the parish or died the 'school' which had existed was liable to collapse because it was in no way institutionalised. Of course, some of these schools were quite longstanding affairs where the schoolteacher remained for a long time in the parish, but their future was always uncertain. Thirty-five of the schools in Stafford archdeaconry were of this type; twenty-nine of those in Derbyshire; twenty-one of those in Coventry and twenty-two of those in Salop. In these archdeaconries the number of *unlicensed* schoolmasters running such schools, respectively, were 16, 3, 6 and 6 of the totals given. Therefore there were a substantial number of licensed schoolmasters apparently functioning outside the schools.

More difficult to treat are the 93 instances of parishes with at least a continuing educational tradition and probably a proper establishment. The archdeaconries were represented in this way: Stafford, 35; Salop, 23; Coventry, 17; Derby, 18. This number exceeds the number of endowed grammar schools listed in either Carlisle's *Endowed Grammar Schools* or W. A. L. Vincent's *The State and School Education*. It is probable that some of these schools, at least, were not grammar schools with a foundation. For instance, in 1606 George Minors obtained a licence to teach boys at Cheadle, Staffordshire; in 1620 he appeared as 'puerorum instructor' in an establishment of two teachers – the curate, James Holmes, being named as 'ludimagister'. The school was still in existence in 1639. No traces of its foundation survive. It was probably a small school with a grammar master and a teacher for the petties. It may or may not have been private or supported by village subscription. The school kept at St Alkmund's Shrewsbury, and St Chad, Shrewsbury, seem to have been strangely placed, within the same town as the well-known and large Shrewsbury Grammar School. Yet they appear to have been established feeder schools for this prominent endowed school.

Having said this, most of the established schools were either endowed grammar schools or town schools. If one looks at the geographical distribution of these established schools within each area, one observes a certain rough pattern. Stafford archdeaconry had within it eighteen market towns: fifteen of these had a continuous tradition of educational facilities; a further one probably possessed a grammar school by the end of the period; and the remaining two, Penkridge and Betley, had a school teacher of their own for at least a part of the time. Over half of the schools in Coventry were situated in market towns (all being grammar schools). Salop archdeaconry was not rich in market towns and such as existed were well served: nine schools existed in seven market towns. The market towns in an area were normally the largest parishes in terms of population, although this was not true of all (for example, Cheadle, Staffs.; Burton, Staffs.; Southam, Warws.; and Rugby, Warws., were small even by the standards of the day). Education developed in the market towns in response to internal population pressure but the market town, however small, also acted as a focus for the rural population of its hinterland.

Locatelli's discussion of the importance of trade routes for the development of education in France seems as relevant to the English situation. Each market town had its hinterland and there is every reason to believe that this was as true of education as it was of trade and religion. The southern part of the archdeaconry of Coventry, for example, was poorly served in educational terms: there was an absence of significant market towns and a low population density. The school at Southam, one of two small market towns in the south east of Coventry archdeaconry, can scarcely have developed in response to internal demand. As a town it was scarcely to be differentiated in terms of its size in 1563 from the surrounding rural parishes, but as the market town it had several built-in advantages in terms of communications, facilities, lodging opportunities and tradition. No doubt the same arguments pertain to the growth of Rugby School within the same deanery. The prominence of the market towns on the educational scene was, of course, not new. It was a continuation of the pre-Reformation situation. Market towns had been a focal point for craft and guild activity and for chantry foundations. Where a chantry school had once existed the population had become accustomed to the presence of educational opportunity and predisposed towards refoundation of the chantry school under other auspices or establishment of an equivalent facility.

Established schools also existed outside the market towns, however. Four of Coventry's 'schools' were located in parishes with a population of between 500 and 1,000 in 1563 (a reasonable size for a rural parish in the sixteenth century) but another four were established in parishes with very low population – Willoughby, Burton on Dunsmore, Great Harborough and Brinklow. More mystifying yet is the absence of an established school in one market town (Kenilworth) and in several quite large parishes, such as Wolston, Napton, Hillmorton, Hampton in Arden, Fillongley, Polesworth, Kinsbury and Stoneleigh. Perhaps the absence of a medieval tradition of educational provision explains this situation; perhaps it is more readily explicable in terms of the fact that, while most of the parishes mentioned appear to have employed private schoolteachers to teach the ABC to children, almost all were sufficiently close to a grammar school to make the foundation of a separate school seem unnecessary. Indeed it seems more remarkable that it was felt worth while to found grammar schools in such close proximity as those at Birmingham, Aston, Sutton Coldfield, Solihull and Coleshill. One is led to speculate again upon the extent to which the early modern educational scene was shaped by the medieval traditions of religious and educational life. Parishes with substantial population (by contemporary standards) might manage quite well by sending their children to a grammar school in an adjacent parish but, if they had become accustomed to the convenience of a school on the spot in late medieval times, might persist in this tradition. Then again, the establishment of a school might have more to do with the whim of an individual benefactor than with apparent demand – the large and well-reputed school at Repton, Derbyshire, for instance, was the result of the munificence of a local gentleman and it drew pupils from far afield. An analysis of the distribution of schooling based on economic and geographical factors should not be pushed too far.

The accessibility of schooling

At the same time, some areas were not rich in endowed schools and it is in these places that one might expect the distribution of schools to reflect demand. Leicestershire, for example, had few grammar schools endowed by generous individuals but a number of grammar schools in small market towns, financed by the town estate either in the form of endowment or direct funding, specifically for the education of freemen's children.[4]

Such local studies indicate that only a small proportion of the rural population was geographically distant from access to any kind of formal educational provision. One in four of the parishes of a far from progressive diocese maintained institutionalised schools, most of them grammar schools or town schools. Even in parishes without such a school there was commonly provision for the young to acquire basic literacy skills where the population warranted it.

Geography, however, does not provide the whole of the story. Even a distance of a very few miles from the nearest school might necessitate boarding and raise perhaps insuperable problems of finance. The 'tabling out' system was common – it was probably taken advantage of by the children of neighbouring parishes as well as by 'foreigners' from other counties. It should not be used as evidence of a particularly wide catchment area. As many schools adopted a sliding scale of fees which discriminated against children from other parishes and other counties, the costs of 'tabling out' added to the financial burden. At Shrewsbury school in the 1570s, for example, the sliding scale of fees read thus:

1. Son of a lord   10s.
2. Son of a knight   6s. 8d.
3. Eldest son of a gentleman   3s. 4d.
4. Younger sons of a gentleman   2s. 6d.
5. Those of lower degree born outside the county
   of Salop   2s.
6. Those of low degree born in Salop   1s.
7. Inhabitants of Shrewsbury   8d.
8. Sons of Shrewsbury burgesses   4d.

These were entrance fees and there is no suggestion that any pupil at Shrewsbury had to pay fees for tuition until the eighteenth century. The entrance fees levied appear to have been fairly typical. At Shrewsbury 'tablers' in the town were carefully controlled under the terms of Thomas Ashton's ordinances of 1578. As a large number of boys did come from outside the town, the problem of supervision must have been great for school and parents alike.

Tabling out, with all its attendant problems, was very common. Shrewsbury was a fashionable school, as was Repton, which contained as many as 340 pupils in 1622, of which 140 were tablers. Such schools attracted the sons of nobility and gentry in some numbers. But even a local school like that at Bridgnorth contained numbers of boarders, probably drawn from the surrounding parishes. Sometimes a family would circumvent the financial problems incurred in sending a child to a distant grammar school. Simonds D'Ewes lived with his grandfather. James Whitehall, native of Staffordshire and later Rector of Checkley, Staffordshire, was sent from home at the age of seven in 1586 to Atherley to attend school there and probably lived with relatives. In 1588 he moved again to Yeldersley, where he remained for three years. In 1591, at the age of twelve, he was transferred to the grammar school at Loughborough, where he tabled out and studied for six years. Those with sufficient funds and conveniently placed relatives could afford to choose schools further afield. The cost of tabling out varied. A gentry family might expect to pay approximately £18 p.a. (plus an additional £12 for clothing) for a son to 'table out', whereas a yeoman child might be boarded out for between £4 and £6 (presumably excluding the cost of cloth-

ing). It would thus cost as much to support a child living away
from home as it would to press a suit for recovery of a debt of £100
through the courts, which it has been speculated was beyond the
means of husbandmen and artisans worth £20 a year or less. Such a
cost would doubtless also put a strain upon the finances of a rural
middle-class family, although, in fact, the practice of 'tabling out'
did not become the preserve of the gentry until much later. Nevertheless, one senses that the economic pressures upon parents of the
yeoman/upper-artisan classes might have been sufficiently severe to
make them restrict the length of a son's stay at a grammar school
and to prefer the services of a local freelance teacher when they
were available.[5]

Schools which were geographically accessible to most of the rural
population were not, therefore, economically accessible to the
equivalent number. Sending one's children to a school of any kind
after the age of six disadvantaged many parents economically without
offering any obvious or immediate compensation, especially in rural
areas where the children were more useful than they were in urban
occupations. Other local studies have indicated that the relationship
between schooling and prosperity was high in early modern European society. In 1695 the bishop of Auxerre enjoined that every parish set up two schools, one for boys and one for girls, that all should
attend until the age of fourteen, and that a schoolmaster should be
appointed. The responses were diverse and reflected not only the
use which the population might make of education in its working
life but also the general prosperity of the area. For instance, whereas
urban areas, particularly market towns, responded well to the direc-
tive, the response was even better in the most prosperous part of
the diocese, which possessed no towns.[6]

In rural Cambridgeshire the availability of schooling varied even
within the county. Fen and valley areas in the west and east, which
were expanding economically in the late sixteenth and early seventeenth centuries, were well provided with institutionalised schools
whereas boulder-clay settlements to the west, economically in decline, had few such facilities although many employed a freelance
schoolmaster at one time or another. Work on three specific villages
indicated that in general it was the prosperous yeomen of these rural communities who demanded education and made most use of
the facilities. For example, the school in the prosperous fen village
of Willingham was endowed by public subscription in 1593: this support came primarily from half-yardlanders in the community who
could afford to subscribe an amount equivalent to two years' rent.
Many midland parishes supported a schoolmaster out of the parish
rates. Boys from some of these schools in Leicestershire attended a
grammar school before going on to university but in some cases
such a school would send a boy direct to the university, suggesting
at least some grounding in latin.[7]

Who then attended the schools of early modern England? One variety of freelance schoolteacher clearly serviced the demand among the husbandman and yeoman classes for reading skills. We can be reasonably confident that the school which Anna Hassall ran in 1616 in Staffordshire was such a school (and it is interesting to note that she taught boys). Similarly, the school held by the recusants Richard and Alice Cox in the same county in 1623 was probably of this elementary variety. Curates who also acted as schoolteachers may have offered more varied services – the teaching of reading and perhaps writing in the vernacular to some children, preparation for a classical education for some others. Twenty-two curate schoolmasters are locatable in Coventry and Lichfield diocese between 1600 and 1640; thirty-two occur between 1660 and 1700. But these are minimum figures.[8]

Perhaps the schools run by beneficed clergymen (not to be confused with the clergymen who also held schoolmasterships in endowed schools) more commonly restricted themselves to preparing boys for university with a classical education, although we cannot be certain of this. Richard Baxter, for example, was coached by a local clergyman in the early seventeenth century. The distribution of such schools and their frequency is uncertain. Boys from 145 unendowed schools were sent to the three Cambridge colleges of Caius, Christ's and St John's, as compared with 127 endowed grammar schools. Some of these unendowed schools undoubtedly were run by clerics. For example, a school run by Matthew Stonham of St Stephen's, Norwich, sent no fewer than thirty-eight boys to university from 1626 to 1637, during which time Norwich Grammar School sent up only eleven. The dominance of the unendowed schools in this diocese is evident, yet it is not possible to provide precise statistics as to the number of incumbent clergymen involved in them. A study of unendowed schools in Coventry and Lichfield was able to discover no more than three incumbents recorded as vicar or rector and schoolteacher in the visitation material for the period 1600 to 1640. This number rose to nine between 1660 and 1700. Yet, as we have said, the absence of any such mention may be a dangerous argument to employ against the view that the beneficed parochial clergy were deeply involved in the education of children. As with preaching, many clergymen regarded themselves as within their rights to teach school within their own parishes and resented the requirement that they pay for and exhibit a licence. In a system where the cost to the teacher would almost certainly be passed onto the pupils in the form of increased fees, one may suspect that few parishioners were eager to present the incumbent for holding a school without licence. Where there was no school building, it was relatively easy to evade the eyes of the visitors. It is probable that, where there was a demand for education of boys in the classics, the local clergy would respond when endowed facilities proved inadequate or inconveniently located. Some parents may have preferred this system because it most often amounted to tuition in small groups and because it was more easily controlled by consumer tastes than were the endowed schools, bound by statutes and the supervision of school governors.[9]

There is painfully little evidence available regarding the clientele of individual endowed schools, either of the petty or grammar school variety – certainly far too little to make any statistical assessments. What we do know seems to support further the argument that after an opening up of educational facilities to a broad section of the community in the 1560s, there was a certain closing up of educational opportunity thereafter. As early as 1562 Shrewsbury Free Grammar School had 266 pupils, and this at a time shortly after its re-foundation and when it had no 'accidence school'. At the start the student body had quite an aristocratic air about it – both Philip Sidney and Fulke Greville attended it in the 1560s – largely due to the interest shown in it by the Lord President of the Council in Wales. But of the 266 boys, exactly 133 were inhabitants of the city of Shrewsbury. The school clearly had tremendous initial support from within the urban community. The fact that not all of the remainder were Shropshire born should not disturb this point unduly for Shrewsbury served the surrounding counties of Herefordshire and North Wales, as indeed the Dean and Chapter of Hereford acknowledged when they petitioned for their own school 'to serve as commodiously for the training of the youth of South Wales as Shrewsbury doth for the youth of North Wales'. It seems significant that the proportion of town boys dropped during Thomas Ashton's Headmastership in the 1560s – of 663 boys entered between 1562 and 1570 only 106 came from Shrewsbury itself. The balance between townsmen and outsiders appears to have been restored under Headmaster Thomas Lawrence in the 1570s – of a list of 201 boys entered from Christmas 1571, only 93 were aliens. But if we analyse the social origins of pupils during the 1580s we discover that this restoration of town support did not imply the dominance of the sons of traders and artisans. During this period the school prospered in terms of numbers. In 1581, for instance, there were approximately 360 pupils (presumably including the Accidence School) and indications are that numbers in the Upper School normally exceeded the 270 mark until the 1620s when the school entered a period of decline. For the year 1589/90 118 new boys were entered. An analysis of this number revealed that 33 were sons of Shrewsbury burgesses; a mere 5 were sons of inhabitants of Shrewsbury below gentleman status; 18 were boys below that degree born in Salop; 28 boys below the rank of gentleman came from other counties (not stipulated); and the entry fees of 30 gentlemen's sons, 3 lord's sons and 1 knight's son were also recorded. Similar rates of entry prevailed until 1621 when the number of recorded fee payments fell to 79. Again a high proportion were sons of gentlemen (22) and sons of burgesses (26) although the number of other inhabitants of Shrewsbury had risen (9) at the expense of those who were Shropshire born (8) and those who came from outside the county (14). At first glance it may, therefore, appear that Shrewsbury lost its aura of high fashion after the sixteenth century (when the numbers of boys attracted from outside the county fell) and became even more of a town grammar school. Yet this impression is partly illusory. The sons of yeomen, tradesmen and artisans were certainly not excluded from Shrewsbury but it was essentially a school for the rural and urban élite of Shropshire (and especially Shrewsbury). At least a proportion of the pupils of below gentleman rank were the sons of clergymen and other minor professionals.[10]

Another school within the diocese of Lichfield also appealed to the gentry: Repton in Derbyshire. Here the expenses of 'poor' scholars were paid in accordance with the original endowment but families such as the Sleighs, Burdetts, Harpurs and Stanhopes certainly sent their sons there to be educated and boasted of its superiority to Derby Grammar School. William Ullock came there from Cumberland. The only definite estimate of its size which survives is that of 1622 which suggests a student body of 340, of whom over half came from the immediate neighbourhood and the remainder found it necessary to 'table out'. Another old Reptonian, John Bradshaw, later maintained that the school had three hundred scholars towards the end of Whitehead's headmastership in the 1630s. It is intriguing to note that Repton, an endowed grammar school, nevertheless appears to have been sensitive to consumer demand and to have educated at least some boys in vernacular skills to a high level.[11]

It is tempting to work only with the more prominent endowed schools, which were more fashionable and presumably more attractive to the well-to-do. Yet where comparisons are possible with less eminent endowed or town schools, the student body seems remarkably constant in composition.

Fashionable Bury St Edmunds School in 1656 showed 'not a single recognisably poor child on the roll'. Five pupils were sons of knights, twenty-five of esquires, fifteen of gentry and one of the Governor of a Caribbean island. The precise social breakdown was as follows:[12]

Aristocratic	52%
Clergy/Professional	17%
Tradesmen*	16%
Yeomen	c. 15%
Husbandmen	0

* Drawn from upper ranks of Bury's shopkeepers and tradesmen

The situation was not significantly different at Colchester Free Grammar School, more typical of the average market town. The admissions register of the school, from 1637 to 1645, recorded the names of 165 boys, whose social breakdown was as follows:[13]

Aristocratic	31%
Clergy/Professional	20%
Tradesmen*	37%
Yeomen	12%
Husbandmen	0
Labourers	0

* This number includes a few children of artisans and clothworkers.

The differences in the composition of the student body of Colchester reflect its relative lack of appeal for the upper aristocracy and the openness of this school to a wider segment of the urban community – as opposed to Bury, a few children of clothworkers and artisans did attend the grammar school. Nevertheless, the school at Colchester served the rural community scarcely at all. Significantly enough, in the 1670s even yeomen admissions to the school ceased, leaving the urban grammar school exclusively to the rural gentry and to the urban middle classes. The situation at both St Alban's and Lavenham was similar. The statutes of The Perse School, Cambridge, stipulated that 100 boys from Cambridge, Barnwell, Chesterton or Trumpington be taught gratis 'and no more nor any other'. But by 1622 this rule had been modified to allow the admission of fee-paying students provided that the master paid for additional assistance. Further it was laid down that no place on the foundation be given to the child of a rich parent if a poor man's child were a candidate. This suggests that, between its opening in 1618 and these new rules, the middle classes were already seeking to adapt this charitable foundation to their own purposes. Most foundationers during the seventeenth century were the sons of urban tradesmen, college servants and professionals. At least 100 boys went from the Perse to Cambridge between 1618 and 1636, some on Perse scholarships.[14] Harborough town grammar school was founded in 1614 to accommodate 90 children but provided free education for only 15.[15]

Given these detailed studies we are probably safe in regarding town grammar schools in average market towns, with no reputation for fashionability, as similar to Colchester in their composition in the seventeenth century. For example, Wolverhampton, which had two masters and 69 pupils in 1609 probably had a much more urban complexion than Repton or Shrewsbury, despite the absolutely higher numbers of urban youth at both the latter. And we must beware of thinking that the curriculum at such urban grammar schools was strictly classical. Although it was apparently unusual for boys not intending to go to university to stay beyond the age of 14, William Lilly at Ashby in 1618 complained that he was the only boy in the top forms who was not to attend university.[16] A school list for Wolverhampton in 1609 (Table 3.1) shows that about half the pupils who took latin studies under the master from the ages of 9–14 left before entering the two top forms. In addition the usher at the school taught a much larger number of 8–13-year-olds and a small group of petties.[17]

Table 3.1 Wolverhampton 1609

	Class	Age-range	Number of pupils
Master	2 top forms	14–18	9
	2 next forms	9–14	19
Usher	2 forms	8–13	30
	Accidence class	6–13	11
			Total 69

All the evidence appears to point to the conclusion that, gentry apart, the grammar schools (whether fully endowed or supported by town corporations) failed to accommodate pupils from rural areas in large numbers. They possessed, with the exception of a few fashionable schools, a lower-upper-class/middle-class complexion. Seemingly, such members of the yeomanry as wanted a classical education sought it in their villages – either by supporting a freelance schoolteacher or private school or by banding together to subscribe to a village school. As we noted in the chapter on literacy, the indications are that very few below yeoman level required a classical education and were, therefore, influenced by Renaissance currents of education in any direct sense.

Number and distribution of schools in Wales

The outlook was rather less rosy in Wales than in England. Certainly a number of grammar schools had been endowed during the period 1540 to 1640. These included prominent establishments at Bangor and Carmarthen. But these endowed schools served the towns only and the countryside remained neglected. As the population was scattered and as access to towns was often much poorer than it was in England, the situation was serious. Moreover, there were no opportunities for the children of Welsh-speaking parents.

The situation was temporarily improved under the Commonwealth and Protectorate governments. Approximately sixty new schools were established by the Commissioners for the Propagation of the Gospel in Wales between 1650 and 1654. Most of these were founded in the larger towns and in the market towns and villages. Some, such as that at Wrexham, offered the full range of subjects to university level while others, that at Carew, Pembrokeshire, for example, simply served these larger grammar schools. The Commissioners normally ordered quite good provision and endowment for these schools.

The schools were not always wisely sited, however. Not a few of the country schools failed because they were too inaccessible. Llangorse and Bottwnog grammar schools, for example, were themselves so far away from housing that pupils could not even table out in the vicinity. At the same time, the transfer of responsibility for the maintenance of these schools and their schoolmasters from the Commissioners to the Trustees for the Maintenance of Ministers in 1654, hit the foundations hard. By the Restoration only twenty-one of the original sixty foundations still survived. Certainly this represented an improvement over the sixteenth-century position. Wales now had twenty-eight more schools than it had in 1600, if we include early seventeenth-century endowments. Nevertheless, it was cause enough for concern that in a country with such poor communications a county like Brecon retained only two of its nine mid-century endowments.[18]

Insufficient work has been done on early schooling in Wales for us to arrive at any hard and fast conclusions regarding the distribution of schools and their geographic and economic accessibility. Nevertheless, such work as has been done suggests that the mere presence of a grammar school in a market town did not necessarily meet the educational requirements of a community. In Wales, the Welsh speaking community was entirely unserved; the grammar schools catered for an English-speaking gentry. In addition, remote country areas were also out of reach of schools. In some respects Wales was a special case – not every region of England had a similar language problem, for example – but in others it resembled other areas of Britain. One wonders whether some of those areas of England characterised by geographically large and sprawling parishes suffered similarly when it came to the children therein actually reaching a 'local' school. Certainly it is important to count the number of parishes with schools in any one area, but some knowledge of the topography and geography of the region is required before one can estimate the accessibility of such schools and their probable clientele.

Comparison with the situation in the later Middle Ages

Attempts to impose a pattern on the forms of early modern education available are doomed to failure – what one is faced with is not simply a division between an endowed and a private sector. In a way difficult to comprehend today, individuals and isolated communities were influencing the forms of education as much as educational theory was influencing them. Freelance teachers and schools were sensitive to educational demand: to some extent, they were also responsive to institutional pressures (for instance, to that from the universities) but this was a far less marked influence than it is today, when national examinations and standardised tests dictate what is taught in schools. Even endowed schools, although bound by their statutes, made concessions to parental wishes and community requirements. And so the historian, who loves to categorise, is faced with a multiplicity of types of school, each the product of differing traditions as well as of the interplay between these traditions and specific circumstances. Yet this is an accurate portrayal of the provision of education at the elementary/grammar level in early modern England and Wales.

We have described the provision of educational facilities and concluded that, on the one hand, schooling was geographically accessible to most of the population and, on the other hand, that it was economically inaccessible and/or less coveted among some sections of the population than others. Yet we must not see this issue out of context. Does it represent a dramatic change since the later Middle Ages or since the Reformation? It was once believed that the Dissolution of the Monasteries by Henry VIII and of the Chantries by his son, Edward VI, destroyed a lively tradition of education while neglecting to replace it with the new schools for which the commonwealthmen longed. This view came under attack in the mid twentieth century from historians who suspected that there had been no significant educational provision by the monasteries and chantries on the eve of the Reformation, no matter what the situation in the fourteenth century, and who claimed that real strides were made in the direction of widespread educational provision in sixteenth- and early seventeenth-century England and Wales, despite the failure of the state to finance a 'national' system of schools and colleges. Evidence for this argument was supplied from many quarters: the endowment of grammar schools throughout the country, especially from the reign of Elizabeth onwards; the large numbers of young men entering the universities and the Inns of Court during the same period; the great interest in the issue displayed by educational theorists and social reformers. Since the mid 1970s this position has been made considerably less secure. As Chapter 5 suggests it may well prove impossible to argue a discontinuity with the medieval period based on evidence from the universities of the 1560s, 70s and 80s. It is impossible to estimate with any degree of accuracy the undergraduate population of Oxford, for example, before the introduction of the first matriculation statute of 1564. Equally, as we indicated in Chapter 2, the interest in expanding the total number of schools and in extending education to all classes was far from constant during the period between the Reformation and the Civil Wars. And work on educational provision spanning the period between the early fifteenth century and the Reformation indicates that schooling was more accessible in late medieval England than has been allowed in recent times.[19]

The tradition of the secular endowed grammar school was already prospering in the fifteenth century, although most schools were dedicated still to the education of priests and clerks. A brief study of pre- and post-Reformation schools in Berkshire and Oxfordshire suggests that the medieval tradition was continued and enhanced in these counties. Before the Reformation there were fourteen established schools. Two of these were attached to important religious houses and trained novices and choristers. In 1437 a school was founded at Ewelme to educate local children in grammar. A school established at Childrey in 1526 combined instruction in latin grammar and the vernacular. In the 1480s Magdalen College School was the first grammar school offering free education to all comers in Oxford. There were nine other schools which were totally dependent upon chantry foundations. After the Reformation most of these schools continued. Newbury and Chipping Norton (former chantry schools) continued under state patronage. Five other chantry schools were refounded between 1550 and 1670. At Burford the townspeople had endowed the guild of Our Lady in order to support a schoolmaster and, when the school was refounded in 1571, the town corporation assumed the management of the school. Local interest in Chipping Camden school was also evinced: in 1572 the townspeople bought a messuage and garden to provide for a well-qualified schoolmaster; in 1606 a charter confirmed corporation control of the school. Similarly, Henley, Oxford, Banbury and Wantage all petitioned for royal charters to establish their control over the local schools. Numerically, the number of grammar schools in the two counties increased over the period between 1547 and 1670, from fourteen to twenty-five, although it is unclear whether the Chantry certificates of 1547 would have revealed the existence of non-chantry foundations. In any event, clearly every market town of standing had a school by 1547. The new schools were founded on the personal initiative of gentlemen, merchants and local clergy. In two of the ten cases mentioned, a merchant refounded a chantry or monastic school. These schools fit into the picture which we have sketched of urban grammar schools satisfying the demands of the gentry and of the merchants and new professionals (clergy, attorneys, clerks). They tell us a good deal about the new interests of these groups, about the newly created demand for an educated parochial clergy, and about the prominence of the market towns as educational/cultural centres. But they do not indicate a development which affected other levels of town society or rural areas. For that, we would need evidence of an enormous increase in the provision of basic education in rural areas, and this is absent.[20]

The records which survive of educational provision in late medieval England are not rich. Nevertheless, it has been demonstrated, for example, that every fifty years between 1250 and 1500 the number of grammar schools in the large diocese of York increased by two. In fact, the number of such schools increased twofold in this 250-year period. There was a more marked threefold increase in the first half of the sixteenth century, especially between 1530 and 1550. The data for song and reading schools shows that such elementary institutions tripled in number in the fifteenth century and increased approximately sixfold between the fourteenth century and the Reformation. In 1500 the elementary institutions in York diocese were three times more numerous than the grammar schools; the elementary institutions were still twice as common as grammar schools even after 1500 when more attention was being given to the establishment of grammar schools. And the absolute numbers involved in each case were far from small. Excluding the city of York, 36 song schools, 38 reading schools and 22 grammar schools were traced in the diocese between 1450 and 1499. In this diocese at least there was a lively medieval educational tradition. An examination of education in Cornwall, Devon, Dorset, Gloucestershire, Somerset and Wiltshire between 1066 and 1530 revealed the existence of at least 66 secular and 38 religious establishments, most of them dating from the late Middle Ages. Taken together with the evidence for rising rates of lay literacy in the later Middle Ages, such information suggests that the improvement in educational provision in the later sixteenth and early seventeenth centuries was the intensification of an existing trend rather than a dramatic development which emerged 'out of the blue' with the Renaissance. There was a rise in the number of schools in the Elizabethan and early Stuart periods but this rise was not sudden, nor was it entirely due to the impact of Renaissance conviction that gentlemen must be properly educated to serve the state. Some schools in England and Wales undoubtedly bore the imprint of Renaissance humanist theory, but many more continued in the tradition of earlier centuries, serving the utilitarian requirements of their patrons and absorbing such of this new attitude to education as was appropriate to this task.[21]

Chapter 4

Curriculum and method in schools, c. 1550–1650

The teaching of reading

By studying how youth was taught we can discover something of the intention behind school and university education; discover how these pupils were prepared to accept learning or reject it as integral to their lives; and learn a little about contemporary attitudes to youth and the learning process. The *how* should be studied simultaneously with the *why* and the *what*. Just as curriculum and method are associated in twentieth-century education, so they were in early modern education.

In this chapter I shall be summarising our knowledge to date of the curriculum adopted at all stages of schooling, and noting the motivation of which contemporaries were conscious. But most of all I shall be examining such indications we have of the teaching methods employed in each context and the extent to which these support the theory that education was an agent of revolution. Much of what is said here is applicable to methods of teaching employed in the universities also but specific consideration of university teaching is contained in Chapter 6.

In the early modern period it was the responsibility of the Church (through curates) to catechise children prior to confirmation. English Protestants undoubtedly attached a good deal of importance to education in the battle against Catholicism. Although many Protestants criticised the Bishops of the Church of England for neglecting the confirmation of children, this concern arose from the increased interest in the religious instruction of children during the Reformation period. Education was now a tool of conversion. In 1523 Wynken de Worde had issued a primer containing the Lord's Prayer in English. In c. 1534 the first wholly vernacular and approved primer was written by John Byddell for William Marshall. This first Primer contained English prayers but no prefatory alphabet. It was, of course, not only intended for the use of children but for the religious instruction of all Christian people.[1] The 1536 Injunctions ordered that the clergy should teach the youth of the parish the Lord's Prayer, the Creed and the Ten Commandments in two ways.

The clauses of the prayers should be recited in sermons (to be duly repeated by the congregation) until the whole was learned by heart. Written versions of the same should be made available to those who could read for private study.[2]

Injunctions of 1538 stipulated that recitation of the contents of the Primer was necessary before a child could be admitted to communion and ordered that the petty teachers of the Church should be responsible for ensuring that all the children knew the creed, Lord's Prayer, Ten Commandments and Ave Maria in English.[3] Apparently it was accepted that children should learn to read the same because it became common for primers to contain a printed alphabet. Attempts were made to control the form of the primer and catechism – in 1545 King Henry's *Primer* introduced a set form.[4] Some primers contained not only an alphabet but also a syllable table and in *c.* 1547 an official A.B.C. was issued which offered simple spelling exercises also.

Licensed catechisms were an important part of this religious instruction of the young. Catechisms took the form of a debate: a question was posed and an answer supplied. The catechism was then (and is now) an oral exercise in which the memory plays a great part. The ability to read for oneself the text of the catechism was merely an aid to learning the questions and appropriate responses. This form of debate or disputation was part of the fabric of the learning process in medieval and early modern England: it was common at every level, ABC School, grammar school, university; it placed a premium on memorising *accepted* thought and frowned upon free thinking.[5] Attention has been drawn to the existence and persistence of the oral method of study and learning in England.[6] Even those who could not themselves read were introduced to the world of the mind by attentive listening to those who could and did read aloud; by memorising long passages of books read; and by discussing what was read in a group situation. Learning and reading was much less a personal, private activity (an isolated and isolating activity) than it is for today's children. Even when one had learned to read (today a group activity) one continued to read aloud and to share one's reading with others. In the diocese of Salisbury in the early fifteenth century, Lollards were meeting together to read the Bible – an activity which involved listening and discussing as well as reading the symbols. Foxe's account of the Lollard community in the Chilterns indicates how widespread reading was among the Lollards and mentions one family in particular. Richard Collins owned and taught from several English books. His wife, Alice, knew by heart much of the Scriptures: when a conventicle was held in Burford she was sent for to *recite* the Epistles of Peter and James and the Ten Commandments. Their daughter, Joan, had learnt some five chapters of St James's Epistle and other prayers and passages.[7] Reading, teaching and memorising, therefore, were part of a longstanding tradition and were more closely interconnected than they are today. Reading was a communal activity. Yet the extent to which contemporaries wished reading to be an active process, a two-way communication between reading material and reader, is doubtful. Clearly the 'establishment' did not wish reflection upon the authorised readings to constitute any more than acceptance of their contents. While some of the Elizabethan and Stuart church hierarchy saw the religious reformation as a continuing process, those in command regarded it as accomplished and sought to curtail further change. In any event, none considered further reformation to be the concern of the ordinary 'reader'. The Protestant emphasis on educating the laity in religion, therefore, consisted of a stress on the acquisition of knowledge and approved doctrine and not on a cultivation of critical and creative techniques.

Catechisms became very popular in the sixteenth century and made considerable sums of money for those printers who had the monopoly of producing them. The first Book of Common Prayer of 1549 had an English catechism and in the 1570s Dean Alexander Nowell's catechisms were recognised as authoritative, despite their unofficial status. Booksellers carried numerous copies of these primers and catechisms. In 1595 Andrew Maunsell's catalogue listed no fewer than sixty different catechisms on sale. A Warrington bookseller in 1648 had a stock of more than 1,200 volumes, among which were a sizeable collection of primers, psalters, Bibles, catechisms, puritan sermons and devotional guides.[8] Diligent ministers produced their own catechisms to counteract the ignorance and irreligion of their parishioners, young and old. Some of these reached a wider public through print but it is probable that many more were used within one parish alone. Immanuel Bourne, rector of Ashover, Derbyshire, circulated his own catechism to try to counteract local superstition and then printed it for wider circulation. He was following in the steps of his father, who had also written and circulated a catechism. In the 1620s Bishop Thomas Morton of Coventry and Lichfield is said to have purchased some 500 copies of a catechism and distributed them among the parishes of his large diocese.[9] Although it was the responsibility of the curate (or the reader) to catechise the young and ensure that they could repeat the responses correctly, this responsibility was shared by fathers and masters of households who engaged in family prayer and catechising sessions. When John Stalham, vicar of Terling from 1632 to 1662, published a catechism in 1644 he did so 'at the desire of divers for the private instruction of their little children and more ignorant servants ... because sufficient written copies cannot be procured', which in itself suggests, tantalisingly, that many manuscript copies of such catechisms and guides were produced. Alice Wandesford described in her autobiography how her father, Sir Christopher Wandesford, a Laudian, held family prayers three times daily at 6 a.m., 10 a.m. and 9 p.m. After his death, her mother assumed this duty. Contemporary handbooks, such as William Gouge's *Of Domestical Duties* (1622), reinforced this religious role of the father with their advice and as late as 1715 Daniel Defoe's *The Family Instructor* was attempting to shore up this ancient practice.[10]

Some children learned to read during this religious instruction. But other ways to literacy were open to the children of town or village. Children might attend a Dame school, petty school or ABC school. It is impossible to establish how much attempts to teach poorer children to read as well as to spin and knit were motivated as much by the need to keep very young children willing to sit still and quiet as by the Protestant ideal of a people able to read the Bible for themselves. It is at least interesting to speculate that reading was a by-product of many Dame schools rather than their principal purpose. Recently Margaret Spufford has argued that children were not an economic asset before the age of seven and that, as a consequence, many relatively poor children did manage to master the art of reading. Her assumption is that reading was commonly taught either at home or in school before that age. Writing, she asserts, was taught during the eighth year and was thus put out of reach of the poorer children whose labour was needed at home. Unfortunately, the argument is based upon evidence from a rather small sample of highly unusual people – autobiographers. Nevertheless, this work does suggest that purely passive literacy may have been more common than David Cressy is willing to allow. Of course, the Dame and ABC schools were often transitory and they charged fees. For this reason a child's school experience might be brief and/or irregular. Depending upon the aptitude of the child, he or she might learn to read or merely to recite the alphabet after such a schooling.[11]

How was reading taught? Pupils were introduced to the limited vocabulary of parts of the Church's liturgy via the ABC and syllable tables printed in either the primers or the hornbooks. The approach was a combination of look-and-say, familiarity with the material, and phonetics, and was often not very considered. There was little intention that in learning this task pupils would be fitted to read other books. Few considered that in reading the Scriptures the pupils might feel emboldened to challenge the interpretation offered by churchmen and, specifically, their parson. But for many children the effect was, eventually, just that. The children applied their new skill to other books. Some of them thought about what they read; some of them began to challenge accepted opinion.

One of the most interesting developments in early modern education is the emergence of printed manuals of instruction for teachers in the mid sixteenth century. The earliest of these to be published were John Hart's *Orthography* (1569) and *Method* (1570). Some of these books, notably Ascham's *The Scholemaster*, were intended not only for use by the schoolmaster himself but for use in lieu of a schoolmaster by adult pupils – they were 'how to' books rather than simply 'how to teach' books. But all encouraged practising teachers to consider purpose, material and method in the light of current educational thought.[12]

The most popular manual of reading instruction was that produced by Edmund Coote, a teacher in the free school of Bury St Edmunds, Suffolk. This book, *The English Schoolmaster*, went through twenty-six editions between 1596 and 1656 and was still in use in the early eighteenth century, the last edition appearing in 1704. The content of Coote's book was typical of reading manuals of the late sixteenth and early seventeenth centuries. The child is first introduced to the upper- and lower-case alphabets; then he is taught vowels and consonants; then he proceeds to graded vocabulary exercises (using verses to facilitate learning) which introduce words of one, two and three syllables and which stress mechanical accuracy rather than comprehension; next the pupil is taught to syllabify using a catechistical method.

Scholar Sir, I do not un-der-stand what you mean by a syllable?
Master　A syl-la-ble is a per-fect sound, made of so ma-ny let-ters, as we
　　　　　spell to-ge-ther: as in di-vi-si-on you see few-er syl-la-bles.
Scholar How ma-ny let-ters may be in a syl-la-ble?

Then the child learns rules of pronunciation, engages in a spelling contest with other members of the class, practises his reading skills via a catechism and primer, learns rules of behaviour and gains some understanding of number.[13]

John Brinsley's method

But, if Coote's *The English Schoolmaster* was the most commonly adopted method of teaching reading, John Brinsley's *Ludus Literarius* is one of the most intriguing introductions to the thought of a progressive teacher.[14] Brinsley presented his manual in the form of a lively dialogue between two schoolmasters, Spondeus, who has had a dispiriting teaching experience, and Philoponus, who has discovered a successful method or approach. The design of the book is valuable for our purposes because it sets out existing practice (*c.* 1612) as well as Brinsley's recommendations for a new approach.[15]

Spondeus For the time of their entrance with us, in our country schools, it
　　　　　is commonly about 7 or 8 years old; six is very soon. If any begin
　　　　　so early, they are rather sent to the school to keep them from
　　　　　troubling the house at home, and from danger, and shrewd
　　　　　turns, than for any great hope and desire their friends have that
　　　　　they should learn anything in effect.

Phil.   I find that therein first is a very great want generally; for that the child if he be of any ordinary towardness and capacity, should begin at five years old at the uttermost, or sooner rather.
My reasons are these:
1. Because that then children will begin to conceive of instruction, and to understand, and be able not only to know their letters, to spell and to read, but also to take a delight therein, and to strive to go before their fellows. . .
2. Very reason must needs persuade every one of this. For if they be apt much before five years of age, to learn shrewdness, and those things which are hurtful, which they must be taught to unlearn again; why are they not as well fit to learn those things which are good and profitable for them, if they be entered and drawn on in such a manner, as they may take a delight and find a kind of sport and play in the same. This delight may and ought to be in all their progress, and most of all the first entrance to make them the better to love the school, and learning, as we shall see after.

Very early in *Ludus Literarius* we become acquainted with some of the assumptions which Brinsley confronted in contemporary attitudes to teaching the very young to read and the premises upon which he himself acted in his capacity as schoolmaster in Leicestershire. Early childhood was evidently regarded as a period of play – Spondeus objected that parents would claim that 'it will hinder the growth of their children to be sent to school so young' and Brinsley's own argument was that learning itself was and should be a form of play and that it could no more hinder their growth than 'their play doth, but rather further it, when they sit at their ease'.[16] Brinsley clearly shared the views of William Perkins and Richard Greenham regarding the education of the young. If children did not learn profitable things in their early years, then they would certainly learn bad things, which would have to be unlearned at great cost. Schooling at an early age would keep children out of bad company and prevent them from associating pleasure with idleness. At this early age it was much easier to shape the child in a particular way because he was at his 'most pliant'.[17] In addition, claimed Brinsley, early education would reap dividends later on – the child would be prepared earlier for university or vocation. Moreover, it was the parents' responsibility to educate the children while they were yet alive – at a time when life expectancy was low, this argument was probably a telling one.[18]

Brinsley's approach to the teaching of reading was derivative from Coote's but he made some interesting statements concerning the application of this method. For instance the child was not only sent to recite the ABC front to back and back to front but also 'to find out, and to show you which is a, which b, which c, which f, and so any other letter. First to find them in the alphabet, then in any other place' – a game played by children in early learning situations today.[19] Interestingly, the child was to learn to spell before he could read. Spelling was a collective activity: 'Let so many as are beginners, or who cannot read perfectly, stand together, and then parse them without book, one by one.'[20] The child was to engage in half an hour's drill of spelling words and syllables daily, using Coote's *The English Schoolmaster*. Such a method emphasised the connections between pronunciation and spelling.

Brinsley went in to some detail regarding suitable reading matter. First the child was to read the ABC and the primer, preferably twice over, 'For the second reading of any book doth much encourage children, because it seemeth to be so easy then; and also it doth imprint the more.'[21] But then the child would read other material, again chosen because it was easy to learn and therefore encouraging for the beginner – 'Amongst which the Psalms in metre would be one, because children will learn that book with most readiness and delight through the running of the metre, as it is found by experience' and then the New Testament.[22] Brinsley also recommended some more secular socialising material – *The School of Virtue* and *The Schoole of Good Manners*. Coote had offered:[23]

The School-master to his scholars

My child and scholar, take good heed,
unto the words which here are set:
and see you do accordingly,
or else be sure you shall be beat.

First, I command thee God to serve,
then to thy parents duty yield:
Unto all men be courteous,
and mannerly in town and field.

Your clothes unbuttoned do not use,
let not your hose ungartered be:
Have handkerchief in readiness,
wash hands and face, or see not me.

Lose not your books, inkhorn nor pen,
nor girdle, garters, hat nor band:
Let shoes be tied, pin shirts and close
keep well your points at any hand.

If broken hosed or shoed you go,
or slovenly in your array:
Without a girdle, or untrust,
then you and I must make affray.

If that you cry, or talk aloud,
or books do rend, or strike with knife,
Or laugh or play unlawfully,
then you and I must be at strife.

If that you curse, miscall, or swear,
if that you pick, filch, steal or lie:
If you forget a scholar's part,

then must you sure your points untie.

If to the school you do not go,
when time doth call you to the same:
Or if you loiter in the streets,
when we do meet, then look for blame.

Wherefore (my child) behave thyself
so decently at all essays,
That thou mayest purchase parent's love,
and eke obtain thy master's praise.

The emphasis within this poem on corporal punishment should not blind us to the significance of the schoolmaster's claim to socialise the child. Through attendance at school a child learns to become a good Christian and a good citizen; he learns the mores of the society in which he lives. In a society (such as that of the Middle Ages) when schools were clerically orientated, such aims were only occasionally voiced, although 'household education' was specifically designed to socialise the child. It is in the sixteenth century that the *concept* of the school as a superior agent of socialisation and acculturation is fully developed alongside its academic functions. The claim had a certain novelty in a society where schooling outside the home was still not accepted as the norm. The process whereby both the academic and the social 'bringing up' of children increasingly was moved out of the family and into the schoolhouse was one of the most distinctive contributions of early modern educational thought. What is most intriguing is not that schools performed this socialising function, for medieval schools had done that, but that a coherent theory was developed which rationalised this dual purpose.

John Brinsley's chief interest for the historian has been said to lie in his treatment of Lily's Latin Grammar and its central role in the curriculum of the early seventeenth-century grammar school, but his comments on the simultaneous maintenance of competence in the vernacular seem equally notable. His view that the instruction of the young in English was essential to later learning and that it could not be neglected even in the absence of special ABC and Petty schools was not unusual, but his insistence on the need to maintain vernacular literacy was. Spondeus complained that once they began work in Latin, children lost their ability to read English while parents asked that he prevent this occurring by arranging daily Bible reading at the expense of their Latin studies. Philoponus replied that the vernacular was important and that learning of it could be maintained during the child's learning of Latin. The pupil should read Lily's rules, practise orthography, translate from Latin into good English prose and verse. He should learn to write letters to his friends in both languages. Pupils would take notes on sermons, declare the best ways of saying things, and read directly from Latin into good English. Brinsley recommended, for example, that the children learn to précis stories in the best English possible: 'Amongst some of them, the reporting of a Fable in English, or the like matter, trying who can make the best report, doth much further them in this.' And, of course, parents can help by encouraging home Bible reading, which is primarily a parental responsibility.[24]

Brinsley's detailed instructions regarding religious education are equally revealing. He recommends that half an hour a week should be spent learning and answering the catechism: each child should read and learn a set amount of the catechism and repeat this cumulatively, so that eventually the whole catechism will be known by heart. The ushers or senior members of the class were to test knowledge of the catechism and then the master would step in and test those whom he suspects of knowing it rather less than well. The pupils were also expected to attend and listen attentively to sermons on Sundays: the monitor supervised their attendance and note-taking. Even those who could not read could take memory notes – some three or four points which they were expected to memorise and repeat in the classroom the next day. Those who could write even a little were to memorise five or six points and, when they came out of church, to discuss them with their friends and note them down. Those who were more advanced were to make their notes according to a pattern: text; theses (doctrines asserted); proofs; the use of these proofs. In the very highest forms of all more detailed notes were expected, in which not only the content of the sermon would be indicated but also its import and application. Pupils would thus be taught to set out their notes in a way conducive to learning and would be taught mnemonic devices such as the use of marginalia. Eventually they would be expected both to understand and to repeat the sermon and to translate it into Latin either in writing or in speech, 'according to their ability'.

Brinsley made it clear that his interest was not only in rote learning and, equally, that he was not concerned to encourage speculation on the part of pupils. The techniques which he recommended had several purposes: the pupil would be encouraged to be more attentive; to understand and to see the import of the sermon; to make 'good notes', that is notes which aided the understanding and the memory; and to make progress with his Latin and his English. The subject matter – the sermon – was the same for all pupils from the five-year-old beginner to the boy on the eve of university, and the learning process was one which took place in an assembly of the whole school, but the methods cultivated differed according to the stage of education which the individual pupil had reached. Brinsley had a clear notion that the same material can be experienced at different levels.[25] Brinsley's counsel on the teaching of religion is not important solely because it demonstrates how well the future clergyman was coached in relevant skills but also because it indicates that this education was common to all.

Ludus Literarius had as one of its basic assumptions the contention that children are encouraged to learn through competition.
Learning is not only a game, it is a highly competitive game. At the
start of his book Brinsley commented that he found his chief delight
in observing his children hard at work, competing for place, and
watching their progress. Continual competition between and examination of pupils, and placement in class according to performance should be the norm. The child who did extraordinarily well
should be accelerated to a higher form. Once every quarter a competition, with prizes, for the victorship (in the form of a disputation
between rival teams of 'seniors') should be staged. This would be a
dress rehearsal for university. The discipline in such a school would
be that of promotion and demotion according to merit and performance, not sarcasm and punishment. The master would avoid argument with his scholars for this was demeaning and ineffective. He
would also avoid anger. Yet there would be times when corporal
punishment was necessary as a disciplinary measure, although not as
an aid to learning.[26]

That Brinsley was basing his advice on what he considered to be
the best practice is evidenced in more than one quarter. For example, John Stow described a competition between seniors from four
of London's free grammar schools in the sixteenth century:[27]

As for the meeting of the schoolmasters on festival days, at festival churches, and the disputing of their scholars logically, etc., . . . the same was long
since discontinued; but the arguing of the schoolboys about the principles of
grammar hath been continued even till our time; *for I myself, in my youth*,
have yearly seen, on the eve of St Bartholemew the Apostle, the scholars of
divers grammar schools repair unto the churchyard of St Bartholemew, the
priory in Smithfield, where upon a bank boarded about under a tree, some
one scholar hath stepped up, and there opposed and answered, till he were
by some better scholar overcome and put down; and then the overcomer
taking the place, did like as the first; and in the end the best opposers and
answerers had rewards, which I observed not but it made both good schoolmasters, and also good scholars, diligently against such times to prepare
themselves for the obtaining of this garland. I remembered there repaired
to these exercises, amongst others, the masters and scholars of St Paul's in
London, of St Peter's at Westminster, of St Thomas Acon's Hospital and of
St Anthony's Hospital; whereof the last named commonly presented the
best scholars and had the prize in those days.

At the present day, even in schools which cultivate given forms of
competition (stars for good performance, competitive sports and so
on), competitiveness between children is frowned upon. If this is
true in a society which, at least on cursory examination, appears to
be firmly rooted in competitiveness, it is at least interesting to
speculate why sixteenth- and seventeenth-century educators should
have sought to cultivate and profit from such a spirit.

Brinsley's outline of 'preferments and encouragements' and disciplinary techniques should remind us of the context in which he wrote. Children were at school for long hours. Despite Brinsley's insistence that learning was play, this must have been a difficult concept to realise in practice when recesses were so short and holidays so occupied with sermons and serious-minded activities. Competition was one means by which children could be urged on to attend and learn in this environment and through which their aggressiveness could be channelled. Brinsley also advocated regular but short periods of study in any one subject and insisted that understanding was the key to both learning and enjoyment. There are occasional indications that rhyme and music were emphasised in the teaching of reading; that games were used (spelling-bees); that plays were performed; and that pride in the presentation of work was encouraged. But the competitive emphasis and the resort to physical punishment only in times of necessity must also have had a great appeal for parents who wanted to be assured that they were obtaining value for money and who yet deplored the fact that many teachers taught little and punished excessively. Brinsley's words on the relations between school and parents indicate some of the problems which teachers encountered in this area and we have evidence of complaint from other sources.[28]

But there may have been other reasons for contemporary emphasis on competition than its promotion as an alternative to corporal punishment. Sixteenth- and seventeenth-century society was certainly competitive – the examination system of the nineteenth and twentieth centuries was absent but in its place was the competitive patronage system. Those boys who attended school and university with a view to social advancement had every reason to be competitively inclined. By displaying their talents and not hiding them under a bushel they could attract coveted patronage – and there was only so much to go around. The early modern schoolmaster would certainly have disadvantaged his pupils had he sought to diminish their competitive urges and their opportunities to shine.[29]

Various techniques for the teaching of reading

During the sixteenth and seventeenth centuries teachers were experimenting with various techniques for the teaching of reading and other basic subjects. In Mulcaster's *Elementary* he recommended that the material given to children should be modified to suit their interests and abilities.[30] Brinsley noted the desirability of graded vocabulary exercises and anecdotal material in the teaching of reading, although he, like his contemporaries, graded vocabulary according to number of syllables rather than comprehension.[31] It had long been accepted that children would learn both English and Latin better if the subject matter were entertaining – witness the colloquies used in so many sixteenth-century schools and the fables which Brinsley recommended.[32] Other methods were adopted by some to make the learning of reading easier. With the availability of printed books for the classroom, there was a heavier reliance on visual aids. Englishmen appear to have lagged behind their continental counterparts in pioneering such developments. The pictorial ABC book had appeared in Bavaria as early as 1477 in the form of Christopher Hueber's ABC.[33] One picture primer which appeared in 1496 contained miniatures which have been attributed to Leonardo da Vinci.[34] Marcum Schulte published a picture alphabet in 1532 which significantly used the illustrations to demonstrate the sound of the letter and which also used rhyming couplets to make learning easy. By the later sixteenth century picture alphabets, with accompanying verses, were very common in Germany. There had been a long tradition of rhymed alphabets in England (stretching back at least until the *ABC of Aristotle* of Master Bennet of Essex (in manuscript *c.* 1430) but the pictorial form was not copied until the mid sixteenth century, when it appeared in *Alphabeticum Primum Becardi* (1552) and other versions.[35]

In the early seventeenth century the importance of illustration for teaching whole words or sentences was appreciated by Lubinus in *The True and ready Way to Learn the Latin Tongue* (1614), which was translated by Hartlib and published in English in 1654. Comenius's *Orbis Pictus* (1657) merely elaborated on this exposition of the look-and-say method, which emphasised that the child learned better through visual and tactile experiences. But in his discussion of this development Frank Davies, the twentieth-century authority on the teaching of reading in early times, indicates that pictorial vocabularies were used in England in manuscript form in the late fifteenth century.[36] When Tobias Ellis published his *The English School* (an interesting title in that it suggests that the book might be regarded as a substitute for the institution), he published alphabetised lists of common, syllabified words and, alongside them, shorter lists with accompanying pictures.[37]

The use of phonics was also pioneered in Germany but soon found its niche in England. John Hart's *Method* (1570) used a combined pictorial and phonetic approach. Bullokar (*Book at Large*), Coote and Brinsley all emphasised the sounds of the letters and the importance of pronunciation. At times it seems that the hornbook was set to music.[38] Some gimmicks were employed in the teaching of reading; each represented the techniques which individual masters had found valuable in their own teaching and now tried to market as a new and perfect method, apparently discounting the importance of their own personalities in making their methods work. Some of these gimmicks achieved respectability – the shape-of-the letter approach described by John Buno in 1650 which illustrated each sound in a hieroglyphic manner did not achieve popularity until the later seventeenth century.[39] Petrus Jordan and Wolfgang Ratichius both stressed the interaction of reading and writing in the learning process. Vives in the early sixteenth century accepted that writing a point down fixed it the more in the pupil's memory and this was an idea accepted implicitly by Brinsley, Coote and Mulcaster.[40] Nevertheless, as has been noted, English educationalists appear to have seen writing as a skill independent of reading and generally acquired subsequently. Children in the seventeenth century were also given educational games, although we do not know whether they were used in schools – packs of cards bearing pictures and letters of the alphabet; dice games; reading wheels; an archery alphabet and so on.[41]

The schooling of Adam Martindale

Contemporary accounts of elementary schooling are few and far between. The account of his early schooling by Adam Martindale (born in 1623) is, therefore, the more valuable.[42]

About the same time, when I was near six years old, one Anne Simpkin, who was one of my sureties at the font,. . . bestowed an A B C upon me; a gift in itself exceeding small and contemptible, but in respect of the design and event, worth more than its weight in gold. For till that time I was all for childish play, and never thought of learning. But then I was frequently importunate with my mother that had laid it up (thinking I would only pull in pieces) to give it into mine own hands, which being so small a trifle she accordingly did; and I, by the help of my brethren and sisters that could read, and a young man that came to court my sister, had quickly learned it, and the primer also after it. Then of mine own accord I fell to reading the Bible and any other English book, and such great delight I took in it, and the praises I got by it from my parents, which preferred my reading before any other in the family, that I think I could almost have read a day together without play or meat, if breath and strength would have held out, and thus it continued to the end of the first seven years of my life.

This son of a Shropshire yeoman, then, learned to read at home, using the ABC and primer and progressing to read the Bible and anything which he could lay his hands on. Interestingly enough, he was helped by siblings (including sisters) who could already read and was encouraged by parental praise for his efforts. We know that in many cases the first of the three Rs was learned at home. In Ralph Josselin's diary we are allowed glimpses of the early stages of his children's education, although it is not always clear whether this was at home or in the Earl's Colne school which Josselin himself kept. At the age of three years and ten months his daughter, Anne, went 'to learn her book', by which is meant, presumably, the ABC and primer.[43] In June 1646 Mary, just over four years old, showed a 'towardliness to learn'[44] and by November of that year had acquired 'an aptness to her book' (again the ABC and primer).[45] The girls clearly were encouraged to read as much as the boys. Moreover, the language of the diary indicates that Josselin watched for signs of reading readiness in all his children. His son, Tom, began school itself at the age of five. Tom was bought a Bible soon after he began school, indicating that he had already mastered the ABC and primer, and before he was six was showing an academic aptitude of a kind which pleased his father – proficiency in reading and spelling and accidence. He seems, however, to have been a rather withdrawn child at this stage.[46] At the age of six years and two months Tom was learning his accidence by heart.[47] Josselin's children evidently began their education at an earlier age than did Adam Martindale, something perhaps to be explained in terms of their father's own superior education and his involvement with teaching. The autobiography of one of the well-born, Sir Simonds D'Ewes, tells us relatively little of this gentleman's son's early education but D'Ewes does ascribe his proficiency in the vernacular to his schoolteacher, Mr White. He appears to have attended school at the latest by the age of seven, and to have lodged either with his grandfather or with the schoolmaster, the Reverend Richard White of Chardstock. 'At school also with Mr White, though I had a pretty while been entered into the grammar [Latin], yet the chief thing I learned was the exact spelling and reading of English (in which I have known scholars themselves that were not well taught at first, too backward to their dying days in the writing of it).'[48] This suggests that D'Ewes could already read when he went to Mr White but that considerable time was spent improving his English skills at this school.

The accounts which we have show that, wherever and whenever the child learned to read, the same books were used – ABC, primer and Bible. It is also clear that there was no fixed age for beginning school – the petty class must have contained scholars between the ages of four and eight at varying levels of proficiency.[49] Nevertheless, as Ariès observed, a child would normally be given work which suited his own stage of development – Tom Josselin was set to learn his accidence before Adam Martindale had begun school. Skipping forms was common, if the French example may be applied to England.[50]

When he was seven years old, Adam Martindale was sent to school in St Helen's, 'almost two miles from my father's house, a great way for a little fat, short-legged lad (as I was) to travel twice a day; yet I went it cheerfully . . . such was my innate love of learning'. In assessing the time he spent at school, Martindale concluded that time which could have been spent profitably was wasted generally because of five factors:[51]

.My hindrances were many, as, first, many teachers (five in fewer years).

Secondly, these none of the best. Thirdly, a tedious long method then and there used. Fourthly, dullards in the same class with me having power to confine me to their pace; for when the lowest, who was presumed to be the weakest, said, *Satis* the ablest must take no further. Fifthly, many sad providences making great gaps in this seven years, as will appear hereafter.

In his account Martindale points to some of the defects of education in seventeenth-century England. It does indeed seem to have been common for children to be sent to a number of schools in a short school life – a fact attested to by college records and by the careers of individuals such as Martindale, James Whitehall and Simonds D'Ewes.[52] Many schools were kept not for love but for money – Martindale's first master 'having a good full school, but so bad a husband, that he quickly spoiled all and left us'. Other schools were transitory by their very nature, being kept by a peripatetic schoolteacher who was not licensed to teach. The second master, who taught him the accidence 'without book' was 'an old humdrum curate', a 'simpleton' and a 'tippler'.[53]

At one point Martindale was taught by a woman, 'daughter to a famous schoolteacher, that had some smattering of Latin'. This teacher used the English rules for Latin grammar and sometimes set him to read English, 'so that with her I did something better than quite lose my time, but not much.'

After a period with this schoolmistress, Adam was placed with another schoolmaster at St Helen's chapel, a young man who had been educated at Winwick school, a great grammar school foundation in Lancashire which was renowned for preparing youths for the university and priesthood despite a short existence (it was founded in 1619), and who, according to Adam, had Winwick's method down to a tee:

but they were usually of good years before they were fitted, the method where they were taught being very long. This master of mine had the Winwick method right enough, and was scholar sufficient for me then . . .

but Martindale balked at the master's capricious behaviour, his habit of making new rules and the way in which he favoured those pupils whose parents paid him most:[54]

being a married man without charge, and very poor, he lay open to impressions from such as could fee him well, to carry partially amongst his scholars, so that the whole school could not but be aware of the grossness of it.

On one occasion Martindale was placed high in the school because of his ability and performance but, when the fathers of two 'arrant dunces' paid the master a hefty sum and 'prevailed with him to thrust me down below them', Adam was distraught.[55]

And to continue the wrong, he peremptorily denied me the liberty (which I

never heard denied to any before or since), to strive with the young fellow
for recovery of my place above him, and when I had actually gotten it again
from the gentleman by very fair play and odds enough, (yet for sooth) because he cried, I must still be kept below him.

This I confess I could not brook, but complained to my father, who removed me to Rainford, a school somewhat nearer than St Helen's, but
more costly, because no free school as the other was.

That this incident still rankled in the memory of the ageing Martindale is significant. The competitive system which Brinsley and
others encouraged could be corrupted easily in a society where the
schoolteacher was of a lower social status than many of his pupils
and often dependent upon their parents for his living and his
furtherance. Although we cannot know how many teachers were
open to bribery and how many discriminated between fee-paying
and free scholars, the system was certainly open to abuse. Throughout his career the eminent Elizabethan educationalist, Richard Mulcaster, was under financial pressure which tempted him to actual
theft, embezzlement and the taking of numbers of private fee-
paying pupils against the statutes of both Merchant Taylor's and St
Paul's schools.

Martindale's experience with his fifth schoolmaster, whom he later followed to St Helen's Free School, was more favourable. The
master, again a product of Winwick, taught grammar well and introduced Martindale to the catechism. Nevertheless, this master had a
fierce temper and beat the boys in a passion 'for small or no faults at
all', suggesting perhaps that it was expected that corporal punishment would be administered dispassionately and only for major
offences.[56] His time with a sixth master, a university man, at Rainford was yet more worthwhile.[57]

It is probable, of course, that the first five teachers were (with the
exception of the curate) young men, even mere boys, who had the
equivalent of a grammar school education and no maturity or, in the
case of the woman, even less: they knew scarcely more than the
boys they taught to read English and the Latin accidence. Adam
Martindale himself provides an example of the grammar-school-
educated schoolteacher. Few contemporary eyebrows would have
been raised at such a situation: in the schools, as in everyday life,
those who had learned were considered qualified to pass on their
learning to those who came after. Richard Mulcaster, Christopher
Holden, William Malim and Ralph Waddington were all leading
Elizabethan schoolmasters who obtained their first experience of
teaching when they served as 'praepositores' in the seventh form at
Eton in the 1540s. The account of Martindale's schooling cannot be
regarded as typical – each of his teachers had different faults – because we simply do not have enough similar accounts to check it
against, but it does provide us with a refreshing reminder that the
ideal sketched by Mulcaster, Coote and Brinsley was often fallen

short of in practice.[58] Martindale's early teachers seem to have thought little about humanist theory, method, justice or the need for the child to enjoy learning. Martindale's 'innate love of learning' must have been strong indeed to compensate for the agony of these early educational experiences.

The schoolroom

If we have few accounts of actual schooling experiences, we do possess some illustrations of Elizabethan and Stuart classrooms which help us to understand the conditions in which youngsters learned their lessons. It is, however, difficult to interpret the wood-cuts which survive: were Elizabethan schoolrooms as cramped and crowded as some suggest? We do know that the ratio of boys to teachers was often very high (although this would vary enormously from school to school). It must have been hard indeed to learn in a crowded schoolroom and the noise level, even in a strict regimen, must have been stressfully high. One schoolroom shows five groups of boys rehearsing their lessons.[59] One of these groups is reading from individual books and being heard by the master. A boy (perhaps a senior pupil or an usher) is reading to a small group of children with hornbooks in their hands. An usher appears to be teaching number of some kind to boys at the back of the room, while another group may be seen reciting or engaging in a spelling-bee while their teacher writes at a desk. In the lefthand foreground a couple of boys are being whipped on their bare buttocks. The range of visual aids which the room contains suggests that these played a real role in the teaching of the young. In the left-hand corner of the back of the room a large sheet of paper is hung on the wall, which bears writing of some kind. On the wall in the right-hand back corner are a clock face, an hour glass and a music score. The usher is standing before a tall and narrow board and writing upon it for the benefit of the boys behind him (perhaps demonstrating the casting of accounts). Group teaching using a board or a visual aid was seemingly common. And we know that pupils were helped to learn by a variety of individual visual aids – the picture alphabet, flash cards, illustrated books, religious pictures, diagrammatic ex-planations of difficult concepts (witness the visual aid in William Perkins' popular *Works* which demonstrates the paths to salvation and damnation), and the tactile counting frame.[60]

The teaching of writing

We have concentrated thus far upon the teaching of vernacular reading and the accidence in early modern England, but what of the second 'R', writing? Writing was not accepted as one of the skills taught in the elementary school. More commonly, writing was taught by a peripatetic scrivener for a fee. Some schoolmasters, however, did feel strongly that the teaching of writing belonged in the school. Brinsley complained that writing required constant practice and that boys who had been taught briefly by a scrivener soon forgot how to write well.[61] Perhaps Simonds D'Ewes provides us with an example here: in his *Autobiography* D'Ewes writes that he 'learned to write a good Roman, secretary and Greek hand, all which by disuse afterwards I in a manner lost'.[62] Brinsley recommended that the key to good writing habits lay in proper equipment and constant practice. The teacher should instruct his pupils on how to prepare pen and ink; provide each pupil with an individual copy book on good paper to encourage pride in the work; and allow one hour's writing practice per day. The paper for writing practice should be divided into squares to facilitate properly forming letters. The child should be encouraged to write straight, but 'practice will bring facility' in this respect. The child will practise until he can form each letter separately. Tracing the letters will increase his ability to do this, as will the making of writing patterns. Meanwhile the master will walk among the students to see how they are faring and he will take any one of the scholars, 'chiefly one of them who write the best' to help him direct the rest. But if writing was to form an accepted part of the curriculum of the early years at school, the Elizabethan and Jacobean schoolroom was ill designed for its practice. There were no desks.[63]

The teaching of arithmetic

Even in Brinsley's school it is clear that writing is a subject which is learned after reading has been mastered. The same holds true for the teaching of arithmetic. During the reign of Edward VI Robert Recorde produced what was to prove a highly influential defence of the teaching of arithmetic in English schools. This defence was based upon the antiquity of the subject and its evident utility. Recorde discussed the use of pen-arithmetic and arithmetic by counters. He introduced the reader to the meaning and use of symbols. By means of visual aids he showed the reader how to cast accounts, making it clear that numeracy was accessible to the illiterate as well as the literate.[64] The teaching of cyphering and, particularly, of casting accounts required considerable facility and practice. For this reason it was not uncommon for the subject to be taught by a 'specialist'.

Many schools did teach both types of arithmetic. It was laid down in a number of late-sixteenth-century school statutes that the master should be qualified to teach arithmetic, and the statutes of Black-

burn Grammar School (1597) even ordered the teaching of geometry. Some teachers, such as Adam Martindale, displayed a particular enthusiasm for the teaching of the third 'R', probably because
they appreciated its commercial potential. Martindale realised the
deficiencies of the available textbooks and when he started teaching
set out to compile his own textbook for use with his pupils. Yet
Martindale, by his own admission, was at that point no mathematician. He concentrated on vulgar arithmetic and fractions because he
'knew nothing of decimals, logarithms or algebra' and he did not remedy this lack of knowledge until after the Restoration, when he
was about forty and became dependent upon mathematics for his
livelihood. But Martindale early accepted that the parents of his
scholars were especially concerned with the practical aspects of their
sons' education. He therefore concentrated on the practical applications of mathematics for the gentle and trading classes – surveying
as well as casting accounts – and was to produce a textbook for the
teaching of surveying later in his career. When the Test Acts denied
Martindale the right to a church living or to a regular teaching post,
he supported himself and his family as a peripatetic teacher, staying
for six months here and three months there instructing youths in
mathematics.[65]

Even the teacher without any special enthusiasm for mathematics
was expected to provide his pupils with a grounding in the subject:
Brinsley advocated that all children be taught the Roman numerals
(for use in locating the psalms and chapters correctly) and the arabic
numerals as well as the fundamental skills of casting accounts.
Brinsley was, of course, commenting on the ideal situation – probably there were still many schools which did not follow this advice.
In any event, there can be little doubt that arithmetic was left until
reading and the accidence had been learned and, moreover, that
those boys who concentrated on classical subjects suffered with regard to mathematical facility. Although all three of Sir Gervase
Sleigh's children attended Repton (as we have seen, a Latin grammar school of some reputation) in the early seventeenth century,
and although all stayed there until their late teens, only two of the
boys followed the classical curriculum and went on the higher
education and the professions, whilst the youngest learned reading,
writing and casting accounts in preparation for his employment as
the apprentice to a merchant factor.[66] This distinction between the
curricula followed by boys intended for different vocations once
mastery of reading and accidence was achieved may well have been
common even within the so-called grammar schools, so that the
same school fulfilled a number of differing functions. For example,
the statutes of Aldenham, Herts, in 1597 stipulated that the school
was for the 'free instruction of 60 scholars in purity of life, manners
and religion, and in Latin, English, writing, cyphering and accounts', and the 1596 statutes of Northampton Grammar School

ordered that there either be one master to teach all subjects (including writing, cyphering and casting accounts) or 'otherwise that there be one schoolmaster to teach the Latin tongue and one other distinct schoolmaster to teach to read, write and cast accounts'. The schools established by Cromwell in 1653 in Essex were expressly to provide an education in reading, writing and accounts *or* grammar learning for the poor children. Some schools accepted that the able should learn classical subjects and the less able, cyphering and casting accounts. For instance, the Charterhouse orders of 1627 recommend that 'It shall be his care [i.e. the master's] and the Usher's charge, to teach the scholars to cypher and cast an account, especially those that are less capable of learning, and fittest to be put to trades.' In some free grammar schools, writing and arithmetic were regarded as extra subjects for which parents paid a fee: perhaps this was why Martindale was so enthusiastic about the mathematics side of his schools. There were private schools for the teaching of pen and counter arithmetic just as there were private writing schools and private writing masters before the Restoration.

The grammar schools and comprehensive education

Historians writing about education in English schools before the eighteenth century have assumed that the various levels, or forms, coincided with chronological age. Boys (and some girls) learned to read either at home or at a school (petty, ABC, dame, parish) somewhere between the ages of four and eight; very occasionally reading was actually taught on the grammar school premises in a petties' class; boys were admitted to the accidence forms of the grammar school once they could read and spell (around the age of seven or eight) and here they learned first English grammar and then proceeded to classical studies. As was established in the preceding chapter, the situation was much more complicated than this – differing types of school abounded. Moreover, there was no accepted school age – even young adults attended schools in the lower forms where need so dictated and it was difficult still to age-group the pupils strictly. Also, social class had a profound impact upon schooling. At a time when the idea that each child was designed for a specific vocation was in vogue, it was accepted that each child had different educational requirements. Vocation was determined not only by merit, aptitude and ambition but also by social class. As was observed earlier, the schools catered to the varying needs of the market. It was not considered unusual that boys in the lower Latin forms should continue with their vernacular studies; in the 1660s it seemed natural that boys from Manchester Grammar School should be sent to a private master to learn writing and arithmetic. Schools which were founded by subscription provide the perfect example of the interaction between schools and schooling and the felt needs of society but the endowed grammar schools and the private schools of every description also demonstrate this sensitivity to the wishes of the clientele.

W.A.L. Vincent argued in *The Grammar Schools* that the teaching of vernacular subjects had no place in the sixteenth- and seventeenth-century grammar schools and that the inflexibility of the schools in this regard contained the seeds of their post-Restoration decay.[67] Tempting though this hypothesis is, it assumes that the grammar schools were what their statutes said that they should be. It seems true that a rigorous classical curriculum was offered in the endowed grammar schools to boys whose parents demanded it but the evidence of co-existing English and Latin schools at Chigwell, Exeter, Lewisham, Repton and other schools in the first half of the seventeenth century and the general acceptance in the country grammar schools that they should be responsible for the tuition of petties indicates that the grammar schools were betraying their classical origins.[68] Whereas Vincent is undoubtedly correct in ascribing to men like Dury a conviction that education should be closely geared to the vocational needs of the individual pupil, he is incorrect when he maintains that sixteenth- and seventeenth-century Englishmen were not equally convinced of this fact. What really occurred was a subtle shift from humanist and Protestant humanist views of the need for a general education for all vocations (views from the top, if you will) to mid- and late-seventeenth-century arguments that education should be more specifically vocational or practical. This latter view was related to the upsurge of 'class' feeling during the English Revolution, to the rise of the mercantile economy and so on, but it was none the less in a line of natural progression from ideas held earlier in the century. Above all, the novel contribution of John Dury's *A Supplement to the Reformed School* of 1650 was his contention that '*all* the subjects thereof should in their youth be trained up in some schools fit for their capacities, and that over these schools some overseers should be appointed to look to the course of their education, to see that *none* should be left destitute of some benefit of virtuous breeding . . . ' This suggestion of the need for and desirability of universal education for all male youth was truly significant and foreign to the essentially élitist humanist attitude to education. But, as we shall see in future chapters, the flexibility of the English grammar schools, far from being increased somewhat at the Restoration, as Vincent appears to contend, actually disappeared. Whether as a reaction to the years of warfare and uncertainty or not, the experiment of 'comprehensive' education in the town or country grammar school ended in the post-Restoration years.

It is artificial to represent curriculum arrangements in schools of the sixteenth and seventeenth centuries as consisting of a lower vernacular school and an upper classical school. In actuality schools generally departed more dramatically from the Renaissance pattern. Early modern schools were created and run to fulfil the needs of a community which was often not much in touch with the ideas of Renaissance educators. One must beware of contrasting the so-called 'private' schools with a mythical 'public' school system.[69] Many of the more famous endowed schools were founded in the spirit of the Renaissance and their masters imbued with the theory of prominent educators and social humanists but there was, in no sense, a grammar school system imposed from above. There is a strong case to be made for the idea that during the late sixteenth and seventeenth centuries the gentry classes (and I include here the lawyers, clergymen and doctors) increasingly saw education as the way to confirm rather than to modify the ramifications of the hierarchical social structure. In their view, education had its value for all classes of society above the very poorest but the education offered would not always be classical – rather it would be designed to serve the needs of the vocation for which the particular youth was destined. Such a view did not contradict directly the social humanist view that through education the individual would be brought to 'virtue', but it did make it clear that class and patronage determined the path to virtue which each youth would adopt. Education would help to improve society but it would not help to revolutionise it.[70]

Curriculum and method in the grammar schools

Much has been written about the curriculum followed in classical subjects in the English grammar schools – more in fact than upon any other aspect of early modern education in England. It has been assumed that vernacular subjects were taught in the schools only with the intention of enabling the teacher 'to get on with the real business of the day, the study of Latin grammar'.[71] Renaissance theorists certainly believed that to be the case and it is difficult to find a contemporary author who did not pay lipservice to this view. Indeed, for most schoolmasters the preparation of boys for university through a rigorous classical curriculum was the most important aspect of their job. In his *A Consolation for Our Grammar Schools* (1622) Brinsley made it clear that he saw the grammar master's chief priority as the fitting of youth for university:[72]

For this is a thing notorious, that in the greatest part of our common schools abroad, (some few of principal note excepted) the scholars at fifteen or sixteen years of age, have not commonly so much as any sense of the meaning and true use of learning, for understanding, resolving, writing, or speaking, but only to construe and to parse a little, to steal an exercise, and to write such Latin as any of judgement will disdain to read. That in respect of being fit to be sent to the Universities with credit, that they may proceed with delight and understanding, when they come there, they are commonly so senseless, as that they are much meeter to be sent home again. And if they be admitted into the Universities, it is not without the grief of all who respect the credit thereof. So as that they enter commonly with foul disgrace, and continue with much contempt, to spend their friends' money and their own precious time, which might have been far better employed. That they become there a great deal more ready to any kind of exercise than unto the study of good learning, the ignorance whereof proves such a reproach unto them. Hence also after sundry years so evilly spent, many of them return home again, almost as rude as when they went thither, or are sent abroad to be unprofitable burdens, both of the Church and Commonwealth perpetually. Or if such do light into the hands of painful and conscionable tutors, and fall to their studies, yet their tutors must then act for them the schoolmaster's part, which must needs be very harsh and unpleasing, yet rare to be found amongst them. So that in stead of their academical readings, they must be enforced to supply that which was wanting in the Grammar School. Such scholars must likewise use extraordinary pains and industry and be of most happy capacities, if ever they shall come to that pitch and height of good learning, which being trained up rightly from the beginning, they might very easily and in shorter time have attained unto.

But in the course of his complaint he indicated just how far the majority of such schools had neglected this priority. From the sort of evidence examined already in this chapter it is evident that considerable pressures were placed upon the schools to provide an education in subjects which were more obviously useful for the non-professional, non-gentle classes. For some teachers, the importance of Latin must have been eclipsed in practice if not in theory by the very profitability and popularity of other subjects, more geared to the needs of their clientele. The pre-eminence of Latin in the grammar school curriculum on a continuing basis was determined to a great extent, of course, by the fact that the universities required it. Its continued importance was also ensured by the hierarchy within the schools themselves: it was accepted that the brighter pupils or seniors would teach the boys how to read and spell under the supervision of the usher – in some schools a second usher was hired specifically to take charge of the teaching of vernacular subjects; the usher (under master or *hypodidasculus*) was responsible for helping the boys to build up a Latin vocabulary, parse and construe, and make Latins. Only the Master would teach the true classical subjects – Latin composition and rhetoric, Greek and, very rarely, Hebrew. The subjects themselves marked the stages in the hierarchy of both teachers and pupils.[73]

This acceptance of Latin as the be all and end all of grammar school education was at odds with reality in many cases. Even writers such as Brinsley laid more and more emphasis upon the necessity of vernacular studies for their own sake – every effort must be made to see that the pupil does not lose his ability to read and write good English in the attempt to learn Latin; through English the child will be socialised and will come to an understanding of the Scriptures and religious instruction and of the content of major classical works. Mulcaster even suggested that teachers of vernacular subjects should be paid more because their task was more difficult than that of the Latin masters.[74] The Protestantisation of education in England must also have had its effect upon the place of classical studies in the grammar schools in a subtle but real manner. It has often been noticed that Renaissance textbooks were sometimes replaced in the schools by the works of English or continental Protestants. In 1600, for example, Richard Mulcaster published *Cato Christianus*, which was used as a textbook at St Paul's and was designed to combine the teaching of the fundamentals of Latin composition with the Christianising of Cato according to Protestant humanist principles. In other words, it would be an appropriate text for impressionable youth. As Head of Eton from 1528 Richard Cox (later Bishop of Ely under Elizabeth) used textbooks such as the *Paedologia* of Peter Mosellanus, which attacked the ceremonial of the Church as pagan and showed the way to a new piety via the new learning. Such a curriculum had a profound impact upon some of the more important teachers of the Elizabethan period. Classical languages were taught in many late-sixteenth- and early-seventeenth-century schools less as a way to open classical texts to the pupils than as a way into the ministry. Once at the university, in theory, the scholar would progress to read the Testaments and the Fathers in the original. John Strype (whose father had told friends that 'these little fists shall thump the pulpit one day' and who had instructed his wife to direct John towards the ministry) learned Latin, Greek, Hebrew and Syriac at St Paul's in the later 1650s. Now there is certainly little doubt that this religious emphasis coexisted with the Renaissance emphasis on the classics, which, in England, had always stressed the relevance of classical writings to Christianity. But when we see Brinsley's emphasis on the translation of the New Testament into and from Latin and Greek by his scholars; when we see the detailed instructions given to pupils on note-taking to be done at sermons; when we note the tremendous stress on understanding of the classical texts, on their import for Christians and on the expurgation of classical authors, we cannot be surprised that a Simonds D'Ewes or a John Manningham (both lawyers and both products of the English grammar schools and universities) displayed a tremendous interest in religious issues and sermons which was at least as evident (and probably more so) as their interest in the classics.[75]

During the sixteenth century practitioners attempted to produce new textbooks which would facilitate the learning of Latin by schoolboys. The teachers of Magdalen College School, Oxford, produced a series of Latin grammars, based on the grammar of Donatus but, nevertheless, dedicated to simplifying the learning process. John Holte, an usher at the school and specifically responsible for the teaching of fundamental rules of accidence and syntax to the lower forms, produced his *Lac Puerorum or Mylke for Children* in 1479. This book broke away from tradition by explaining the rules of Latin accidence in English and by using visual aids to help the child memorise cases and declensions, and it was evidently popular. Both John Stanbridge and Robert Whittinton produced popular grammars which pioneered new teaching techniques: for example, Stanbridge's *Accidence* (*c.* 1520) made a tabular display of the conjugation of verbs. Colet produced a short accidence for use by the pupils at St Paul's School, while William Lily produced two works on syntax, one for use by the lower and one for use by the upper forms. The confusion caused by the multiplicity of grammars and therefore of teaching methods forced the Church to take action: in the late 1530s, through the influence of eminent churchmen and the interest of the King, a royal committee was set up to produce a royal grammar based on the St Paul's texts of Colet, Lily and Erasmus. The result was what became known as Lily's Latin Grammar, which was prescribed for use in English grammar schools until 1604 and continued in regular use until the mid eighteenth century. At a time when editions of books normally consisted of some 1,250 copies, 10,000 copies of Lily's Latin Grammar were produced annually.[76]

Children in the accidence forms also began to build a Latin vocabulary through the making of vulgars – collections of Latin sentences with appropriate English translations. This method of teaching was common in the early sixteenth century and suitable collections of sentences were supplied by John Anwykyll (*Vulgaria Terentii*, 1483), John Stanbridge, Robert Whittinton and William Horman. It was such a tedious approach, however, that Vives roundly denounced it and encouraged a tendency to use the method of double translation, which stressed not the teaching of rules but a mother tongue approach. Thus Erasmus had written, 'it is not by learning rules that we acquire the power of speaking a language but by daily intercourse with those accustomed to express themselves with exactness and refinement and by the copious reading of the best authors'. Roger Ascham was a keen advocate of this method in *The Scholemaster*, which was first published in 1570. Texts such as Cicero's *Epistles*, the *Colloquies* of Erasmus, Mosellanus and Corderius and Aesop's *Fables* were used for these exercises.

In the more advanced forms the emphasis was upon the speaking and writing of Latin – rhetoric and composition. Erasmus's *De Duplici Verborum ac Rerum* (*De Copia*) of 1512 was the standard work throughout Europe and went through no fewer than 100 editions before the end of the sixteenth century. The work contains an ex-

tended vocabulary, designed to indicate alternative ways of express-
ing the same sentiment and also a guide to literary arrangement of
such sentences. Early in the century it was common for teachers to
supplement this work with other continental texts: Vives even recommended that Mosellanus's *Tabulae* might be used as a teaching
aid in the classroom, 'hung up on the wall so that it will catch the
attention of the pupil as he walks past it and force itself upon his
eyes'. But later on English authors produced textbooks compiled
from these authors – for instance, Richard Sherry's *Treatise of
Schemes and Tropes* (1550) – and even from writers of antiquity
(Richard Rainolde's *Foundation of Rhetoric* was a free translation
of the work of Aphthonius of Antioch, who lived in the third century A.D., through a sixteenth century edition). Traditional works
on the teaching of rhetoric and logic, such as Thomas Wilson's *Rule
of Reason* (1551) and *Art of Rhetoric* (1553) were popular. The
work done in this area in the schools remained in this Aristotelian
tradition for the most part. Nevertheless, the influence of the
methods employed by Peter de Ramèe (Ramus) can be seen in William Kempe's *Education of Children in Learning* (1588), in the
Rameae Rhetoricae (1592) of Charles Butler (Master of Basingstoke
Grammar School) and in teaching manuals of the seventeenth century such as Brinsley's *Ludus Literarius*. The Latin scholar had at
his disposal also texts demonstrating the art of writing letters – the
most popular of which remained Erasmus's *De Conscribendis Epis-
tolis* (1521) – and dictionaries.

   Although Renaissance educationalists recommended that boys
learn Greek and Hebrew to the same level as Latin, it is probable
that few schools taught these subjects before the late sixteenth century, when, presumably, the universities had begun to produce
more teachers capable of instructing grammar school pupils in the
same. Richard Mulcaster, for instance, had learned no Greek at
Eton in the 1540s and yet his education in that tongue at Cambridge
was sufficiently good to enable him to teach Greek at Merchant
Taylors' School to a high enough standard to please the examining
committees first of the Bishop of London and then of members of St
John's College, Oxford. Even in the seventeenth century Greek was
not normally begun until the fourth form. The Greek New Testament was the basic text used in the increasing number of schools
which did stipulate the teaching of Greek in their statutes – the
advantages of using a text which the pupils already knew and understood were obvious enough. Moreover, it was in order to study
sacred texts that, in practical terms, the student needed to learn
Greek. *Camden's Grammar* (1597) was to the study of school Greek
what *Lily's Grammar* was to Latin studies. The study of Hebrew at
school level also appears to have been a late sixteenth- and early
seventeenth-century phenomenon. Hebrew was taught at Retford
from 1552, at Westminster from 1560, at Merchant Taylors' from

1561 and at Newport Grammar School, Essex, from 1589. Evidence exists (either in the statutes or in occasional references) of the teaching of Hebrew at the following schools at different dates: Blackburn Grammar School (1597), Heath Grammar School, near Halifax (1600), Market Bosworth (1601), Hampton Lucy, Warwickshire (1635), Newport, Salop (1656), Felsted, Essex (c. 1630), St Paul's (1646, 1657, 1662–3), St Alban's (1660s), Bristol (c. 1666), Guisborough, Northamptonshire (1667–8), Brigg Grammar School, Lincolnshire (1669), Bulwell, Nottinghamshire (1669) and Martock, Somerset (1662). Is it safe to assume that Hebrew was not being taught in those schools which do not appear on this list? Doubtless further examination of surviving correspondence and other documentation would produce chance references to Hebrew at other schools. Nevertheless, it does seem probable that Hebrew (and to a lesser extent Greek) was crowded out of the grammar school curriculum by the excessive demands of the Latin course. Hebrew was taught only from the fourth form at Retford and from the seventh form at Westminster. For many schoolmasters it was clearly difficult enough to bring their hostile pupils to something approaching true proficiency in Latin, let alone to teach them additional languages. And it must always have been more difficult to recruit schoolmasters capable of teaching this subject.[77]

The historian, however, is able sometimes to look beyond the writings of educational theorists and prescriptive literature to actual practice in the schools. Once again, Adam Martindale provides us with a description of his own course in the grammar school of St Helen's, Lancashire:

As for the proficiency I made under him 'twas this: He received me when I was learning in As in praesenti and Cato, and instructed me for prose in Corderius, Aesop's Fables, Tully's Offices, epistles and orations, together with Aphthonius for Latin in prose, and the Greek Grammars of Camden first and Clenard afterwards, together with a Greek Catechism, and lastly the Greek Testament (for I proceeded no further with him); and for poetry in Mantuan Terence, Ovid's Epistles and Metamorphosis, Virgil and Horace. The rhetorics he read to us were Susenbrotus first and Taloeus afterwards. Mine exercises were usually a piece of Latin (of which he himself dictated the English) every day of the week save Thursdays and Saturdays; and besides somewhat weekly as I rose in ability, first a dialogue in imitation of Corderius, or Pueriles Confabulatiunculae [Brinsley, 1617], then an epistle wherein I was to follow Cicero, though (alas) at a great distance. Then Themes (as we called them) in the way of Aphthonius, consisting of many parts, and taking up one side of half a sheet pretty thick written, and (towards the latter end) good store of verses on the back side, most hexameters and pentameters, but some Sapphics and Adonics. All that were presumed by their standing able to discourse in Latin were under a penalty if they either spoke English or broke Piscian's head; but barbarous language, if not incongruous for grammar, had no punishing but derision.

Martindale's marginal comment on his tuition in Greek is revealing of his attitude to the teaching methods of the day – 'the old saying is Gutta cavat lapidem non sed soepe cadendo: "The soft drop wears the hard stone by frequent falling". So a long tedious method, well plied, at length brought us to somewhat.'[78]

In this grammar school at least rote learning and repetition were the chief methods employed and 'delight in learning' was a very secondary consideration. Martindale's teacher clearly put a great deal of effort into preparing work for his pupils – he wrote out English passages to be translated into Latin by the children and one can scarcely blame him if on occasion he dictated the work to the form, although this must have added greatly to the tedium of learning.[79]

Books and school libraries

Interestingly enough, Martindale makes no mention of the use of a dictionary or of the individual work on commonplace books, designed to extend the vocabulary. Perhaps such work was emphasised more commonly at a later stage – John Baret wrote in the preface to his *Alvearie* (1573):[80]

About eighteen years ago, having pupils at Cambridge studious of the Latin tongue, I used then to write epistles and then together and daily to translate some piece of English into Latin, for the more speedy and easy attaining of the same. And after we had a little begun, perceiving what great trouble it was to come running to me for every word they missed (knowing then of no other dictionary to help as but Sir Thomas Elyot's Library which was come out a little before), I appointed them certain leaves of the same book every day to write the English before the Latin, and likewise to gather a number of fine phrases out of Cicero, Terence, Caesar, Livy etc. and to set them under several titles, for the more readily finding them again at their need. Thus within a year or two they had gathered together a great volume which (for the apt similitude between the good scholars and the diligent bees in gathering their wax and honey into the hive) I called the book their Aviary [Alvearie, sic], both for a memorial by whom it was made and also by this name to encourage others to the like diligence for that they should see their worthy praise for the same unworthily drowned in oblivion.

We are not sure how widely used books were in the schoolroom. There are some indications (such as this) that reference books were in short supply – particularly dictionaries which might cost as much as 15s. apiece. Where this was so, the task of preparing 'work sheets' and reference aids lay squarely on the shoulders of teacher or pupil. Even then, books still had their influence – Baret adapted the idea behind Elyot's *Library* for use in his classroom. In this way sophisticated techniques of alphabetising, indexing, categorising and classifying knowledge were introduced to grammar school and university students. Many Elizabethan and Stuart schoolboys carried these study habits into adult life with them – they proved useful and influential in the working life of the lawyer, the clerk, the merchant, the preacher and the landowner and they may well have boosted the manifest 'bureaucratisation of life' – filing, classifying, recording, storing, systematising. This was a skill which was acquired by many young women of the period who compiled commonplace books for pleasure and for work (recipe and remedy books were arranged in this manner). Truly, once an idea appeared in print it provided a model for many to copy. We may also find another point of interest in Baret's example. Implicitly he was encouraging his students to discover for themselves, to be independent learners, and was accepting that the pupil would remember more clearly words for which he had had to search.

Yet there is also evidence that schoolbooks were produced and used. Elyot's *Library* went through several editions, especially as revised and enlarged by Thomas Cooper, Master of Magdalen School, Oxford, 1549–67. Of all dictionaries, John Withal's *Short Dictionary for Young Beginners* of 1556 was probably the most widely used in the sixteenth century, although other dictionaries designed to facilitate the preparation of latin themes in the upper forms of grammar schools were clearly in demand. Richard Huloet's alphabetically arranged *Abcedarium Anglico-Latinum* (1552) for example was enlarged in 1572 by John Higgins to include French. Huloet produced another dictionary which gave multiple Latin translations for a variety of English sentences and phrases. Baret's own *Alvearie* (a triple dictionary) was itself revised and enlarged by Abraham Fleming in 1580. Thomas Thomas's *Dictionarium Latinae et Anglicanae* (1587) went through numerous editions, suggesting widespread usage. We know that Felsted School, Essex, owned a copy, as did St Albans and Colchester schools. When increasing emphasis came to be laid upon vernacular skills, a demand was created for reference works such as Peter Levins's *Manipulus Vocabulorum. A Dictionarie of English and Latin Words* (1570) which was arranged alphabetically in English.[81]

Moreover, we know that many of the urban grammar schools possessed libraries and made provision for the purchase of books. At the Restoration Charles Hoole recommended that every grammar school should have its own library of specific reference works for each class (he listed a total of 250 desirable books) and a more advanced library for the Master's use. Occasional evidence survives of the provision of grammar school libraries – Shrewsbury, Felsted, St Alban's, Colchester. Sometimes these libraries were established as the result of a bequest. Abraham Colfe provided the Master of Lewisham grammar school with both a library and a house and William Adams at Newport, Shropshire, gave £100 to purchase a library. Sir Roger Manwood's statutes for Sandwich Free Grammar

School in 1580 stipulated that free scholars should give a benevolence at the end of every quarter 'towards buying and providing of such dictionaries and other books as shall be for common use of scholars'.

Nevertheless, it is probable that schools, unless they were large and exceptionally well endowed, were poorly protected against inflation with respect to their libraries. Book supply at Martindale's school of St Helen's was probably not atypical – as the Wase Manuscript returns confirm. By 1679 we find the pupils of Sherborne, Dorset, being required to pay 6d. per annum towards the cost of books – a very necessary step.[82]

More so by far than today, the teacher in early modern Britain had to experiment, use his imagination and adapt available techniques to use in the schoolroom. There were probably many practical teaching manuals in manuscript form. While it is true that the printing press increased the tendency to uniformity of teaching methods and materials in the schools and meant that educational theorists and practitioners had wide influence through their printed works, it would be unwise to exaggerate this power of the press prematurely. The influence of a new book might be considerably delayed, for instance. Secondly, many poorer schools could not afford textbooks. Thirdly, the teacher might be eclectic in his use of such works and produce his own materials.

The method of teaching Latin

Historians used to assume that Latin was taught by the mother tongue method, which was advocated by Vives, Erasmus and Ascham and was the aim of grammar school Latin studies. But, as Kenneth Charlton has pointed out, developments in the teaching of Latin in England emphasised the use of the vernacular in communicating rules to the pupil and in helping him to understand the content of the material used. From both Martindale's and D'Ewes's accounts of their Latin studies we can detect that composition and declamation (oratory) were emphasised at the expense of conversation. At St Helen's the abler pupils only were expected to be able to converse in that tongue; Simonds D'Ewes left one of his masters well versed in themes, epistles and dialogues and able only to 'discourse a little in that tongue' at the age of twelve. The writings of Comenius and others in the mid and later seventeenth century recommending the advantages of 'mother tongue' language teaching in themselves suggest that this ideal had been lost sight of along the way. The classical curriculum was designed to enable pupils to read and write in Latin – to produce future theologians, preachers, lawyers and gentlemen – not to make Latin a living language. At this time Latin was a dying language but still breathing. Medieval

Latin, for instance, was used in the ecclesiastical courts. It is intriguing that Gabriel Harvey obviously found the prospect of pleading his case to Mr Young of Pembroke Hall, Cambridge, in Latin totally daunting. He wrote in English 'that I might the better and more fully open the matter as it standeth . . . '. The English version covered ten folios (recto and verso) of his letter book. Even the scholar found it a strain to write freely in Latin. Martindale's master does not appear to have objected to his pupils coining new Latin words from the vernacular as long as these obeyed the rules and were used grammatically! We may assume, however, that this was not the sense in which Renaissance educationalists had conceived their hope that Latin alone would be used as the means of communication in school. There was every reason why the ideal could not be realised at school level: few saw its utility – while the scholar might love Latin for its own sake, society as a whole valued Latin for its usefulness (one needed to know Latin in order to get at the meaning of certain words) and this utility lay in being able to read and understand. Even when the scholar needed Latin for oratory, it was accepted that he would make a formal declamation based on a written composition. This is not to deny the tremendous impact which the Latin language and its forms had upon English oral and written culture.

Much of what has been said already of the method of teaching vernacular subjects is also applicable to the teaching of the classical curriculum. Against the background of the texts used and the exercises formed by the pupils, we see that monitors were used in each form (under, Brinsley advised, the close supervision of master and usher to guard against abuse); reliance on group methods of teaching; the encouragement of competition for place among the pupils; the employment of various forms of discipline – sarcasm, derision, positive reinforcement, corporal punishments of varying degrees of intensity; and the encouragement of learning by more positive means – short recesses, half-day holidays, regularised periods of 'misrule', praise, competition between teams, more interesting content and so forth. John Brinsley advised that pupils learned more readily if they understood what they were learning and if each point to be mastered was broken down into its simplest parts. He suggested that the long day's monotony could be broken by brief recesses and short periods of concentrated study on the individual subjects.[83]

The length of the school day

Indeed the length of the early modern school day never has been adequately explained: the sudden distinction between the life of leisured play (which Martindale conjures up) and the life of school work must have been traumatic for children.[84] Was it a matter of economics? Were parents anxious that their children should learn as much as possible within the brief time which they were able to afford at school? Or was the long day a result of the total lack of appreciation of the child's or the youth's ability to study for long stretches of time? But perceptive and experienced (and often compassionate) teachers such as Mulcaster and Brinsley did not fail to notice that the child flagged during the latter part of such a long workday. Colloquies used in contemporary schools indicate that teachers were well aware that children stayed up too late at night, and suffered for this in school. Richard Mulcaster pleaded for a more leisurely day at Merchant Taylors' School, London, (with no success) but managed to alleviate the monotony and rigour of the school day both there and at St Paul's by the introduction of amateur dramatics into the curriculum. A more satisfactory explanation of the long day may be that the curriculum was almost always put before the child and this curriculum was very demanding. Masters in the classical tradition were not concerned with the 'development' of the individual in the modern sense but with the acquisition of a given body of knowledge by that individual. If a youth were to achieve the sort of mastery of two, three, even occasionally four, languages in a few years, then every moment was indeed precious. At the same time, the child was often viewed as a small adult, without special requirements. The realisation that a child was different in kind from the adult was reached only after the experience of trying to teach this rigorous Latin curriculum. The writings of teachers such as Brinsley and Mulcaster come to fruition in those of Comenius. Keith Thomas has argued persuasively, moreover, that during the period learning was seen as equivalent to discipline. Children were subjected to a factory-like routine in preparation for a life of renunciation. He quotes the comments of Sir John Eardley Wilmot, Chief Justice of Common Pleas, in the eighteenth century:[85]

Obedience is one of the capital benefits arising from a public education, for though I am very desirous of having young minds impregnated with classical knowledge, from the pleasure I have derived from it, as well as the utility of it in all stations of life, yet it is but a secondary benefit in my estimation of education; for to break the natural ferocity of human nature, to subdue the passions and to impress the principles of religion and morality, and give habits of obedience and subordination to paternal as well as political authority, is the first object to be attended to by all schoolmasters who know their duty.

There were, indeed, objections to the methods used by many schoolmasters to accomplish this socialisation of children and youth (from parents and teachers) but at the same time there was a common acceptance that this socialisation process was one of the prime functions (and virtues) of the school. What we have to remember is that the society for which these boys were being prepared was not such a one as our own.

Conclusions

There will always be tantalising gaps in our knowledge of what went on in early modern schools. Nevertheless, we know enough to draw some important general conclusions. The sixteenth and seventeenth centuries certainly represent a milestone in the attempt to 'school society'. Many Englishmen believed that, by a deliberate effort, expressed through an academic curriculum, new generations could be fitted for society. Many of those who wrote on this subject, who founded English grammar schools or who taught in the same, were deeply influenced by the ideas of social humanism. The classical curriculum would be used to fit each boy to fulfil his vocation within society. But there was a subtle interaction between the 'new' ideas of the Renaissance, the novel demands of the Tudor and Stuart monarchical state and the traditional demands of English society. Hierarchy was not overthrown and education was used to modify and bolster the existing class structure. At the same time, while education was an essential agent in the defeat of Catholicism and the conversion of the people to a distinctively English form of Protestantism, no one ever suggested that through education young people would be enabled to make religious choices. Education would be used to acquaint the people of England with a new social and religious creed – service to the state to the best of one's ability and within the limits set by one's station in life and conformity to a new set of religious beliefs. Knowledge and improvement are the ends of the educational process, not revolution. In the preceding pages it has been shown that early modern teachers and writers concerned themselves, above all, with perfecting teaching techniques. It was hard to achieve success with the Latin curriculum – demanding as it was – especially given the half-hearted commitment to it of many parents and, indeed, of society itself. Experimentation was rife – authors were preoccupied with ingenious ways of presenting material and with ways to discipline youths into concentrated effort. 'Creativity', individual development, free expression were concepts unknown to the Tudor and Stuart educator and, therefore, unconsidered in his writings. Joy in learning meant no more than the delight obtainable in the acquisition of knowledge. Simultaneously, educators were pulled in other and occasionally contradictory directions by the idea that schooling was chiefly valuable for its disciplinary effects and by the demands voiced by many parents for a different kind of curriculum. Neither force was revolutionary in its implications.

Such conclusions may lead us to speculate on the extent to which early modern school education marked a sharp break theoretically with the situation in the late Middle Ages. Was it not rather that the schools now sought to serve a different political and religious situation and, in so doing, adapted Renaissance educational theory and existing educational ideas and techniques? The historian should be impressed by the self-conscious approach of early modern educators, by their conviction that so much could be achieved through formal schooling rather than by the often illusory novelty of the theory itself.

Chapter 5

The role of the ancient universities to 1640

Oxford and Cambridge and their relations with the crown and the church[1]

The Universities of Oxford and Cambridge traditionally served the ecclesiastical estate and were essentially ecclesiastical institutions. They arose as societies of masters or teachers, who were clergy in the medieval (and not the post-Reformation) sense of that word. Oxford had grown up in the late twelfth century and Cambridge in the early thirteenth century. The guilds had considerable autonomy and control over the admission of others to their privileges but they owed allegiance to the Church. The teachers of the universities were subject, as clerks, to the jurisdiction of the ecclesiastical authorities and their courts. After a time the Chancellor of Oxford, originally a representative of the Bishop of Lincoln, and the Chancellor of Cambridge, a representative of the Bishop of Ely, became the chief officials of the universities. The Church successfully maintained control because it continued to have a monopoly of the licensing power: although the universities trained recruits to their number, the Church alone, through the bishops and their commissaries, the Chancellors, could give them the authority to practise teaching. But in the thirteenth and fourteenth centuries the Chancellors, especially of Oxford, 'spearheaded the campaign for university freedom from ecclesiastical control and by so doing they further cemented the chancellor-guild cohesion'. In other words the Chancellors became more identified with university than with Church interests. This tendency was accentuated as members of the universities began to exercise some influence in the selection of their Chancellors. There were attempts to slacken the hold of the bishops on the universities. Initially these were directed against the power of Lincoln and Ely in university affairs and jurisdiction: the universities claimed first that they came under the jurisdiction of the Archbishop of Canterbury and then, having won this case, of the Pope alone. At the same time, the universities derived some of their privileges directly from the Crown – the Chancellors, for example, also exercised civil jurisdiction as Justices of the Peace – and in return gave the King due fealty. Nevertheless, the placing of the universities under the direct jurisdiction of the Papacy must be regarded as one of the most important steps in the history of the institutions as we consider their changing place in English and Welsh society and their changing function in that society. For when the monarchs of England became Heads of or Supreme Governors of the Church in England they commanded the entire obedience of the universities of England. As the institutionalised Church became more and more equivalent to the pastoral ministry, the monasteries could be dissolved as of no utility and institutions such as the universities could be adapted to serve a new purpose, no longer necessarily primarily religious. This is not to say that the universities would cease to perform religious functions or that the church hierarchy would acknowledge that they were no longer within the church's direct jurisdiction, but it is to say that the new situation offered a certain potential for secularisation.

The uneasy relationship between the universities and the Church during the sixteenth and, particularly, the seventeenth centuries owed much to the fact that the universities, after the dissolution of the monasteries and collegiate churches, were unique among ecclesiastical institutions in their direct relationship with the Crown. The Church continued to use the universities for the training of future ministers – indeed the concept of a university education became integral to the project of an educated parochial ministry in a novel fashion – but the Church's hierarchy was unable to assert direct institutional control over the teaching institutions themselves. In this situation it was possible for the universities to nurture, if not nonconformity, then criticism of the established church; to regard the production of ministers as only a part of their *raison d'être,* and to introduce into the universities elements of both curriculum and life which seemed iniquitous to the hierarchy. This is a point important to bear in mind when we come to consider apparently contradictory statements such as the description of the universities as 'seminaries for young ministers' or as 'nurseries for the gentry'; as both religious and secular institutions; as in the grip of the civic or, on the other hand, the ecclesiastical authorities. Only by understanding the relationship between the universities and, on the one hand, the Crown and, on the other, the Church can we come to grips with these assessments. Similarly, some understanding of the dual nature of the royal supremacy in England is necessary. The Crown is not simply head of the English state in which the Church exists, thus demanding the allegiance of all citizens, secular or religious. The Crown is rather Head of the State and also of the Church which exists within and of it. The Crown has rights within the Church which exceed those of demanding the loyalty of its personnel as citizens – the Crown's rights include those of Government, of direction and initiation. The Crown's role in the Church, as in the state, is active as well as passive. Thus, to say that the universities now confess the jurisdiction of the Crown instead of the Pope is not to say that the universities have become secular as opposed to ecclesiastical institutions but it is to say that, because the Crown is both a spiritual and a civil ruler, the universities have a potential for secular *and* ecclesiastical use which they did not have previously.[2]

The new relationship between the universities and the other institutions of state had other implications. In 1571 both universities were incorporated.[3] They now stood in the state in much the same relationship to the Crown as the municipal boroughs, with charters which confirmed privileges, liberties and franchises. All these privileges were seen to derive from the Crown (in Parliament) alone. The universities after 1604 each sent two members to Parliament to represent their community and their vested interests. The universities, however, had no representation in Convocation. This confirmed independence of the interference of Church hierarchy (especially Canterbury) and Convocation probably permitted the teachers of the universities to develop as a profession distinct from the Church in a way which had not been possible previously.[4] This development was gradual but it was real. The professionalisation of university teachers in the modern sense was realised only after the universities had thrown off all external control other than the ultimate control of the Crown. The shaking off of ecclesiastical controls may have been implicit in the Acts of Supremacy and the Acts of Incorporation but these were built upon by future developments. For instance, most of the chancellors of the universities after the Reformation were laymen. Significantly enough the two ecclesiastical chancellors of Oxford, Richard Bancroft and William Laud, were the two most anxious to retrieve the old relationship between the universities and the Church. After the reign of Laud, Oxford never had another ecclesiastical chancellor. In 1635–36 William Laud attempted to visit the universities in his metropolitical visitation. He could have done this on the strength of a royal commission, thus pleading the royal prerogative, but instead chose to claim the right to visit of his ordinary authority. This was a deliberate bid for ecclesiastical control over the universities and their personnel. Although Laud won recognition of his right to visit from Charles I, he never had time to carry out the intended visitation and so the victory was a hollow one, soon forgotten. Similarly, as we shall see later, the lay character of the universities was further accentuated by changes in the composition of the student body and, as both cause and consequence of this, by the change in attitude to the role of the universities within society.[5]

In many ways the approach of the Crown to the universities was similar to its approach to the Church at the same time. The Crown favoured oligarchical, and on occasion monarchical, forms of government within the Church. Institutions or movements which promised more influence to the bulk of the English and Welsh clergy were not popular with Elizabeth or the Early Stuarts. The Crown wanted to control the life of the country and sought to exercise this control to some extent through the parochial clergy. It was far easier to deal with a small group of men, close to the hub of government and the concerns of the Crown, than with the masses when seeking to influence the clergy. For this reason the great institutions of the state had in their decision-making apparatus as well as their bureaucratic machinery a developed tendency to replicate the decision-making machinery of the polity. This made for efficient government but it also made for less democracy and less opportunity for the thwarting of royal wishes (at least in theory). The government of the Church became increasingly centralised and oligarchic. The powers of convocation and movements for increased clerical participation in Church decisions were discouraged. Similarly with the universities. The Colleges had been gaining steadily in importance in the life of the universities during the latter half of the sixteenth century but the society of Masters still effectively governed the universities – this was still a guild fellowship. But in 1570 new statutes for the University of Cambridge changed this situation. The Regent Masters were stripped of most of their old powers and new powers were conferred upon a fresh oligarchy within the university community – the heads of the colleges. Collectively the heads of colleges, who had had no official status in the university outside their own colleges before this date, now became the chief governing body of the university, who nominated that candidate for the vice-chancellorship annually whom the regents and non-regents elected, and who also controlled elections to the *Caput*, the steering committee which passed on business to the congregation of regents. Similarly the heads of colleges gained control over the proctorships of the universities. Measures such as these did not take root in Oxford until the Laudian period, when the Hebdomadal Council, consisting of the vice-chancellor, the heads of colleges and two proctors, was created as a committee to examine matters of importance and to bring these forward before the Convocation, the legislative body of the university. The Hebdomadal Council was especially powerful because it met weekly and had great administrative, disciplinary and academic influence in the university. By this process, the guild organisation of the universities was subtly altered. It was an alteration which recognised certain changes in the academic and social composition of the universities as well as the needs of the Crown for a more easily manageable institution.

These changes in the relationship between universities, Church and Crown were not in themselves, of course, the result of changing attitudes to education and its role in society. As we have hinted, however, there is a sense in which such changes were hastened by fresh thinking on these very issues of education. Moreover, it is essential that we grasp the nature of these changes in the government of the university because they provide more than just a backdrop to any educational expansion which occurred in the ensuing two hundred years. If they did not *cause* change they, at the least, permitted it to occur and, at the most, facilitated its occurrence.

The changing function of the universities: a debate

The functions of the universities certainly appear to have undergone a sea change during the years 1540 to 1640, although the exact nature of that change and the speed and suddenness with which it occurred are more difficult to fathom. There are two schools of thought on the issue. On the one hand, there are those historians who chart an enormous increase in undergraduate numbers at both universities from 1560 onwards and, moreover, an influx of well-born lay students, whose presence was not apparent in the medieval universities.[6] This change, they say, was due to the impact of external factors upon the university scene. England's ruling élite became convinced of the appropriateness of a humanistic education within a university setting for its sons. The universities, or rather the colleges, accommodated this movement by providing personal and academic tuition for young gentlemen and young nobles within a congenial atmosphere and approved discipline. On the other hand there are those, myself included, who feel that the situation is exaggerated when put in these terms. The increase in the size of the undergraduate body was more apparent than real. Expansion there was, but it was far more gradual than historians have allowed since the early 1950s. Likewise, the change in the social composition of the universities may also be partly illusory.[7]

In the medieval period the undergraduate body of the universities was accommodated in a variety of inns, hostels and halls. At least 20 per cent of the population of the University of Oxford had been assigned to study there by a religious order. Students in the monastic colleges did receive a special kind of supervision. At Oxford there were three such monastic colleges (Gloucester, Durham and Canterbury) and two houses for canons (St Mary's and St Bernard's). At Cambridge there were no monastic colleges as such although four orders of friars and the Benedictine order of monks were well represented in the student body. Here, however, it is worth making two points. Firstly, many regulars had no college affiliation whatsoever and secondly, most were not undergraduates in the Arts Faculty or even bachelors but were in one of the higher faculties – especially theology. The other early colleges within Oxford and Cambridge were intended for the study of theology or, more occasionally, law (both in the higher faculties). Oxford, before

1379 when New College was founded, had a very tiny undergraduate *college* population. In 1379, of 90 college members, only 10 were undergraduate.[8]

We note, on the other hand, that Oxford had 120 halls in the year 1300. This number fell (probably chiefly in the early fifteenth century) to around 69 in 1444. Even so, a breakdown of the student population of Oxford in 1438 reveals 200 college residents; 100 monks and friars; and 700 students in lodgings, hostels and halls. T.H. Aston thinks that 1,200 students in halls is a more realistic figure for Oxford in 1450. At this date Cambridge accommodated as many as 800 students in halls. These halls were not teaching institutions (although they sometimes provided teaching) but residential houses. They normally possessed no endowment and were, therefore, very much subject to closure at short notice when student numbers dropped or times of hardship hit the hall concerned. More important, however, is the fact that the halls were affiliated to various faculties. When John Rous made a listing of Oxford and Cambridge halls in 1440–50 he divided Oxford halls as follows: 6 Grammar halls, 4 undesignated; 25 Arts halls: 2 Theological halls and 34 halls for Lawyers. At Cambridge 6 of 17 halls were for Artists and 6 for Lawyers. Perhaps significantly, the legist halls accommodated, on average, 80 students each whereas the arts hostels gave housing to only 25 to 30 young men apiece.[9]

Quite clearly, if we are looking for undergraduates we should look for them in the hostels and in private lodgings and not, at this stage, in the colleges. Supervision of the undergraduates within the university was poor, with the exception of a few students supervised within colleges of religious orders or a few aristocratic students who possessed personal tutors. Students were expected to fulfil the statutory requirements of the university but were given little or no direction or moral supervision. The university authorities were continually faced with disciplinary problems, which were not assisted by the fact that the university had no accurate measurement of the size of its student body and no check upon the whereabouts of students in halls or private chambers. Students were not made to matriculate at Oxford until the first matriculation statute of 1564/5 was passed. At Cambridge, compulsory matriculations date from 1544.

Meanwhile the situation was worsening because of the decline of the existing halls and the consequent resort of even more students to private lodgings in town and because of the failure to revitalise the academic teaching system of the universities. A.B. Emden's biographical register of the University of Oxford between 1501 and 1540 indicated that only 30 per cent of known members of the university were college linked, with a further 37 per cent having no institutional connection whatsoever. When one reflects that almost any biographical data concerning *alumni* from a period when matriculation was not compulsory must be biased in favour of members with an institutional connection in the first place, these percentages seem highly significant.[10]

Throughout the fifteenth century there is evidence that the university authorities were anxious about discipline among university members and concerned to revitalise the academic system. Probably Cambridge was more successful in this respect than was Oxford. A new school of Theology was built at Cambridge in 1400; schools for Canon Law complete with library were erected in 1438 and schools for Philosophy and Civil Law again with a library were built between 1458 and 1470 – 71. In 1473 a new general range with a library was completed. At Oxford the rebuilding of the schools and the expansion of the Bodleian Library came too late to revive the university teaching system. But we must stress that, whereas Cambridge may have tackled the problem earlier because of its rising numbers in the fifteenth century, it can also be argued that its success in handling the matter was only partial.[11]

In fact, a rival teaching system was fast taking root at both universities. In the late thirteenth and early fourteenth centuries a number of colleges were founded in both Oxford and Cambridge. In Cambridge, for example, Peterhouse, Michaelhouse, Clare Hall, King's Hall, Pembroke Hall, Gonville Hall, Trinity Hall and Corpus Christi were all founded by 1352. In Oxford five colleges were already in existence by the end of the thirteenth century – University, Balliol, Merton, Gloucester Hall (monastic) and Durham College (monastic)[12] Royal, noble and eminent ecclesiastical personages were responsible for the endowment of such colleges and they often had mixed motives in so doing. For example, Archbishop Chichele commented that the members of his college were, 'not so much to attend therein to the various sciences and faculties but with all devotion to pray for the souls of glorious memory' of the House of Lancaster, for those who fell in the French Wars, and for All Souls. These colleges represented a natural extension of the predominant patronage system. For example, Clare College, Cambridge, was seen by Lady Clare and Lord Howard as a means to educate members of their retinues. King's Hall, Cambridge, was an extension of the Chapel Royal, in which the monarch demonstrated his vested interest in the education of future bureaucrats. New College, seen by one historian as the type of the new college, was in its origin also an extension of an episcopal household.[13] Each new college had statutes laid down for it by its founders, which reflected concern that the college be conducted in accordance with its intentions. In other words, the ideas of control and careful supervision were implicit in the collegiate movement. This aspect of college development is either missed or underestimated if we stress the nature of the college as a corporation of university teachers, founded out of a desire felt among the Masters of Arts to associate. Members of the early colleges lived a carefully regulated life and were bound by a debt of gratitude such as was felt by all clients of noble patrons.[14]

Until the fifteenth century the colleges were not intimately involved in the teaching of undergraduates. King's Hall, Cambridge, took some undergraduates in the fourteenth century. When William of Wykeham founded New College, Oxford, in 1379 he provided for a warden and some seventy scholars. Wykeham made it clear that the undergraduate members of the college were part of the scholarly community and part of the responsibility of the fellows, when he stipulated that money was to be taken from the college funds to pay the fellows and scholars for teaching the undergraduate elements within the college.[15] The fifteenth century itself witnessed a piecemeal transfer of the undergraduate population from halls to colleges (Table 5.1). Colleges were increasing the number of undergraduates in residence but they were also annexing the halls which still existed. Merton College annexed St John's, Nunn, Knyght, Colishalle and St Alban's Halls. In general, all those halls which accommodated young Arts students came under the control of the colleges. Only the law halls remained independent and their demise was made certain by the abolition of canon law studies at the universities and a decline in the study of civil law. There can be little doubt that, in annexing the halls, the colleges were seeking to exploit the demand from parents of prospective undergraduates in order to supplement the colleges' own ailing finances. The advantages of the close moral and educational supervision offered by the monastic colleges and by the secular colleges to a very few youths were clear to the parents of young Arts students.[16]

Table 5.1 Decline in the number of halls at Oxford

Date	Number	No. of colleges*
1300	120	3
1444	69	15[†] (9 sec.; 2 mon.; 4 acad. halls)
Late fifteenth century	50	16
1511	25	17
1514	12	17

*approximate; †the short lived London College, 1416–21 is not included.

That the colleges subsumed the membership of the old halls has often been noted: what has less frequently been taken into account is the fact that the increase in the number of colleges housing and teaching undergraduates off the foundation coincided chronologically with the official 'hounding of town dwellers' or 'Chamberdakyns'. Elizabeth Russell has observed that in all probability fifteenth- and sixteenth-century colleges were taking in and teaching ever larger groups of 'commoners' well before the reign of Elizabeth.[17]

During the fifteenth and sixteenth centuries the teaching duties of the colleges expanded greatly. It has been argued that King's Hall, Cambridge, set the new trend by inaugurating a system by which tutors taught undergraduates who were not of the foundation for a fee (dating from circa 1430). Tutors of such students collected their college fees and acted as their guarantors or sponsors as well as their teachers. Some years later, in 1479/80, Magdalen College, Oxford, endowed college lectureships which began to attract undergraduates away from the university's own public lecture system. Magdalen's lead was followed by other colleges so that by the mid 1550s most colleges at Oxford had organised full systems of undergraduate tuition. At Brasenose, Oriel and Corpus Christi students were examined internally and there is evidence that at Christ Church in 1550 students were made to take a collegiate examination before being allowed to supplicate for a degree in the university. By the later sixteenth century, college teaching rather than university teaching of undergraduates, on a decentralised pattern, was established at both English universities.[18]

Elizabeth Russell argues convincingly that an important element in this rise of the colleges as a predominant undergraduate teaching institutions was official pressure from both within and without the universities for the control of multitudinous and potentially troublesome chamberdakyns. She sees the two matriculation statutes of the university of Oxford as direct attempts to measure the presence of 'commoners' in the university and thus control them. The first matriculation statute of 1564/5 insisted that even town dwellers both subscribe and also have and name a tutor with a college or hall affiliation. Convocation ordered on 27 June 1580 that future supplicants for the degree must be members of a college or hall with an official signature from a member of that institution as surety. The second matriculation act of 1581 ordered that students subscribe to the Thirty-nine Articles, the Royal Supremacy, and to the orders and statutes of the university. Through the colleges and surviving halls, the University of Oxford was asserting a new control over university membership.[19]

That the same was true of Cambridge is probable but not proven. In 1377 the total population of Cambridge is estimated at 700, as against 1,500 at the university of Oxford. During the fifteenth century Oxford was affected by a relative malaise, accentuated by continuous plague and presumably by the fact that the population of England as a whole did not begin to recover until the later century. Cambridge, on the other hand, increased her numbers considerably. By 1450 Oxford appears to have had in the region of 1,700 resident students and Cambridge 1,300. Cambridge continued this expansion in the period 1450–1550. Unfortunately these estimates rest upon the assumption that both universities had tiny numbers of students in private lodgings. Whereas it may well be that Cambridge was more successfully institutionalising her student body than was Oxford, there seems no obvious reason why we should believe that this was the case. There were early attempts at Cambridge to register student presence in a systematic way. Students were required by statute to enroll their name with a regent master within fifteen days of coming up to the University. Compulsory university-wide matriculation, however, was introduced in 1544 and it is from this date that the matriculation registers exist. We have no means of knowing how successful these earlier attempts at recording student identities were although they demonstrate the same concern for student discipline as was noticed at Oxford. Perhaps it is significant also that late fifteenth-century college statutes were already recognising the presence of pensioners in the Cambridge foundations (for example, at God's–House in 1495/6). Of course, this was a special case, for God's–House was set up specifically to train grammar schoolmasters, who were of necessity Arts students. But it is important that this was one of the first colleges to inaugurate a college lecture system, which dated from 1451. All in all, the evidence points to a picture of an expanding university and a commensurate anxiety for the preservation of discipline and the development of mechanisms such as the colleges to enforce university discipline.[20]

The main point, of course, is this: although a case has been made that Oxford and Cambridge suffered an influx of well-born undergraduate commoners, who belonged to colleges but were not on their foundations, after 1560 in the case of Oxford and after 1540 in the case of Cambridge, it may well be that any such influx is indeed 'an optical illusion'. For it is clear that, prior to 1564/5 (Oxford) and 1544 (Cambridge), we have no statistically reliable or representative information about the composition or size of either university outside its institutional organisation. A statement to the effect that the rise of the colleges 'brought a rise in entry numbers at each university from 150 a year in 1500 to 400–500 by 1600' is thus of very uncertain validity. We know that the size of the universities had always fluctuated from year to year, from decade to decade: war, plague, demographic change, secular and religious politics had all taken their toll at various times. It becomes dangerous, therefore, to contrast the flourishing state of the two universities in the late sixteenth and early seventeenth centuries with what may well have been a very temporary slump in numbers in the mid sixteenth century.[21]

It is entirely possible that the universities contained considerable numbers of well-born youths prior to the late sixteenth century. T.H. Aston has indicated that few below the upper yeomanry could have afforded to attend the university because the chief means of student support was the family. In addition, we know that fourteenth- and fifteenth-century colleges themselves were accommodating the sons of upper-class laymen. For example, 88 members of noble families can be shown to have attended the two universities between 1307 and 1485: 69 of these were at Oxford and 19 at Cambridge. The Nevilles, for instance, sent eight or more youths to university over two centuries. The majority of noble university students were younger sons. Fifty-one of these students had gone to university in the fourteenth century; thirty-seven in the fifteenth century. Before we jump to the conclusion that noble interest in a university education was falling in the fifteenth century we should recall that the size of the English nobility was dramatically reduced in the period after the Black Death and, moreover, that it is chronically difficult to recover the identities of early students. Not only were a small number of aristocratic boys already educated in the colleges, but also gentry and professional interest was evident. From the late fourteenth century onwards a growing number of government officials were sending their sons to Oxford. Business administration was taught in Oxford for intending bureaucrats. T. H. Aston was able to recover the names of sixty upper-class and gentle youths who attended Cambridge in the fifteenth century from evidence heavily biased in favour of the colleges and halls. Some prominent lawyers were sending their own sons into the law via the university and the Inns of Court by the late fifteenth century. Thomas More, whose father was a Judge of the King's Bench, attended Oxford before Lincoln's Inn. The sons of William Paston, Justice of the Common Pleas, were educated at Cambridge before being admitted to the Inns of Court. During the later fifteenth century a number of members of Parliament were also giving their sons an Oxford or Cambridge education. It has been argued persuasively that the illiterate aristocrat of the fourteenth and fifteenth centuries was not a typical figure. When we recall that most of this information pertains to Oxford and Cambridge students with a college or hall affiliation, it seems reasonable to suppose that many more noble and middle-class youths had private chambers in town and thus escaped the records.[22]

Thus, while we may accept J. H. Hexter's contention that aristocratic interest in the universities increased during the sixteenth century and Lawrence Stone's argument that gentry interest in a university education also burgeoned, we must surely do so with reservations. It seems probable that the numbers of commoners in the universities had always been sizeable and that the dramatic nature of the increase in their numbers in the later sixteenth century is indeed more apparent than real. Until the undergraduates who were not on the foundation of a college or resident in hall were brought under the auspices of a teaching college, their presence in the university went unrecorded. Even the introduction of compulsory matriculation may not have achieved consistent and accurate results immediately. Thus it seems improbable that we shall ever be able to compare accurately the numbers of upper-class students at either university before and after 1560. Unsatisfactory though it may be, we shall have to content ourselves with the statement that it is more probable that the increase in the number of commoners at the universities after 1564 was an intensification of a well-established medieval trend rather than a dramatic revolution in the way in which these classes viewed university education. We should not forget that the surviving literary evidence dates the upper-class invasion of the universities from the reigns of HenryVIII and Edward VI. Both Roger Ascham and Hugh Latimer bemoaned the usurpation of the places of the deserving poor at the universities by the wealthy and indolent, while Thomas Lever was more specific. According to him a decline in the number of divinity students had been effected by the decay of hostels: the occupants of these hostels 'be either gone away, or else fain to creep into colleges, and put poor men from bare livings'.[23]

The function of the universities in Tudor and early Stuart England: educating the upper classes

By the early sixteenth century, then, the role of the colleges in the teaching and supervision of undergraduates in the Arts Faculty was established and the matriculation regulations forced into these societies students who had previously lived in private lodgings in town. The facilities were there for the large-scale accommodation in the colleges of lay youth. This in no sense explains, however, why the population did take up the idea of a university education so wholeheartedly.

Initially the English humanists did not themselves see the universities as appropriate for this function of training statesmen or gentlemen. In his *Dialogue* (1533–36) Thomas Starkey made it plain that the universities were designed to educate churchmen and not gentlemen. A separate academy (in the capital) was necessary for the education of the élite. Does this mean that the English humanists were counselling against the prevailing trend? Starkey, Thomas Elyot and Richard Morison were all advising Henry VIII in the 1530s to adapt the education offered at the Inns of Court to include the teaching of civic and Christian humanism. Their ideas had some considerable influence upon Thomas Cromwell. It seems probable that the government itself planned to found such a college in 1539 when funds became available from the dissolution of the monasteries. In response, a close associate of Elyot, Thomas Denton, put forward a detailed plan, in the form of a petition, for a House of Students, modelled on the Inns of Court, which would attempt to remedy the defects of upper-class education. Within the timetable of the 'House of Students', rhetoric, modern French, Latin and Greek, the Scriptures and martial and physical activities all found a prominent place. The legal curriculum itself, while based on that of the Inns, would be designed to profit those who would serve the King in public affairs. For example, two students would accompany embassies abroad; some others would be sent to record military exploits; and two would compile an impartial history of the kingdom. All this may be seen in the light of a programme of humanistic educational and legal reform, using the revenues of the dissolved houses and the royal acquisition of the existing Inns and sponsored by Thomas Cromwell. This programme collapsed when Cromwell was disgraced and finally executed in 1540. Many other schemes for academies were proposed during the sixteenth century. In all cases the recommended curriculum was dissimilar to that adopted at the universities. One can only speculate that the annexation of the universities as a training ground for gentlemen occurred by default as far as the humanists were concerned. When the proposed academies failed to materialise and the Crown declined to adapt the Inns of Court, the gentry utilised the existing institutions – the universities – which, despite their concentration on the education of ecclesiastics, had experience of educating members of the lay élite and, moreover, appeared anxious to extend this experience.[24]

The process by which social humanism took a hold on the gentry and aristocracy is a separate though related question. Social humanism was a missionary creed. Historians are currently making much of the influence of the humanist John Tiptoft and several of the fifteenth-century upper-class bishops (especially William Gray) in preparing court circles. The blow to traditional feudal values struck by the political and economic developments of the late fifteenth and early sixteenth centuries, together with the demand of the Tudor State for a different kind of servant, were crucial. Henry Tudor would not tolerate a nobility which conceived of itself as standing in a feudal relationship with the Crown. The bond of fealty in the Tudor State was to be much stronger than in the preceding Lancastrian and Yorkist periods – there was to be no divisive aristocracy, vying for the loyalty of the King's subjects. That this ideal did not materialise precisely is beside the point. Henry VII and his successors, themselves converts to social humanism, were not slow to see its value in diverting the energies of the upper classes into safer channels, which emphasised the concept of service to the state (or at least the monarchy) and under-emphasised motives of private gain and aggrandisement. But as the events of the sixteenth and seventeenth centuries were to show, it might be a simple matter to convert the ruling classes to the wisdom of a university education but the education of the same men in the new ideology itself was a much more gradual process. The appeal of the Earl of Essex under Elizabeth may be the chief reminder of the late survival of the bastard feudal vision but it was by no means the only one. Nevertheless, in this new ideology the ruling classes found a fresh and convincing justification for their position of influence, which rested not

on birth alone nor yet on the ownership of land but on the possession of virtue, achieved through education, which allowed them to
exercise leadership and patronage in both state and church. When
William Springe recommended his son to the care of William Sancroft at Emmanuel in 1630 he asked that the youth leave that college with his innocence intact but with 'some addition of helps of
art, which may apt him to the *service* of his country' and that he
'may above all learn to be good and religious and so be better able
to do good *service* to God and his country' (author's emphasis).[25]

Although we have challenged the view that the influx of well-
born students into the universities between 1560 and 1580 was novel
and dramatic, there can be no doubt that the social composition of
the student body was altered significantly between 1450 and 1650.
This change was gradual but it was none the less important. In the
years 1575–79, for example, 39 per cent of Oxford matriculants
were gentlemen or above; in 1580–89, 41 per cent; in 1590–99, 50
per cent; and in 1600–09, 52 per cent. Even if some of this rise was
attributable to a greater tendency to claim gentle status, it must
have had a dramatic impact upon the social and academic atmosphere of the universities. Throughout the second half of the sixteenth century there was a continuous stream of complaints about
the frivolous behaviour and lack of scholarship among such students. In 1577 William Harrison wrote in his *Description of England*.

most of them study little other than histories, tables dice and trifles . . . . Besides this, being for the most part either gentlemen or rich men's sons they
oft bring the university into much slander. For standing upon their reputation and liberty, they ruffle and roist it out, exceeding in apparel and hunt-
ing riotous company, (which draweth them from their books into another
trade) and for excuse they are charged with breach of one good order think
it sufficient to say that they be gentlemen which grieveth many not a little.

Clearly, the disciplinary problems of the university authorities had
not been solved entirely by bringing well-born students within the
fold of the colleges.[26]

Demonstrably the universities became socially segregated communities. Thrown into close proximity with men of plebeian origin,
the sons of nobility and gentry were warned about the consequences
of mixing with the same. For instance, Henry Peacham's *The Compleat Gentleman* (1622)[27] urged strict class segregation: 'For the companions of your recreation, consort yourself with gentlemen of your
own rank and quality; for that friendship is best contenting and last-
ing. To be over free and familiar with inferiors argues a baseness of
spirit, and begetteth contempt . . . .' and later, Simonds D'Ewes,[28]
ever conscious of birth, warned his brother Richard at St Cather-
ine's, Cambridge, to remember that, 'You are maintained with the
best of your rank, dishonorate [sic] not your self by your unseemly

associating with pensioners and subsizers though of other colleges.'

When the son of a prominent member of the aristocracy entered college as a commoner (fellow-commoner), perhaps his most important privilege was that of commoning (eating and associating) with the fellows and master rather than the undergraduate body. Depending upon the college, the son of a nobleman entered as a fellow-commoner could safely associate with approximately 10 per cent of the student body.[29] Parents and guardians were also anxious that their sons should come under the influence of appropriate tutors. The boy was 'to get his Latin tongue' from someone 'of your own rank, I mean gentlemen of good quality' and 'of good fashion and demeanour, for it is commonly seen, that of such behaviour are children to those with whom they most converse'. In other words, upper-class parents were determined that university education should not undermine the value system which they held most dear. Perhaps as a consequence some tutors specialised in looking after the sons of aristocrats, as did John Preston. Certainly the masters of colleges were actively interested in this class of student, as Thomas Crosfield's diary attests.[30]

For the universities such attitudes had a real importance. Teaching accounted for a good deal of the college fellow's income – in money, and perhaps in kind, it spelt the difference between meagre and tolerable lifestyle. It presented opportunities for further preferment when the pupil was well connected. Edward Gellybrand of Magdalen College, Oxford, was prepared to go to law to retain tuition of John Foxe's sixteen-year-old son, Samuel, in 1576 despite mutual dislike and the boy's lack of progress under his supervision. During the seventeenth century tutors were especially eager to attract gentle or noble pupils to their colleges. Not only did this benefit individual tutors; it also profited the college as a whole, because a few noble pupils one year might set the tone for future years. As a consequence one meets with a number of complaints that tutors were neglecting their responsibilities to plebeian students in the interests of those from the upper classes. In 1587 Burghley, at the time Chancellor of Cambridge, maintained that,

> through the great stipends of tutors and the little pains they do take in the instructing and well governing of their pupils, not only the poorer sort are not able to maintain their children at the university, and the richer be so corrupt with liberty and remissness, so that the Tutor is more afraid to displease his pupil through the desire of great gain than which he hath by his tutorage than the pupil is of his tutor . . .

The accommodation of well-born students in the college structure clearly had potentially adverse implications for student discipline and standards.[31]

Richard Tyler discovered that some 70.8 per cent of fellows at Jesus, King's, St John's and Emmanuel Colleges, Cambridge (1590–

1640), were themselves of gentle or clerical birth and noted that, 'presumably these dons could meet the pedagogical and social criteria of the early seventeenth century'. But the situation seems to have been rather different in at least some Oxford colleges in the later sixteenth century (1577–1603/4). For example, only 47.4 per cent of foundationers at Corpus Christi College came from these two classes; only 31 per cent at Trinity College; only 19.2 per cent at St John's; 27 per cent at Exeter; 27 per cent at University and 25 per cent at Magdalen. In some cases the overwhelming number of plebeian foundationers is explicable in terms of the statutes: at St John's, for example, thirty-seven fellowships were reserved for pupils of Merchant Taylors' School, London, and the remainder for youths from Bristol, Reading, Coventry and Tonbridge and for kin of the founder. Many of these boys would be the sons of wealthy merchants or the prosperous bourgeoisie and yet would be accommodated in the matriculation lists as plebeians. The declared intention of Fox in the statutes of Corpus Christi to use the college to produce preachers may have had a similar effect upon the type of student elected to the foundation. But it is less easy to explain away the markedly unaristocratic complexion of Magdalen, University and Exeter Colleges in this way. Certainly the students at these colleges who were not on the foundation were noticeably higher in social status than the majority of the fellows: it was not that the college tutors had less need to deal with fashionable students than did their Cambridge peers. Possibly the discrepancy can be best explained in terms of the time difference. It may have more common for students to bring their own tutors to Oxford in the late sixteenth century than to rely upon tutoring provided within the college. In other words, there may have been less onus on the fellows to cater to the whims of parents than was later to be the case. Moreover, we have some evidence to suggest that the threat of upper-class usurpation of places intended for the poor was a feature of the early seventeenth century rather than of the late sixteenth.[32]

Whatever the answer to this dilemma, the evidence is incontrovertible that certain colleges made a good deal of their ability to cater for the fashionable student, particularly in the seventeenth century. For example, when at Queen's, Oxford, John Preston announced his intention to concentrate on the education of the gentry and nobility, in the interests of the spread of reformed Protestantism. Accordingly, he admitted sixteen fellow-commoners to that college in one year. Jesus, Cambridge, for other reasons, established a tradition of gentle education. We know that individual fellows would compose special instructions and reading lists for their gentle undergraduates.[33] When in the Bagot manuscripts we read that the President of Trinity College, Oxford, advised the young Harvey Bagot to leave Oxford for the Inns of Court, we become aware that the university teachers themselves were thinking in terms of the current conception of gentry education rather than in terms of seeing all their students through an academic degree course. As contemporaries undoubtedly regarded the education of the élite in the universities with ambivalence, it is small wonder that modern historians find it difficult to determine whether their presence dominated the development of university education at the time or not, and whether their attendance was beneficial or not.[34]

The social segregation of the different classes within the undergraduate body was in a sense confirmed and in another sense mitigated by the heterogeneous character of both Oxford and Cambridge colleges. While it used to be assumed that a single college's social composition could be assumed to be representative of the entire student body of a university, more detailed studies have made it difficult to adopt such a view. No longer would we urge that Caius, with its rising tide of gentle students, epitomised a movement throughout Cambridge nor that the heavily middle-class origins of students at St John's College, Cambridge, indicated that Cambridge itself was predominantly a middle-class university with a student population almost wholly orientated towards the Church.[35] Instead we recognise that the various colleges displayed distinctive patterns. For example, while the gentry occupied 30 per cent of places at Emmanuel, Jesus, St John's and King's, there were significant differences in the actual configuration of the student body (Table 5.2).[36] And even these statistics require elaboration. Emmanuel drew upon a more comfortable economic base, that of the gentry, while St John's, despite its lower percentage of students from gentle families, had a qualitatively more aristocratic student body than Emmanuel. All in all, Emmanuel and King's appear to be much more homogeneous socially than either Jesus or John's. At both the latter there were significant groups of both gentle and plebeian students, maintaining a kind of social balance. This probably helps to explain why the rate of degree taking was so much lower at Emmanuel than at the three other colleges. The lower rate at Emmanuel may also be explicable in terms of the higher incidence of religious heterodoxy there.

Table 5.2

	Emmanuel (%)	Jesus (%)	St John's (%)	King's (%)
Gentle	63.0	49.0	48.0	58.0
Clergy	17.0	18.0	15.0	20.0
Plebeian	20.0	33.0	37.0	21.0

From such evidence we may conclude that the extent to which members of different social classes mingled or were thrown together varied considerably with individual colleges. Some colleges were much more fashionable than others. Moreover, the living and boarding arrangements were commonly designed to placate anxious parents. The statutes of Emmanuel College, for example, stipulated that a fellow-commoner had to be MA, BD or DD or a gentleman of knightly or noble birth unless the Master and Fellows made specific exception.[37]

Such restrictions were imposed because fellow-commoners were a privileged group within the college: they ate with the dons, were permitted to keep sizars and paid higher fees for tuition. Yet in point of fact places as fellow-commoner seem to have been subject to outright purchase at Emmanuel: some 220 of 328 did not have acceptable birth or degree status.[38] It is unclear whether wealth was an acceptable substitute for birth at other colleges in the early seventeenth century. College living arrangements could also be made to serve sectional religious interests. Nicholas Cobbe, ex-fellow of St John's Cambridge, entered Gonville and Caius College Cambridge as a fellow-commoner in 1564. He probably came from a Catholic family in Essex and his first students, with one exception, were taken from his home county, were well born and of strongly recusant stock. It is entirely possible that Cobbe was 'hired' to attend Caius and supervise this particular batch of students and no other. For instance, four of the students (William Greene (19), Thomas Crawley (14), Richard Greene (11) and William Stoorton (16)) had been educated in the home of Mr Greene at Sampford, Essex. With the exception of Stoorton, they entered Caius as fellow-commoners and shared Cobbe's suite of cubicles. Three sons of esquires (one of whom had also been educated at home and of Catholic (persuasion) shared the fifth lower cubicle with Stoorton. The extent to which Cobbe was a *college* teacher is, therefore, questionable. He seems to have had few institutional links with the college itself and to have been brought in from outside to supervise the scions of respectable Essex Catholic families, previously preserved from Protestantising influence by a home education and now bent on the same at Cambridge.[39]

The problems involved in ascertaining the social origins of university students are as nothing when compared with the difficulties in establishing the social destination of such youths. Only a very little work has been done in this area. Contemporaries in the sixteenth and early seventeenth centuries often charged that the secular professions were drawing off promising graduates who would normally have entered the Church. Historians have tended, erroneously, to agree with this assessment, particularly where the mid sixteenth century is concerned.[40] Some work on the social origins of secular professionals (particularly of lawyers) has suggested indirectly that this cannot have been an important drain on the intellectual resources of the ministry – future barristers as well as 'social members' of the Inns were drawn overwhelmingly from social classes which were not important traditional feeding grounds for the ministry.[41] More recently, in his work on the fortunes of Emmanuel, St John's, Jesus and King's Colleges, Cambridge, Richard Tyler has produced statistics which give the lie to the impression that the Universities were sending significant numbers of men into secular professions and government work. For instance, of a total of 7,039 men at these colleges between 1590 and 1640, only 264 (3.8 per cent) held political positions (including membership of Parliament, positions on the Commissions of the Peace and office holding). Socially these men were drawn from the élite (only five sizars entered state service) but were, in themselves, a very small proportion of upper-class students in the four colleges. Further, Tyler demonstrates that 41.3 per cent of the men took orders and that 47.5 per cent of the men who took degrees held at least one living. Only 281 (4.0 per cent) of the students entered the secular professions from university (physicians, attorneys, schoolmasters, non-clerical academics) although some 126 entered the squirearchy via a call to the Bar and 36 more attended the Inns of Court as a prelude to their careers. As against this 7.8 per cent of students who entered secular professions and government, and 41.3 per cent who entered the ministry, perhaps as many as 50 per cent (3,391) entered college for a short period only in order to achieve a veneer of humane learning and the increased status which went with it. The percentage of non-graduates was highest of all among the fellow-commoners (84 per cent as against 58.5 per cent of pensioners and 24.1 per cent of sizars).[42]

Richard Tyler's comment that 63.6 per cent of fellow-commoners left no record 'of ever applying their learning to anything', similar in kind to Lawrence Stone's statement, 'Demand for university education for prospective country gentlemen is entirely a matter of social convention, since the training obtained has no obvious utility whatsoever', deserves further scrutiny. While it is true that these youths did not apply their learning in the modern sense to an occupation, there can be little doubt that they and their parents regarded it as strictly utilitarian and geared closely to their vocation or profession as gentlemen. James McConica has described the manner in which the extension of university (or, more properly, college) education to the well-born layman enabled many more young men to benefit from the type of education which only the wealthiest homes could have provided on a private basis. In stressing the utilitarian nature of this education one does not mean, of course, that the majority of gentle students took their studies seriously, although some did.[43]

Whatever the motivation behind their going, the attendance of upper-class youths at the universities certainly had its impact upon the government of the country as a whole. The proportion of members of Parliament who had attended university escalated during the period 1563–1642: for instance, of 420 MPs in 1563, 110 had matriculated at the university; by 1584, 145 out of 460 MPs had done

Table 5.3

Date	Kent %	Norf. %	Northants. %	Soms. %	Worcs. %	N.R. Yorks. %	Total %	Diff. incr. %
1562	2.27	5.88	5.88	3.44	5.26	11.76	4.89	
1584	16.38	41.66	16.66	15.38	15.38	38.63	23.17	18.28
1608	40.20	59.61	18.91	35.55	20.58	56.25	40.51	17.34
1626	62.71	52.94	53.70	50.00	51.72	58.82	55.47	14.96
1636	68.25	67.30	71.79	54.90	50.00	48.71	61.65	6.18

so; by 1593, 161 out of 462 MPs; and by 1642, 276 out of 552 MPs (26%, 32%, 35%, 50%). Although it is true that matriculation did not necessarily imply attendance, probably most of these men did spend some time in residence.[44] J. H. Gleason drew up a table (see Table 5.3) of the university experience of working members of the Commission of the Peace in various counties during the years 1562–1636.[45]

Similarly, J. H. Hexter discovered that, in the early seventeenth century, over half of the prominent county-landowners who served as Lords Lieutenant or Deputies had been educated at university and he suggested that the same applied to Justices of the Peace.[46] T. G. Barnes estimated that some 74 per cent of Somerset JPs had had a university or Inns of Court affiliation between 1625 and 1640, and Lawrence Stone felt that this was an under-estimate, himself positing a figure of at least 80 per cent.[47]

Quite clearly the ruling classes in both Court and country did feel that the universities were offering a desirable commodity. This fact must not be allowed to obscure, however, the interruption in the so-called secular boom at the universities which occurred between 1590 and 1615. Did this reflect a disillusionment on the part of the upper classes with university education? Stone suggests that the root of the slump lay in economic depression and, moreover, that it hit the plebeian students at Oxford much more than it did the gentry and esquires. Similarly, he demonstrates that the depression affected the growth of the number of 'cultural' students rather than the growth of serious professional students – that is, those bound for the ministry.[48] While one might well quarrel with his use of these concepts, it remains true that the number of graduates rose during these years and that this rise was absorbed by vacancies in the Church. Yet, despite a possible short-term halt in the growth of admissions from the gentry class and above to the universities during these years, an overall view of élite admissions suggests that the rise in their numbers at the university in proportion to the size of the élite group in the nation as a whole (which stood at 3.5 per cent in the 1590s) more than kept pace between 1603 and 1630 with the tremendous increase in the size of that group (due to the inflation of honours).

The effect of university education upon the élite

What effect did university education have upon the ruling classes and, indeed, upon England herself? Historians have sometimes asserted that through the universities England was made a more homogeneous nation. A common educational experience dissolved local and class loyalties. We have already observed the extent to which social humanism was being used in the service of the Tudor state. Chapter 7 discusses the degree to which the clergy wished to see themselves as a part of gentle society as a result of sharing a common humanistic education. Curriculum aside, the evidence of social segregation at the universities (and perhaps especially at Oxford) is, however, convincing. And there is certainly good reason to suspect that the relationship which evolved between the gentry and particular colleges reinforced local loyalties.[49]

Victor Morgan has emphasised that 'university men' were, in reality, 'college men': it was the college, physically, which drew men's loyalties.[50] If we concentrate too much on the curriculum taught and its possible implications, we are in danger of missing this important point. Typical student unrest in the late sixteenth century was intercollegiate violence – the men of Trinity battling against those of St John's. A game of football or a public disputation provided the occasion for intercollegiate rivalry. And these competitions reflected the regional complexion of the colleges. Whereas Wilbur Jordan claimed that endowments to the university were made to benefit the whole nation, in truth they were made for the benefit of students from particular counties. Through their endowments, the colleges became landowners with vested interests in their localities, while these areas in their turn developed equivalent interests in the colleges. College endowments tended to be regionally concentrated and at least some of the fellows would visit the counties concerned each year, making contacts with tenants and with estate administrators. Local gentlemen administered college estates. Alumni in the counties concerned loaned money for college building projects and were rewarded with beneficial leases or other perquisites, sometimes to the long-term disadvantage of the college itself. Grammar schools with closed scholarships to particular colleges formed another link between local community and college, a tie often made by an individual. In counties such as Yorkshire, the establishment of endowed grammar schools to Protestantise the area, with accompanying closed scholarships to Cambridge colleges, created a system of 'feeder schools' which ensured a continuing regional connection between the North and Cambridge. In a county such as Norfolk, however, the local influence of educated clergy who were Cambridge alumni, and the fact of proximity to the university made the bond between schools and colleges much more dependent upon individuals. Contemporaries were well aware that the college affected the character of the local community and vice versa.

A student's experience of college life reinforced these local connections. Undergraduates, for example, were constantly reminded of their dependence on local munificence by a proliferation of portraits of benefactors and frequent prayers for the founders. Regional dialects were perpetuated in the colleges, making the distinction between one house and another more apparent. Latin and Greek pronunciation, word selection and syntax may have been standardised by university study during this time but there is little evidence that this standardisation affected the vernacular. Meanwhile, Parker's endowments at Corpus required that all Norfolk scholars be taught by Norfolk fellows. The fellows there assigned Norfolk scholars studies in their own chambers. The records of Gonville and Caius indicate that such a practice was by no means uncommon.

Once a student left the university his college and university connections were not severed. The Great Commencement in July provided the occasion for a meeting between clerical alumni and members of the colleges. Stourbridge Fair in September presented a more informal opportunity. During the Long Vacation, which had by the 1570s become normal, university fellows were drawn into the life of the counties. They attended the Midsummer Quarter Sessions, the festivities surrounding the summer Assizes, and house parties given by the gentry (often the parents of their pupils). For many this was an opportunity to agitate for clerical preferment, by giving sermons before potential patrons. Meanwhile, alumni carried their early interests in learning, in university theology and in college politics into their lives in the country.

In truth there seems every reason to accept that the experience of the universities obtained by the gentry and clergy through the medium of the colleges did underline regional loyalties. Yet there are some questions which demand an answer. Did some colleges provide a route to social and geographical mobility for large numbers of their recruits from backward areas of England and Wales? Did Jesus College, Oxford, for example, send back into Wales well-educated local preachers or divert these talents into more profitable employment elsewhere? The ordination lists of London, for instance, certainly suggest some significant geographical mobility via the universities into the south-east from Yorkshire.[51] While it is true that individual colleges favoured scholars from a given county or counties, no college was exclusively composed of students from such a restricted area. The commoners of Trinity College, Oxford, in the later sixteenth century were drawn from no fewer than twenty-nine counties. As a consequence there was ample opportunity for the young gentleman therein to broaden his experience and for the servitor or plebeian student to form patronage connections outside his native area.[52] Then again, we must not ignore the role of the curriculum which the universities offered and the ethos which they espoused in giving students and graduates a common 'intellectual baggage' which was at least as pervasive as their sense of regional distinctness. Whereas it is certainly illuminating to regard the college as an extension of and a reinforcement of pre-existing local ties, it was much more than this. If England did not become a homogeneous nation as a result of the common education of her rulers, then she was at least less heterogeneous as a consequence.[53]

Educating the clergy

A good deal of attention has been given by historians to the secular boom in the universities during the sixteenth and early seventeenth centuries. This attention is justified and we shall, in the next chapter, be examining the extent to which the universities sought to meet the intellectual requirements of the ruling classes and thus to influence the mental processes of the country's governors. Yet it is all too easy to permit this emphasis on the education of the upper-classes to eclipse other important functions of the universities.

For at the opposite pole from the well-born students were the plebeians. In the 1570s and 80s at Oxford, for example, 50 per cent of the student body was of plebeian origin. At this time it was still within the financial means of the upper artisan or yeoman to send his son to the university with the aid of patronage, servitor- or sizarships, scholarships and so on. There were in existence between 1560 and 1640 at least 500 scholarships which would help to cover the expenses of 'poor' students. It seems certain that most of these students of plebeian origin wanted to enter the Church and, therefore, aimed for a degree. The numbers granted a BA rose sixfold between the 1520s and 30s and the 1620s, echoing the increased demand for educated ministers from the Church. Very little of the Church's need was fulfilled by recruitment from the upper ranks of society. We have no figures for the period 1520–90 but it is noteworthy that only 11.8 per cent of gentle youth at Emmanuel (1590–1645) entered orders and only 17.2 per cent of gentle youth at King's, Jesus and John's. By this date each of the colleges mentioned contained a considerable proportion of sons of the clergy – a feature which was not present earlier in Elizabeth's reign. We may safely assume that in the earlier sixteenth century the majority of graduates entering the ministry sprang from plebeian stock. In the period 1590–1645 over 41 per cent of students at the four Cambridge colleges took orders, a small proportion of which were drawn from gentle families. A glance back at the table on p. 93 suggests that the sons of the clergy now compensate for a decreased proportion of plebeian students. In other words, whereas the new Protestant career route to the ministry was open to plebeian groups at large in the 1560s, 70s and, to some extent, the 80s, by the earlier seventeenth century the career ladder is *relatively* more closed – recruitment is coming increasingly from the families of the clergy themselves. If it is true, as I believe, that the status of the parochial clergy rose during the later sixteenth and early seventeenth centuries, this change in the recruitment base of the clergy itself represented a type of upward social and occupational mobility for the first generation of Elizabethan clergy who went through the universities. It was not long, however,before the new clergy themselves set up boundaries which prevented excessive mobility into their ranks.

This tendency, of course, was not deliberate but it is well documented. For instance, as late as 1577 the sons of clergy constituted only 3 per cent of matriculants at Oxford and only 5 per cent in 1600, yet by the 1630s the sons of the clergy made up at least 15 per cent of the student body. This trend was even more marked at Cambridge and within individual colleges at both universities. And at Emmanuel College, Cambridge, we know that at least two-thirds of these sons of the clergy themselves became ministers. Half of the sons of the clergy attending Jesus, John's and King's, Cambridge, also entered the Church. This suggests both that the clergy as a group tended to favour university education for their children and also that the Church was regarded as a natural destination for them. There are indications that Emmanuel College was particularly sought out by those with a strong commitment to puritanism, which may account for the higher rate of clerical recruitment into the ministry at that college.[54]

It has often been suggested that the gentry were depriving poor students of the opportunity to study at grammar school and university but rather less attention has been accorded to the role of the clergy. When 686 scholars at Cambridge between 1596 and 1645 were analysed it was found that the following pattern emerged. The status of 265 of the scholarship holders was known: 98 were gentle, 111 were clerical and 56 were plebeian. Similarly, when 751 holders of college fellowships were studied, it was found that the clergy controlled over one third of the places. The importance which one attaches to this phenomenon hinges to a great extent upon one's view of the social status of the clergy. Some scholars would still label the clergy a low status, plebeian group. Others, myself included, would dub them a once plebeian group, newly 'arrived' via education and Protestant ideology. Nevertheless, whatever one's stand on this particular point, it still seems evident that the clergy as a group were restricting the opportunities available to youths from the lower classes as a whole. It is significant, for example, that a majority of élite positions in the Church's hierarchy, from prebends up, were occupied by ex-fellows of university colleges.[55]

The clergy, once a clearly demarcated estate divided vertically from lay society, do not, of course, correspond to any one class within society. Bishops, deans and archdeacons possessed considerably more status in lay society than did rectors, vicars, or lecturers, who, in their turn, commanded more social respect than mere chaplains and curates. It is interesting, therefore, to analyse the social breakdown of the sons of the clergy at the universities. By far the greatest majority sprang from the households of the beneficed parochial clergy – rectors and vicars – although the exact proportions seem to have varied between college and college. Very few dignitaries, for example, sent their sons to the 'house of pure Emmanuel', renowned for its puritan leanings, while quite a number of lecturers and preachers did. The fact remains that only a small proportion of these sons of the clergy could be equated with the gentle classes of lay society.[56]

It is well known that certain colleges and halls in both universities were famous as seminaries. As mentioned above, both Corpus Christi College and St John's College, Oxford, were founded specifically to improve the quality of the parochial clergy (in 1517 and 1557 respectively). Magdalen Hall, which was one of the largest institutions in early seventeenth century Oxford, produced significant numbers of puritan ministers. Similarly, Emmanuel College, Cambridge, and the smaller Sidney Sussex College had the reputation of drawing clerical recruits of puritan persuasion. St John's College, Cambridge, another large college, produced numerous clerical recruits. On occasion this productivity could be explained in terms of the wealth of the foundation itself: St John's, for instance, had 54 fellowships and considerable support in terms of both teaching and finance to offer the undergraduate. But Emmanuel had only 14 fellows on the foundation: there was, according to Benjamin Whichcote, enormous pressure on the fellow as undergraduate tutor at Emmanuel, leaving little time for study. In the case of both Emmanuel and Sidney Sussex the large numbers of clerical recruits in attendance appear to have been the product of the intention of the founders and the subsequent reputation of the college. Within twelve years of its foundation Emmanuel was one of the most crowded colleges in Cambridge. This popularity strained Emmanuel's ability to house and tutor large numbers of freshmen in particular years, when other colleges were suffering less acutely. The renown of the college as a puritan seminary derived from its statutes, from the dominance of both Lawrence Chadderton and John Preston as Heads of the college, and from the 'contemporary advertisement network'.

When the schools of 1,090 freshmen at Jesus, King's, Emmanuel and John's were examined, it was found that 800 of these freshmen had attended schools with intimate links to Cambridge itself and that 606 had attended schools with a specific connection with the college chosen – be it through patronage, the education of the schoolmaster, the existence of a closed scholarship, or the presence of a particular college tutor who had taught boys from the school before and was, perhaps, himself an old boy. In perhaps 40 per cent of cases a boy's school helped to determine the college selected. Other sources of information were important – a potential university student might have a relative or friend who had attended a given college or a local minister who advertised the merit of one particular college or another.[57]

Such a network of connections helped to perpetuate existing characteristics of individual colleges and to strengthen their geographical exclusiveness in many cases. In part the geographic insularity of Oxford and Cambridge was determined by poor transport. Students attended where it was feasible. Oxford, for instance, drew most of its student body from the Oxford area and the region north-west, south and south-west of Oxford. Cambridge drew equally heavily on the north and east and the area around London. But individual colleges were linked closely to particular catchment areas by the terms of their statutes and factors such as those mentioned above. St John's, Oxford, reserved 37 of its 50 fellowships for pupils of Merchant Taylor's School, London, by its statutes of 1566. Trinity College, Oxford, drew heavily upon Oxfordshire and London. Exeter College, Oxford, had statutory connections with Devon. Emmanuel provided 16 scholarships for youths from Norfolk and 10 for youths from Suffolk. Jesus and King's Cambridge favoured boys from Yorkshire, Wales, Essex and Lincoln. Because students sought colleges where there were reasonable opportunities for their personal advancement (and might actually migrate for this reason), students from specific geographical areas tended to cluster where there was this provision on the foundation. (Although, as McConica indicates, in colleges where there were numerous commoners who were not on the foundation, these students tended to be drawn from diverse geographical locations.) The religious complexion of a college might add to this geographical distinctiveness: for instance, Gonville and Caius had a definite appeal in the later sixteenth century for recusant Essex families, whose sons often brought local boys with them to act as their sizars. Walter Bagot sent his son Harvey to Trinity, Oxford, in 1608. He appears to have been guardian of Thomas Broughton, younger brother of his son-in-law, whom he also sent to Trinity, at Bagot's expense. When Wat Edge's father died, Bagot hurried to the boy's rescue, and secured him a room and patronage at Trinity, probably as Harvey's sizar. Harvey's brother, William, followed him to Trinity. In this way the apparently insignificant connection which the elder Bagot had formed with the President of Trinity gains importance in directing a small number of Staffordshire boys to the college.[58]

Although it may seem that the universities, in acting as seminaries, were merely continuing their traditional role as educators of the clerical estate, this was in fact not the case. The medieval universities had educated the clerical élite – the dignitaries of both the regular and secular branches of the Church; the rectors; the scholars; the future teachers of monks. Few resident beneficed clergy were university graduates although the number was rising in the early sixteenth century. Foundations such as Corpus Christi College, Oxford – designed to produce educated parochial clergy – represented a small move in the right direction. The sixteenth- and seventeenth-century universities (from the reign of Elizabeth to the Civil War), much larger, concentrated a high proportion of their energies on the education of the pastoral ministry. They were, in other words, participating in a major revolution in what society was asking of its clergy. The extent to which the universities and their personnel actively promoted this revolution is a debatable point and one which will be considered at a later point in this book.[59]

Educating plebeians with no clerical ambitions

It is probably reasonable to assume that most students at the universities from non-gentle origins intended to apply their learning to some career, usually in the Church. We have already concluded that, by the early seventeenth century, recruitment from within the Church itself was restricting to some degree the number of opportunities for plebeian boys in the Church and education, but there were still opportunities for the determined. David Cressy has estimated that 16 per cent of all Cambridge admissions were made up of sons of tradesmen and merchants but that few of these sprang from the homes of mere artisans or rural craftsmen. Similarly, while sons of middle- and lower-class rural dwellers accounted for 15 per cent of the Cambridge student population, most of these were the sons of yeomen rather than of husbandmen or below. Proportionately, neither the bourgeois groups in society nor the rural groups were particularly well represented in the university. The peasantry, for example, made up between 60 and 70 per cent of the nation but only 15 per cent of the student body. Margaret Spufford's excellent study of the schooling of the peasantry in Cambridgeshire suggested that only a tiny proportion even of the prosperous yeomanry were able 'to take the final step in social aggrandisement of sending their sons to college'. Different social structures in communities within a region had a considerable effect, even so, on the number of boys who would be able to benefit from a university education and pursue a gentlemanly vocation.[60]

Such plebeian students as there were at Oxford and Cambridge did take their work seriously. For them the degree was a meal-ticket. Of peasant entrants at Caius 82 per cent took their degrees, as compared with some 50 per cent among the student body as a whole. However, Richard Tyler's figures for the four Cambridge colleges indicate that the rate of plebeian degree taking was not as high as that among clergy sons. He claims that in the university as a whole, 34.4 per cent gentry sons took degrees; 82.5 per cent clerical sons; and 77.4 per cent plebeian sons. This small but significant difference may reflect the considerable difficulties which many plebeian students experienced in keeping up their studies, as the sons of the clergy joined the sons of the gentry to try to monopolise the sources of college finance. Similarly, it may be that the system of sizarships and servitorships at both universities proved the undoing of many a plebeian student.If the fellow or fellow-commoner upon whom the sizar was dependent left the university, the sizar might well be left without means of support or, perhaps, bound to follow his erstwhile student master elsewhere. There are many examples of students, both pensioners and sizars, who interrupted their university studies to undertake employment to underwrite further periods of study. Such a system was bound to result in a relatively high rate of drop-outs even among a determined and persistent group.[61]

When one examines the evidence regarding the university education of the plebeian groups in English society one can scarcely avoid the conclusion that to a greater extent than has sometimes been appreciated these groups were excluded from the expansion in higher education. This is not to ignore the relatively high proportion of plebeian youths at the universities themselves – for, taken as a percentage of their social groups as a whole, they represent an infinitesimal proportion of the plebian population of England as a whole and, even so, appear to be skimmed from the more prosperous elements within it. Even the halcyon days of the 1560s, 70s and 80s, with their open recruitment into a Church emphasising the need for a graduate ministry, were past. Opportunities for plebeian youths were contracting rather than expanding in the early seventeenth century. The percentage of plebeian students appears to have fallen as the percentage of clerical sons rose.[62]

Conclusions

The problem before the historian is twofold: he must disentangle the relationship between the universities and society on the one hand from the internal composition of the universities and their function on the other. The universities drew at least 50 per cent of their student bodies from social groups which made up no more than 5 per cent of the total population – gentry, clergy, professionals. The remainder were drawn in the main from the more prosperous elements among the peasantry and the bourgeoisie. University education was scarcely open to all in the late sixteenth and early seventeenth centuries. On the other hand, the universities did educate distinct groups of students for different roles in society: the gentlemen; the clerical and plebeian entrants to the professions. They combined the roles of fashionable colleges for young gentlemen and secular seminaries for determined professional recruits in a manner which has both fascinated and confused historians.

Chapter 6

Teaching and learning in the Tudor and Stuart Universities

The university curriculum

The Tudor and Early Stuart universities clearly both grew in size and altered in character. It was widely felt that a university education fitted the sons of gentlemen to serve the state in several capacities and to live the lives of gentlemen more appropriately. Many felt that the same institutions prepared professionals to perform their vocations adequately, although not everyone was satisfied that this was the case. Hence the two universities educated two, in theory distinct, groups of student. There was, however, no intention that university-level education should be open to all.

We have touched already upon the manner in which the universities, through the colleges, accommodated the new wave of secular, well-born students in the sixteenth and early seventeenth centuries. We have indicated also that this development did have definite late medieval antecedents. But there was more to educating young gentlemen than merely providing them with housing and supervision; more to educating clergy and other professionals than creating collegiate communities with suitable reputations. How far were the university and college authorities willing to bend the curriculum and requirements to the needs of the new gentry and the new Church?

According to the university statutes of 1570 the Cambridge arts course covered seven years of study. At the end of four years the student might determine BA and proceed to study for the MA degree. In other words, the course was an arts course, a seven-year unit, of which the BA degree was but an important stage in the student's total progress. The student studied rhetoric, logic and philosophy for the first four years and proceeded to study further natural, moral and metaphysical philosophy, astronomy, drawing and Greek for three years for the MA. At Oxford during the reign of Elizabeth the student studied grammar, rhetoric, dialectics or logic, arithmetic and music and, when he proceeded BA after four years, studied Greek, geometry, astronomy, natural philosophy, moral philosophy and metaphysics.[1]

The arts course was very conservative. It has been said that much of the course simply repeated ground covered in the grammar school. In fact, however, the Cambridge statutes forbade the teaching of grammar as a subject except at Jesus College and to the boy choristers of Trinity and King's, and the main part of the course at Cambridge stressed the study of philosophy. At Oxford a gentleman was permitted to take his BA degree after three instead of four years. Presumably this was allowed because such a student had had sufficient schooling to proceed directly to the study of dialectics and logic without hearing lectures in grammar.[2] Although there were certainly very many young students in the universities – in the late sixteenth century, for example, 9 per cent of Oxford freshmen were aged 13 or below and 18 per cent aged 14 or below – the median age was quite high, about 17.1 years in 1637–9. There is good reason to believe that the majority of matriculating students who intended to pursue a university education seriously were between 17 and 18 years of age. The first four years of the arts course, therefore, took cognisance of the fact that most such students already had reached an acceptable standard in some parts of the course. This was a rather different situation from that at Paris, where the university was forced to provide the equivalent of a grammar school education for its very young students.

It is appropriate to make two further points here.[3] Firstly, it is probable that we today do not allow sufficiently for the irregularity and flexibility of the university system in the Tudor-Stuart period. Many students were not affected at all by the statutory requirements of the university curriculum, which point will receive attention below. But equally clearly the pacing of study was much more flexible than that in England today. One student might not have achieved grammar standards appropriate to university study and might make up the ground with a tutor, while attending university lectures; another student, well prepared, might do relatively little work in this area. One student might follow the BA part of the course in uninterrupted residence; another might be absent frequently, paying his way by taking by-employment and perhaps requiring longer than sixteen terms to obtain the degree. Secondly, however, the student was expected to study the subjects of the curriculum consecutively and not simultaneously. It was a course with a clearly marked progression. For example, at Oxford the undergraduate spent two terms studying grammar, four terms rhetoric, five terms dialectic or logic, three terms arithmetic and two terms music. Such an arrangement permitted shortening of the course and also, presumably, meant that if a student left university after two years it was clear to all how far he had progressed through the arts course. The word course had a significance which it has perhaps lost today – running the course was impossible if you had not traversed the whole route. But the situation for a student who left to teach school after two years (either to earn enough money to continue the course or as a drop-out) was that he was as well equipped to teach grammar or rhetoric as he ever would be after four or seven years. Similarly, the university student who chose to go to the Inns of Court had reached *graduate* standards in a restricted number of subjects.

The curriculum was modified during the course of the period. For instance, at Oxford the foundation of the Savilian Chair of geometry in 1619 added geometry to the curriculum of the third-year undergraduate. And the Laudian statutes of 1636 ordered undergraduates to study Greek. Work in history, Arabic and Hebrew was added to the MA curriculum. Similarly, by 1628 ancient history became an integral part of the Cambridge MA syllabus. Most of these changes, however, affected the education of future clergymen.[4]

Historians have raised the issue of the relative importance of the statutory curriculum of the universities at this date given the expansion of the teaching functions of the colleges and the growth of what we might call non-serious student numbers. Certain factors do point to the decreasing importance among students of the university curriculum and degree requirements. For example, some tutors' study guides appear to ignore admonitions to students to fulfil the university requirements of attendance at specified lecture courses and performances in university exercises. Such guides sometimes emphasise a much more modern course of studies – history, literature, geography, travel, divinity, modern philosophy and so forth. Students were encouraged to attend the many sermons given in pulpits throughout the university communities and to enter into discussions based upon them. Some historians have concluded that the sixteenth and early seventeenth centuries saw the expansion of the BA degree as an end in itself at the universities, through collegiate teaching, at the expense of the concept of the arts course expressed in the university statutes. There is indeed much truth in this assessment but there are problems involved in accepting this interpretation as it stands.[5]

Firstly, the student guides may well have been designed to meet the needs of the non-serious student, who found the BA degree as irrelevant to his needs as the seven-year MA course. Mark Curtis gives Simonds D'Ewes as an example of a student who clearly did not perform the university disputations in the manner prescribed by the statutes but D'Ewes himself stayed at Cambridge for only two years and afterwards attended the Inns of Court.[6] D'Ewes was, in other words, a student who treated his two university years as a preparatory course for the study of the law. Unfortunately, also, Curtis built much of his case for the extra-statutory education of undergraduates upon the assumption that Richard Holdsworth's *Directions for a Student* were penned before the Civil War. There are, in fact, serious objections to this point of view and relatively little evidence to suggest that students studying seriously at the university were doing much outside the university curriculum.[7]

Secondly, even if we accept that college tuition was making the undergraduate course more interesting and relevant for the student than the university statutes provided for, we are still a long way from proving that the BA had now become an end in itself. On the contrary, while this may have been true in the late sixteenth century, there are signs that the full MA course also became increasingly popular. So many clergy took MAs (after 1600 and 1608 taking advantage of the formal relaxation of all residence requirements for the degree, no doubt) that it seems that the natural progression from BA to MA was still accepted by students with career needs. By the Restoration the MA was the most popular clerical degree and, as Curtis himself suggests, more clergymen were also taking the degrees of BD and DD. Of course it is true that absentee students had less influence in the university than resident students. It was assumed, presumably, that after the BA part of the course the student for the MA could study independently successfully. This must have rendered many lecture courses aimed at the MA student redundant or, at the least, poorly attended. It perhaps quenched the enthusiasm of the men responsible for teaching at this level. The present situation, where the Oxford and Cambridge MA is a purely formal degree obtained on payment of a fee after a given lapse of time and with absolutely no course or residence requirements, has its origins in this movement towards the absentee study for the MA degree but they were no more than beginnings. In effect, the concept of the seven-year arts course was given a new lease of life in the late sixteenth and seventeenth centuries.[8]

So it may well be that we ought to modify Curtis's thesis to read thus: as the universities took increasing numbers of students requiring a liberal humanist education and not intending to proceed beyond the BA (if that far), and as the colleges became involved as teaching institutions in the care of such students, a new emphasis was undoubtedly put on undergraduate studies. In addition, the curriculum was modified in practice for these students both by the seeming irrelevance of university requirements to the student who did not intend to take a degree and by the colleges' attempts to supplement university teaching provision and cater for the individual needs of the student as paid for by the parents. On the other hand, one must be careful not to forget that the colleges also had to cater, again individually, for the needs of students who intended to enter the professions – chiefly the Church – and that some colleges had statutory provision for the tuition of such students *en masse*. For large numbers of students the concept of the seven-year arts course continued to have meaning and was made to have more relevance for the training of a Protestant clergyman. Generalist education had been grafted onto the universities during this period – it was never formalised and it withered away and died when the gentry fled the universities after 1642. The seven-year arts course gripped the universities in the ultra-conservative atmosphere of the late seventeenth century.[9]

The true significance of these developments in the long term probably lies in two directions: on the one hand, despite attempts to introduce new subjects into the arts course as a whole (particularly in Oxford), attempts to modernise the curriculum, and efforts to breathe new life into the MA part of the course, such modifications were destined to comparative failure because of the abolition of residence requirements and the power of the colleges *vis-à-vis* the universities: on the other hand, the studies of generalists within these colleges may have had an impact upon the studies of intending professionals. The universities certainly fulfilled a dual or even a triple function in society – providing general education for no paper qualification; a basic curriculum for the BA; and preparation for the MA at one and the same time, using the same institutions to accomplish all. As such, they seem to parallel the Inns of Court in their various provisions for the education of young gentlemen. As we have suggested, though, the clergy were so anxious to ape the gentlemen with whom they studied and use the degree as a means to social aggrandisement as well as occupational security, that the emphasis on contemporary and frivolous studies may have affected the serious students also.[10]

If we feel bound to modify the view that the BA degree as an end in itself mattered most in the early seventeenth-century universities, we must still agree that the university requirements were being evaded by a large body of students. They were made to seem less important than college requirements to many others who still, nevertheless, aspired to BA and MA statutes. This point is best made perhaps through an examination of teaching methods at the universities during the period. The two main methods laid down in the statutes of the universities were the lecture and the disputation or exercise. A case could be made for the continuing vitality of the university lecturing system on the basis of the large number of new endowments during the period 1540–1640. Regius Professorships of divinity, law, medicine, Hebrew and Greek were founded in 1540. In Elizabethan Oxford the arts lectures were put on a sounder footing and in 1579 the Rede lectureships in philosophy, rhetoric and logic were endowed at Cambridge. The second and third decades of the seventeenth century witnessed an injection of new blood into the lecture system of both universities: at Oxford we note the Savilian Professorships of geometry and astronomy in 1619, the Sedleian Chair of natural philosophy in 1622, the Tomlins lectureship in anatomy in 1622 and the Camden Readership in history in the same year. At Cambridge, a history lectureship was established in 1628 (in ancient history). The furore caused by Thomas Cartwright's divinity lectures in the 1560s and similar controversies sparked off by university lectures lead one to believe that the system was still full of vitality. But, if we look more closely, we can see that few of these lectures impinged upon undergraduate life – only the arts lectures at Oxford and the Rede lectures at Cambridge. Moreover, as early as 1547 Walter Haddon was led to complain at a Cambridge Commencement that some professors were addressing audiences of one! Despite this warning, by the late 1590s it was so common for students to pay fines for non-attendance at the arts lectures in Oxford that, in 1599, some of their number defended their continued absence on the grounds that they thought the fine was a licence for non-attendance. When such attitudes were prevalent, one wonders just how many undergraduates actually fulfilled the residence requirements of even the BA part of the course.[11]

The tendency for students to neglect university lectures was probably heightened by the more satisfactory teaching provision made by the colleges. For example, the college lecturers in logic and sophistry at Clare College, Cambridge, in 1551 were to lecture daily after prayers, first examining the class catechistically for three quarters of an hour and then lecturing formally for half an hour. College lectures catered for small groups; the lecturers knew the students and a personal and flexible approach was made possible. In this context the position of the university lecture had become similar to that which it occupies today – an optional way of obtaining information and ideas which was peripheral to the more fundamental approaches of the tutorial and the college lecture. As early as the 1570s many colleges – for examples, Balliol and Brasenose at Oxford – formally instituted the tutorial system under which every student would be assigned to a tutor. Had the universities permitted more methodological experimentation, the university lectures at undergraduate level might yet have had a new lease on life. But when Edmund Gunter tried to demonstrate practical methods of lecturing in his interview for the Savilian chair of geometry, Sir Henry Savile criticised his approach.[12]

The university statutes emphasised the role of disputations or exercises in the teaching of the arts course. University disputations began in a student's second year at Oxford, when he was expected to begin regular attendance at exercises performed by third- and fourth-year men, as he himself began the study of logic. Disputations of sophists took place on Monday, Wednesday and Friday afternoons. After this year of observation, the sophist was expected to participate twice, as both an opponent and a respondent. He would then be made general sophister. After this he had to continue attending disputations until he graduated and to participate actively once a term. He had also to respond twice at the Lenten disputations of determining bachelors before he could petition the Congregation of Regents for a degree. At Cambridge the requirements were similar, but the Cambridge undergraduate had two *viva voce* examinations in the arts school before he was allowed to participate in the required Lenten disputations.

The oral disputation was the ordinary means of scholarly communication in the Elizabethan and Early Stuart period: it was firmly embedded in the medieval tradition of the universities. As we shall see in our study of training for the law, the disputation was copied by the lawyers (and the law courts) in the form of the moot. The contemporary Church adapted the scholarly exercise in the guise of the clerical exercise or prophesying. Students who intended to take the BA degree could not evade this part of the course as they could the requirement to attend university lectures. Student notebooks are dominated by work for the disputations. This preoccupation continued during studies for the MA and divinity degrees also. For instance, John Day of Oriel, studying for his MA, listed over one hundred disputation articles on Aristotelian themes. Once again, the colleges built upon this system – arranging internal disputations within their walls. Clearly the methods adopted by college lecturers (and, to some extent, tutors and readers) were designed to prepare the student for this activity. By the 1640s and 50s the performance of exercises mattered much more to the authorities than did either fulfilment of residence requirements or attendance at university lecture courses. Thus Adam Martindale, who had never matriculated at either university and who had undertaken a course of study entirely independently, was permitted to fulfil the exercise requirements and take his degree at Oxford in 1645, 'dispensed with as to time'.[13]

For the student who intended to take the degree, then, the disputations remained important academic hurdles to be jumped. Yet a situation had arisen where preparation for these university exercises was coming increasingly under the province of the colleges. Moreover, there were now large numbers of students who could ignore these public displays of learning in their own education.

College teaching

How were students prepared within the collegiate system. We have already noted the prevalence of the college lecture, provided for in the statutes of Christ's, Trinity, and St John's at Cambridge and of Christchurch, Oxford, and part of the provision of all subsequent university colleges. Robert Norgate, Master of Corpus Christi, Cambridge, 1573–87, left a detailed account of teaching within that college. There were three lectures daily: a 6 a.m. lecture on Aristotle's Natural Philosophy, Aristotle's Organon and Seton; a 12 o'clock lecture on Greek, which covered construction as shown in 'Homer or Demosthenes or Hesiod or Isocrates' and grammar; and a 3 p.m. lecture on rhetoric, using 'some part of Tully'. This steady diet was supplemented by an early morning exposition of a passage in Scripture on Wednesdays and Fridays by one of the fellows 'in his order', and by a number of regular exercises in the afternoon. For example, on Monday afternoons the 'scholars' sophism' took place, and on Thursday afternoons there was 'a problem for the bachelors of art and general sophisters'.[14]

The unique contribution of the colleges to teaching method, however, was the one-to-one relationship of student and tutor. This tutor guided the course of a student's studies, offered moral and spiritual supervision, and sponsored the student (that is, he guaranteed to the college authorities that the student would pay all his dues). The Clare College statutes of 1549 stated that tutors were to 'teach diligently the things which are to be taught, and... instruct and put in mind those things which are to be performed', sentiments echoed in other college statutes and in the University statutes of 1570, which also said that the tutors 'shall not allow them to wander idly in the town'. This blend of academic and supervisory responsibility is of extreme significance – it meant that the tutor's concern would be for the needs of the individual student and his purpose in attending the university. So we are not surprised to see President Kettle of Trinity College, Oxford, advising Harvey Bagot to leave the university for the Inns of Court or to see William Bagot stay with his tutor in Oxford throughout the summer of 1621 for additional tuition.[15]

This meant that the quality of a student's education came to depend upon the conscientious behaviour of his tutor. Christopher Guise, for example, had a tutor who was so absorbed in college politics that he did not fulfil his obligations to his pupils. As a result, Guise spent his time carousing and wenching. At Cambridge in the 1570s Gabriel Harvey criticised the fellows of Pembroke for neglecting the teaching of Latin and Greek. But some tutors and college lecturers were diligent and effective – Thomas Allen of Corpus Christi College, Oxford; Joseph Mead of Christ's Cambridge, Richard Holdworth of Emmanuel; Thomas Hill, John Cotton and James Duport of Trinity College, Cambridge, were such men. Joseph Mead was known for attending to the individual needs of his pupils: at the end of each day he would converse with each pupil privately concerning their academic progress. Archbishop George Abbot wrote a geography book for the use of his students when he was a fellow. During the period before the Civil War, Ralph Verney's tutor, John Crowther, sent him astronomy notes and suggested private instruction in geography at Verney's home during the coming vacation. Such references in private collections and tutor's notebooks are too numerous for individual quotation.[16]

How did students learn within the collegiate system? Once more, we must continually remind ourselves that students studied according to their needs. Many of the more detailed accounts of student studying patterns pertain to students who never took a degree and who, therefore, took rather less part in the exercises required by the university statutes and were less concerned to prepare themselves in the conventional way. Such a student was Simonds D'Ewes, who was at Cambridge from 1617 to 1619. D'Ewes, as a fellow-commoner at St John's, developed an interest in contemporary theological controversy, listening to sermons, keeping a detailed theological commonplace book, and daily reading the Scriptures and discussing such matters with his tutor, Holdsworth, and his tutor's friends.

My other studies for the attaining of humane learning, were of several natures during my stay at the university, which was about two years and a quarter, although Mr Richard Holdsworth, my tutor, read unto me but one year and a half of that time; in which he went over all Seton's logic, exactly, and part of Kerkerman's and Molineus. Of ethics, of moral philosophy, he read to me Gelius, and part of Pickolimineus; of physics, part of Magirus; and of history, part of Florus, which I after finished, transcribing historical abbreviations out of it in my private study: in which also, I perused most of the other authors, and read over Gellius's Attic Nights, and part of Macrobius' Saturnals. Nor was my increase in knowledge small, which I attained by the ear as well as by the eye, by being present at the public commencements, at Mr Downes his public Greek lectures, and at Mr Harbert's public rhetoric lectures in the university; at problems, sophisms, declamations, and other scholastical exercises in our private college; and by my often conversing with learned men of other colleges, and the prime young students of our own.

My own exercises, performed during my stay here, were very few, replying only twice in two philosophical acts: the one upon Mr Richard Saltonstall, in the public schools, it being his bachelor's act; the other upon Mr Nevill, a fellow-commoner and prime student of St John's College, in the chapel. My declamations also were very rarely performed, being but two in number; the first in my tutor's chamber, and the other in the college chapel. But my frequent Latin letters, and more frequent English, being sometimes very elaborate, did much help to amend and perfect my style in either tongue; which letters I sent to several friends . . .

In assessing what D'Ewes has to say, we should recall that he was writing from memory and that he was assessing the value of his time at Cambridge in the context of his life rather than seeking to describe the curriculum or his study methods. In many ways D'Ewes conveys the impression that he was a passive learner rather than an active participant in his education. He was read to, lectured at, and told what to read. He took part in few university or college exercises. It is clear that D'Ewes did not neglect the university requirements. He singles out the rhetoric lecture of Herbert as being of particular use, but laments the lack of formal opportunity to improve his Latin and English writing style.

On the other hand, it is equally evident that D'Ewes found the unofficial part of his studies far more interesting. He revelled, for example, in history and in theology. He enjoyed writing letters in both English and Latin.

Recently it has been argued that there was a marked difference in the curriculum followed by lay and clerical students. 'Lay and clerical students shared a common curriculum in logic, religion, Latin and Greek. While the clerical students moved on to acquire proficiency in Hebrew the lay students continued to polish their fluency in Latin. And while the clerical students were moving beyond logic to ethics, physics and metaphysics, the lay students were breaking out of the scholastic tradition and studying history and geography.' Unfortunately, it seems clear that D'Ewes, for example, did not regard his studies in history as a substitute for the formal university curriculum. For him it was the enjoyable frosting on the cake. In fact, his tutor, concentrated not on working through the general reading list but on preparing D'Ewes in the areas prescribed by the University statutes. It has also been suggested that clerical and lay students shared tutorials in the first year only with separation of the two groups thereafter. This explanation is, on the grounds already stated, unsatisfactory. In fact, although D'Ewes complained about the non-participatory nature of his role, he did perform no more and no less in the way of exercises than the university demanded. This participation was all demanded in the *second* year and not the first of university study. Moreover, a large number of lay students (with no clerical ambitions) simply left university before the end of the third year.

And are we correct in assuming that tutorial supervision of a close kind was common throughout the student's time in university? Holdsworth retained a general supervisory role for the whole of D'Ewes' stay but *read* to his student for only a part of that time. The tutor helped the student to read a given text intelligently, to comprehend what he read (with eye and ear) in the context of his other learning and the contemporary framework of thought. Holdsworth assigned two books for each subject of the curriculum. The books which D'Ewes was assigned in logic and philosophy were in line with the scholastic framework of seventeenth-century university studies. After this careful teaching, the student was left to apply what he had learned to the next stage of his university learning – from the end of the fourth term. D'Ewes continued his required studies. He read privately and compiled notebooks. He discussed his work both inside and outside his college. He heard lectures. He kept commonplace books. He read from his general reading list. He participated in necessary exercises. He concentrated on improving his written style in Latin and in English.[17]

We can learn a good deal from the notes of tutors themselves about the operation of the tutorial/college lecture system. Daniel Featley left a notebook pertaining to the years 1604–5 when he was MA and tutor at Corpus Christi, Oxford.[18] Featley reported that he

wrote a compendium of physic for his students between October
and December 1604. In February he recorded writing numerous lectures for his students and of having read to them. Having students
was a matter of importance to college fellows. At some time between 1607 and 1610 Featley directed a series of letters to Dr
Spencer, President of Corpus, concerning problems over his students with other fellows and tutors. The meaning of these letters is
not altogether clear but it seems that Mr Brian Twyne and Mr Jackson were attempting to claim some of Featley's pupils for their own
(and thus the £5 per annum payment which a tutor received per student). It is in these letters that we read of the possible separation
between the supervisory and academic duties of a college tutor:

[I] would most willingly refer myself to your determination since in my absence he took upon him against my will the tuition of Allen and for a slight
cause very sharply whipped him not without reproachful speeches against
me and Mr Allen his brother and cousins, saying the college was never
without a fool which was an Allen, which far more grieved the soft natured
and truly religiously affected lad than his sharp punishments or Mr
Browne's either. Here their proceedings fane me to exclaim: Me me adsum
qui feci in me converse tela.

I laboured to compose the matter with Mr Jackson for quietness sake
'and *offered him to yield unto him the reading unto Colmer and all the commodity [partly legible] reserving unto myself only the paying of his battles that
I might not altogether forgo my right and prejudice myself in my other scholars,'* but he will not be beholding unto me, he will have him as due by statute . . . [italics added]

Similarly, in a draft letter to Sir Walter Raleigh concerning the latter's son, Featley hints that there was indeed sometimes a separation between these duties:

there things befell which I am sorry '*when I was his reader but Mr Hookes
his tutor, under whom he lay, above whom he studied, coming within my
sight only at the hours of my reading to him, when Mr Hookes told me from
you that he was absolute tutor and I but a subaltern under him, wherefore
also controlled my course and hours of reading and seemed to mistake the
subject of his authority, supposing himself my tutor not Wat's . . .?* [italics
added]

Equally interesting is one of the reasons which Featley gives for not
wanting to lose his pupils: 'I have given them many notes and directions of mine own which I would be loath other teachers should
oversee and, although peradventure they might direct them in a better course, yet that course being contrary to mine and altogether unknown to them, it is not likely they will so well go forward in it.
Especially seeing with me they have divers who run with them in the
same race, whose industry may stir them by emulation or by
shame.' Here we have a university teacher who feels that he has a
distinctive teaching style and syllabus, to which his students are
accustomed. He believes that a change of direction cannot but do

them harm. Moreover, he stresses the value of the competitive, yet collaborative atmosphere which he has cultivated among the pupils in his chambers. We remember that Simonds D'Ewes studied with his companions at both Cambridge and his Inn. Moreover, Featley was very secretive about the written material which he had given to his pupils.

Thomas Newman, who was probably an undergraduate of Exeter College, Oxford, in 1624, penned a doggerel verse to describe his tutor's teaching efforts:[19]

> My tutor telling me I was not sent
> to have my time there vain and idly spent
> from childish humour gently called me in
> and with his grave instructions did begin
> to teach and by his good persuasion sought
> to bring me to a love of what he taught.
> Then after this he laboured to impart
> the hidden secrets of the logic art.
> Instead of grammar's rules he read me then
> Old Scotus, Seton and new Kirkerman.
> He showed me which the praedicables be
> as genus, species and the other three.
> So having said enough of their contents
> handles in order the praedicaments.
> Next post praedicamenti with priorum
> per harm [menias] and posteriorum
> he with topics open and discried El [   ], full of fallacies.
> There to unfold indeed he took much pain
> but of the meaning were as far to seek
> as Coriats horse was of his master's Greek
> his infinities, individuities
> contraries and subcontraries
> divisions, subdivisions and a crew
> of terms and words such as I never knew.

Poor Newman continued 'in that amazed plight' until he was forced to perform an exercise in the schools and work matters out for himself.

> I reached my books, that I had cast about
> to see if I could pick his meaning out
> and prying on them with some diligence
> at length I felt my dull intelligence
> begin to open and perceived more
> in half an hour, than half a year before.

As Newman cheerfully admitted, he was not the most apt of students and knew 'little in philosophy'. Nevertheless, he did detect the deficiencies of relying upon the teacher's skills alone and came to see the remedy in private study. The Oxford system, which placed so much emphasis upon passive receptivity in the first two years of the arts course, contained certain dangers for the student who went no further. His attitude to learning might for ever remain passive, his experience of learning be, at best, sterile and puzzling, at worst, hostile.

We can see from these examples that it was the custom of the tutor to design a course of study for the student or students in his care (probably expressed in the form of a reading list and perhaps a guide) and to prepare predigested materials for the students to use. This material might take the form of lectures or digests of the tutor's own reading of the set texts or other books. Brian Twyne of Corpus, for instance, allowed his students to share in his personal interest in mathematics. He lent one a table for use in multiplication and division.[20] Although printed books were by now widely available to both tutors and students, it was still possible to hire texts in Oxford for the purpose of copying. The student was expected to make digests from the books which he read and commonplacing was an entrenched study method. Holdsworth expected students to read some books and merely to refer to others. Within the college context, the tutor was always a student himself. As he acquired skills and knowledge in pursuit of a degree he passed these on to his own undergraduate pupils.

Did the undergraduates produce written work for their tutors? John Gandy, a student at Oriel in about 1620, evidently prepared work for a tutorial in written form, which was then perused and commented upon by his tutor, Mr Mead.[21] In 1609 Harvey Bagot wrote to his father from Oxford, reporting that he was performing his exercises (disputations). His father demanded some written proof of his son's diligence and achievements and was rewarded by carefully penned Latin theses and poetry.[22] It was evidently customary for students to read out their theses in the exercises – because they were spoken aloud, we should not be misled into thinking that students did not write out their arguments. For example, at the Inns of Court Simonds D'Ewes took it for granted that he would write out his case for the moot.[23] But nowhere in the college statutes (and certainly not in those of the university) is there any mention of what we today call the weekly essay – the staple fare of the tutorial system. This is the more interesting because the statutes of Trinity College, Dublin, so closely modelled upon the college system, specifically required that the student write such a weekly essay for his tutor.[24] We can only speculate whether this was an extension of some go-ahead practice at the ancient universities or whether it was something new at Trinity.

Library facilities

Clearly it is important to discover both what books students and fellows read and the facilities which the colleges and the universities provided for study. Colleges founded in the medieval period had had chained libraries. For example, Oriel had such a library in 1310 and Merton possessed a chained library at least as early as 1338. A statute of University College, Oxford, for 1292 stipulated that the best or only copy of any book should be chained in the library building and that duplicates should be made available for borrowing. This system was adopted at most colleges, although Trinity Hall, Cambridge, in 1350 decided that all books belonging to the Hall should be kept in the library to facilitate common access, although provision would be made for private borrowing. Much more typical was the existence of a separate circulating library of duplicates and less valued books. These circulating libraries were of the utmost importance to the senior members of the colleges. Few fellows were able to acquire substantial libraries of their own during their tenure. They were able, however, to borrow on long loan (normally for a year) books which they needed for teaching purposes. A fellow was bound to submit an indenture for the books which he borrowed and to return the books at the annual *electio*. The books which were loaned tended to reflect the academic requirements of the fellow or undergraduate. Masters would receive works of theology; bachelors works of philosophy, and undergraduates and bachelors would share books pertaining to the first part of the arts course. At an *electio* at Merton on 13 January 1452, 224 books were distributed: they were mainly texts of or commentaries on Aristotle. The importance of the works of medieval scholastics in the curriculum of Oxford is illustrated by the contents of the chained library of New College which was, by medieval standards, well stocked. The library was weak in the writings of the early Fathers but strong in those of Aquinas, Duns Scotus and Peter Lombard. When fellows of Lincoln College made bequests to the college library they were often of books of scholastic theology. Lincoln's library was dominated by such works.[25]

In the sixteenth century the colleges were presented with a problem. There was increasing enthusiasm for classical and patristic studies as the century wore on but the facilities for such studies which the universities provided were plainly inadequate. Existing library holdings of both chained and loaned books were designed to complement the traditional medieval curriculum. Medieval college libraries had, for the most part, relied wholly upon gifts of books. Their libraries were unplanned. The extent to which humanistic studies infiltrated individual college libraries in the period 1500–1535 was also a matter of chance. Thus when Dean Fleming of Lincoln gave Lincoln college sixty-six manuscripts in the 1470s and 80s which represented, among other things, his interest in Greek and in the contemporary writings of Boccaccio, Bruni, Valla and Guarino da Verona, the bequest did nothing to influence future acquisitions.

Early sixteenth-century fellows of Lincoln were apparently buying and borrowing works of medieval scholasticism, almost untouched by contemporary interest in textual criticism and the classics. But gradually, as interest in a different kind of scholarship became established, there was a movement to control the contents of the college libraries and to bring them into line with a changed curriculum. The indications are that the Henrician and Edwardian visitations of the mid century provided the incentive. Between 1535 and 1550 Magdalen College, Oxford, spent over £73 on printed books. In 1544/5 New College spent a more modest £27 on additions to its collection. Merton and All Souls also bought books.[26]

The effect of this planned activity is well illustrated by the case of All Souls. By 1546 the college library accorded proportionately far less space to theology than it did to civil law. The new law books included modern commentaries and the only English volume in the library, Berthelet's Statutes. A collection of classical texts and reference works was also established. A working library, closely associated with the modified curriculum, was in the process of being accumulated. Just as in the university curriculum scholasticism remained important, so it did in the holdings of the college libraries. But the deliberate acquisition of patristic, legal and classical materials is notable and significant.[27]

The colleges had to find a way to finance book purchase. Many colleges sold plate for the purpose – Oriel in 1544, Merton in 1549 and, perhaps, All Souls in 1548. In the late sixteenth century fines paid to All Souls' College on the grant or renewal of beneficial leases came to be reserved for book acquisition. By the early seventeenth century All Souls was frequently spending money on books: £12 in 1607; £20 on law books and £8 on arts and divinity books in 1612; and £20 on divinity books and £10 on law books in 1613. St John's College, Oxford, appears to have adopted a different approach. It continued to rely on donations but appears to have solicited gifts of books and counselled donors on the books which would be acceptable to the college. The result was a library with surprisingly little duplication and, from the seventeenth century, useful content in the context of the contemporary university and college teaching requirements. Thus, while the initial holdings of the library were not designed to suit a humanistic approach to learning, being heavily dominated by the bequest of the medieval monastic library of Southwick Priory, these deficiencies were remedied from 1595 onwards. In the 1590s, for example, St John's used a bequest from Robert Dowe, Merchant Taylor, to buy civil law books which would complement existing holdings and aid the studies of its twelve law fellows. At the turn of the century the college obtained bequests of books of reformation theology and in the seventeenth century built up a collection of contemporary controversial writings. When the donation of 135 books in 1601 by Henry Price revealed many duplications, the college responded by selling off the unwanted books and purchasing others. The new emphasis on the value of books to the community was illustrated by the introduction of the custom whereby new gentlemen-commoners gave the college books instead of plate for batteling at the Master's table.[28]

The changing physical appearance of the college libraries bears witness to the changing nature of their holdings. College libraries increased in size over the period of their existence as a whole but especially from the introduction of the printed book. Merton College owned approximately 340 books in the mid fourteenth century, of which only 42 were chained in the common library. The number of chained books had grown to 100 in 1385. The number of books for loan seems to have grown apace so that by 1500 the circulating library was 500 strong. All Souls began its library in 1438 with some 49 manuscripts and it built a library, modelled on the purpose-built library of New College, to hold fewer than 500 manuscripts. By 1440 the number of chained works had increased to 204 and there were 164 books for distribution. This was a good working library, particularly strong in law. It contained no printed books in 1480. Until the college began to purchase its own books the growth was slow indeed. By 1502 there were only 250 manuscripts and 100 printed books for common access. New College Library, which had been particularly fortunate in the size and number of its bequests, had overflowed its library capacity of 500 volumes by the late fifteenth century and built an extension in 1479/80. The advent of the printed book meant that it was possible for a college to overcome its problems of storage: even without design modifications in the storage of books it was possible to store three times as many printed books as manuscripts in a medieval-style library. As books became cheaper and more reliably printed it was also feasible for a college to build up a substantial collection of required texts and commentaries, reference works and what might be regarded as luxury purchases, which bore no certain relation to the university curriculum. In the 1590s St John's College had received some 300 volumes at most but during the period 1595 to 1612 it has been calculated that the college received 1,500 volumes. New College Library grew much more rapidly during the early modern period.[29]

To accommodate the increased holdings the colleges began to introduce organisational innovations and also to build new libraries and extensions. New College built a second library extension in 1585/6. St John's College built a new library between 1595 and 1602 and a further library in 1636. But new building was a temporary solution only. New College Library was a well appointed medieval library, fitted with double-sided lectern desks to which manuscript volumes were chained. Each such desk might accommodate a maximum of 30 volumes and the library itself had room for 500. Clearly there would be a continuing problem of storage despite new building. In 1589 Merton College introduced an important new method of organisation – the library was fitted with double-decker book presses or stalls, which could accommodate three times as many books as the old lecterns. Between 1596 and 1598 Queen's, All Souls' and St John's Colleges followed suit. In 1598 Thomas Bodley fitted the restored Duke Humfrey Library with triple-decker book presses. As need dictated the colleges adopted this design.[30]

It was in the latter years of the sixteenth century and the early years of the seventeenth century that the libraries began to be organised to suit the needs of scholars more effectively. More systematic cataloguing and shelving was introduced. In 1598 Thomas James, Bodley's first librarian, compiled a list of manuscripts in New College Library, which was published in 1600 as part of a collection of listings of manuscripts in Oxford and Cambridge college libraries, *Ecloga Oxonio-Cantabrigiensis*. In 1605 Thomas Man produced the first catalogue of the holdings of the Bodleian Library. In 1624 he listed the manuscripts of New College and gave them subject classifications and numbers. He was a fellow of New College from 1615 to 1632 and its first Librarian-Fellow. This appointment of Librarian-Fellows was apparently begun by Magdalen in 1550 and copied by St John's in 1586, Christchurch in 1599, Trinity in 1629 and All Souls in 1637. The colleges gradually introduced alphabetical cataloguing of their holdings, in imitation of Thomas James's author catalogue of the Bodleian Library in 1612/13 which was published in 1620. If a library were to be efficiently used such a catalogue and shelf marking was essential: All Souls' produced its first such listing in 1635 when it possessed 1,229 volumes.[31]

The question of library usage is an intriguing one. According to the medieval statutes of most colleges all foundation members of the community had a key to the library and free access at all times. Occasionally access to the library necessitated an interview with the master and the award of the key. As the early colleges were essentially graduate institutions, access was effectively restricted to bachelors and above, with the addition of a few junior members. Because the colleges had few undergraduate members, the undergraduate population of the university was left without library facilities. The University of Oxford itself had no library building until the Duke Humfrey was built in 1481. This was despite the fact that Duke Humfrey of Gloucester had bequeathed his collection of books to the University in 1435. It is improbable that undergraduates were allowed to use this library either, except with special dispensation. The libraries of the colleges were clearly used by graduate members. On occasion the college would instruct certain of its members to read in the library. For example, in 1549 the bachelors of Merton were ordered to read in the common library for a month in June, from 7 to 8.30 at night. In 1612 a young fellow at Lincoln was ordered to study in the library for two hours a day, excepting

Saturday and holidays, from 8 to 9 in the morning and from 1 to 2 in the afternoon, as a punishment for ill behaviour.[32]

Were fellows and junior members of the individual colleges able to borrow books in the sixteenth and seventeenth centuries? It is probable that, with the advent of more easily housed printed books, the colleges began to store all books in the common library. This was probably a gradual process. We know, for example, that at the Merton College *electio* of 1519 138 books and 7 astronomical instruments were loaned temporarily to members of the college; 101 books were loaned to 4 new bachelor fellows and 197 theology books were shared among five senior fellows. The system of loaning books resulted in quite heavy losses and we may speculate that, once lost, the books tended not to be replaced and fed into the circulating library. In addition, it has been suggested that many manuscripts from these libraries, often in an unbound state, were simply sold or destroyed at the Reformation. Evidence of the circulating library at Lincoln College in the later sixteenth century suggests that this was perhaps the case. In 1543, 92 books were loaned; in 1568 only 30; and in 1595, 18. In 1543 the books lent to fellows were predominantly books of medieval theology and included seven volumes of Aquinas and four of Duns Scotus. The collection in 1568, although much smaller, reflected a change in the needs of scholars. Aquinas had disappeared (although Duns Scotus remained) and five volumes of Cicero, the letters of Politian, and some Greek works had entered the list. The 18 books lent in 1596 were largely patristic and conservative in character, reflecting the traditionalist character of Lincoln itself. The decline in the size of Lincoln's circulating collection probably reflects a tendency for the college not to repurchase lost books which were now no longer useful for the fellows' studies and to place new printed works in the common library. St John's College, founded in the mid sixteenth century, made a provision for an *electio* in its statutes but no circulating library appears to have functioned. Members of the college were made to read in the library building and, if they could so afford, to buy personal copies of much used books.[33]

The Duke Humfrey Library fell into considerable disrepair in the sixteenth century and was certainly disorganised and depleted. Between 1598 and 1602 Thomas Bodley felt impelled to restore it completely. It was under Bodley's direction that the university library became the centre of scholarly activity. By its reopening in November 1602 the library contained a collection of 2,000 volumes. In 1610 Bodley reached an agreement with the London Stationers' Company whereby the library would receive one copy of each new book printed by a member of the company, except in Cambridge. Effectively it had become a copyright library. By 1612 the accommodation offered by the Duke Humfrey Library was already inadequate; Bodley financed the building of Arts End in that year and in

1640 the West (or Selden) End of the library was opened. During the late 1620s and 30s the library received huge bequests of manuscripts.[34]

Access to the Bodleian Library, however, was restricted. Under the statutes of 1610 the library was opened from 8 to 11 in the morning and from 2 to 5 in the afternoon. Access was limited to doctors, masters and bachelors of the university who had paid a membership fee of 12 pence. Sons of lords and of donors were also accorded the privilege of reading in the library. Other students were only to be admitted by Grace of convocation. There was no lending whatsoever. Undergraduate use was similarly restricted at the Cambridge Library.[35]

During the sixteenth and seventeenth centuries, therefore, the library collections of individual colleges and of the university itself had grown considerably in size and had been planned to meet the needs of a modified curriculum. The libraries were now better organised and were cared for by specifically appointed fellows. The college lending libraries, once so common, had gradually fallen into disuetude. While fellows and foundationers of the colleges had easy access to working collections of books, the undergraduate population of the colleges was not well provided with library facilities. Only a few of the wealthy and prominent might gain access to the university or college libraries. Undergraduates had to rely upon book purchase, borrowing among themselves or from a tutor, and hiring texts from bookshops in the town. Copying of texts was still widely practised by early modern students.

Student book buying and what it has to tell us about the studies of students

It has been suggested that a study of student book purchases may have a good deal to tell us about the real difference in the curriculum followed by lay and clerical students. An analysis of the accounts of Joseph Mead, tutor at Christ's College, Cambridge, 1613–38, has been used to indicate that lay students bought significantly more history, geography, and Latin books than clerical students who, on the other hand, bought more works of Hebrew, physics and metaphysics. Clerical students bought books in geometry whereas lay students favoured arithmetic books. As we have said above, this information has been used to argue that lay and clerical students shared a core curriculum of logic, religion, Latin and Greek for only one year before a real parting of the ways.

It is doubtful whether records of book purchases even of tutor-assigned readings can be used in this way. On the one hand we do have snippets of evidence which suggest that lay students did continue to follow the university curriculum proper after the first year, even though they did not proceed to a degree, and that more modern studies were regarded, perhaps regretfully, as additional subjects. On the other, we can scarcely discount the opposing arguments regarding alternative student access to other books as easily as the proposer of this thesis. Lay students may well have chosen to buy books which they would value in later life rather than dry texts which they could gain access to in the library or in their tutor's rooms. The wealthier the student the more probable that he would gain access to the university library or to the college library for a fee. It may also be true that some of the required texts were already in the student's possession when he entered the university. Borrowing among students must not be discounted either. Clerical students, often less wealthy, might be forced to buy books which were set texts and to forego the luxury of buying books on optional subjects. While it is true that the tutor held the student's purse strings while he was at university, it is entirely possible that students purchased books during vacations and at other times.

In total, it seems that a study of student book purchases really tells us little more that is certain about the varying studies of lay and clerical students than does a more impressionistic approach. Indeed, it is perhaps more dangerous as it suggests certainty where there is none. In fact, what it does reaffirm is the suggestion that the poorer student (and, by definition, many of the clergy) was unlikely to be introduced to non-required works very often because he could not afford access to them and because they played no direct part in his formal education. The existence of cheap printed texts and their availability through second-hand and new booksellers and through borrowing and copying probably meant that the basic texts were within reach of the poor.[36]

Adaptation of the curriculum to suit new needs

While numerically the significance of the gentle student was enormous, the universities (and colleges) did not concentrate all of their energies on adapting the system to meet their needs. Such adaptations as were made were informal. The well-born student would mix in better company; live in a fashionable hall with his peers; be given, perhaps, a more appropriate reading schedule and be less pressured to work hard. Apparently a father or patron would make clear his desires for a boy before entering him into college. In 1635 Richard Holdsworth wrote to William Sancroft, Master of Emmanuel (1625–37), asking him to take care of the son of a friend at Emmanuel and making it quite clear that 'His father means not to have him a scholar by profession but only to be seasoned with the varnish of learning and piety which is remarkable in many under your government.'[37] Thus all was arranged informally. But the universities and the colleges within them were committed to teaching the seven-year arts course. This course had been modified to suit the humanist and Protestant ideology of the sixteenth century – shared by both lay and clerical students. The arts course, in part or in its entirety, served the needs of gentry and future clergy. Like the universities, the course was multifunctional. In maintaining that the universities responded most urgently to the needs of the newly established Church of England, functioning as a new kind of seminary, one is not denying that the universities also acknowledged a deep commitment to the needs of the lay élite. It was felt, quite simply, that these needs were complementary and not contradictory.

This assumption was novel. Certainly some students were dissatisfied with the provision made for lay students. Robert Devereux, for example, complained that the curriculum was irrelevant for the young gentleman. This was true, he said, even in those subjects which he deemed potentially useful to the man of affairs, because the tutor and lecturers emphasised the wrong aspects. But some contemporary tutors were conscious of the need for a utilitarian education for the gentleman student which they grafted on to the university curriculum. Gabriel Harvey wrote to Arthur Capel in 1573:

In good sooth my purpose is nothing else but this: I would have gentlemen to be conversant and occupied in those books, especially, whereof they may have most use and practice, either for writing and speaking, eloquently or wittily, now or hereafter. Farewell, good Mr Arthur, and account of learning, as it is, to be one of the fairest and goodliest ornaments that a gentleman can beautify, and commend himself withal.

The curriculum was also under pressure from another group of students – the future clergy.[38]

Is it possible to detect real changes in the design of the basic university curriculum during the sixteenth and seventeenth centuries? At first glance, the university curriculum in the arts course smacks little of the Renaissance and much of the Middle Ages, containing as it did studies in the traditional seven subjects. A sixteenth-century student was certainly intended to hear lectures in five or six of the liberal arts.

Yet there were important distinctions between the course in medieval Oxford and early modern Oxford, for instance. The principal difference seems to have lain in the way in which time was apportioned between the various areas of study. In the fifteenth century logic and metaphysics assumed such colossal importance that other subjects were cast into shadow. Students studied grammar briefly, using the *De Constructionibus* of Priscian and the *Barbarismus* of Donatus; they then proceeded to an exhaustive study of Aristotle's *Organon*. A treatment of natural philosophy via Aristotle's

De Physica, De Anima and *De Generatione et Corruptione* completed the first part of the arts course, that leading to the BA. It was not until the Elizabethan period that rhetoric, arithmetic and music became part of the undergraduate curriculum. Moral philosophy and Greek formed no part of the statutory curriculum of Oxford until they were introduced in the Laudian code in the reign of Charles I. In Elizabethan Cambridge, however, both Greek and rhetoric were added to the undergraduate syllabus. In the university course itself, then, the balance of the teaching changed somewhat. And innovation was even more apparent in the teaching which the colleges offered to prepare the student for the degrees of BA and MA. By the end of the sixteenth century also, even the poorest Oxford colleges had provided for at least one reader in humanity.[39]

The teaching of grammar at Oxford was reformed during the later sixteenth century. Students used Linacre's humanist grammar and the works of Horace, Cicero and Virgil. They spent little time on formal grammar study after entering university, however, and educationalists such as Brinsley assumed that this was the function of the grammar schools and not the universities. Rhetoric assumed a new importance. This skill was cultivated by gentlemen and preachers alike. Greek and Latin grammar, classical literature and ancient history were all the handmaids of rhetoric. Logic itself remained important and assumed a new relevance, as Aristotelianism was first challenged and jostled by Ramism (especially in late sixteenth-century Cambridge) and then revived.[40]

It seems that the attack upon Aristotelian metaphysics and logic by Pierre de la Ramée gained a tremendous foothold in Cambridge and in Magdalen College, Oxford, in Elizabeth's reign. Ramism appealed to extreme Protestants. It was antihierarchical and based upon the idea that knowledge was accessible to all men, however humble. There was within it an emphasis upon the utility of knowledge. Dudley Fenner's translation of de la Ramée in 1584 enhanced his appeal for radical Protestants by substituting Scriptural for classical examples. An earlier translator, Roland MacIlmaine, had tried already to show his readers how to model sermons upon de la Ramée's method. Through the media of English Protestant translations the ideas of Ramus affected numerous sermons and printed works.

In the universities Ramism became closely associated with clerical puritanism. For this reason, perhaps, it appealed to many at Cambridge and to far fewer at Oxford. It had slight appeal for those who wished to support the academic and professional *status quo*.[41]

There can be little doubt that the principal producers of clergy were under Ramist influence in the late sixteenth century. Ramism dominated the thought of influential preachers such as Thomas Cartwright, Arthur Hildersham and William Perkins. St John's and

Emmanuel, which turned out considerable numbers of clerics each year, were Ramist. Yet Ramism found no place in Trinity College, Cambridge, which was a bastion of Aristotelianism and has been identified as the focal point of the seventeenth-century Aristotelian revival. At Oxford the challenge to teaching was less evident, except at Magdalen College in the late sixteenth century. At Corpus the fellows were divided between the Ramist Rainolds and the Aristotelians. In 1606 Daniel Featley attacked Ramus in an oration in praise of Aristotle. Brian Twyne, then a student at Corpus, studied Aristotle with a non-Ramist commentary. John Day's Oriel notebook was crammed with Aristotelian theses.[42]

But the late sixteenth and the early seventeenth century saw a pronounced reaction against Ramism and return to scholasticism which was in common with that of much of Europe. Only a few years after the death of its Ramist president, Laurence Humphrey, Magdalen College, Oxford, was purchasing scores of scholastic folios. Such purchases continued down until the late 1630s. John Whitgift's tutorial accounts for the 1570s at Trinity show him buying Ciceros galore for his students and John Seton's *Dialectica* to make Aristotle intelligible, in addition to Aristotle's *Organon* and *De Physica*. Robert Norgate, Master of Corpus Christi College, Oxford, lectured for one hour a day on Aristotle's natural philosophy. A bequest to the St John's College, Cambridge, library was partly spent in 1633: much of the money went to buy works of scholastic theology. Students at Queen's and Oriel, Oxford, and at Christ's Cambridge were reading Aristotelian works. Preston of Queen's was dubbed by his biographer one who 'adoreth Aristotle as his tutelary saint'. Aristotelianism was dominant at both Balliol and Emmanuel in the late 1630s.[43]

Some have identified Ramism as country logic in the same way that puritanism has sometimes been called country churchmanship. By the same token, revived scholasticism has been equated with 'court' philosophy and 'court' religion. This identification is open to question. It is true that Laud was opposed to Ramism and sought to rout it from the universities and from Gresham College but it does not follow that all Aristotelians were Laudian. On the contrary many, like Richard Holdsworth and Joseph Mead, were moderate Protestants who adhered to the pre-Laudian, even pre-Whitgiftian, concept of the Church and shared the same theology if not the same churchmanship as the supporters of Ramism. Politically and ecclesiastically they were more conservative than their Ramist counterparts, who tended to a much more radical response to society and church.[44]

There can be little doubt that the impact of Ramism was far greater than the brevity and incompleteness of its reign in the university of Cambridge might suggest. Ramist approaches were taken and adapted to specifically English uses by puritan academics and preachers. These same men educated hundreds of young clergymen, who themselves spread this approach to further puritan recruits. Such developments probably had an influence upon sermon style and content within a puritan ambience. Influenced by the thought of Ramus, puritan writers such as Perkins and Greenham developed a distinctive concept of *calling* which they, in their turn, communicated to others. Men did not inherit a position in society; they chose or were chosen by God for a position. Talent and individual aptitudes were stressed, birth was made to seem relatively unimportant.[45] It is exaggerating a little to equate the thought of Perkins with that of the modern world, which stresses individual achievement over inherited social status, because Perkins made God's choice the crux of the whole matter.[46] Nevertheless, it is true that he did emphasise calling according to talents and the importance of gifts. The anti-hierarchical approach of Ramus himself appeared to challenge the accepted government of Church and State.

By formally releasing the Elizabethan academic from the Aristotelian system, Ramism did much to legitimise and make respectable the pre-existent tendencies of English clerical puritans and to extend their influence. It may be seen to have facilitated the Protestant Churchman's attempt to adapt the English University system to the needs of the Church as he saw them. The reaction against Ramism may be seen in the same way—as a reaction against a radical look at Church and society. It was a reaction which might be espoused by moderates and conservatives but also by extremists who wanted radical changes in an entirely different direction. Most interesting of all would be an examination of the impact of Aristotelianism upon clerical puritanism in the seventeenth century, which seems to have swung away from an earlier anti-professionalism towards an exaggerated enthusiasm for professionalism. What part, if any, did the Aristotelian world view play in reinforcing this tendency?

The colleges spent a good deal of their time preparing the undergraduate according to the university syllabus. Yet the colleges also mediated this syllabus and occasionally subtly transformed it. It was through the dominance of the tutorial system that the education offered might differ in emphasis from that laid down in the statutes. Holdsworth, for instance, accorded rhetoric a higher place than logic, thus reversing the emphasis of the university statutes and, in a sweep, making the course more humanistic in tone for his students at least. Through the collegiate system some colleges gained a reputation for anti-Aristotelianism, despite the fact that the university statutes of both Oxford and Cambridge remained constant in their devotion to Aristotle.[47]

Conclusions

During the sixteenth and early seventeenth centuries the curriculum of the arts course at both universities did undergo some modification at the level of the statutes. As a result the tone of the course was more humanistic. While university teaching lost its hold on undergraduates during the sixteenth century, there is little evidence that the university curriculum or requirements did. The colleges took over and mediated the university syllabus to students.

The colleges had to cater for two main groups of undergraduates: the sons of the gentry and the nobility, on the one hand, and the sons of plebeians who intended a career in the Church of England. Various arguments have been put forward to the effect that gentle students had no interest in pursuing the arts course as laid down by the university, at least after the first year of study; that they failed to meet the statutory requirements; and that they industriously applied themselves, with their tutors' help, to an entirely different course of humanistic, modern study, more suited to the life of a gentleman than a scholar. In fact the evidence does not really point in this direction. The tutor's responsibilities were never entirely academic. He had, in modern terminology, a socialising function and the parents of his charges expected him to produce young gentlemen as well as young scholars. Perhaps he realised this by encouraging his gentle students to read modern works on what constituted a gentleman, contemporary controversies in theology and politics, and the workings of national and local government. Gabriel Harvey bade Arthur Capel read about Mary Queen of Scots and familiarise himself with John Cheke's *The Hurt of Sedition*; Roger Ascham's *The Scholemaster*, Castiglione's *The Courtier*, Marshe's *Mirror for Magistrates*, and works by Sturn, Ramus and Osorius. Other tutors recommended Bodin, Camden, Buchanan, Elyot, Fortescue and Machiavelli as suitable reading.[48] But, and it is a big but, are we really proving more than that the student was urged but not compelled to read widely in modern works?

In fact, a rather stronger case can be made for the concern which was shown in the colleges for the education of future clerics. The statutes of the colleges and the flexibility of the tutorial arrangements made modifications of the university curriculum entirely possible.[49]

Finally, it seems important to emphasise the multiple functions of the college tutor at this time (academic, moral, spiritual, financial) and his rather ambiguous status in the university. This status allowed him to respond to the particular wishes of parents and students as well as to the demands of college and university statutes. The system was both more flexible and more rigid than is today the case: the tutor was then so much more *in loco parentis* as well as being the representative of an institution. Because there was, at certain social levels, at least as much consumer as institutional control over the individual's studies, it is simply not possible for us to assert that all gentle students received one particular type of university education and all clerical students another. There were a wide variety of individual experiences, which were easily accommodated in these expanding and developing universities.

Chapter 7

Educating clergymen

As we saw in Chapter 5, a majority of those students who took degrees at the university appear to have entered the Church. This fact alone would justify an examination of the education of ministers. In addition to this, however, the Protestant Church of England was in the process of developing a distinctive attitude to education, an attitude which is of great significance when we set out to discuss the nature of educational change. The Church, of course, had traditionally needed the world of learning – it had been the world of learning. Nevertheless, both grammar school and university education had been reserved for a clerical élite among both the regular and the secular clergy. Only rarely did the clergy who performed the true pastoral work – the poor vicars, curates and parish priests – possess more than a modicum of education.[1] When the ancient justification for the clergy was undermined at the Reformation, a vacuum was created in the thinking of Protestant churchmen. This void was filled in the mid sixteenth century by the insistence upon the need for a pastoral, preaching ministry, commissioned to teach and convert the laity and minister to their spiritual needs. In this context, both hierarchy and puritan activists concentrated upon ways to provide the Church with such ministers. Education was seen, essentially, as a means to this end. The Church attempted to control and exploit the existing educational institutions to produce suitable new recruits, while simultaneously experimenting with a variety of programmes of in-service education. With the departure of the zealous first generation of Elizabethan bishops, however, this attitude on the part of the hierarchy changed. Frightened by the spectre of nonconformity, both Crown and hierarchy took refuge in the idea that the clergy should be well-educated, conformist pastors who supported the political, religious and social *status quo*, who did not open their mouths on controversial issues, and who made their separation from the laity quite plain. As the hierarchy began to lose interest in the vocational content of institutionalised education for the ministry, the potential recruits to the ministry themselves often became more interested in the rise in social status which a university education proffered them. Of course, there were many exceptions to both of these generalisations: there were Jacobean and Caroline bishops who despaired of the vocational inadequacy of candidates for orders who yet possessed BA degrees; there were young clergymen who sought via their university experience the way to a successful ministry of God's word and the sacraments. Nevertheless, it appears true that the education which had earlier been seen as a means of improving the ministry was now increasingly regarded as the means to consolidate the clergy's claims to be a gentle profession. Ironically enough, tendencies in this latter direction were enhanced by the views of social humanism, which so influenced the sixteenth- and seventeenth-century gentry. After a lengthy period when truly vocational education for the clergy was little experimented with, there were movements in post-Restoration and eighteenth-century episcopal circles to wrest the responsibility for education of the clergy from the universities and to vest it in Church-controlled seminaries.[2]

This chapter will focus on a number of specific issues. Firstly, it will outline the manner in which the Protestant episcopate during the reign of Edward VI and the early years of Elizabeth attempted to exploit existing educational institutions and traditions in the interests of the spread of Protestantism. Secondly, it will suggest the manner in which the emphasis upon a graduate clergy evolved and the way in which this emphasis co-existed with clerically controlled programmes of education. Then it will focus on the triumph of the idea that the Church should rely entirely upon the grammar schools and universities for the training of its personnel, outline the implications of this triumph for the Church and for its relations with the majority of the population. The chapter then proceeds to examine the continuing, simultaneous influence of alternative traditions of education within the Church. Finally, late seventeenth- and eighteenth-century attempts by the Church to regain control over the education of its personnel are briefly examined.[3]

The education of serving parish clergy in the early sixteenth century

In the early sixteenth century the education of the clergy who actually resided on their cures was not regularised. The better of these resident priests had a grammar school or monastic school education; the worst were barely literate in a functional sense. Historians have tried to decide where the balance lay – recently it has come to be accepted that serving parochial clergy were probably not so badly educated as was often assumed in the past. Yet this was the result of accident rather than of design. Ordination examinations, the chief mechanisms by which bishops could control admissions into the ministry, appear to have been neglected and, when held, to have taken a perfunctory form. As far as is known, there were no large-scale attempts to educate the clergy once they were ordained. The situation changed somewhat during and after the Reformation. Once the Reformers defined the ministerial role in terms of a service being offered to the laity, it became even more evident that the clergy were ill-equipped to perform such functions adequately. How could men poorly versed themselves in the Scriptures explain the same to laymen? How could priests steeped in Catholicism convert the population to Protestantism?[4]

Protestantism and an educated pastoral ministry

The Protestant Church did not reject the great heritage of Biblical scholarship, rather it emphasised its importance for the practical work of the parish priest. Instead of despising learning and encouraging the idea of a revivalist ministry, most English Protestants adopted the rationale that the clergy needed a strong intellectual background and carefully supervised training in order to perform their pastoral functions satisfactorily. The Edwardian and Elizabethan bishops used a variety of methods in their attack on pastoral inadequacy.[5] Some of these do not concern us directly here – for example, the attempts to ensure that each parish was served by a resident, non-pluralist minister. For a good while the whole situation was complicated, of course, by the issue of allegiance. To the bishops it was more important that a minister be Protestant and resident than that he be Catholic or non-resident and well-educated. Education was viewed as the handmaid of Protestantism and no more. Yet it was important from the start to provide worthy labourers in Christ's vineyard. The problems were manifold. The system of freehold beneficing of clergymen in the English Church meant that it was relatively difficult to oust an incumbent from his benefice so long as he was outwardly conformable. Early Protestantism was faced with a Church served by thousands of conservative clergymen, poorly educated, little interested in Protestantism if not covertly Catholic in sympathy, and certainly ill-prepared to act as missionaries for the new faith. The major task before the bishops was, therefore, that of reshaping the existing parochial clergy into an acceptable format. Bishop John Hooper tested Scriptural knowledge among his diocesan clergy and then laid down practical remedies for their woeful ignorance of the English Bible.[6] It is well known that fewer candidates were admitted to holy orders under Edward VI than was normal under either Henry VIII or Mary I, but historians have no reliable way of assessing whether this was because the clerical vocation appeared less attractive to young men in those uncertain times or because ordination examinations were being conducted in a more rigorous manner.[7]

Control of recruitment into the pastoral ministry

With the reign of Mary these attempts to improve the qualifications of the parochial clergy were forgotten and it is not until the late 1550s and the 1560s that the issue again became of paramount importance. Although at that time the prime concern of the government was to see the parishes served by men loyal to the new régime, and its second and parallel concern was to ensure that they were served at all, it was not long before the archbishops and bishops began to turn their attention to the control of initial recruitment into the Church.[8] If life experience and connection mattered as much as paper qualifications to these bishops and their archdeacons when they examined prospective candidates for ordination, scriptural competence and a sense of vocation were their criteria for excellence. For a long time historians believed that ordination examinations were still in abeyance in the reign of Elizabeth; that they were conducted on an informal basis if at all. There are many indications that this was not so. For instance, in September 1560 we find Thomas Bentham, bishop of Coventry and Lichfield ordering his archdeacon to examine candidates for suitability before sending them to the bishop for ordination. At the same time Archdeacon Mullins was examining candidates in the diocese of London.[9] As early as August 1560 Archbishop Parker of Canterbury was urging Bishop Grindal of London and other bishops of the southern province to call a halt to indiscriminate ordination of candidates. Bishops were to concentrate on long-term commitment to the clerical vocation and on scriptural knowledge as their criteria for success in the examination.[10] We see this order taking effect in Ely diocese, where competence in scriptural knowledge and training up for the clergy from an early age appear to take priority over university education and patronage considerations. Ely may present a somewhat atypical picture of admission policies (in that ordinands from the University of Cambridge were ordained by the bishop of Ely traditionally) but sufficient examples survive for ordination examinations and rejections during the later sixteenth century at Lincoln, Norwich and elsewhere to suggest that the examination procedures were regarded seriously as an effective means of admission control.[11]

The entrance requirements of the Church changed somewhat during the reign of Elizabeth, tending to become more rigorous as time went on. From the first, however, there were three general categories of qualification: reputation, vocation and education. Each of these categories provided a check upon the validity of the others. For example, knowledge of the candidate's reputation through letters of recommendation provided a check on the strength and duration of his vocation; the information that he had been trained up since childhood for the ministry in school and perhaps even university suggested that he would not lightly take upon him the ministry or turn away from his vocation. Education, then, was valued not only because it enabled the minister to fulfil his function but also because it confirmed that the ordinand had a lifelong commitment: it was a way of sorting out the sheep from the goats, the dedicated professionals from the mere opportunists. The knowledge that a candidate had not been trained in a craft or trade was, therefore, as important almost as the knowledge that he was functionally literate. At the beginning of Elizabeth's reign many mature, even old, men were ordained into the ministry. It was not long, however, before the hierarchy called a halt to this practice, fearing the admission of men possessed of no real vocation or educability but rather of the simple, opportunistic desire to capitalise on the chances of a better livelihood presented by the Elizabethan Church's shortage of manpower. At least two factors were at work here. The profession is a mystery (like the crafts): people who are admitted to the mystery are made privy to its secrets; those who desert the mystery are despised and feared. For these reasons it is all-important to control entry. Secondly, the profession needs to establish a right to monopoly in this particular area of activity – the ministry – in the eyes of society as a whole. It is anxious to preserve its good image; the points of distinction between itself and the Roman ministry which had preceded it; its claim to authority and respect; the good education and reputation of its practitioners.[12]

In the 1560s and 70s it would have been futile to demand that all ordinands have a university education. Indeed, one is uncertain whether the desirability of such a course would have been obvious at this early date, had not the new Church's leaders been university academics. In any event, such an insistence would have resulted in a diminishing rather than an increase in the number of ordinands presenting themselves. Instead the Church laid down minimal standards. In the 1560s the interrogatories administered at ordination conformed to Edwardian standards: they were designed to establish the name, age, dwelling place, reputation, literacy, religious zeal, seriousness of vocation and knowledge of Latin of the candidate. Gradually these rules were modified to take account of changing circumstances. In 1571 ordinands were required to make an account in Latin of their faith in a manner which accorded with the Thirty-nine Articles of the Church. An ordinand had to present letters dimissory from his diocese of origin or long habitation if he sought to be ordained elsewhere. No one could be admitted to orders unless he had a benefice or title. This provision certainly constituted an attempt to control the numbers of recruits and to ensure that all were financially provided for but, first and foremost, it was an attempt to define the ministry in terms of pastoral activity. These same rules urged that, where possible, ordinands should be graduates of the university. This was the first formal recognition of the standing of the universities as seminaries for the pastoral ministry – not only the theologian and prominent churchman were to study in the university but also the average parish priest was to be encouraged to study there to help prepare him for his ministry. In 1575 entry into deacon's orders was further regulated: a deacon had to be at least twenty-three years of age and to serve one year before being admitted to the priesthood. Gradually the diaconate was coming to be regarded not as a distinct order but as a period of apprenticeship for the priesthood. In a Church wherein minor orders had been abolished, such a late age of initial entry to orders and such simultaneous insistence on the protection of future clergy from the corrupting influences of manual labour left young candidates for the priesthood little alternative but to involve themselves in prolonged periods of education at grammar school and university or as teachers. These rules were reiterated in 1585 in such a way as to reinforce the idea of the diaconate as a probationary, apprenticeship period. In addition the articles of 1585 again saw an entirely graduate clergy as the ideal. At the very least the clergy should be well versed in the Scriptures and able to give a good account of its faith in the Latin tongue.[13]

It appears that when the rules for admission were first formulated the intention was that the Church would then build upon this basic framework, using a system of in-service training. Such an idea was by no means novel in Tudor society. Indeed it was far more traditional than formal schooling: apprenticeship involved the passing down of skills from the master to the apprentices at work. Even the educational system of the universities and the Inns of Court bore strong resemblances to this system although they did isolate the world of learning from the world of work. What was more natural in that society than the use of the skill of key clerics (archdeacons, rural deans) to instruct further the raw, under-educated recruits of the Church and also the dead-wood of past years? We can see attempts of this kind in the Edwardian Church (under Hooper) and in the very early Elizabethan Church (Bentham of Coventry and Lichfield, for instance, used the ruridecanal chapter as the basis of such an attempt). Royal injunctions in both reigns had ordered that clergy with dubious academic qualifications should undertake supervised biblical studies. In the 1560s and early 70s the responsibility for overall supervision in this area was delegated to the archdeacons: testing of the clergy and their progress took place within the visitation system. In the diocese of London, Archdeacon Mullins met twice yearly with the non preachers of the archdeaconry, setting them scriptural assignments, testing their understanding and offering help with difficult points. The group made steady progress through the New Testament and the Apocalypse. Yet this approach had no impact upon the inadequate licensed preachers in the archdeaconry, who were not required to attend. In 1581 a more rigorous form of the same system was put into effect in the arch-deaconry of St Albans, Diocese of London, where non-preach-ers and BAs had to submit, in writing, evidence of their studies monthly to a neighbouring preacher or MA, and where all were examined quarterly by the official. In the mid 1580s Bishop Aylmer tightened up the exercises within London in response to directions from Archbishop Whitgift and convocation. He appears to have laid greater emphasis upon the conformity of the preachers and MAs who acted as supervisors and upon the quality and conformity of the work acceptable to the official. Evidence of such schemes may be found in many other dioceses – York, Durham, Chester and Lincoln are often-cited examples.[14]

What did the Elizabethan bishops hope to achieve thereby? Were they trying to produce ministers who could preach or ministers who could read the homilies intelligently and offer minimal extempore instruction to the laity within a parish? There is no doubt that, at least under Parker and Grindal, the English bishops had as their goal a preaching ministry – hence the initiation of or sympathetic attitude towards the prophesyings, and the suggestion that a minis-ter required no licence to preach within his own parish. For the ear-ly Elizabethan episcopate there was no true ministry but a preaching ministry. For such bishops and clergy the homilies and the printed catechism represented a temporary stopgap in the absence of an educated, preaching ministry – a guard for the purity of the Church's teaching during the period of transition, not a straitjacket for the ministry or an excuse to cease training preachers.

But during the 1570s the Queen and some of her advisers became convinced that the system, particularly as manifested in the prophesyings, was in the hands of dissidents. The development of prophesyings was curtailed and attempts made to tighten episcopal or archidiaconal control of in-service education. The emphasis pass-ed from preaching to conformity and respectability, except in the North of England where conversions from Catholicism remained an important issue.

The Church's need to control university education

The hierarchy of the Elizabethan Church, deeply influenced as it was by the English social humanist tradition of the universities and by the view of Continental reformers, had long held up as its ideal the university-educated preacher/pastor. As we have suggested, this ideal was unrealistic during the early years of Elizabeth's reign. The universities had declined in size and reputation during Mary's reign. They had never been used to produce graduate clergymen for the pastoral care of the English population but rather to educate an élite for scholarly and administrative service in the secular and regular wings of the Church and the government.[15] Moreover, at a time when the Church needed more control of the universities, these institutions were falling more and more under secular control and were being commandeered by the nobility and gentry to provide their sons with a liberal classical education.[16] The Church hierarchy certainly could not have direct control over the shaping of the education offered to potential clergymen at the universities. As we have noted earlier, Cambridge had no ecclesiastical Chancellors after the Reformation, while Oxford boasted only Archbishops Bancroft and Laud. While to some extent the Crown fought the battles of the Church, the universities and colleges remained in jealous control of the curriculum. The Laudian Statutes of Oxford in 1636 probably deserve more attention than they have received as an expression of the Church's determination to exercise greater control over the education of its personnel.[17]

While there can be no doubt that the Church favoured a graduate if not necessarily a preaching ministry, it is equally certain that university education for intending clergymen was the product also of more generalised forces within society as well as of professional initiative. A university education, if not a degree, had become the hallmark of the gentleman and, particularly, of the aspiring gentleman – it was, in short, a passport to social status. It was also the passport to office and position in the Church of England. Plebeian students flocked to the universities to take advantage of the situation. Their path to improved social status and career prospects was smoothed by the opportunities for cut-rate education offered by positions as battelers, servitors and sizars – opportunities arising from the simultaneous expansion of gentle numbers at both universities. By the 1620s graduates in the Church were so commonplace that it was no positive competitive asset to possess a degree but, nevertheless, remained a detriment not to have it. Richard Baxter feared that he would not go far in the Church without academic credentials. Later, Adam Martindale indicated that neither laymen nor clerics would count his experience, learning or dedication for ought unless he had a degree to cap them, when he insisted on obtaining his degree from the university. It was necessary to have the seal of approval. Nevertheless, the contracting opportunities in the Church as well as the impact on it of Whitgiftian policy do seem to have been reflected in a reduction of plebeian numbers at Oxford between 1590 and 1615.[18]

By the 1620s recruitment into the Church was almost entirely graduate throughout the country, although there were still many poorly educated clerics lingering in benefices.[19] The Church was over-producing for its needs and some graduates were kicking their heels in inferior and insecure positions before finding placement. In this situation the bishops appear to have abandoned programmes of in-service training for their diocesan clergy. Yet many bishops continued to complain about the inadequacy of ordinands.[20]

Why was this? To be certain, such a complaint was not necessarily a reflection upon the quality of university education in the abstract at this date. Most graduates entering the Church's parochial ministry from the 1550s right down to the Civil Wars were Bachelors of Arts or Masters of Arts of the university. The problem was that in neither case had the university curriculum provided for scriptural training or advice on pastoral/preaching work.[21] Students were, of course, versed in some of the techniques required for Scriptural study – knowledge of Latin and techniques of criticism and translation – and were trained in the oratorical skills deemed necessary for the contemporary preacher – rhetoric, logic and so forth – but undergraduates knew nothing of Scripture or Hebrew and little of Greek at the universities' hands, except by observation. They had, perhaps, the preaching technique but not the word to preach. Only at Cambridge was a candidate in the higher faculty of divinity actually required to preach.

Whether the skills which students did acquire at university were appropriate to the task before them in the English provinces is a matter which we will consider shortly. In any event the degree of preparation specifically for the ministry which an undergraduate received beyond this depended largely upon chance, unless his parents purposefully placed him in a college which emphasised proper training.[22] Some colleges employed a theological lecturer or catechist. Lincoln College, Oxford, hired such a catechist in 1561. At Corpus Christi, Oxford, the fellows took it in turn to expound a portion of the Scriptures after morning prayers on Wednesdays and Fridays. The life of many of the college communities remained rooted in the festivals of the Church's year even after the Reformation. Religious controversy often loomed large. But it was the puritan colleges which attempted a genuine practical pastoral training. Parents who sent their sons to Emmanuel, Cambridge, could take comfort in the fact that

in establishing this College we have set before us this one aim, of rendering as many persons as possible fit for the sacred ministry of the word and the sacraments; so that from this seminary the Church of England might have men whom it may call forth to instruct the people and undertake the duty of pastors (a matter of all things most necessary).

Mildmay admonished Fellows and Scholars of the College who held their places to pursue no other ambition. Realising that there had to be some institutionalised support for such a position, he added:

And lest we should charge the whole burden of this duty upon their own unaided consciences, although we desire them to be learned in philosophy and the other arts, and wish the custom of the University to be retained in this, both in the hearing of lectures and in other exercises, as also in proceeding to those degrees which are proper in the arts, yet we decree that the fellows of the aforesaid college shall every week hold one disputation in Theology, in which each in his turn shall be respondent; and there shall be two opponents, which place shall be filled by each fellow in turn according to the custom usual in other colleges.

The Master of the College was given full authority to devise and require specific forms of exercise designed 'for the promotion of the study of theology and for the training of ministers of the word'. The Bible was to be read before and after every meal in College. In order to reduce the opportunities for abuse of these statutes, Mildmay also laid down that the four senior Fellows of the College should be in holy orders; that Fellows must resign within a year of receiving the doctorate of theology; that strict discipline be maintained; that meetings for any purpose in the rooms of college members below MA in rank be forbidden; that Scholars 'shall be chosen from among such young men as are distinguished by poverty, honesty and outstanding ability, persons of good character, talents, and promise, not Bachelors of Arts nor yet admitted to the sacred ministry, but who intend to take up theology and the sacred ministry; and they shall be at least moderately instructed and skilled in Greek, rhetoric and logic'.

Emmanuel's 1588 statutes clearly illustrate the sense in which a sixteenth-century college was essentially a community of Fellows and Scholars, supported by the foundation. Emmanuel owed a good deal to the earlier example of Christ's College, Cambridge, but it is significant that Mildmay provided for no Fellowships or Scholarships in Law or Medicine. Those on the foundation were dedicated to the service of God: the promotion of the study of theology and preparation for the ministry of the word and sacraments were all-important. Provision for the pensioner or sizar undergraduate is not central to the purpose of the college. The Ministers among the Fellows are charged with their pastoral oversight; Bible-reading at mealtimes clearly falls upon their ears also; and rigorous moral supervision would presumably have its effect, but for the ordinary undergraduate at Emmanuel it was undoubtedly the religious milieu of the college rather than its specific teaching provisions which benefited the potential cleric.[23]

In general, even when the prevailing system permitted the motivated student to take advantage of college facilities and study subjects relevant to his ministerial vocation, there was still no provision for specific training in the art of preaching, except by example and analysis and through the close modelling of the sermon style on ordinary classical oratory, or in pastoral work and responsibilities. This was a strictly academic regimen. Incidentally many students, particularly those from poorer families, acquired some experience in these areas by working their way through university as schoolteachers, curates and readers (lectors). But, however well the college system worked on occasion, it is clear that arrangements were insufficiently institutionalised and the degree requirements too secular to ensure uniformly high standards among prospective ordinands. It was entirely possible for a young man to obtain a degree at the university without undertaking any formal studies related to the ministry or professing any commitment to such a vocation and then to use this same degree as an entry qualification for orders. Some bishops viewed the degree as an adequate educational background for a minister – perhaps they had to when it was difficult to obtain sufficient ministers to serve all the parishes in a remote diocese. But other bishops were more discriminating and looked behind the mere possession of a paper qualification for evidence of vocational training, aptitude and commitment.[24]

Repercussions of the classical education of clergymen

The academic and classical emphasis of the university preparation of ministers prior to 1640 contributed a good deal to the anti-ministry lobby of the late 1640s and 1650s. The Church had created a *mystery*. The clergy seemed determined to hide the secrets of the Scriptures from the people behind obscure language and incomprehensible scholarly techniques so that they could justify their own monopoly of religious teaching in the state. The clergy were charged with keeping the laity out of the Church instead of teaching the laity in simple language in order to bring them into the Church as full participants. All this seemed to many to be strangely at odds with the original message of the Reformers. One can sympathise with such a view after reading the obscure, laboured sermons of contemporaries, strewn as they are with references to scriptural, traditional and classical sources, and couched as they are in the language and style of scholastic disputation. Education, which had been seen by many in the mid sixteenth century as an agent of social mobility and of ease of communication, was now seen as the buttress of monopoly in many areas of human activity. In the traditional social structure men controlled power when they controlled land. Land provided the governing élite with its authority. Gradually, education joined land as a source of authority and power. It was important, therefore, for an aspiring élite to gain control of education and restrict access to it from among other social groups. This was precisely what the sectaries felt had happened by the mid seventeenth century. Education and access to education, therefore, was very much a social issue. Through their monopoly of university (and to some extent secondary) education the gentlemen and the aspiring gentlemen were able to create monopolies of the practice of law, ministry and medicine as well as government, and to oppress the lower classes within society. In order to succeed, plebeian youth had to move out of its class and assume the education, manners, lifestyle and values of gentlemen. Within the universities potential clergymen eagerly pursued the arts course in the company of young gentlemen, acquired patronage connections, and trusted that some of the status of their fellow-students would rub off on them.[25]

Attempts to improve pastoral performance

Were all clergymen of the pre-Restoration English Church hopelessly out of touch with their congregations? The training of the Church's personnel, even where effective, suited young men to a pastoral ministry among scholars and gentlemen rather than among the yeomen and husbandmen, the artisans and tradesmen, and the urban and rural uneducated poor who made up the bulk of the population. The question of widespread technical literacy becomes relatively insignificant at this point: one required much more than the ability to read and write to understand the sermons of the age – one needed the points of reference provided by a classical grammar school and university education. Occasionally a clergyman might have an audience well versed in the classics; more often he would live in a parish where he himself, the curate (if he had one), the schoolmaster and the gentry were the only ones with a grammar school or equivalent education. This situation created a barrier between the minister and his flock when it came to communicating the word of God through sermon or advice and when it came to social relationships. The clergy tended to marry within educated circles, often among themselves. Their social life often revolved around their professional life. The diary of Ralph Josselin, vicar of Earl's Colne, Essex, in the mid seventeenth century allows us a glimpse of the social milieu in which such men lived and the difficulties with which they met in establishing lines of communication with the majority of their parishioners. Such problems were made worse when the clergymen concerned were displaying anxiety to 'keep their distance' from the ordinary parishioners, to emphasise the prestige of their profession, to accentuate their affinities with the gentry.[26]

When ministers overcame these impediments to successful pastoral ministry it was either because of personal qualities or because they came under the influence of a non-academic tradition, that of the reformed pastor, which operated through personal contact and the printed word, but little through institutionalised channels. There was no way in which either hierarchy or 'puritan' caucus could ensure the participation of ordinands and recruits in this tradition – it was voluntary but influential; a seam within the Church rather than the whole garment. It made the ministry less pastorally deficient than might have been the case but had no machinery of enforcement. This movement was not academic in its emphasis but vocational.

In the 1560s and 70s the prophesyings developed out of the traditions of in-service training in the Church and the desire to emphasise the preaching of the word as the prime function of the ministry. In the prophesyings ministers preached, expounded, debated, censured the recalcitrant and errant brethren, and fraternised. The informal disciplinary function of these conferences assumed heightened importance in the later 1570s, the 1580s and 90s, when they often operated under different names. There was not only communication and teaching but also advice and control over performance. The Dedham Conference (records survive for this conference in the 1580s) is the best known. Professor Collinson has indicated that this conference was not strictly speaking Presbyterian in either structure or intent.[27] Certainly one senses that there were many later conferences of local clergy, often bearing other names, which resembled it closely and which may have been every bit as organised. Often these associations were centred on the market town – Southam, Warwickshire, in the sixteenth century and Chesterfield, Derbyshire, in the seventeenth century are examples – but these towns were often also used as official or unofficial divisions of the various dioceses, as the heart of the local ruridecanal chapter. It must, therefore, have been especially easy for the participants to organise conferences or lectures by combination within the pre-existent structure of the Church, within the traditions of that Church and certainly without arousing hostility from above. It was quite normal, therefore, in the 1640s for Mr John Billingsley, minister of Chesterfield, to challenge James Nayler, the Quaker, to a formal debate with the ministers of High Peak, with Immanuel Bourne, rector of Ashover, as their champion. It was not extraordinary either for ministers like Ralph Josselin, apparently rooted in independency, to meet regularly with their fellow clerics to discuss points of doctrine and practice. Richard Baxter's Worcestershire Association and others like it were but an indication of the discomfort which many ministers felt in the 1650s in the absence of an institutionalised church structure and the machinery for clerical association and conference which that had always furnished. Clergymen who were active as leaders in such groups may well have led the field, as did Baxter, in the production and circulation of manuals, catechisms and guides. This movement culminated in but did not begin with Richard Baxter's pastoral literature, which consisted of exemplary writings for use by his fellow ministers as much as for use as devotional literature by pious laymen.[28]

At a more personal level it is clear that there were many ministers of a puritan persuasion who welcomed young men, graduates among them, into their own households for pastoral training. The works of Samuel Clarke are our chief source for such activity and, of course, we must be aware that he may well have exaggerated the extent to which this was customary among puritan candidates for the ministry. But we do know, from other sources, that eminent puritan divines were approached frequently to educate particular individuals for a more successful ministry. For instance, Henry Holland's introduction to the works of Richard Greenham (1599) states that Greenham was often approached by the godly to 'train up some younger men to the ministry, and communicate his experience with them'. Equally, Samuel Ward's diary suggests that William Perkins took responsibility for the pastoral training of young graduates in the later sixteenth century. Robert Harris was trained in the puritan household of John Dod and in his turn trained graduates of Oxford University for the ministry. Richard Blackerby, deprived minister, turned to educating grammar-school-age boys and graduates of Cambridge when he could not obtain preferment in the Church. 'Divers young students (after they came from the University), betook themselves to him to prepare for the Ministry, whom he taught the Hebrew tongue, to whom he opened the Scriptures, and read Divinity, and gave them excellent advice for learning, doctrine and life; and many proceeded from this Gamaliel.' Bernard Gilpin lodged in his family twenty-four boys who attended the grammar school which he had founded. He emphasised their religious training within the household.[29]

Clerical associations, supervision by an experienced minister and preacher, and pastoral manuals provided the most important sources of vocational education available to the late sixteenth- and early seventeenth-century clergyman. All sprang, significantly enough, almost exclusively from within the puritan wing of the Church. The fact that there was an extremely zealous element among the parochial clergy, actively committed to improvement of the pastoral ministry and, therefore, to providing supplementary vocational education is of extreme importance to the history of education for the professions during this period. Any history which concentrated entirely upon formal provision for the preparation of ministers in schools and universities would miss an essential point: a good deal of vocational as well as purely academic education had to take place, as it were, on the job and through uninstitutionalised channels.

As has been indicated, the years 1640 to 1660 witnessed the formation of an anti-ministry lobby. This variously opposed the idea that ministers needed 'humane learning' and, therefore, a university education; the belief that ministers need formal approval by other men as well as a call from God before practising (that is, ordination); the concept of a settled, full-time ministry; and the support of this same ministry through tithe on parishioners' produce. The claims of the sectaries that no human education was necessary to become a minister brought forward spirited and articulate replies from the established clergy. For example, in 1646 Giles Workman produced a reasoned justification for the cleric's need for a thorough grounding in Greek, Hebrew and Latin because of their Biblical applications. In 1650 Thomas Hall in Warwickshire attacked unlearned sectarian preachers and stimulated replies from both William Hartley and Thomas Collier. Hartley professed no antagonism towards the universities, only to the training of the ministers therein: he called for a radical reformation of the universities and the total abolition of the study of theology there. Collier in his turn charged that education was of no use to the clergy except as a means of ensuring their monopoly and of enslaving the laity. These views were then countered by a second wave of defence from the conservative puritans, only to be in their turn countered by more outbursts from the sectaries. The conservatives misrepresented the sectaries' position, claiming that they not only wanted to abolish training for the ministry but also the universities themselves:

> Wee'l down with all the Versities,
> Where learning is profest,
> Because they practice and maintain
> The language of the beast;
> We'el drive the Doctors out of doors,
> And parts what ere they be;
> Wee'l cry all Arts and learning down
> And hey then up go we.

But in fact the most sweeping criticism of the education offered at the universities in general was offered by members of the universities themselves – such as Sidrach Simpson and his opponent Seth Ward – and the sectary John Webster. Meanwhile the outcry of the sectaries bore no real fruit – the settled, educated ministry remained.[30]

The post-Restoration universities and the production of clergy

After the Restoration of the monarchy in 1660 the universities continued to produce large numbers of prospective clerics. Indeed it has been suggested that the social appeal of the universities disappeared after the interregnum, making them even more exclusively seminarial in character. John Pruett maintains that the chief distinction between the pre-war and post-war situations was not that fewer clergymen now had university degrees but rather that there were fewer plebeian clergymen. He maintains that university education after 1660 was so costly that it was beyond the means of most plebeians. This suggestion is borne out by Lawrence Stone's conclusion that the proportion of plebeians at Oxford fell progressively from 55 per cent (1577–79) to 37 per cent (1637–39) to 27 per cent (1711) and that the costs of university education were rising rapidly at a time when private aid for the poor student (in the form of patronage) was dwindling. Moreover, the cost of preparing a boy for university at a time when the grammar schools were in serious decline were prohibitive. It is significant that the proportion of clergy sons among freshmen at Oxford steadily rose: 5 per cent (1600); 15 per cent (1637); 21 per cent (1661); 29 per cent (1810). The clergy was becoming even more inbred (this is particularly true when we recall that such figures ignore other kinship connections) and the opportunities of plebeians yet more restricted.[31]

The universities, then, continued to produce graduates for the Church's parochial ministry but the word 'seminary' has connotations which are inappropriate. As we have stressed, the universities provided little in the way of formal vocational education; some of the colleges provided rather more; and some students were able to take advantage of good tuition. By the later years of the seventeenth century many churchmen were dissatisfied by the extra-curricular provision for intending ministers at the universities. Standards of supervision were criticised and gone, we sense, was the absorption of society in general in sermons and theological debate. What was left was an academic syllabus which made few demands upon the student and left him ill-suited to pastoral responsibilities. Interest in the study of theology at the universities had waned during the interregnum and was not fast to revive.

Post-Restoration bishops did what they could to control ordinations but this was little in the face of poor university education. Some clerics were turning their thoughts towards forms of more truly vocational education and there were some interesting small experiments in this area. They indicate a growing determination on the part of the Church to gain control of the education of future clergymen. Perhaps the best known experiment is that of Richard Sherlock, rector of Winwick, Lancashire, from 1662 to 1689 who trained young curates, already in orders, to improve their pastoral ministry in a sort of 'priests' house'. Somewhat later Bishop Gilbert Burnet of Salisbury (1689–1715) resolved to supplement the deficient training of the clergy by establishing a 'nursery at Salisbury of students in divinity who should follow their studies and devotions till I could provide for them'. For five years he and Daniel Whitby, precentor of the cathedral, provided an education in divinity and pastoral care for ten students per annum at a cost of £30 a head. The students received individual tuition for one hour a day in 'matters of learning and piety and particularly of such things as related to the pastoral care'. The experiment was in fact an institutionalisation of the old tradition of the bishop's household, which had provided for a group of episcopal protégés and which had given them an environment conducive to learning and debate as well as opportunities for preferment, when well organised. But Burnet was forced to discontinue the project because of extreme opposition from the university of Oxford. Burnet approached ordination examinations with an unusual degree of seriousness. He tried to establish the names of prospective candidates a full year before they presented themselves, to provide supervision by beneficed clergymen, and to insist that referees write letters of recommendation honestly. But he saw all these measures as a stopgap until the universities were reformed and seminaries 'can be raised for maintaining a number of persons, to be duly prepared for Holy Orders'.[32]

It was, however, Thomas Wilson, Bishop of Sodor and Man (1698–1755), who made the greatest strides towards introducing institutionalised vocational preparation for ordinands. Candidates for orders were brought to the attention of clergy at the annual diocesan synod. The clergy were to observe the candidates over a lengthy period and base their references upon what they noted. Meanwhile the ordinands were taken into the Bishop's own household for daily instruction for a year prior to ordination. What was, in effect, the first diocesan theological college was thus founded in 1699.[33]

There can be little doubt that the rigorous standards set by some diocesans in examining ordinands led to a raising of standards among candidates. The compact entered into by Sancroft; William Lloyd, Bishop of St Asaph; William Lloyd, Bishop of Peterborough and Norwich; Thomas Ken, Bishop of Bath and Wells; and Francis Turner, Bishop of Rochester, to resist laxity in admission to orders is well known. Bishop Wake of Lincoln routinely failed candidates in the 1700s; Bishop William Thomas of Worcester was notoriously searching in his examinations; Bishop Nicolson of Carlisle (1702–18) set standards for ordinands which had to be met and rejected the unsuitable. Successive archbishops wished to institutionalise these personal initiatives and in 1695 such efforts were augmented by William III's Royal Injunctions urging more care in ordinations. Despite these manifestations of concern on the part of the hierarchy for the state of professional education, it was from a layman, Robert Nelson, that the strongest plea for seminaries for the English clergy emanated in 1713.

In the absence of widespread formal provision for vocational preparation these years saw a flood of printed manuals designed to fill the gap. We know of lists of suitable reading distributed by various bishops to prospective ministers. Clearly some young men tried to follow this advice in as systematic a fashion as possible. Perhaps professional commonplace books of the type produced by Matthew Wood in the early years of the century were common. Certainly the earlier traditions of Tudor and Stuart education had encouraged young men to compile their own compendia of *useful* information, carefully indexed and annotated, as well as to collect literary snippets. The urge to give the university curriculum a more vocational emphasis was also felt within those institutions by the mid eighteenth century. Beilby Porteus's sermon of 5 July 1767 advocated professional teaching and Herbert Marsh's *An Essay on the Usefulness and Necessity of Theological Learning to those who are Designed for Holy Orders* (1792) urged the grafting of divinity onto the existing BA syllabus. This movement bore fruit in the later eighteenth century with an improvement in university provision for theological training. Prior to this the lectures in divinity given at the universities had fallen into disuse. The Norrisian Chair in revealed religion was founded at Cambridge in 1780 and it had occupants who actually lectured. In Oxford the lectures of the various Regius Professors of Divinity and the series of Bampton lectures raised the level of theological education offered to young men with the Church in mind as a career. As a result, the bishops claimed, standards of academic achievement and scriptural knowledge improved markedly among recruits at ordination examinations.[34]

The desertion of the ancient universities by the nobility and gentry presumably compensated the Church to some extent for the fact that it still did not have direct control over the universities which trained its clergy. The dons of the universities were now more susceptible to ecclesiastical pressure regarding the curriculum simply because there was not the same competing pressure from secular students seeking a liberal education. As the outcome of the Burnet experiment indicates, the universities now were certainly not willing to stomach the suggestion that clerical education should be taken over by the hierarchy itself. They were, however, prepared to consider conciliatory reforms.

Protestant churchmen in sixteenth-century England wanted to use education to a revolutionary end – to produce a new sort of ministry in line with reformed doctrine. They were prevented from so doing by a multitude of factors. From the beginning Elizabeth I did not sympathise entirely with their desires, was determinedly conservative in her attitude to the ministry and soon cultivated a leadership within the Church which was ambivalent in its attitude to the reformation of the ministry. At the same time the universities, chosen instruments for this reformation, had but recently achieved independence of a sort from the Church – an independence to which they were determined to cling. Simultaneously they were, as institutions, coming increasingly under the influence of the gentry and nobility, who successfully demanded that the universities and colleges care for their educational needs as well as those of the Church. The result was that while the universities continued to educate clergymen in large numbers through the later sixteenth century and the entire seventeenth century, the amount of control which the hierarchy of the Church exercised over this process was erratic and, for the most part, indirect. During the mid seventeenth century the role of the universities in the preparation of ministers was sharply criticised. Criticism came from other quarters – from the bishops and higher clergy – during the later seventeenth and eighteenth centuries but the universities were determined to maintain their monopoly. The university of Oxford fought Bishop Burnet's attempt to provide an alternative or supplementary form of clerical training. The hierarchy were forced to give most of their attention to attempts to influence the universities themselves in the direction of appropriate reform. For as long as the universities remained on the periphery of national life, the institutions were willing to conciliate the hierarchy and reform their approach to the training of potential ministers but, once the universities came to be used again by young men with other careers in mind, in significant numbers, the universities would again become highly unreliable allies in the fight to defeat vocational inadequacy.

Clearly, if we compared the early seventeenth-century parochial clergyman with his serving early sixteenth-century counterpart we would be aware that a revolution in educational standards had taken place. Nevertheless, this revolution was not such a one as the mid sixteenth-century Protestant reformers had in mind. Seventeenth-century clergymen were incomparably better off educationally in humanist terms; vocationally they may not have been much better prepared than their predecessors. Such improvements as had occurred were due not to the efforts of the universities or the grammar schools but to the influence of in-service training and the puritan tradition as expressed in both clerical and lay attempts to give the clergy vocational preparation and support. There is a danger, therefore, that the undoubted revolution in numbers which occurred in the number of graduate parochial clergy during this period will obscure the true picture. Only those Churchmen who believed that it was adequate for a cleric to receive an education identical to that of a gentleman, which at the universities was general and not strictly speaking vocational, could believe that a satisfactory reformation had occurred. Unlike the law, the Church during this period did not succeed in appending a period of strictly vocational training to the period spent studying the arts curriculum at the universities. Politics and tradition stood in the way. Crown and dominant hierarchy regarded loyalty as the prime qualification for a clergyman. The universities were determined to cling to their traditional monopoly of clerical education. The clerical profession, highly organised though it was at this early date, suffered because it could not control the recruitment and education of its own personnel.

Chapter 8

Legal change and the education of lawyers before the Civil Wars

The ascendancy of the common law

Religious life in England underwent a momentous change in six-teenth century England. This period also saw something ap-proaching a revolution in legal life, which has been less empha-sised by historians. We tend to assume that English common law, which triumphed in the later seventeenth century over other forms of law practised in the kingdom, always had been supreme. But this was not the case. During the sixteenth and seventeenth centuries the common lawyers were fighting a battle for ascendancy which only in retrospect appears to have been won already. England pos-sessed many different legal systems, in which differing types of law were practised – civil law, canon law, common law, equity. While canon law was no longer taught in the universities, it was practised in the numerous ecclesiastical courts of the realm by men trained in the civil law. These courts had jurisdiction over spiritual and moral cases but they also had cognizance over some categories of 'civil' suit – tithe claims, cases of defamation, marital suits. Roman or civil law was practised, for example, in the Court of Admiralty. In the la-ter sixteenth and early seventeenth century attempts were made to expand the equity jurisdiction of the Lord Chancellor: the Lord Chancellor reserved to himself the right to hear and pronounce on cases which had been heard and pronounced upon already in a com-mon law court. The equity side of Chancery expanded particularly between 1616 and 1625. During the sixteenth and seventeenth cen-turies, many common lawyers moved towards the position where they claimed that common law was not only supreme but the only law of England. These common lawyers did not speak with one voice and different segments of the common-law profession would have accorded other types of law varied positions in the scheme of things. But, in any event, the development of common-law claims was gradual.

Education was extremely important in this process. The other forms of law practised in England had an ancient educational lineage. Canon law was no longer taught formally in an educational institution but there was a written corpus of canon law, a venerable code of practice and a university trained personnel in key positions. The civil law retained its importance as an academic discipline. Although there were few courts in the realm which practised Roman law *per se,* for as long as the ecclesiastical courts retained power, the civil lawyers were secure. The common law, however, was not and never had been an academic discipline. Indeed, it might be possible to argue that, while there were common lawyers and a common-law practice, there was little clearly definable, written common law. The place of statute in common law was uncertain in the fifteenth century. Until the sixteenth century precedent mattered relatively little. Common lawyers learned technique rather than law.

In this chapter I want to sketch in briefly the major milestones in the educational revolution which shook the English legal world. It was a revolution which did not necessarily have very immediate effects – contemporaries were often slow to absorb its implications. For example, in the late 1620s Thomas Powell in his *Tom of All Trades* (a manual for parents seeking advice on careers for their children) clearly envisaged the civil lawyers as the élite of the legal profession. When Tom described the 'laws promotions' he advised that there were more certain promotions within the civil law than the common law:

It is to be confessed, the charge of breeding a man to the Civil Law is more expensive, and the way more painful, and the books of greater number, and price than the Common Law requireth. But after the Civil Lawyer is once grown to maturity his way of advancement is more beneficial, more certain, and more easy to attain, than is the Common Lawyer's, and all because their number is less, their learning more intricate. And they admit few or no solicitors to trample between them and the client. So that the fee comes to them immediately, and with the more advantage.

In order to begin a career in the civil law, the youth will be sent to Trinity Hall, Cambridge, or to New College, Oxford (with the benefit of a scholarship from Winchester), because 'for breeding of your youth in the civil law these are two colleges of especial note in our universities'. The civil law, then, was reserved to the wealthy and the clever. For the many who could not meet these requirements, Tom advocated the common law. Tom's advice probably seemed sound in view of the apparently flourishing state of the ecclesiastical courts, upon which most of his civil lawyers were dependent for a living. Yet there had been developments in the common law which might have suggested to him that the common law had become or was about to become an élite profession in its own right. A decade later his advice would be outmoded.[1]

It was during the reigns of the Tudors and the early Stuarts that major issues in the common law were being thrashed out: the standing of statute law; the role of the judges and barristers as interpreters of statute and other law; the relationship between the judges and the official policies of the reigning monarch; the distinction between an administrative and a legal career; the place of precedent in law.

The development of common law as an intellectual discipline

Developments within the legal profession during the period had tremendous repercussions for the development of the law itself and vice versa. In the fifteenth century the Inns of Court already had a developed function as teaching institutions: early in the century most of this teaching was oral and aural. Inner barristers were learning how to plead – skill and technique were stressed and the nature of the law itself under-emphasised. Barristers and Serjeants-at-Law did use the Yearbooks, but mainly to learn how to plead rather than to seek precedents. The arrangement of the early Yearbooks and the manner of their production precluded such a usage: medieval law reporters rarely recorded final verdicts; there was little attempt to be up to date – a fifty-year-old case was regarded as as useful as a case heard and decided yesterday; cases were not numbered and were not arranged for easy reference. But during the reign of Edward IV (1461–83) paper pleadings were introduced; the reporting of these pleadings eventually encouraged the use of the Yearbooks as a source of authority as well as of 'tips for advocates'. This development, however, was still slow. In the early sixteenth-century the Yearbooks were still reporting cases heard in the reign of Henry VI (1422–61). It was not until Tottel's printed version of Fitzherbert's *Abridgements* that cases were numbered for easy reference. Nevertheless, there was an increasing tendency towards uniformity in the style of reporting in the late fifteenth- and early sixteenth-century Yearbooks. Fortescue indicates that students of the law were now encouraged to study writs and the remedies which they afforded just as much as technique. It has been suggested that the Yearbooks were compiled in the Inns of Court and were concentrating on their teaching functions and the study of law. These Yearbooks were compiled essentially for the instruction of students of pleading and they still emphasised the study of past law rather than current legal practice.[2]

Such Yearbooks met the requirements of legal practitioners reasonably well until the early sixteenth century. Probably barristers and serjeants had kept notebooks for their own use. But the early years of Henry VIII marked a watershed in the development of English law. The spate of legislation guided through the Parliament by Thomas Cromwell, which included important statutes relating to treason, proclamations, wills and recoveries and the creation of new courts of law, made demands upon the expertise of the legal profession which it could not meet with its existing equipment. The profession had to find a way, quickly, to deal with entirely new legal contingencies. Some lawyers hesitated to accept the supremacy of statute law but it was difficult to avoid giving serious attention to the implications of the view that Parliament was the chief legislative body which could introduce 'new law' out of government or other initiative for the view that English law was customary law, unchanging and stable. The creation of new law itself established a demand for new books – case books compiled by eminent practitioners who might be expected to know how to deal with this new phenomenon and explain to the younger practitioner how to apply statute law in the courts and to help him to sort out the increasing complexity caused by the proliferation of courts and overlapping jurisdictions. Edmund Plowden, for example, attempted in his *Commentaries* to provide practising lawyers and judges with a set of rules for the interpretation of statute law. According to Plowden and others, the lawyer possessed an expertise upon which he could draw to explain obscure words and passages.[3]

Lawyers did not deliberate upon the meaning of statute law within a theoretical vacuum. The courts reacted to individual cases brought before them; in their reactions they interpreted statute law in such a way that justice seemed to them to be done and the intention of the legislators honoured. Plowden did not discourse upon the meaning of statute law in general. He provided the means by which practising barristers and judges could profit from precedent (experience) and also a guideline to future response in similar instances. In an increasingly complex situation, precedent and authority were becoming much more important to the lawyer than they once had been but attention was also paid to the individual's qualifications and judgement. It is easy to see how the concept of the expert both came into being and was expanded upon. Not only did Plowden report cases in such a way as to make clear his view that it was legal training which enabled the lawyer to interpret statute law and his duty to do it in such a way as would contribute towards the public good, but also was careful to report leading cases in detail, to stress their authority and to create a sourcebook which was available to practising lawyers. In ways such as these the common lawyers were developing an intellectual discipline and, as a consequence, a concept of appropriate legal education.[4]

The Inns of Court as educational institutions

This emergence of the intellectual discipline of the common law took place within the context of the ancient Inns of Court. By the late fifteenth century the Inns of Court were fulfilling an important educational function. During the fourteenth century the dozen or so Inns which were associated with the apprentices (barristers) in common law grew up. Of these four had a responsible function from the mid-fifteenth century – the Inns of Court called apprentices to their bars as licensed pleaders from *c.* 1454–55, when the word barrister is first encountered. The Inns of Chancery had no such licensing power. (This fact, in itself, does much to explain the decline of the Inns of Chancery.) With the assumption of this licensing role the membership of the Inns of Court came to be much more limited than that of the Inns of Chancery – essentially they numbered among their members students and licensed apprentices. According to whether one was licensed or not, members of the Inns were seated on forms (*barrae*) within the hall: the junior members sat 'within the bar'; the senior members 'without the bar'. Students came to be called 'inner barristers' and those who were called to the bar were known as 'utter barristers'. The bar to which they were called was the bar of the Inn but this awarding of the degree of barrister within the Inns of Court conferred upon the apprentice the privilege of pleading in the Court of King's Bench and other central courts, with the exception of the Common Pleas. The licensing system had introduced yet another hierarchical element into the profession of the law – a clearly defined student body. Quite naturally this licensing system gave rise to the further development of an educational system within the Inns.[5]

This system bore more similarities to that of the late medieval universities than to that of the teaching colleges of the sixteenth and seventeenth centuries. The standard teaching method was the reading or lecture; student participation was achieved through the moot – a vocational adaptation of the scholastic disputation or exercise. The Inns never provided their students with tutorial supervision: when a student at the Inns possessed a tutor it was without exception the result of private initiative on his own or his kin's part. Neither did the Inns bend over backwards to provide an environment suitable for students of tender age – Dr Prest has observed that it was difficult, given the location of the Inns and the maturity of many of their occupants, to exclude from their premises prostitutes and knaves, and the exposure to metropolitan forms of culture and society was regarded as one of the advantages of attending the Inns.[6]

On the other hand, the system owed much to traditional forms of qualifying for the law, and indeed any trade or craft, in the Middle Ages. The essential form of the time was apprenticeship – not academic training. Within the Inns academic education itself was organised along the traditional lines of the master/apprenticeship relationship: the more senior members taught the more junior – at a term-time moot the benchers acted as judges, the barristers argued the cases and the students recited the pleadings which they had learned by rote; in vacation moots the barristers trained to be benchers by acting as judges while the students prepared to be barristers by arguing the cases for themselves. Some few barristers were eventually appointed Readers and thereby called to the Bench of the Inn. The Reading was thus simultaneously a recognition of the barrister's fitness for the bench and a learning exercise for inner barristers and utter barristers who provided him with an audience. At after-dinner discussions during term, the inner barristers presented cases and learned from the comment of the utter barristers. One is scarcely being accurate, therefore, if one assumes that a 'student' ceased being a 'learner' once he became an utter barrister – rather he became a combination of student and teacher within the Inn. And the ultimate ambition of every utter barrister until the seventeenth century remained to be called from the bench of his Inn to become a Serjeant-at-Law entitled to plead in the Court of Common Pleas. While this teaching arrangement in some ways resembled the master-apprentice relationship, it did not, of course, duplicate it: the essentially personal relationship of the master and apprentice was missing and the student was one among many, sharing the disadvantages and the advantages of group learning.[7]

Apprenticeship

If the Inns provided an amalgam of academic and practical training through the readings, moots and discussions, they did not provide all the education necessary for the young student of the common law. The surviving diaries indicate that attendance at court was still considered to be a vital part of every intending lawyer's preparation. During the law terms Simonds D'Ewes made it a practice to attend the proceedings of Star Chamber on Wednesday and Friday mornings; he also spent time in the High Court of Parliament, the 'sessions house' and the Court of Wards. That he was by no means unique in spending much study time in the courts during term-time is suggested by John Manningham's earlier accounts of the boatloads of students attending the courts of Westminster, particularly Common Pleas and King's Bench. The law student was very much a student in the courts of law as well as a student of the Inns of Court – an indication that the educational functions of the Inns had been grafted onto an existing system of legal training in an attempt to supply its remedy.[8]

Change in the education of barristers

It is important to emphasise the fact that the aural education of the late fifteenth- and early sixteenth-century lawyer concentrated not so much upon the nature and content of the common law as upon the art of pleading in the central courts. The Yearbooks reported cases which had been heard years before, neglected to record decisions and took little account of the lawyer's need for a knowledge of precedent. Similarly, when a barrister was chosen to read, he commonly chose as his subject for the reading a statute which had no contemporary relevance. Inner barristers were apprentices, seeking practical expertise, rather than students working in an academic milieu.[9]

During the sixteenth and seventeenth centuries this situation altered. Historians have focused their attention upon the issue: did the education offered by the Inns of Court decline in quality in the sixteenth century? Writers on the law such as Holdsworth argued that, after a period of medieval excellence, the aural exercise system deteriorated. This decline paralleled another in the aural system at the universities and it was aided by the spread of the printed word, which turned a society accustomed to oral debate and listening to lectures into a society which drew its knowledge from books and studied independently. Kenneth Charlton modified this thesis somewhat by claiming that this movement away from education by exercise at the Inns of Court had already occurred by the beginning of the sixteenth century. But Wilfrid Prest argued very persuasively that what occurred at the Inns of Court during the sixteenth and seventeenth centuries was not a deterioration and collapse of the system of education but rather an adaptation of that system to changing circumstances and needs. He demolished the cornerstone of Holdsworth's argument – a comparison between the criticism of readings in the 1550s for excessive zeal and obscurity and the unduly formalistic orders of 1591 regulating the length and the expense of readings – by establishing that the orders of 1557 related not to readings in the Inns of Court but to grand moots in the Inns of Chancery. He agreed that readings certainly took up less time than formerly and were rather less intricate in the early seventeenth century than in the sixteenth. But he urged that it was never difficult to obtain readers (except for Inn-of-Chancery) moots; that students continued to pay considerable attention to both moots and readings throughout the period up to 1640; and that the conscientious would-be lawyer spent a good deal of time preparing his own exercises in mooting and case-putting.[10]

In fact what had occurred was not an eclipse but a revolution. The place of the aural exercises within the overall education of a lawyer changed. This was not simply because the printed book and observation of the system at work in the central courts came to play a larger role in the student lawyer's education, although both may have been important. Lawyers were becoming more interested in the law itself, and relatively less interested in technique. As we noted earlier, law reporters such as Edmund Plowden and James

Dyer reported the activities of judges when called upon to interpret
and apply particular laws to particular cases. Such reporters found
a ready market among both inner and utter barristers. The judg-
ments and statements of senior barristers, serjeants and judges had
the greatest appeal. There is evidence that lawyers at all stages of
their careers were concerning themselves with contemporary legal
decisions in the interests of their practices. Over 300 collections of
unprinted law reports survive for the period 1485–1603, two- thirds
of which fall into the period 1575 to 1603.[11] The legal education at
the Inns of Court emphasised the student's obligation to attend the
central courts and note down proceedings and decisions. Sir James
Dyer, John Manningham and Simonds D'Ewes are examples only of
what seems to have been common practice. When D'Ewes left the
Middle Temple in 1626 he lamented leaving 'his reporting of law
cases at the Court of Common Pleas'. The law reporting which he
practised was of the new variety – interested in precedent established in contemporary cases. It has been assumed that students
were encouraged also to consult and make extracts from their spon-
soring barristers' commonplace books. Thomas Egerton, later Lord
Ellesmere, compiled a carefully referenced commonplace book which
gave him easy access to the *Commentaries* of Plowden, the *Tenures*
of Littleton and other key works. But throughout a long career, a
barrister would compile his own reports – concise, factual notes,
often carefully referenced in the new style – and would, on occasion, have the same copied by a scrivener and circulated within the
Inns. In general only those 'private' reports produced by senior
lawyers would be printed but there was, nevertheless, a good deal
of co-operation among practising lawyers which consisted in part
of the exchange of manuscript reports and of discussion of contemporary cases.[12]

The impact of printing should not be underestimated. By the early seventeenth century serious students of the law like D'Ewes were
making use of the legal libraries of their Inns and building up legal
libraries of their own. In the second and third decade of the sixteenth century there began to come from the printing press books
such as Germain's *Doctor and Student* (1523) which increased the
range of literature available to students. By about the middle of the
century it became necessary for students to be advised not to rely
entirely upon book learning but also to participate in discussions –
certainly a reversal of the situation prior to the invention and introduction of printing. The printing of the first systematic legal textbook in 1600 (Fulbecke's *A Direction*) was undoubtedly a landmark
in the history of legal education but it marked not the beginning but
the culmination of a movement towards private study among law
students. The systematic textbook made private study easier, especially in the absence of a tutor.[13]

By the late sixteenth century it was common for students to study in the universities for two years or so before going up to the Inns of Court whether, as in the case of D'Ewes, the student had been destined for a career in the law from birth or not. Students at the universities studied the arts curriculum – particularly those parts of it which treated rhetoric and logic. Why did this arts prefix to legal vocational training become the norm? It seems to have arisen out of the preoccupation of the gentry classes with the social humanist view of education as a preparation for the active life in pursuit of virtue. It was accepted that the arts curriculum at the universities, as now taught in the undergraduate colleges, was designed to produce men equipped for responsibility in the state in a general sense – the Inns of Court added to this training a more particular vocational preparation. It was similar to the pattern adopted in the American colonies and perpetuated until the present day, where professional education follows on from a more liberal education. But sixteenth-century gentlemen who were interested in a career as a barrister were taught to regard their education at the universities as 'vocational' also.[14]

This use of the universities as preparatory schools for lawyers had an incalculable influence upon the educational system of the Inns themselves. These same students came to the Inns heavily imbued with what they had learned in college and university, and accustomed to given study methods which differed radically from those traditionally practised at the Inns. The student was already used to private study – to relying on books, reading guides, private discussions with tutors and fellow students, commonplacing, cataloguing and listening to informal lectures rather than upon lectures and learning exercises.

The impact which commonplacing had upon the Tudor and Stuart mind is obvious indeed to anyone who has read widely among private papers of the period. These are strewn with commonplace books or notebooks. As early as March 1557 John Foxe was to publish (in Basel) a notebook of commonplaces for students at the university. The pages were blank for the students to fill in; only headings and sub-headings were supplied. Commonplacing learned at school and at university had a profound influence upon the study habits of all professionals – clergy, physicians and lawyers alike.[15]

The student had been through school and university acclimatised to the idea of education as an intellectual process: even had the authorities so wished, it would have been difficult to wean him from such an attitude at this stage. So we see D'Ewes adopting a method of study common among university students when he attends the Inns of Court – he studies law in the mornings and, when the pressure of moot or case-putting is upon him, follows more humanistic studies in the afternoons and devotes himself to religious exercises and to listening to sermons. D'Ewes is no less a professional law student for this but we should, nevertheless, view his approach to legal studies against the background of the sixteenth and seventeenth-century gentleman's approach to the whole question of vocation and vocational education. For D'Ewes non-legal studies did not simply provide a diversion, a broadening of the mind, but were part of the total education of a gentleman lawyer. At the admittedly more aristocratic Gray's Inn, Edward Waterhouse gave the beginning of the day to the law, then practised 'harmless acts of manhood', academic learning in rhetoric, logic etc., civil visits to friends, reading of history, romances and poetry, and religious exercises for the remainder of the day. In this scheme only three hours were allocated to the study of law out of an active day which began at 5 a.m. and ended at 9 p.m.[16]

Other functions of the Inns

Dr Prest has shown us that the overwhelming majority of students admitted to the Inns of Court in the period 1590 to 1639 were of upper-class origin (in the sense of belonging either to the peer-esquire group or the gentry). We do not know the precise breakdown of non-professional as opposed to professional students at the Inns of Court at this time but we do know that they were being used increasingly as finishing schools for youths who had no intention of ever following a career at the bar. The presence of these aristocratic students at the Inns raised the social tone of the Inns and of the common law itself. While it is clear that professional students tended to mix with other professional students, young law students from gentry backgrounds brought with them gentry assumptions, emphasised the non-manual aspects of the legal profession and regarded their legal studies in much the same way as their preparatory classical education in school and, often, university. Such students either wished to raise their social status by studying the common law or, at the very least, to maintain their pre-existing social status. The traditional model of a legal apprenticeship (which stressed technical skills and practice and regarded the academic training of the Inns as a support system) gave place to a new form of higher education for gentlemen lawyers, which was more strictly academic in content. In this context it was possible, indeed perhaps desirable, for large numbers of youths who had no intention of ever practising the law to study in the Inns of Court as a postscript to their humanistic education at the university. The common lawyers, in the accepted Tudor/Stuart mould, confessed to no change. According to Fortescue, the Inns of Court had always been a third university in the realm. Certainly no contemporary common lawyer would have acknowledged that this emphasis on intellectual training was innovatory in the least.[17]

It is interesting to note, in this context, the futility of the practical lawyer's complaints that the Stuart lawyer is not being adequately trained to practise the law. Thomas Powell was willing enough to endorse the academic training programme advocated by Dodderidge, for example, but felt compelled to urge that academic training was but one part of the barrister's training:

[1] commend the ancient custom of breeding of the younger students. First in the Inns of Chancery, there to be the better prepared for the Inns of Court. And this must needs be the better way, seeing too much liberty at the first proves very fatal to many of the younger sort. I have observed and much commend also the breeding of some common lawyers in this kind, viz.

That when they have been admitted first into an Inn of the Chancery, they have been withall entered as clerks in the office of some protonotary of the Common Pleas to add the *skill of the practicke* [sic] *to their speculation*. And if a student be thus bred, by his foundation in the one, and his experience in the other, he shall with more facility than others, who step into the Inn of Court at first, attain to an ability of practice (author's own emphasis).[18]

Powell's comments possessed a certain validity. For the common lawyer, unlike the civil lawyer, preferment was not certain. Although the Inns called an increasing number of students to the bar during the period 1590 – 1639 (reaching a peak of 511 in 1630–39), there were places for very few in the central court system. It has been estimated that only 458 barristers practised in the Westminster Courts between 1603 and the Civil War. In this situation, without legal connections, it was difficult for a beginning barrister to build up a practice which would bring in sufficient income for his support. As a consequence, practice in the central courts in London was probably the preserve of youths who had considerable financial backing to tide them over the early, precarious years of practice. But it was possible that earlier practical training and the simultaneous acquisition of useful connections in the court system would facilitate the young utter barrister's progress.

The Common lawyer is to be bred only upon the purse. The charge most at the first. For after he hath spent some few years effectually he may attain to the employment of some private friends, for advising with, and instructing of greater Counsel, whereby he shall add both to his means and knowledge.[19]

Failing this, the young barrister must seek a clerkship in one of the offices of state to supplement his meagre income from court work. Gaining experience was all-important: 'if the Common Lawyer be sufficiently able in his profession, he shall want no practice: if no practice, no profit'.[20]

But, valid though it may have been, Powell's advice was swimming against the tide. The Inns of Chancery underwent no revival in the mid and later seventeenth centuries. Many students sadly neglected the practical aspects of the law.

The trend towards a system of legal education which depended more and more upon the private study of the students was fraught with dangers for the legal profession. Dr Prest has shown that the Inns, despite their physical similarities to colleges at the universities, possessed no tutorial or supervisorial system; that the barristers and benchers rarely offered advice to students, except perhaps for a fee; and that few students were admitted to the Inns even with a private tutor. Private study of the common law was complicated both by the nature of the law itself and also by the rather limited value of the guides which men like Dodderidge and Abraham Fraunce produced to aid students. When all is said and done, standards of legal preparation even among industrious and able students cannot have been high after only a few years at an Inn. There is no evidence that, once the formal requirements for admission to the Bar tended to be dispensed with, students were rigorously examined before admission. It was possible to obtain a licence to plead in the central courts of the land on the strength of four to six years of unsupervised, undirected and often part-time study of a subject which was already extremely complicated. Observation of the system in progress depended entirely upon the initiative of the individual student. It had even become acceptable for the student to buy his way out of participating in the learning vacations. One is forced to conclude that by the Civil War educational standards for admission to the Bar were not high and that by the later seventeenth century they had fallen yet further, as exercises fell into disuetude. The new barrister acquired most of his practical knowledge on the job.

When we study the common lawyers in England (that is those who practised the law) we are dealing with a group much smaller than that involved in the study of the clergy. At any one time there were approximately 8,000 to 9,000 beneficed clergymen in the kingdom. In addition, there were an indeterminate number of unbeneficed clergymen, who were part of the profession. Most barristers aspired to practise law in the Westminster Courts. But in those courts there were few opportunities to practise – 458 lawyers practised therein in a forty-year period – although presumably an unspecified number of assistants (already trained barristers) worked for these court barristers in the wings. The Assize Court circuits were staffed by lawyers from the central courts rather than by a bevy of local lawyers. It is interesting to note that Sir Thomas Egerton had a legal practice based on work before the Council in the Marches of Wales, the Western Circuit of the Assize Courts, the Court of Chancery and the Court of King's Bench. There were, of course, openings for barristers to serve in manorial courts; the courts of Stannaries and the Cinque Ports; as recorders in corporate towns and so on.

In addition, many trained common lawyers held clerkships in the offices of the central government and of the provincial councils. Clearly, whereas there were relatively few career opportunities for common lawyers in the court system, the excess was absorbed successfully into quasi-administrative, quasi-legal work. The education offered by the Inns of Court becomes more important in the context of English educational history as a whole when we observe the fact that extremely large numbers of young men came under the influence of the common-law mind whether or not they eventually practised law in the courts.[21]

While it is possible to chart the escalation in student numbers at the Inns of Court over the two centuries under consideration in this chapter, the records prevent us from separating exactly in the statistics those students who were serious law students (who were called to the Bar but who may never have practised law in the central common-law courts) from those young men who treated the Inns as finishing schools. This is an important distinction, because some of the evidence indicates that non-serious students deliberately shunned the company of professional students, the educational endeavours of the Inns and, indeed, the physical premises, because they despised the social milieu of the Inns, and used them only as a springboard to London society. Most of these students came into only minimal contact with legal education. The remainder of the student body, whatever their future careers, may be said to have been influenced considerably by the 'common law mind'. While we cannot be precise in a statistical sense, we do know that calls to the bar between 1590 and 1639 ranged in number (by decade) from 380 to 511. The ratio of calls to admissions during this same period was 1: 5.9 overall. Significantly, at the fashionable Gray's Inn, the ratio stood at 1: 10.9, while at Lincoln's Inn it was 1: 3.7. Over the period 1590 to 1639, 2,138 out of 12,163 students at the Inns were called to the Bar. These figures represent a minimum number of young men who were affected in some way by a legal education at the Inns. These men did not necessarily remain within the ambience of the legal profession but they were influenced by it at an impressionable age.

Our interest in the education of barristers at this time is not justified by an interest in social mobility. The common law did not present opportunities for the plebeian student. During a part of the period the social origins of the students admitted may appear to have fallen, but this seems to have been attributable to the rising intake of sons of lawyers, an ambiguous category. The common law was a gentle profession – this remained the case because of the methods of career advancement, the expenses of training and the determination of the practitioners to maintain and, if possible, to improve their social standing.

Conclusions

What is fascinating about the case of the common law is the manner in which common lawyers used contemporary educational thought, aristocratic interest in higher education, and political developments to bring about a change in the social and professional standing of the common lawyer. It was acceptable within society for a young gentleman to attend university to acquire the education necessary for service in the state. Similarly, the common lawyer was now portrayed as a professional, serving the state, who through a long period of essentially intellectual training acquired expertise. The physical presence of the aristocracy within the Inns of Court lent them an air of respectability and fashion, upon which the lawyers capitalised, while continuing to run the Inns as professional clubs and training schools. Simultaneously, the lawyers, in meeting the requirements of the spate of new statute law, brought into being the corpus of written material necessary to create an academic discipline out of the common law. It appears that the real issue is not whether the educational system of the Inns was in decline, it is rather to what social and professional ends was this educational system put. In line with so many occupations in early modern England, the common law barristers were consolidating as a profession and using education as one of the chief building blocks.

Chapter 9

Was there a teaching profession?

Did the teachers professionalise during the early modern period? Were they, as a group, characterised by organisation, altruism, and internal control over admissions and discipline? In 1967 Kenneth Charlton first asked this question and sufficient work has been done by a number of historians, including Patrick Orpen, Richard L. DeMolen, Alan Smith and myself, perhaps to allow us to draw some conclusions.[1]

The status of teachers in the later Middle Ages

In the Middle Ages grammar schools were attached both to the universities and to the Cathedral foundations. In the fourteenth century the masters serving these schools were well educated. The University of Oxford's statutes assumed that they would be Masters of Arts. In the latter half of that century, however, graduates who wished to become schoolmasters were apparently in short supply. By the fifteenth century the Chancellor of Oxford was licensing some grammar masters who had no degree.[2]

Endowed grammar schools became much more common in the fifteenth century. The grammar schools eventually became the linchpin of the social humanist programme which so gripped the sixteenth- and seventeenth-century gentry. The ethos of the humanist grammar school had to be shared by the masters who served within them or die. How could the governors of the schools recruit such men?

The secular cathedral schools of the later Middle Ages were normally kept by clerics, as were most of the new endowed schools of the fifteenth century, although there was no hard and fast rule about this and men in minor orders or married men sometimes found positions. On average, a schoolmaster probably earned about £10 a year in the fifteenth century. This was probably not too poor a salary before the price rise. It came either from fees collected from parents or from the endowment of the parent institution. Nevertheless, grammar schoolmasters *were* more poorly paid than the more prosperous parochial clergy and it is certain that educated clergy (those from whom the grammar masters were to be recruited) gravitated towards these wealthier livings. It would be difficult to attract graduates to a full-time and long-term commitment to teaching as long as this was the case. The pattern of treating teaching as an apprenticeship for the ministry was thus set early in England.[3]

Renaissance commitment to vocation

The idea of vocation, which was so closely associated with that of profession in its altruistic sense, emerged most fully in the context of Renaissance and Reformation. It was not until the idea that *every man* must have a calling spread through *lay* society that a teaching profession was likely to appear as a distinct alternative to the clerical profession. The commitment to vocation was absorbed by pupils of the humanistically orientated grammar schools and universities of the sixteenth century. It was quite natural for such youths to talk of their vocation and of their specific preparation for its realisation. For some, this vocation would be in the state's service; for some, in that of the church; for some, perhaps, in teaching.

There is no doubt that laymen thought teaching a much more important function than they had when few laymen attended school or university. The teacher became an important person because he was responsible for the success of the humanist and Protestant programmes.

Yet we should be cautious. Ascham's famed *Scholemaster* presented a 'plain and perfect way of teaching children to understand, write and speak, the Latin tongue', but Ascham's commitment to teacher training was less certain than his commitment to humanist content and methods. He was not convinced that youth needed any other schoolmaster than his book. It was, in many ways, a 'teach yourself' manual, being 'specially purposed for the private bringing up of youth in gentlemen and noble men's houses, and commodious also for all such as have forgot the Latin tongue, and would, by themselves, without a schoolmaster, in short time, and with small pains, recover a sufficient ability to understand, write and speak Latin'.[4]

Some humanists seemed to want to obliterate the personal element in teaching. The emphasis was upon a standardised curriculum, method and purpose. When good teachers were few on the ground the printed book could come to the rescue. Even in Richard Mulcaster, writing much later than Ascham and often regarded as the archetypal professionaliser of early modern education, we see this fear of the individual and of experimentation in teaching. Early writers on education advocated the most rigid kind of control over the content of the curriculum.

Richard Mulcaster

When we discuss the professionalisation of teaching, Richard Mulcaster's ideas must assume pride of place. A teacher himself, he served as headmaster of Merchant Taylors' School, London (1561–86) and St Paul's School (1596–1608), although he also held an ecclesiastical living. Mulcaster tackled some of the problems facing humanists who wished to realise their goal through education – ill-qualified and uncommitted teachers; poor method which turned pupils away from learning. He suggested several approaches to correct these faults. He advocated uniformity in both curriculum and method and laid down an acceptable curriculum for both petty and grammar schools. He would have had little sympathy with the masters of town grammar schools who often diluted the classical curriculum to meet the wishes of parents. Perhaps most significantly, he proposed a reform of the universities. A college for teachers would be founded within the reformed institutions. 'Why should not teachers be well provided for, to continue their whole life in the school, as Divines, Lawyers, Physicians do in their several professions? Thereby judgement, cunning, and discretion will grow in them; and masters would prove old men, and such as Xenophon setteth over children in the schooling of Cyrus.' In this teachers' training college students would be divided into groups of potential elementary, grammar and university teachers. They would receive instruction not only in the classics but also in appropriate teaching method. The status of teaching would be raised in the process by the difficulty of the training and by a parallel increase in teachers' salaries. Mulcaster believed that the recruitment of able teachers of elementary children was essential to the success of the humanist programme and so he recommended that such teachers actually receive a higher rate of pay than their colleagues in the upper forms of the grammar schools.

Clearly, Mulcaster did want teaching to become a full-time commitment on the part of its practitioners and to see an end to its use as a by-employment supporting the impoverished clergyman, the itinerant recusant, the poor scholar or the spinster. Teachers had to be committed to the transmission of a particular value system via a specific curriculum and methodology, 'I conclude therefore that this trade requireth a particular college . . . for the subject being the means to make or mar the whole fry of our state.'[5]

Mulcaster addressed the question of the teaching profession and its relationship to humanist ideals with a peculiar directness but he was by no means alone in his wider conception of the place of teaching in society and among the professions. He was extending to the role of the teachers ideas regarding the specific vocation of every man and its demands upon the individual's time and energy. There was a general tendency towards the division of and control of function. And Mulcaster's plea to the teachers to associate had a direct parallel in William Perkins' advice to the ministers:[6]

Teaching: The last conference I appoint to be between those of the same professions, whereby the general training is generally furthered.
Ministers: Are good ministers too thin sown? Are there so few of them: then let all good and godly ministers give the right hand of fellowship one to another, and join together in love, and by that means arm themselves against the scorn and contempt of the world ... and thus define doctrine and preclude debate.

Remarkable as Mulcaster's ideas were, we must not be deceived into thinking that he was describing what had happened in England. Of course, theory was important. Professionalisation itself is a product of self-consciousness and declared commitment. But one is far from certain that contemporary teachers were very conscious of themselves as a distinct group or that they saw themselves as committed to teaching as their vocation. It may be that a number of historical and contemporary factors militated against the development of such an attitude.

Employment patterns among teachers

Field studies have been undertaken to discover whether teaching had become the full-time, permanent commitment of late sixteenth- and seventeenth-century graduates. (This was certainly not the case in the so-called ABC or Dame Schools, where teaching was commonly combined with some other rural occupation such as farming or spinning.) Patrick Orpen divided his sample of Worcestershire and Warwickshire teachers into three broad categories – professionals (those who taught for their whole careers); temporary professionals (who taught for a period before finding other employment) and clericals (who combined teaching and an ecclesiastical career simultaneously). He discovered that one fifth of his sample fitted into the professional category. The number of clericals increased significantly over the seventeenth century. Lengthy careers in teaching characterised less than half of the professionals. Even half the temporary professionals taught for over ten years 'and presumably they brought some measure of commitment to their schools'. On occasion a clerical clearly regarded teaching as his chief profession and his benefice as the sinecure and by-employment.[7]

On the face of it there is a strong case for arguing that there existed an important nucleus of men who made teaching their life's work and brought to it commitment and dedication. But there are some flaws in this argument. Schoolteaching provided a haven for the graduate and the student at a time when ecclesiastical preferment was hard to obtain. It would not have been easy for a temporary professional to extricate himself from a teaching career once he was in it, because he was competing with younger men for church preferment. A ten-year teaching span might or might not indicate a degree of commitment to teaching. We shall probably never know how many of these temporary professionals were always 'clergy at heart'.

Who did the teaching?

As we noted earlier, the curate of a parish was responsible for the religious instruction of the young. Catechising the youth of the parish required no special licence. In theory other types of teaching, including that by the incumbent of the benefice, did require a licence from the bishop or ordinary. In practice it is probable that such licences were rarely applied for. For this reason one should remain sceptical of the significance of the low numbers of curate and vicar school-teachers which emerge from visitation records. For instance, of 382 clergymen serving in Salop archdeaconry between 1584 and 1639 only 21 appear as licensed teachers in the records. On the other hand we know that many clergy ran schools in Norfolk – significantly the information was gleaned from college and not from church records.[8]

A group of schoolteachers which has been relatively neglected consisted of men who were not in orders but who were, nevertheless, connected with the Church. These were the 'lectors' or readers who, during the acute shortage of ministers in the mid sixteenth century, were frequently employed to read matins and evensong, bury the dead, church women and read the homilies. The duties of these lectors were confined to Sundays and holy days. Their stipends were miserably low. Often they found by-employment in teaching. If the man concerned wished ultimately to enter the Church, teaching was an ideal choice. At this time the Church was trying to clamp down upon the admission of 'mechanics' to orders. Teaching did not soil the candidate's hands with manual labour and could be combined with a variety of other suitable employments. In the late sixteenth and early seventeenth centuries many of the readers were mere boys, some of them still at school. But there was an increasing tendency for the reader to act also as schoolteacher and to enter the ministry after a period. In 1616, for example, William Peake was serving as reader and schoolmaster of Great Arcall, Salop; shortly afterwards he took orders. On occasion the time spent serving as reader and schoolteacher before acquiring church preferment might be considerable: Thomas Wellens was reader at Ruckley and Langley Salop and teacher of Acton Burnell for eleven years before obtaining the vicarage of Cheswardine, Salop, in 1617. Some never took orders. They probably regarded the combination of employments as a reasonably prestigious way of keeping hunger at bay.[9]

Some people who were by any definition lay were also attracted to teaching. This group includes recusants such as Margaret Ford, who was presented at visitation in 1619 for recusancy and teaching children in Tutbury. In 1631 she was again presented for teaching school, being a recusant, at Stoke on Trent and in 1634/5 she and her husband were brought before the Quarter Sessions for the same offence.[10]

In addition to the recusants, there were other laypeople teaching in the schools: youths such as Adam Martindale's teachers who were products of Winwick Grammar School and themselves taught grammar, as well as the men and women who operated ABC and Dame schools. Alan Smith discovered fifty-seven references to such lay teachers in Lichfield over the entire seventeenth century – a number which may include some (like the lectors) who would eventually become clergy. Nevertheless, it is probable that many escaped the net of licensing.

Factors militating against the professionalisation of teaching

For as long as teaching was regarded as a suitable by-employment by the clergy of the Church of England, the professionalisation of teaching itself could only be restricted. For, unlike the Church, teaching was institutionally weak and organisationally stunted. There was no built-in network for the dissemination of the theories or practical advice of Mulcaster, Clement, Coote, Brinsley and Hoole. There was no mechanism for controlling the recruitment of teachers over the nation as a whole or even within one area.

The extent to which schoolmasters were exposed to current educational theory and practical advice is unknown. Of course we know that many of these works went into several editions. Very occasionally we discover evidence of teachers consulting one another about educational practice. In 1573 or 1574 Gabriel Harvey corresponded with Humphrey Hales, a recent graduate of Pembroke, Cambridge, who was now a teacher. Hales had asked Harvey for advice about curriculum and method and Harvey gave him some general advice and sent him two books to assist him further. Harvey apologised that he was unable to lend Hales his copy of Henry Schorus's work (printed in Strasbourg in 1572) because he had lent it to another acquaintance.[11]

Sir Hales, I am not a little glad, I assure you, to hear what pains you take with your scholars; neither doubt I but they profit and go forward accordingly . . . . At some other time . . . I will not steek [sic] to open my mind and fancy unto you, touching the most commodious and compendious way of teaching. In the meanwhile let this suffice, as the specialist property of a good schoolmaster, to teach none but the choicest and purest authors, either for prose or verse . . . . I had thought to have sent you a pretty treatise of Henricus Schorus touching the ordering of his school, being in a manner an extract of Ramus' worthy oration *Pro Philosophica Parisiensis Academiae Disciplina*, but surely it was not to be gotten amongst all our stationers, and mine own I gave away to a friend of mine above a month ago. Wherefore, instead thereof, I thought good to bestow upon you those two books, which in my judgement might stand you in singular stead for the better understanding and resolving of all good authors . . .

Teaching relied not upon organised training in methodology but upon the willingness of the teacher to read the books of the committed few.

In certain respects, the grammar schools (especially the larger ones) offered more opportunities for organisation than the small country schools. But there were features even in the endowed grammar school structure which ran counter to professionalisation. These schools and their schoolmasters were supported by a fixed endowment which, in a time of inflation, affected adversely the teacher's financial standing in society. Patrick Orpen collected statistics which demonstrated that the average schoolmaster earned far less than the average vicar or rector.

Schoolmasters	£17 2s. 0d. per annum
Vicars	£42 2s. 8d. per annum
Rectors	£78 0s. 0d. per annum

Only in the seventeenth century was it possible to attract reasonable numbers of graduates into teaching for extended periods of time – this was because the Church itself could not absorb the superabundance of graduate candidates and not because the rewards of teaching had risen significantly. The more fashionable and well-endowed schools offered the necessary incentive to attract graduates away from the Church in some cases. However, even this was not always true. As first Master of Merchant Taylors' School Richard Mulcaster was awarded a paltry £10 plus residence. He received a £10 supplement from Richard Hilles but it was not long before Mulcaster was in dire financial straits and taking in private fee-paying pupils, to the annoyance of the Court of the Company. A similar situation arose when he became High Master of St Paul's. It is true that Mulcaster seems to have been ill able to manage his financial affairs, but by no stretch of the imagination was he well paid for his labours.[12]

In the light of this sort of information W. A. L. Vincent's contention that the situation worsened for schoolmasters after the Restoration seems suspect. Certainly, some teachers on fixed incomes suffered. Burneston Grammar School was founded in 1688, with a master earning £16 per annum and an usher earning £5 8s. a year. In 1820 the master was still receiving the same salary but his status was reduced to that of a teacher of writing and arithmetic to seventeen boys and girls. On the other hand, some of the more famous Warwickshire schools paid their masters relatively well. The Master at Nuneaton in 1694 received £60 and the Master of King Edward VI Grammar School, Birmingham, earned £50 in 1655 and £88 15s. in 1702. In all probability the average schoolmaster's salary had risen to £40 per annum by the late seventeenth century, but with such a large deviation from the mean that the concept of an average wage is rendered meaningless. The majority of Warwickshire schoolteachers earned less than £20 per annum, with only a few earning relatively good salaries.[13]

As a result it was always difficult to insist that schoolmasters devote all their attentions to teaching. The association between teaching and clerical duties appears to have become closer after the Restoration than it was before. Many masters began to take fee-paying pupils to supplement their earnings and were accused of neglecting their free pupils. In addition, it was very difficult for a schoolmaster to retire: he had no pension benefits and was unable to save to keep himself in retirement. Charles Lee remained Master of Bristol Grammar School from 1764 until his death in 1811 because the Corporation refused him a pension. As Lee became less efficient as a master the number of his pupils declined dramatically.

Of course, the status of a professional was not dependent upon income alone. A learned schoolmaster could earn respect. Nevertheless, the poverty of most schoolmasters did have repercussions on the qualifications of recruits and did lead to a loss of respect within the community.

At the same time some of the endowed schools did put further obstacles in the way of professionalisation. Some like Staveley, Derbyshire, in 1613 and Berkswell, Warwickshire, in 1707, bound their masters to celibacy, often forcing teachers to remain for but a short time in post. Shrewsbury School forbade its teachers to augment their salaries from other sources, without making adjustments to these salaries itself.[14]

Teaching was caught in another trap. It was desirable that teachers should be graduates. Yet these same graduates were the very teachers who stood the best chances of promotion outside teaching. The non-graduate was more likely to be a permanent fixture. The available statistics are insufficient for us to test this hypothesis, which is worth bearing in mind none the less. Whether commitment to a teaching career was necessarily closely tied to the quality of the personnel involved seems certainly to be a moot point.

Statistical studies have their disadvantages and should always be seen alongside personal case histories, which can tell invaluable cautionary tales. Such a case is that of Adam Martindale, one of the few seventeenth-century schoolteachers to leave us full information concerning his life.

Adam Martindale as a teacher[15]

Adam Martindale was born the son of Henry Martindale, yeoman, of Prescot, Lancashire, in September 1623. He was educated at home and at various local schools. When Martindale reached the age of fourteen his father intended him to cease his education and learn his craft. His father seems to have been acutely aware of the problematic nature of making a living from further learning: 'alleging too many instances of such as made no advantage of their learning, though they had been brought up so long to it as to be fit for nothing else'. But Adam was unhappy and his father permitted him to return to school. At 16+ he was considered ready for the university but 'the worst of it was, the University was not so ready for me' because of the civil unrest leading up to the War. Martindale was pushed by circumstances into taking a post as tutor to the intolerable sons of Francis Shevington, a Manchester merchant. He 'looked too boyishly to undertake a school'.

At the age of 19 he was dismissed by Shevington and looked for a school position to avoid impressment into the army. He found one at Holland, which seemed to him promising because of the number of prosperous yeomen in the town. This did not turn out to be the case: the war deterred many parents from sending their children to him, he had miserable living conditions, and he was accused of Roundhead sympathies because his brother was at Bolton. So he left Holland after only one term:

Rainford being still open for me, I removed thither, having the promise of some substantial inhabitants, that they would send me their children upon the usual rates that my predecessors had, and also find me my diet by turns, as was customary also. The first they performed well, and I had a pretty full school; the second they never offered to do, but suffered me to depend upon my father for it . . .

Martindale suffered from recusant complaints and from demands to attend the musters. His excuse to the constable is revealing: 'I excused myself as a piece of a clergyman, and kept away.'

If Martindale had entered teaching to secure himself a living in those difficult times, this did not mean that he was negligent in his duties as a teacher. He concentrated on the teaching of arithmetic and produced his own textbook for use in the classroom.

This mercy befell me as I was following my schoolwork diligently at Rainford, and writing a book of arithmetic for whole numbers and fractions, in the old method of Record, Hill, Baker etc. (for then I knew nothing of decimals, logarithms or algebra) but something more contractedly, with an appendix of mine own invention, touching extracting the roots of fractions.

But soon he had to enter the army as clerk and assistant quartermaster. When he was almost 21 years old he returned to teaching at Over Whitley Free Grammar School, Cheshire. His attitude then was much more enthusiastic:

Being got again into my beloved calling, things went on with me pretty smoothly while I was master of a school newly founded by a neighbour, and the foundation of school-house newly laid, which was built up in my time with my name over the door. The income was not very great but well paid . . . and mine accidental gettings (having a full school, and pretty store of rich men's sons in it, and opportunities for earning monies by making writings for neighbours) were a good addition to my salary. As for my diet, that cost me very little, for provision was very cheap, and a friend that had three sons under my care dealt very kindly with me for it. My scholars were (for all my youth) submissive and reverent . . . and by God's blessing profited so well as to gain me as much respect and interest in the neighbourhood as was good for me.

While there Martindale set himself to learn Greek: '(which besides present profiting my scholars) was to improve myself for my work'.

Martindale's resolve to improve himself in this way was cast aside when a neighbouring minister asked him to enter the ministry. 'I was much startled at a motion to a thing so far above me, and excused myself by my youth, the content I had, and the good I hoped to do in my present situation, my utter insufficiency for want of university learning, and the trouble I knew it would cause if I left that place.' The minister replied that the ministry was a higher calling than teaching, which many were suited to who were not suited to serving God. From then on Adam prepared himself not for teaching but for the ministry, learning Hebrew and philosophy, while he continued to keep school.

From May 1646, when he entered the ministry, until the Restoration, Martindale continued as a minister. Put out of his living by the Act of Uniformity, Martindale turned again to teaching – at first running a boarding school and then going out to teach arithmetic, which he found more profitable. This last decision to teach arithmetic was taken after some heart-searching:

and though I was now almost forty years old, and knew little more than arithmetic in the vulgar way, and decimals in Jager's bungling method, I fell close to the study of decimals in a more artificial manner, logarithms, algebra, and other arts, since by me professed; in which work I was encouraged by my noble Lord Delemer, who gave me many excellent books and instruments . . .

And so we see Martindale following a programme, 'fitting myself for this work', which he did not allow to interfere with his teaching. When the Act against Conventicles forced him to close his school and place his own son at Manchester Free Grammar School he became a peripatetic maths teacher. Eventually he was asked by the Master of Manchester Grammar School to tutor some of the boys in mathematics during the autumn term.

Adam Martindale's autobiographical account can help us considerably in understanding the position of the teacher in rural, seventeenth-century England. His attitude to teaching was ambiguous. First and foremost he loved learning and, though he came to teaching by accident, he grew to love it and to be determined to perform his duties diligently and to the best of his ability. He did find in it a sense of vocation. Yet this feeling was superseded by his commitment to the higher calling to the ministry. After this teaching became a by-employment, which he performed to the best of his ability and which he found congenial.

Despite this, the status of teaching as an independent occupation does not emerge all that clearly from Martindale's account. There was still a strong enough tradition of clerical schoolmasters for Martindale to feel that he was already 'a piece of a clergyman' in his extreme youth. He did not regard schoolteaching as incompatible with or negating his vocation as a minister. In fact, his vocation as minister encompasses his vocation as teacher. The pool of recruitment for teaching and the ministry is identical.

In addition, we should note the manner of Martindale's entry into teaching. When he became a teacher, he was called by the parents of his pupils; when he became a minister he was requested so to do by a minister. The people participated in his call to an individual congregation, but his entry into the profession was controlled by fellow professionals. This distinction is crucial and it is too often neglected by historians. A vocation which was professionalised exercised control over the recruitment, training, admission and discipline of its own members, to a greater or a lesser degree. Both the clergy and the teachers professed a vocation. On the other hand, the clergy exercised considerable control over the admission and discipline of members of the profession (which was institutionalised) while the teachers had no such control and possessed absolutely no machinery for exercising it. When Martindale chose to become a teacher, he did so of his own accord and he set himself, voluntarily, a programme of preparatory work. In contrast, it was the ministers who set him his tasks when he began to study for the ministry. Any incentive to become well prepared as a teacher came from the demands of the marketplace, his own character, and his conviction that every Christian must do what he was called to do to the best of his ability, *not* from within the world of teaching.

On the other hand, there are hints in the later part of the autobiography that Martindale was associating with other teachers. This may have been because of his peripatetic practice. Certainly he was not as isolated as John Foxe had been in the 1540s. He had feared to become tutor to the Lucys of Charlecote in 1545 because of the loneliness of the house. Probably many other teachers feared this situation, which might contrast sharply with the bustle of life at Oxford or Cambridge. There was clearly a community of teachers in the larger towns. The teachers of Manchester, with the exception of Wickes of the grammar school, tried to prove Martindale deficient as a maths teacher and thus to assert their monopoly in the town. Professionalising tendencies were probably more apparent in urban areas which possessed several schools.

Many teachers, like Martindale, entered teaching almost by accident. It is thought that many monks and friars entered teaching because they were unwilling to serve in the Reformed Church. Other teachers were recruited from the universities when they had to resign their college fellowships, because of marriage or, as in the case of John Foxe, lack of orders. Overproduction of graduates in the 1620s and 1630s sent many intending clergymen into the schools. And we know that the Acts of Uniformity forced many well-educated clergy into the dissenting schools and into casual teaching. While such men, like Martindale, might become devoted teachers and good teachers, they were not members of a truly professionalised occupation because they had received no specific training and confessed no particular commitment to a common cause.

Post-Restoration developments in the professionalisation of teaching

Only the better endowed, fashionable grammar schools were able to attract able teachers with good qualifications. Other schools attracted no students and tended to draw teachers with poor qualifications. Such schools were unable to demand the sole attention of their personnel because such poor salaries were offered. An examination of licences granted to schoolmasters in the diocese of London between 1627 and 1685 shows that the number of graduates subscribing declined after the Restoration. Even graduate masters, like James Cartres MA of Rugby and Atherstone grammar schools, had other demands on their time. Teaching was now less a prelude to a clerical career than an employment held in combination with a clerical career. And some schoolteachers were now reduced to combining their office with that of the lowly parish clerkship. In Lichfield diocese in 1773 William Stinton, schoolmaster of Elmley Lovel, was nominated as schoolmaster of Aldridge school, Staffordshire: 'in my judgement well qualified for the business of writing master, as also for that of parish clerk, if he should be called to, and

chosen to undertake that office'. This sort of evidence seems to indicate the reduced rather than the improved status of teaching.[16]

By the early nineteenth century there is evidence that teaching
jobs were in demand. In 1803 there was a contest for the mastership
of the school at Brampton, Derbyshire, which seems to have been
the direct result of advertising in the *Daily Mercury*. George Read,
lately assistant to the Reverend Cursliam in his academy at Sutton
near Mansfield, was appointed by a vote of 21 to 16. Applications
for the post of headmaster of Atherstone Free Grammar School in
1817 were so numerous that the governors had to hold two special
meetings to read the testimonials of the twenty-two men involved.[17]

During the eighteenth century there is some evidence to suggest
that the staffs of the private and dissenting academies may well have
contributed a good deal to the professionalisation of teaching.
Historians of the professions are well aware that the modern concept of profession is based upon the development of a body of
theoretical knowledge pertaining to the occupation concerned,
which professionals learn and seek to apply practically in the course
of performing their services. The development of theory is, therefore, very important in the development of a profession. For many
years the *text book* was the chief vehicle for this development within
education.

In the sixteenth and early seventeenth centuries Ascham, Colet,
Coote, Mulcaster, and Brinsley had all sought to make education
supply the needs of society as seen through Protestant or humanist
eyes. They were especially concerned with the use of classical studies to achieve these ends. After the Restoration classical education
fell into disfavour with many because society now recognised other
needs. Classical education did not lose all its adherents – it remained
relevant for the governing élite throughout the modern period – and
the population was not converted immediately to any other system.
Most of the teachers in the academies, however, were seeking to
meet and define other needs. We witness the burgeoning of a theory
of vernacular and vocational teaching and also the production of an
organised body of knowledge in subjects falling into these categories. Some writers of textbooks laid great emphasis upon the method
of teaching and they saw that the student was not necessarily a good
teacher. Specific preparation was required to fulfil the function of a
teacher.[18]

It has been suggested that one of the chief obstacles to the
realisation of this position may be seen in the organisation of the
national schools and their predecessors, in which mere children
assumed teaching responsibilities, without preparation. If satisfactory results could be obtained using untutored labour, how could it
be maintained that a trained teaching profession was necessary?
This certainly goes some way to explaining the relative ease with
which the grammar school and 'private academies' masters profes-

sionalised and the difficulties encountered by primary and secondary modern school teachers in this area. Even when method was not stressed and specific preparation unheard of for the classics master, he was perforce master of his subject.

This activity in producing new materials for teaching and the increased secularisation of teaching in at least one type of school, must have had long-term significance for the professionalisation of teaching. But there is no evidence that eighteenth-century teachers were associating or providing themselves with an organisation within which they might professionalise. They still lacked the institutional framework necessary from which to control membership. This framework emerged in the nineteenth century (with the intervention of the state) when, significantly enough, teaching appears to have been the first occupation to use the word 'professionalise' to describe the movement towards a particular type of organisation.

Conclusions

The evidence for the development of teaching as a profession in the early modern period is indeed ambiguous. Certainly the teachers never professionalised although many developed a sense of commitment and profession. In other words the groundwork was laid for future professionalisation.

Chapter 10

The education of girls and women in society, 1500 –1800

The vocation of woman

Early modern education was regarded as directly vocational. The classical education provided in grammar schools and universities prepared the individual for a vocation as servant of State or Church. Protestant ecclesiastics envisaged education as opening the Scriptures to ordinary laymen, facilitating the spread of Protestantism, and properly preparing Protestant evangelists. A growing number of people believed that through schooling members of the lower classes might be better trained in necessary skills. While views of society and of society's needs might change, education for society remained the goal of contemporaries. The conservative nature of this concept becomes all the more apparent when we examine the provision made for the education of girls and women.

In order to understand the role of woman in the early modern period, we should appreciate that, traditionally, the activities of men, women and children were directed both inwards towards the economy of the household and also outwards (whether it be towards the lord of the manor, the town government, or the monarch). All other unmarried persons, be they apprentices, domestic servants, farm hands, labourers or soldiers, were subsumed into the economy of some household. There were no *independent* individuals. For example, when a domestic servant received a wage this amount of money was ploughed back into the household economy of the parents. In most cases the woman's work was as vital to the household economy as that of the man. Women were engaged in agricultural labour, in a carefully defined way. In addition to work in the fields at specified times in the agricultural year, they took care of the dairy and garden, took produce to market and were often responsible for purchasing supplies. So important was the woman's role that it was commonly believed that it was impossible for a man to head a household successfully if he had no helpmeet, whereas it was perfectly feasible for a widow to continue to run a farm and manage a household without remarriage. 'To thrive thou must wive' went the old saying.[1]

It is sometimes said that the spread of enclosure and the break-down of the manorial system brought with them significant changes in the working life and value of women. When the male members of the family put themselves up for hire or drifted towards the towns, the women with children found a mobile existence taxing and disruptive to the traditional way of life. There was relatively little which such women could contribute to the household economy. Within the towns the decline of the guild system, the violent fluctuations to which the cloth trade was subject (in which so many women had been employed), and the flood of immigrant males from the countryside in the sixteenth and seventeenth centuries, all made it more difficult for women to maintain their position in urban economic life. The position of the all-round worker was further jeopardised by the increasing specialisation evident in the early modern economy of both town and countryside.

Obviously such changes came very gradually. If, for example, one turns to the Diary of William Stout one finds a description of the working life of women in the late seventeenth century which sounds remarkably traditional. Stout, for instance, commented, 'My father and mother were very industrious in their children's infancy, and in a few years had improved their estate to the double what it was when they were married.' During his youth his mother was 'not only fully employed in housewifery but in dressing their corn for the market, and also in the fields in hay and corn harvests, along with our father and servants'. His parents were strong members of the established church and both instructed the children in the catechism. When William's father died, the widow sorrowed at 'the loss of so loving, industrious and provident a husband and partner . . . she being left with six children, the youngest then about four years of age' but she proceeded to run the household and farm perfectly competently.

Being desirous to continue to manage the estate in husbandry . . . was advised [by the overseers of the will] to get some good servant well experienced in husbandry, and was recommended to William Jenkinson, who had been manager of a good estate for many years, whom she hired, and continued with her some years till her own sons were capable to manage the same.

And she bound her son William apprentice in Lancaster. In the 1640s Adam Eyre's wife also fulfilled a traditional role, caring for the chickens, taking produce to market and spending the money which Adam doled out to her on essential supplies.[2]

Indeed, women were most vulnerable in those situations where complex opportunities outside the household had opened up for their menfolk. For women of marriageable age the only vocation open in the sixteenth and seventeenth centuries was indeed marriage and all that it implied in terms of service in the domestic sphere. For men, many more opportunities were available and, as time progressed, fewer and fewer had a role restricted to the household. This was particularly true in the towns.

The reality of this situation is in danger of being obscured by the apparently expanding number of opportunities for unmarried women outside the home. This, however, is an optical illusion. In the seventeenth century, woman's position in the marriage market was generally unfavourable. It was difficult for a woman to find a husband when there were many more marriageable women than men. Some women actually chose to emigrate to the New World in order to circumvent this demographic problem. The average age on marriage for women was in the mid twenties. This time lag between puberty and marriage left women with a period in which to work or in which to acquire some modicum of education. Many went into domestic service during puberty. This was true both in Ealing in 1599 and in Kirkby Lonsdale in 1695: few households retained daughters aged between 15 and 19 or sons aged between 15 and 24. The lure of the big city to a yeoman's or a craftsman's daughter was clearly great, as Adam Martindale reminds us[3]:

There had lately been a great plague in London, causing many that had friends in the country to come down, who having employments to return unto were full as hasty to go up as consisted with safety; and my sister Jane having conversed with some of them, was as forward as they. Our parents and other prudent friends were against her going for many substantial reasons . . . . But all these would not back her. She measured not a competency by the same mete-wand as they did. Freeholders daughters were then confined to their felts, petticoats and waistcoats, cross handkerchiefs about their necks, and white cross cloths upon their heads, with coifs under them wrought with black silk or worsted. Tis true the finest sort of them wore gold or silver lace upon their waistcoats, good silk laces (and store of them) about their petticoats, and bone laces or works about their linens. But the proudest of them (below the gentry) darest not have offered to wear a hood or a scarf, (which now every beggar's brat that can get them thinks not above her), no, nor so much as a gown till her wedding day. And if any of them had transgressed these bounds, she would have been accounted an ambitious fool. These limitations I suppose she did not very well approve, but having her father's spirit and and her mother's beauty, no persuasion would serve, but up she would to serve a lady as she hoped to do, being ingenious at her needle.

And it evidently offered similar attractions to daughters of professional families, like Anne and Rebecka Josselin. As a servant one's social status and living style were, of course, determined by one's master's or mistress's social standing and wealth. If the candidate for employment possessed a skill or a comely person, she stood a better chance of acquiring a coveted position. Once in good employment she would have the opportunity to find herself a spouse. There was also more chance for work in the retailing trade. In post-

Restoration London the New Exchange or Burse acted as the Bond Street of the day. It was dominated by milliners, and sempsters' shops and its milk-bar was frequented by London lawyers. Even in 1619 it was recognised that the presence of extraordinarily attractive shopgirls lured fashionable custom to the Burse. In 1667 Pepys 'walked up and down to see handsome faces, and did see several' in the shops of the Exchange. By the late 1690s the New Exchange was on the decline: the neighbourhood deteriorated socially and its shopgirls were now known for prostitution. Yet, as the fashionable clientele moved on to St James's Square and beyond, so a new rival shopping arcade grew up in the shape of the Middle Exchange. By the late seventeenth century not only London attracted growing numbers of servants and shopgirls. Bath, for example, had a substantial sex imbalance in favour of women due to the influx of female servants. All the spas (and later the seaside resorts) attracted the establishment of luxury shops and facilities, which required female management. This was presumably also true of the pleasure gardens in the environs of London.[4]

As we shall see, girls were 'educated' for this period in their lives. This was not regarded as their true vocation, however, by either parents or daughters. As a consequence, perhaps, during this period away from home they tended to perform tasks which were but extensions of household activity – housewifery or retailing. Thus the girl was in truth being educated for her eventual vocation as mistress of a household. The removal of so many young women out of the family home and into the towns and cities probably did have unforeseen effects upon their willingness to accept a traditional role in the future but the concept of putting girls into domestic service, cloth trade occupations or retailing was essentially conservative in both intent and effect.

It is, of course, a matter of debate as to whether women were either more oppressed or more aware of their oppression within the early modern household than in that of the later Middle Ages. Marriage had been a property relationship throughout the Middle Ages – a means of passing on wealth from one generation to another. In exchange for the woman's dower and for her services as wife, mother and helpmeet, the male offered physical support for the duration of their lives together and provision for her on his death. During the sixteenth century certain changes were introduced into the conjugal relationship. On the one hand Protestant theology both glorified the institution of marriage and the existence of a love relationship between the married couple. On the other hand, in theory the status of the patriarch within the family was exalted. In such a system the woman might be, at most, the beloved second-in command of a benevolent father and husband. Her marriage represented a disguised form of domestic slavery, which society would not allow her to escape, in which the husband was master, even if he were kind and considerate. After 1562 the Homily on Marriage was regularly read, with its emphasis on the duties of love, honour and obedience which the wife owed her husband. Her life was essentially a private one, lived within the household; his life was a public one, often played out within other institutions than the family unit.

The reality of this picture is open to question. Certainly this was the theory. The relationship between theory and practice, however, appears to have varied enormously. Property did not determine all marriages. Within individual households, women often seem to have been rather dominant personalities who were allowed or claimed a full share in family decision-making. A reader of Adam Eyre's Dyurnall, for example, would have to confess that his wife resisted Adam's will on several important matters and, apparently, succeeded in imposing her will upon him. William Stout had few illusions about the relationship between his 48-year-old brother Josias and his new 30-year-old wife, Sybill. Josias 'was a quiet and easy man, his wife being of a resolute disposition, and he was very condescending for peace sake'. In other households, such as that of Ralph Josselin, husbands appear to have discussed matters with their wives before taking final decisions. Against this sort of evidence we are bound to set other facts which appear to suggest the real subjection of wives. For instance, Adam Eyre never refers to his wife by name – she is defined in terms of her relationship to him. As few female diaries survive (if they ever existed) we do not know whether such an attitude was common to women also, but it does seem significant. Adam's public social round almost excluded his wife (and, for that matter, other women) although they did share some common friends and, when in harmony, spent Sunday afternoons walking in the district together. It seems that the type of evidence available makes it impossible to decide whether the strict patriarchal family model was prevalent or no.[5]

The education of early modern women

Schools flourished when it became necessary to communicate to the younger generation knowledge and skills which few of the older generation possessed, but which many believed to be important. No new skills had been added to the list of accomplishments which the young girl must master. All girls, with the exception of the orphaned or the children of paupers, might learn what they needed for their future life at their mother's knee – sewing, cooking, medicine, all manner of housewifery, accounting and, in the case of the lower classes, certain agricultural skills. Many of the schools which were begun to teach practical skills owed their origins to provision for the orphaned and destitute. Quite commonly instruction in such schools was combined with the teaching of reading, so that the young might read the Scriptures. This was regarded as a form of moral training to counteract the evil influences of poor or absent home life. The school was functioning *in loco parentis*. Similarly, we note that many of the earliest sixteenth-century girls' schools were run in exiled communities. The normal forms of household education had been disrupted when families were separated; there was a felt need to maintain the original culture in this alien land, while inculcating the traditional virtues. The medieval tradition of household education continued in noble and gentry homes. In 1546, for example, the daughter of Thomas Fenton was placed with her godmother, Lady Nevill, in whose care were also three Nevill daughters and three other gentlewomen – Anne and Katherine Topcliffe and Ursula Clifton. In 1551 Sir Edmund Molineux's daughters were placed with a cousin and his wife to be brought up 'in virtue, good manners and learning to play the gentlewomen and good housewives, to dress meat and oversee their households'. They were being well prepared to fulfil the duties expected of women of their sex and class. These duties, in so far as they were responsible, were directed within the household.[6]

Even Renaissance educationalists renowned for their liberal attitudes to the education of women were bound by the common conception of woman's family vocation. It is misleading to see in the period 1520–60 halcyon days for women's academic education. Vives, for example, devoted a large part of his *Instruction of a Christian Woman* to the importance of the maintenance of chastity. For him it was clear that a woman's domestic vocation dictated the limits of her educational needs. He spent more time showing the way to cultivation of correct social behaviour than indicating the way to cultivate the mind. Reading and household tasks were, for the upper-class clientele for whom he wrote, a means to protect the female mind against idleness and sin. The preoccupation with chastity meant, of course, the censorship of reading material and the insistence that the female scholar, however able, should not indulge in vanity or engage in conversation with men outside the family circle. Sir Thomas More combined an appreciation of the abilities of his daughters with an acceptance of the traditional view of woman's domestic vocation and an admonition that Margaret restrict her scholarly activities to within the home.[7]

The species of home academic tuiton provided for the children of intellectuals and princes was certainly atypical. The three More daughters; Lady Jane Grey and her sisters; the Princesses Mary and Elizabeth Tudor; Lady Jane Howard; Frances Brandon; Anne, Margaret and Jane Seymour, daughters of Protector Somerset; the daughters of the Earl of Arundel; Anne and Mildred, daughters of Sir Anthony Cooke; Princess Elizabeth, the daughter of James I; and another Princess Elizabeth, daughter to Charles I, were all the recipients of a rigorous classical education. But, for the most part, these girls were consciously educated for public service as leaders. For More and Cooke, their daughters were guinea-pigs in an educational experiment. The participation of all these young women in society was peculiar among English women. They set no pattern for their sex, as Richard Mulcaster made clear.[8]

It would be incorrect, however, to imply that there was no educational provision outside the home for early modern women or that there was no noticeable change in the type of education offered women over the period as a whole.

In 1581 Richard Mulcaster indicated that boys and girls were commonly educated together in the elementary school. He found it necessary to argue against the further co-education of boys and girls in the grammar schools. By 1589 the statutes of Harrow specifically excluded girls from that school, indicating perhaps some debate about their possible admission. The statutes of Banbury School decreed that girls might attend the petty classes up to the age of nine years for a vernacular education. The records of Rivington Free Grammar School, Lancashire, show that a girl named Alice Shaw attended in 1615 and that two or three more girls were admitted in 1616 and 1617. Twelve girls were admitted to this school in 1672 and thirteen in 1681. In 1645 Sir John Offley founded in Madeley, Staffordshire, two schools divided by a partition wall for boys and girls. The wall marked the sexual and curricular segregation of the pupils. Truly co-educational establishments did not appear until the 1680s, when Waitby and Smardale, Westmorland; Haydon Bridge, Northumberland; and Kingsbury, Warwickshire, were founded as grammar schools. There are, of course, also a number of references to schoolgirls in contemporary literature. Evidence such as this suggests that it was not so much that schools were barred to girls as that education at school was not demanded by their parents. It was simply not necessary for women to acquire more than a smattering of formal academic learning (and by the age of nine adequate levels of reading and numeracy and, perhaps, writing would have been acquired) to pursue their vocation. For economic reasons, many families could not release their daughters for a relatively expensive and 'useless' schooling. Even had they so been able, schooling alongside boys was regarded as dangerous for the preservation of a marriageable girl's most precious commodity – her chastity.

Whereas it is the most common and usual course for many to send their daughters to common schools to be taught together with and amongst all sorts of youths, which course is by many conceived very uncomely and not decent, therefore the said schoolmaster may not admit any of that sex to be taught in the said school.

For those who did require further education for their daughters two avenues were pursued – private tuition within the parental home or in the house of someone of higher or identical social standing; boarding education for girls.[9]

Perhaps the most remarkable development in girls' education in the seventeenth century was the rise of the girls' boarding school. Such schools were an extension of a medieval tradition. In 1537 Polesworth Convent, Warwickshire, for example, was said to have educated some 30 to 40 daughters of gentry families. Godstow, Oxfordshire, reputedly educated most of the daughters of the county gentry. A small house such as Swaffham Bulbeck catered for the daughters of Cambridge burgesses and tradesmen. The education in these convents consisted of religion, morals, the making of riddles, the reading of French romances, French conversation and needlework. Even a staunch reformer such as Thomas Becon commended the convent schools for their good work and recommended the foundation of Protestant girls' schools on the same model.[10] No endowed schools emerged from this proposal and, in fact, few girls' boarding establishments are mentioned between the 1530s and the seventeenth century. Such an academy appears to have existed in Windsor in the late sixteenth century. So Anne Higginson wrote to Lady Ferrers of Tamworth Castle that,

the gentlewoman we spoke of doth continue her course in teaching still, and she saith no more welcome unto her than they shall be of my noting, and because I did write your ladyship was one of my best friends, she saith her best care shall be for their good which she maketh no question of but you will give her great thanks for their good education every way, if it please you to place them with her. Her rates are this, sixteen pounds a year a piece, for diet, lodging, washing, and teaching them to work, reading, writing, and dancing, this cometh unto £32 a year. But for music you must pay for besides according as you will have them learn. She hath teachers for viol, singing, virginals and lute. Which it may be will come near to the other eight pound.

The mistress of this school, shocked to discover that Anne had guaranteed fees of no more than £20 apiece, was at pains to stress that her school was not short of pupils and that many girls paid £20 for board alone, without additional tuition:

she saith she hath now twenty gentlewomen boarders, and half as many more ladies and gentlewomen's daughters come forth of the town and cloisters, for she hath none but such for the meaner sort are not able to reach her rate. She doth protest she hath twenty pounds a year of some that be in her house besides music, but she saith she will set her least rates unto me, as I know she hath of my own kindred which I placed with her four years ago.

The adolescent Ferrers' daughter in question was to receive an education in the social graces most in demand at that time. There is little hint of her learning there how to become a competent mistress of a household or, on the other hand, of her learning to use her mind. Girls' boarding academies were already set in the mould of social finishing schools.[11]

There may have been other girls' boarding establishments in the sixteenth century but, in truth, they appear to have been more characteristic of the seventeenth and eighteenth centuries. In 1617 there was a Ladies' Hall at Deptford: the pupils were taught needlework and produced a masque at court. Dancing and masquing were to become especially fashionable subjects because of the interest in them displayed by Queen Henrietta Maria in the 1620s and 30s. In 1628 we read of Mrs Freind's school at Stepney, where fees of £21 per annum were paid for tuition in writing, needlework and music. By the 1630s the Hackney boarding schools were already well known. In 1667 Samuel Pepys visited Hackney and commented upon the appearance of the young ladies. Hackney academies offered tuition in calligraphy, accounts, cookery, housewifery, music, dancing and sewing. Each of the Hackney schools appears to have had its own distinctive clientele: for instance, Mrs Crittenden's school was patronised by the Court of Aldermen in the interests of their orphan wards and Mrs Slater's school was favoured by the daughters of Hull merchants. Another district within the metropolis which attracted the foundation of fashionable boarding schools was Putney. In 1649 John Evelyn made a special trip by barge to see 'the schools and colleges of the young gentlewomen' in Putney. In 1682 eight-year-old Molly Verney was sent to board at a school in Chelsea.[12]

If London was the natural centre for fashionable finishing schools, there was still room for expansion in the provinces after the Restoration. Oxford supported two girls' boarding schools in the 1670s. From 1638 until 1673 Mrs Parnell Amye ran a boarding school in Manchester, charging £11 per annum. Pupils who wished to study additional subjects – such as writing, dancing and music – paid a separate fee. The core of the curriculum was reading and needlework. In 1680 Mrs Frankland founded a boarding school in Manchester for the daughters of dissenters. It was still in existence in 1714. In 1641 there was a girls' school at Exeter. In Leicester in 1687 it was the wife of the grammar school master, Mrs Angell, who taught gentlewomen scholars. References to such schools only occur incidentally in collections of correspondence, diaries and autobiographies but they do occur in sufficiently great numbers for us to suspect that every town of any size had a girls' academy by the mid seventeenth century.[13]

The frivolous character of the boarding schools met with some criticism during the later seventeenth century. In part this was expressed in Utopian schemes for religious schools for girls. Mary Astell in her *Serious Proposal* suggested such a school for the better training of female teachers. On a more practical level, the Quakers were at the forefront of the provision of schools for 'instructing them in whatsoever things were civil and useful in the creation'. By

1671 of the fifteen Quaker boarding schools in existence, two were for girls and two more were co-educational. In 1696 John Beller proposed a college of industry where both sexes would receive training in languages, science, industrious exercises and literature.[14]

In 1673 Mrs Bathsua Makin began a school for gentlewomen in Tottenham High Cross. She made the most of her earlier position of governess to the Princess Elizabeth (daughter of Charles I) to attract clients to her school. She claimed to introduce her pupils to a wide range of classical and modern languages, sciences and mathematics. Nevertheless, she continued to offer the usual curriculum of non-academic subjects. In point of fact she seems to have tried to show the relevance of modern subjects to woman's traditional role. For example, the realist approach of educationalists such as Comenius was employed to teach girls the recognition of medicinal plants and a knowledge of their usefulness. One of the traditional duties of the gentlewoman was that of tending the sick. Truly academic schools were probably rare indeed in the seventeenth and early eighteenth centuries.[15]

It is interesting to note that several prominent men criticised the type of education offered to gentle and middle-class women in the seventeenth century. John Locke saw the woman as the linchpin which guaranteed either the success or the failure of such projects of home education as he favoured – for it was the woman who, for the first eight to ten years of the child's life, would educate the children. In his view it was imperative that women should receive a better and more appropriate education. A woman must be taught such academic subjects as it was necessary to communicate to her offspring. In this view, Locke was joined by William Law. In fact, others adapted this view to apply to the female school teacher. From now on, a few young women would receive a more academic education to fulfil a particularly academic vocation.

Other notable male contemporaries – namely Daniel Defoe and Jonathan Swift – believed that a woman should be well educated and not simply ornamental so that she could be a better companion for her husband.[16]

In both cases it is clear that the interests of the woman herself were little considered. These views were dictated by a traditional conception of woman's role of domestic service – to the husband and to the children.

There are a few references to girls' schools which offered a more academic curriculum in the seventeenth century. Mrs Draper taught Latin, Italian and geography at her school in Westminster and Mrs Makin offered French, Latin, arithmetic, history, astronomy and geography. But such instances are more commonly noted in the later eighteenth century. In the 1760s Mrs Meribah Lorrington taught a small number of girls classical languages, French, Italian, astronomy and arithmetic in her boarding establishment in Chelsea. The

Abbey House School, Reading, began in the 1740s but saw its peak in the 1790s under Dominic de St Quentin and his wife. At this time there were about sixty boarders in the school. The curriculum included the three Rs, English, French and Latin languages and literature, history and geography and, for some, Greek and Italian. In 1796 or 1797 the school was relocated in Chelsea. Among its more eminent pupils were Lady Caroline Lamb, Mary Sherwood and Jane Austen. A school offering French, writing, geography and English literature in addition to the usual fare was run in Bath in the 1760s. From most such schools science was noticeable by its absence, however. Mrs Margaret Bryan kept a school in Blackheath (1795–1806) and at Hyde Park Corner (1815), where she delivered lectures on both astronomy and mathematics. She then moved the school to Margate. At about the same time the wife of J.B. Florian Jolly kept a girls' boarding school in Leytonstone, Epping Forest, with a curriculum modelled on that of her husband's boys' academy at Bath. This included arithmetic, geometry, trigonometry, astronomy, geography and general science. But such examples are rare indeed.[17]

We must beware of assuming that these more academic girls' schools replaced the traditional finishing schools or schools which taught exclusively domestic subjects. Of thirteen girls' schools before 1782 and twelve after that date which were founded in Chester, many fell into this earlier pattern. In 1775, for instance, Mrs Lucas taught both plain sewing and clear starching to her pupils, actually taking in washing and mending from the townspeople to provide the girls with practical experience. This was in sharp contrast to Mrs Tapley's boarding academy in Newgate Street, where paints, silk and muslin were furnished to those pupils who wished to work with them and could afford to pay. These schools have to be seen alongside those more modern establishments where academic subjects were offered girls. In 1775, for instance, Mrs Briscoe of Queen Street was teaching Latin or English in addition to writing, arithmetic, French drawing and music. In this school pupils had to pay extra if they wished to study needlework and embroidery, lately staples of the curriculum for girls.[18]

Although much work remains to be done on the provision of education for women and, indeed, on the role of women in early modern society, it seems clear that more schooling for girls did not mean more and wider vocational opportunities for women in society. In the eighteenth century women were as much restricted to a private, domestic vocation as they had been in the sixteenth. The case for a more academic education for girls rested on the grounds that well-educated women would mean well-brought up children and contented husbands. Although adolescent and young women were often drawn into the labour market prior to marriage, there was no concept of a vocational choice for women. The old maid was, indubitably, a failed woman by the standards of the day.

The extent to which such schooling affected women

It is hard to discover just how many women in the population as a whole could read and write; it is even harder to estimate how many of the literate had acquired literacy outside the home or even in childhood. Between 1580 and 1700 women appear to have been the most illiterate group in society, irrespective of class, when the ability to write is counted. Of female deponents sampled in Norfolk and Suffolk between 1580 and 1640 95 per cent could not sign their names. The proportion had declined only to 82 per cent between 1660 and 1700. 'East Anglian Women as a whole were no more literate, and had no more need of literacy, than building workers and rural labourers', wrote David Cressy. There does seem, however, to have been an increasing discrepancy between female literacy rates in town and countryside and, especially, between London and the provinces. By the 1690s female illiteracy had sunk to 52 per cent in the metropolis while it remained at the 80 per cent level in the provinces. By the 1720s the illiteracy rate in London was half what it had been in the 1670s. These facts suggest both that the metropolis was drawing into itself relatively able, well educated and adventurous women and also that there was sufficient educational provision for girls in the capital to make some real impact on the female population.

It is true, also, both that female illiteracy was being reduced over the country as a whole between 1600 and 1800 and that the differential between male and female literacy rates was falling. Between 1580 and 1640 there were approximately eight literate males to every literate female. By the end of the seventeenth century this ratio had changed to one of 3:1. The gap was closed further in the eighteenth-century. A nation-wide sampling of marriage registers in 274 parishes in 1754 showed that 60 per cent of males (from all social classes) and 35 per cent of females could sign their names. By 1800 the percentage of men who could sign their names was unchanged (60 per cent) whereas 45 per cent of women could now do so. Clearly female literacy was rising faster than that of men over the country as a whole and over all social classes. So we see that three out of every four women were illiterate in the early Hanoverian period but two out of three by the accession of George III.[19]

There was, therefore, some erosion of female illiteracy during the seventeenth century, especially in London, but a much more marked increase in female literacy during the first half of the eighteenth century. This movement accelerated still further in the second half of the eighteenth century.

Although educational provision in the form of schools was important in the war against illiteracy, these improvements should not tempt us to speculate that girls spent considerable periods in school. It was possible to learn to read well by the age of seven and to learn to write in a short period of private tuition. Moreover, reading and writing were both skills which could be taught by one literate member of a family or workplace to the others.

Many of the forms of school which we have discussed in this chapter obviously appealed to a much more restricted clientele than did the ABC school. Generally speaking, girls' boarding schools attracted daughters of the well-to-do middle classes, the professional classes and the gentry. As time went on the tradition strengthened and more and more parents from these groups sent their daughters away to school. Few gentry or bourgeois parents could afford to support their daughters through an indefinite period of spinster-hood. In the past they had sold their daughters to the highest bidders. Now they were hard put to bid sufficiently high themselves for the eligible males in society. A timely, brief and often minimal investment in an education sometimes appeared to be an appropriate alternative. At best, it might win a girl a husband; at worst, it might win her a means of self-support. It is hard to be precise concerning the level of investment necessary in a girl's education. The cost of sending any child to school varied with the type of institution involved. Excluding the cost of dowries (which a father would have been bound to pay on a daughter's marriage were she literate or no), it seems that Ralph Josselin paid approximately £6 a year for the support of each daughter as opposed to about £10 a year for the maintenance of each son. It was still less expensive to prepare a daughter for her future life and give her some formal education than it was to prepare a boy through apprenticeship. Josselin sent several of his daughters to boarding schools. In April 1656 Jane was sent away to Colchester for four years. Here, at Mr Piggott's school, she learned to write. She left at the age of 14. Her sister Mary boarded out with the minister of White Colne from the age of 10. Her sister Elizabeth at 13 attended Bury St Edmunds School, possibly along with her 10-year-old sister Rebecka. In early June 1675 both Mary and Elizabeth were sent to a boarding academy in Hackney. Perhaps significantly, Elizabeth lost no time in finding herself a husband – she married at the age of sixteen years and eleven months.[20]

Women's expectations

It would be pleasant to draw a simple correlation between the amount of education available to and received by women and increased agitation for a wider participation by women in public life. Unfortunately, there is no such simple correspondence. Curiously

enough, many well-educated women themselves deplored the ex-
altation of intellectual gifts over housewifery and motherhood.
Mary Evelyn is but one excellent example of such a woman who de-
finitely perceived a necessary conflict between learning and
housewifery.[21] No incipient feminist movement may be discerned in
the aftermath of the prominent role which women played in early
English Protestantism or in the civil war turmoil. In the years of civil
war and interregnum many women were involved in the separatist
sects, some even in ministerial capacity. Where participation in the
work of the sect involved family conflict with the husband (master),
the wife had to appeal for the right to decide how she worshipped
and conducted her spiritual life. This sometimes led to the breakdown of traditional family structures but, in general, the women
concerned were not intending to undermine the place of the male in
the family in any other respect. They were simply asserting that one
supreme Patriarch took precedence over a mortal patriarch. Where
God and man came into conflict, God won every time. Women, of
course, were especially active among the Quakers, who held monthly women's meetings. Nevertheless, the work which women performed within this sect was traditional – they were entrusted with
the spiritual care of other women, with traditional hospitality and
medical care.

The Civil War has been presented as posing a politico-religious
crisis for many women. At first numbers of women petitioned for
peace. This was a normal reaction to the hardships imposed by warfare, in the shape of the removal of their menfolk, lack of food and
provisions, harm to their houses and so on. Women had to find
some justification for their action, for men did not acknowledge
their right to petition on their own behalf. The women urged that in
time of crisis, *when the husband was absent*, the wife might speak
for the household and demand protection. Somewhat later, Leveller
women used both secular and religious precedents to argue that they
were citizens of the Commonwealth with a right to certain of its im-
munities and privileges. They did not, however, demand the suf-
frage or deny the essential inferiority of women. In 1653, when
Katharine Chidley's petition to the House of Commons was denied
'they being women and many of them wives', her defensive reply
was 'that they were not all wives, and therefore pressed for the receiving of the petition'. This response indicated an explicit acknowl-
edgement of the subjection of the wife to the husband and of the
contemporary view that it was the male head of the household who
represented the interests of the wife in both state and church when
such active participation was requested. The individual's equal
rights before God and the Law were different in kind. Only the
widow and, in certain circumstances, the spinster were in any real
sense independent. We are forced to the conclusion that these
women were not feminists, seeking female emancipation or a new

role for women. They had no long-term goal. They were responding *ad hoc* to a gradually unfolding situation. In neither case were women led to dream of a real public role for women.[22]

Constantly cudgelled by ideas such as those of Ralph Verney on the proper role of women, and brought up within an environment which assumed the inferior place of woman, it is not surprising that women were as yet unable to shake loose from the traditional conception of their role.

Good sweetheart, believe me a Bible (with the common prayer) and a good plain catechism in your mother tongue being well read and practised is well worth all the rest and much more suitable to your sex; I know your Father thinks this false doctrine, but be confident your husband will be of my opinion. In French you cannot be too cunning, for that language affords many admirable books fit for you, as romances, plays, poetry, stories of illustrious (but not learned) women, receipts for preserving, making creams and all sorts of cookeries, ordering your gardens and in brief all manner of good housewifery. If you please to have a little patience with yourself (without Hebrew, Greek or Latin) when I go to Paris again I will send you half a dozen of the French books to begin your library...[23]

In this atmosphere, some women resigned themselves to the fact that women were denied a public persona but argued that women should cultivate their minds in order to escape the monotony and indignity of the existence laid down for them by society. Through this means, women might be serious scholars. Hilda Smith argues in *Reason's Disciples* that this attitude offered late-seventeenth-century women two benefits: firstly, a personal haven and, secondly, an effective, long-term way of defeating the male argument that women were silly, idle, frivolous and irresponsible creatures. Dr Smith's thesis certainly helps to explain why it was that women demonstrated an increasing interest in academic education and intellectual concerns at a time when vocational opportunities were not opening up in significantly greater variety than in the sixteenth century.

Conclusions

It will always be difficult to assess what proportion of the female population of England received an education before the introduction of compulsory education: even more than males, women were excluded from those institutions which produced records. One is forced to be impressionistic. Yet there are reasonable grounds for believing that a much higher proportion of the female population was literate in 1800 than in 1600 (over all social classes and in the provinces as well as in London). For the middle and gentry classes, it was increasingly common for daughters to be sent away to a boarding school to prepare them for their future marriage and, in part, for the period of often enforced spinsterhood when they would have to be partially self-supporting. As the period progressed, the type of 'finishing' which girls required changed somewhat – the emphasis in such schools was no longer only on needlework, cookery, music and the three Rs but also on modern subjects such as French, geography, arithmetic and astronomy. Hannah Woolley, for example, produced books of direct use to such girls seeking positions as ladies' maids. Many of these changes were dictated by the views of men, who wanted more interesting wives and better educated mothers, or, occasionally, by ladies who wanted 'fashionable' maids.

Broadly speaking, the role for which middle-class and upper-class girls were being finished had not changed at all. And there are only rare exceptions to the rule that most early modern women were contented to accept this. Sometimes there were women who found themselves demanding the right to speak and to be heard, while simultaneously being dedicated to the conception of a male-dominated society. Above all, it was often difficult to reconcile inactivity and inequality in civil society with activity and equality in religious society. But it was rare for women to acknowledge this inconsistency, let alone to agitate for a social revolution.

The education which was extended to women was designed to fit women for those roles which men had designated as specifically theirs and which women implicitly accepted. It produced, at best, intelligent wives, who could converse sensibly with their husbands, run an efficient household, and bring up literate and moral children – or girls who could make an adequate living in the world should they fail to find a husband.

On the other hand, one cannot discount the possible long-term results of expanding educational opportunities for small numbers of women. In the later seventeenth century and in the eighteenth century, contemporary authors became aware of a growing market for publications specifically catering for women. In the 1690s *The Athenian Mercury* was established as a periodical. In the early eighteenth century another periodical, *The Ladies' Diary*, appeared. In 1714 Richard Steele published a collection of items of interest to women in *The Ladies' Library*. These publications were not, for the most part, aimed exclusively at a female readership but they found their natural audience among women, who were denied access to institutional education. Samuel Richardson's heroines, Pamela and Clarissa, who were well educated by the standards of the day, both appealed to and moulded feminine tastes, as did the independent heroines of Jane Austen later in the period. Women also began to form a large portion of the audience for plays and the many lecture courses offered in eighteenth-century towns. When Thomas Sheridan visited Edinburgh in the summer of 1761 he repeated his month-long lecture course on correct English specifically to meet the demand of the ladies. Clearly educational and cultural supply were creating their own demand.[24]

One might make a case for the expansion of women's education in the period 1600–1800, particularly with respect to the middle and gentry groups, and for the spread of literacy, but it would be unwise to suggest that this gave immediate impetus to a commensurate social revolution or even to a revolution in the expectations of women themselves. Many literate and able women were meeting the same fate as William Stout's faithful, invalid sister Elin, who 'was early confined to wait on her brother, more than she was well able' and who continued to do so through her unmarried life. Elin could read and her skills in shopkeeping were at least equal to those of Stout's apprentice. Stout was full of praise for such industrious women, who used their skills in the service of their menfolk, while pouring contempt upon his master's wife who 'was one who took her ease, and took no notice of trade or of anything but indulging her children'. While Stout approved greatly of the conduct of the widow of a neighbour in the early years of the eighteenth century, he spoke with regret of the education of her daughter: 'Her daughter Ann she educated altogether as a gentlewoman, and being her only daughter, humoured her in apparel and diversion without putting her to the exercise of husbandry.' In his diary, bad fortune almost always overtook such frivolous, idle women.[25]

Within the framework of the traditional role of women in the household, it was possible to accommodate all the new developments in female education.

Chapter 11

The educational scene, 1660–1800: an overview

For those historians who see the Elizabethan and Early Stuart years as marked by a large-scale revolution in the provision of and social accessibility of educational facilities, the post-Restoration period will always appear to be one of stagnation and conservatism, even reaction. In view of recent work on the period prior to 1660 this position is becoming increasingly untenable. It appears that the conservatism of post-Restoration Englishmen with regard to the provision of education was a continuation of pre-existing trends. The English élite were already reacting against the idea of extending an academic education to all classes well before the Revolution: the events of that period merely strengthened their conviction that a little learning was a dangerous thing in the hands of the lower social orders. Clearly also, some individuals were critical of the relevance of the classical curriculum to the needs of certain sectors of society. The interest in developing vocational and practical curricula which was certainly evident in the eighteenth century had been evident in the seventeenth century also. An overall view of educational trends throughout the early modern period has been hindered by the excessive periodisation which is rampant in historical studies. Few historians have crossed the divide between the Early and the Later Stuarts.

Declining interest in classical studies

The decreasing popularity of classical studies in late seventeenth- and eighteenth-century England and Wales is clearly documented. It has been called 'The Great Depression' in the history of Oxford: whereas the number of freshmen admitted during the 1660s recovered some of the pre-Civil War momentum, numbers fell dramatically until 1890.

1660s	460 per annum
1690s	310 per annum
1750s	below 200 per annum
1800	below 250 per annum

The explanations for this decline in student numbers have been various. While it is true that the gentry and aristocracy were no longer attending the universities in substantial numbers after the Interregnum, the decline appears to have been most noticeable amongst students who recorded their status as 'plebeian'. In the period 1577–79 some 55 per cent of the freshmen admitted to Oxford were plebeian; this percentage declined steadily and dramatically. In 1637–39 it stood at 37 per cent; in 1711 at 27 per cent; in 1760 at 17 per cent and in 1810 at a mere 1 per cent. These figures support the position that opportunities in higher education were shrinking for the sub-gentry and non-professional classes throughout the seventeenth and eighteenth centuries. Such plebeian students had still formed a substantial proportion of the serious-minded students who took BA degrees down to the end of the second decade of the eighteenth century (36 per cent) but as the century wore on fewer and fewer plebeian students graduated (11 per cent between 1781 and 1800). This may be due in part to the increasingly caste-like appearance of the clergy. By 1810 a full 29 per cent of freshmen were sons of clerics and 28 per cent of all bachelors were the sons of clergymen. These scions of clerical families dominated college patronage of both benefices and fellowships.[1]

For the poor boy the feasibility of attending university in post-Restoration England must have seemed increasingly dubious. It appears that it was more difficult to obtain private support to attend college in the first place. The early seventeenth-century tendency for fellowships and scholarships to be dominated by those with clerical and gentry origins was now intensified and, indeed, those places which were available to the plebeian students were of decreasing value after an age of inflation. It seemed doubtful whether a youth without clerical connections or good birth would find a benefice easily on emerging from the university. We know from Adam Martindale's diary that parents were becoming aware of the problems of a career in the Church well before the war. John Eachard claimed that the universities were producing large numbers of educated clerics who could not find livings: 'we are perfectly overstocked with professors of divinity'. But recent work indicates that far from the number of new ordinands rising, the number of available benefices shrank. In the archdeaconry of Leicester, for instance, a full 32 per cent of benefices were held in plurality by 1670, a percentage which rose to 49 per cent in 1750. This situation was fostered by the poverty of many of the livings concerned – a problem which the Cromwellian government had tried to address through a formal programme of union and division of parishes in the later 1650s. Whereas ordinands in the 1660s appear to have found it possible to obtain a benefice (a situation presumably attributable to the immediate shortage of ordained clergymen after the Interregnum and the vacancies caused by ejections), competition for benefices seems to have mounted thereafter. In the 1660s 91 per cent of ordinands had found benefices: by 1705 the percentage success rate had fallen to 84 per cent per annum. Moreover, the length of time spent between receiving the BA and finding a benefice had lengthened from six to eight years. The indications are that it was the sons of plebeians and the mere BAs who found it most difficult to secure a benefice. Stipendiary curates, largely paid at a rate of £30 a year or less, were drawn exclusively from among the plebeians.[2]

As career prospects for the plebeian student appear to have dwindled, so did college costs rise. In the late sixteenth and early seventeenth centuries the cost of supporting a commoner at an Oxford college had ranged from £30 to £40 per annum. This cost had risen to £50 per annum by 1720, to £80–£100 by 1750 and to between £200 and £250 by 1850. As the cost of sending a boy to Oxford had risen twice as quickly as the general cost of living index and wages index for the period, such a rise was significant for the poor youth in search of a career. When this rise in costs is considered alongside the decline in career prospects for the unconnected graduate, it becomes clearer why we see a marked turning away from the universities by such students. It is also clear, however, that we should see this development as part of a general trend which was observable already in the early seventeenth century.[3]

It would have been atypical had not this decline in plebeian attendance at the universities had repercussions in the grammar schools. It is well known that a sizeable proportion of boys attending the grammar schools were destined for the universities and for careers in the clergy and in what may be called the minor professions. It is entirely probable that the demand for a classical education in the grammar schools contracted dramatically as a result of contractions in the clerical job market. This may have been more particularly the case if the educated clergy tended to prepare their own sons for the universities.

In the 1650s it is true that the endowed grammar schools continued to retain the support of the gentry classes. For example, Pocklington Grammar School admitted 76 boys from the most important Yorkshire families in 1650. Oliver Cromwell is known to have sent four sons to Felsted. Inevitably, fewer educational bequests were made during the Interregnum but the absolute sum was not much below that of the late sixteenth century (1560–1600) and the rate of giving not much less than during the Early Stuart period. The real value of such endowments, however, had declined considerably.

During the decade of the 1660s such gentry support was less forthcoming. In part this may have been a reaction to the political turmoil of the preceding period. When Thomas Hobbes wrote in 1651: 'by reading of these Greek, and Latin authors, men from their childhood have gotten a habit (under a false show of liberty) of

favouring tumults, and of licentious controlling the actions of their
sovereigns; and again of controlling those controllers, with the effu-
sion of so much blood . . .' he may have voiced the convictions of
many of the élite. On the other hand, there were royalists such as
Christopher Wase who argued for the continuation of the classical
grammar school tradition and, indeed, for its expansion. Wase's en-
quiry into the condition of the endowed grammar schools received
the authorisation of the Vice-Chancellor of Oxford, who was influenced possibly by a concern for the lack of demand for places at Oxford and a commensurate decline in clerical candidates. The Vice
Chancellor of Oxford was also the Bishop of Bath and Wells. Wase
generally received assistance from the Bishops and registrars and
hindrance from the governors of the grammar schools themselves.
This type of evidence suggests that for everyone who sought the demise of classical education, there were at least as many who sought
to revive this tradition and to seek out the reasons for its decline.[4]

What precisely happened to the grammar schools in the period
1660 to 1800 is open to debate. A. F. Leach believed that this was a
period of degradation for the endowed free schools. Their numbers
fell alarmingly and many of them ceased to offer classical subjects at
all, being converted into elementary English schools. W. A. L. Vincent agreed with him that the eighteenth century saw the decay of
the grammar schools and sought the seeds of this decay in the seventeenth-century situation. The falling value of grammar school endowment; the corruption and lack of interest on the part of school
governors; the fall in demand for classical eduation; and the difficulties which the grammar schools encountered in adapting their curricula, because of their statutory provisions, all contributed to the
eventual decay of most grammar schools in the eighteenth century.
Competition from other forms of educational provision was, in Vincent's view, negligible. Alternative educational provision was not
sufficiently extensive to suggest that the fall in demand for classical
subjects was compensated for by a rise in demand for other types of
education. Nicholas Hans had argued that the eighteenth century
was an era of unprecedented experimentation with new forms of
educational provision – the private academy (often of a mixed classical, vocational and technical character), the dissenting academy,
and an increased reliance on the private tutor. Whereas Vincent had
accepted Hans's overview of eighteenth-century novelty, Joan
Simon criticised Hans's statistics (which were based on an unrepresentative sampling of entries in the *Dictionary of National Biogra-
phy* and an exceedingly uncritical approach to the reliability and
consistency of that work) and argued that those 'new trends' which
Hans espied in eighteenth-century educational circles were, in fact,
old trends. Richard Tompson concerned himself to show that the so-
called degradation of the grammar schools has been by no means
convincingly documented; that the grammar schools were in fact

adapting themselves to changed demands by attempting to be flexible in their curricula and provision; and that there is some doubt that the grammar schools were failing to fulfil the charitable intentions of their founders.[5]

There can, however, be little doubt that the endowed grammar schools were in an unenviable position in the 1660s and beyond. As we have noted in Chapter 9, the value of the endowment of most schools declined during the seventeenth century, due to a combination of circumstances. Even when the value of school property actually rose, as at Bedford in the late seventeenth century, school governors were not obliged or inclined to pass on the benefit to the schoolmaster. This situation tempted many schoolmasters and ushers to search for alternative sources of income. George Long, master of Solihull, Warwickshire (1663–68), was warned by the trustees 'not to admit so numerous a company of foreign children' that his attention should be drawn away from the education of 'the parishioners' children in school learning and that so far as to fit them for the university'. Early seventeenth-century statutes had also exhibited concern that the schoolmaster should not take in so many fee-paying pupils that the charitable intent of the foundation be defeated. The statutes of Steyning Grammar School in 1614 ordered that the school should admit no more than 6 boarders and no more than a total of 50 pupils so that the master might not 'be oppressed with multitude, and thereby not able to set forward and further his said charge to his credit and profit of his scholars: provided always that no child or youth, which shall be dwelling within the liberty of the said town, and shall be found meet and able, shall be refused to be admitted and received a scholar in the said school'. But such warnings and safeguards had limited success. Free grammar schools which had once offered free tuition to all now introduced graduated scales of fees: Bury St Edmunds Free School now distinguished between the sons of townsmen, who continued to receive free tuition, and foreigners, for whom fees were set [1665]. By these same new statutes an admission fee of 1s. was levied on all sons of townsmen, while foreigners were charged 2s. 6d. Schools offering free tuition to all were, however, relatively rare even in the early seventeenth century. A more common fund-raising device was that of discouraging the registration of 'free' scholars and encouraging the admission of foreigners. Boarding, which had been a feature of many early Stuart grammar schools, now received increasing emphasis. For example, in 1774 Dr John Washbourne, Master of Cirencester Grammar School, Gloucestershire, made it abundantly clear that he did not welcome dayboys from the town. By 1820 Bath Grammar School had no free scholars on its foundation and catered for some 70 to 80 fee-paying 'foreigners'. Boarders paid 55 guineas per annum and dayboys 8 guineas only. Other schools introduced higher admission fees (which could be levied even on free scholars) and a variety of charges to cover books, cleaning and repair.[6]

At the same time there appears to be evidence that the grammar schools were finding it difficult to attract such a monied clientele. One must tread warily here, however, because enrolments in all early modern educational institutions were subject to tremendous fluctuation – a school with low enrolment during one year might be full to overflowing the next. Sometimes this situation was due to a direct economic response but it also owed much to the absence of an established pattern in a schoolboy's career in the days before compulsory education for all. It has also been suggested that falling enrolments reflected parental revulsion against corporal punishment which was commonly practised in the old grammar schools. Objections to the use of flogging to enforce learning may be found in the works of such as Brinsley in the early seventeenth century but they are found in greater numbers from the mid century onwards. In the anonymous pamphlet, *The Children's Petition* (1669), a distinction was drawn between punishment by flogging for serious moral offences and indiscriminate use of the birch to punish stupidity. This view was made widespread by its adoption by John Locke in his best-selling essay on education of 1693. In the eighteenth century *The Spectator* published a number of essays on the subject, including comment by Richard Steele and Jonathan Swift. A former Eton schoolboy described the practice in the following way[7]:

Many a white and tender hand, which the fond mother had passionately kissed a thousand times, have I seen whipped until it was covered with blood; perhaps for smiling, or for going a yard and a half out of the gate, or for writing an O for an A, or an A for an O. These were our great faults! Many a brave and noble spirit has been there broken, others have run from thence, and were never heard of afterwards.

For whatever reason, some of the old free grammar schools were suffering falling recruitment, at least in some areas. What appears to have happened is that many of the schools could not attract pupils to take classical subjects. This led some of them to try to cater for a different clientele. In 1791 Oundle Grammar School had no pupils at all. The school was revived in 1792 when the headmaster offered forty-five boys (including twenty-one boarders) a mixed curriculum of classical subjects, geography, surveying, merchants' accounting and drawing. Manchester Grammar School appears to provide the perfect example of a grammar school which continued to prepare some boys for the universities but simultaneously offered a commercial curriculum. Between 1740 and 1765 it admitted 196 boarders and 477 dayboys. Of these only 100 (a mere 16 of them dayboys) went on to university. The majority of Manchester's pupils were drawn from the artisan and shopkeeping classes, with a smattering of boys from professional, merchant and rural middle-class homes. As a reflection of this intake, a high proportion of Manchester pupils went into industry and commerce. Alumni of the school between 1740 and 1800 demonstrated the same trend. A mere 14 per cent attended university; only 10 per cent entered holy orders. Successive headmasters promoted the study of mathematics, surveying and scientific subjects to answer this demand and, no doubt, to some extent to create it.[8]

By 1802 Bradley Free School had also assumed a mixed character. In that year the schoolmistress, Mrs Webb, was ordered to take into her class *all* children of the parish of four years of age or above and to teach them to read the New Testament. When the boys could read well they were to be handed over to the Master of the Free Grammar School for instruction in reading, writing, arithmetic, grammar and the classics. At Burton-on-Trent the headmaster was in charge of teaching English grammar, reading and classics and the undermaster taught writing, reading and arithmetic by 1814.[9]

A. F. Leach subjectively viewed this process of adaptation by the grammar schools as a degrading one. Certainly the grammar schools were denying the wishes of their founders when they sought to introduce a non-classical curriculum. As important, however, was the fact that the grammar schools were losing their classical clientele and trying to respond to the more immediate needs of both the artisan and shopkeeping classes and the prosperous middle classes. This can be illustrated by the case of Chigwell Grammar School, Essex, where, between 1724 and 1729 there were very few classics scholars. At Maldon, Essex, in 1768 the very few classics pupils were taught in the same room as the more numerous English scholars: by 1770 the demand for Latin had sunk so low that the English school alone continued. The same fate met the grammar school at Higham Ferrers. A rising number of grammar schools introduced non-classical subjects to their curricula during the seventeenth and eighteenth centuries, despite the legal obstacles. Unfortunately, we shall probably never know whether the English and commercial subjects offered in addition to or in place of Latin and Greek were taught at an elementary or a more advanced level. Early nineteenth-century examples, such as those above, seem to suggest the latter. Moreover, a number of new grammar school foundations made immediate provision for the teaching of both ancient and vernacular languages. For example, when Dartmouth grammar school was founded in 1679 it had two masters, one to teach Latin and one to teach English, navigation and maths.[10]

Adaptability had its dangers. If a grammar school attracted more pupils from the artisan and shopkeeping classes by offering vernacular subjects it stood the risk of losing those middle-class and gentry clients who sent their boys as boarders to the schools. Some historians have argued from the absence of gentry pupils in combined English and classical grammar schools that this in fact did occur. But the small numbers of boys studying classics in such schools may indicate not a falling away from the grammar schools for social reasons but rather an awareness on the part of the grammar schools that they could not survive with gentry patronage alone. No seventeenth- or eighteenth-century schoolmaster, after all, was going to kill voluntarily the goose which laid the golden egg. At the root of the grammar schools' problem was the falling demand for classical education. This decline in the popularity of the classics was, of course, relative. While it is possible to list the failure of some endowed classical schools and their conversion to English schools, it is also necessary to remind ourselves of those grammar schools which continued inflexible and prospered. A contraction in the number of grammar schools which offered an exclusively classical curriculum made possible their survival. Thus the song of woe sung about Brailes in the 1670s:

This free school was formerly a grammar school or for Latin, but since the wars learning declining and men's inclination to Latin; English is most taught and nothing above the accidence. The schoolmaster heretofore was either the vicar or vicar's deputy, but since the time of the present vicar who officiates himself but undertakes not for the school either the clerk of the parish or one but meanly qualified for learning hath performed it; the salary being too small to invite any one of parts to court the place. [£8 1s. 8d. p.a.]

was not needed at prosperous grammar schools such as St Paul's:

At St Paul's we teach nothing but the classics, nothing but Latin and Greek. If you want your son to learn anything else you must have him taught at home, and for this purpose we give him three half-holidays a week. Such was the information given to an early nineteenth-century parent.[11]

Similarly many of the old grammar schools continued to teach the classics and to attract pupils from the élite classes while also responding positively to the attacks on the classical curriculum current in contemporary society. Numbers at Rugby, for instance, rose from 66 in 1778 to 245 in 1794 at a time when the school offered a modified classical curriculum. The traditional diet of Latin and Greek was served, with side dishes of Biblical, Roman and English history, the study of Milton, modern geography and mathematics. As additional fare, writing, arithmetic and French were offered.[12]

What factors enabled some of the old grammar schools to survive and even prosper while others either failed completely or modified their character beyond recognition? Clearly the demand for classical education had not disappeared: there was still room for a number of traditional grammar schools. The question of which grammar schools were destined to prosper was less easily decided. The past history of the school was probably an important factor. Shrewsbury, for instance, had long been fashionable and large, despite a seventeenth-century deterioration in her reputation. Location was also important – Westminster and Merchant Taylors' had an inbuilt advantage in their metropolitan location, as did St Paul's. Grammar schools in other rapidly growing urban centres such as Manchester and Birmingham had a natural clientele. Both Eton and Winchester were destined to thrive, at least in part, because of their statutory and historical connections with the universities. It would be interesting to know how close a correlation existed between university connections (in the concrete form of scholarships and exhibitions) and grammar school continuance. Certainly the classical side of a school and its ongoing university connections were less likely to thrive once it ceased to support a graduate master. In Chapter 5 we suggested the importance of the schoolmaster in attracting pupils from a given school to a particular college. As we observed in Chapter 9 it became increasingly difficult for grammar schools in the post-Restoration period and in the eighteenth century to attract graduate personnel. Highly qualified masters flocked to the better endowed schools and fostered the university connection therein. The initiative and personality of individual schoolmasters was probably a determinant in the fate of many grammar schools. Wise decisions made by the headmasters of Manchester, Rugby and King Edward VI School, Birmingham, ensured the continued popularity of these schools in the eighteenth century.

The pattern appears to be one of the survival of the fittest – the larger urban or more fashionable grammar schools – and the decline or changed character of the weakest. A strong argument could be made that it was the smaller rural and town grammar schools which altered their character in the late seventeenth and eighteenth centuries – schools which had all along been less committed to the classical education of the humanist ideal and which had even in the early seventeenth century adapted their curricula to suit the needs of a non-élite, non-professional clientele. With the decline of opportunities in the Church, demand in such local grammar schools for a classical education all but died. Their already prominent vernacular bent triumphed.

For some members of society a classical education was still important and coveted. Perhaps two-thirds of the sons of peers attended the nine great public schools during the eighteenth century and approximately half of them attended Eton and Westminster. In the eighteenth century, 34 of the 47 ministers of state (72 per cent) had attended Eton or Westminster, 1 had attended Charterhouse, 1 Harrow, 1 Seckar's School Norfolk, 1 King's School Canterbury, 2 Dalkeith School and 2 the Hackney Academy. In other words 83 per cent of the ministers had attended one of the more famous English endowed foundations. On average these boys had resided at their schools for just over six years and a number had attended a residential preparatory school prior to this. M. V. Wallbank's work points to a political élite heavily influenced by the traditions of a classical education. There is, however, a certain circularity to his argument: would the 'great public schools' ever have been designated 'great' had they not been patronised by the social élite or been the producers of illustrious alumni? In a sense, such statistics do no more than confirm what we know already. Similarly, we are told that the classical education offered at Eton and Westminster fitted their pupils for their activities in government. Pupils were trained to be highly competitive, diligent and rational. They were taught to speak well, both through oratory and versification. But we are not reminded that these values were important in British political life precisely because they had, throughout the sixteenth and seventeenth centuries, been cultivated in her grammar schools. What we see in the eighteenth century is the self-perpetuation of a political class via the agency of the 'great public schools'. Both Eton and Westminster appear to have done this job efficiently.[13]

A classical education was still necessary, of course, for those who entered the Church. By the later Stuart period the standard degree held by a parochial clergyman was the MA. Whereas it is doubtful whether this meant that the clergy had significantly more theological training than their early seventeenth-century forbears (who more commonly had only a BA degree), it certainly meant that there was a continued demand for a classical preparatory education. It has been suggested that many intending ordinands received their schooling privately from their clerical fathers or from the local clergyman. This seems reasonable but is difficult to substantiate. The number of private classical schools sending boys to Cambridge in the eighteenth century appears to have declined more rapidly than the number of grammar schools doing so. As we shall see later it would be difficult to argue that such private classical schools were in direct competition with the endowed schools. Nevertheless, it does seem that the tradition of small private schools run by clergymen was continued if not actually expanded in the late seventeenth and eighteenth centuries.[14]

William Cowper's lines may seem to present the very antithesis of career advancement by education and talent:

Church ladders are not always mounted best
By learned clerks and Latinists professed.
The exalted prize demands an upward look
Not to be found by poring on a book.
Small skill in Latin, and still less in Greek,
Is more than adequate to all I seek.
Let erudition grace him or not grace,
I give the bauble for the second place;
His wealth, fame, honours, all that I intend,
Subsist and centre in one point – a friend.
A friend, whate'er he studies or neglects,
Shall give him consequence, heal all defects.

His intercourse with peers and sons of peers –
There dawns the splendour of his future years;
In that bright quarter his propitious skies
Shall blush betimes, and there his glory rise.
Your Lordship and *Your Grace*! what school can teach
A rhetoric equal to those parts of speech?
What need of Homer's verse, or Tully's prose,
Sweet interpretations! if he learn but those?
Let reverent churls his ignorance rebuke,
Who starve upon a dog's-ear's Pentateuch.
The Parson knows enough who knows a Duke.

In fact, however, 40 per cent of English bishops between 1660 and 1760 had attended one of the 'great public schools'. All but one had received sufficient classical education to attend one of the universities. Of these bishops 60 per cent held fellowships early in their careers: this provided them with the means of subsistence while they waited to be admitted into priests' orders, for which they were too young on graduation. A goodly proportion of these men possessed scholarly reputations to rival those of seventeenth-century bishops and it was through their educational interests and residence in the universities that they made the necessary connections which would help further their ecclesiastical careers.[15]

Unendowed classical boarding schools, often maintained by clergymen, were, as we have suggested, a continuation of early seventeenth-century practice. By their nature such schools were able to be more flexible in the matter of curriculum. They were established on individual initiative when a demand for classical education was observed. When there was no demand for what such a school had to offer, it either adapted or closed down. The existence of an unendowed school was a testimonial to success; none continued, as did many grammar schools, as memorials to failure. Hans divided the masters of these unendowed classical schools into two groups: the dedicated, professional teachers in orders such as the Gilpins of Cheam, the Burneys of Greenwich and Thomas Horne of Chiswick; and the resident rectors and vicars who performed clerical functions and started a boarding school to supplement their incomes and/or to educate their own children, such as Isaac Milles of Highclere or Ralph Josselin of Earl's Colne. The schools run by the former group tended to have the appearance of an established school and to be longer lived than schools in the second group, which might have no premises other than the vicarage and a life of only a very few years.[16]

Cheam School, of all the eighteenth-century classical schools, demands recognition. It was in existence by 1647 and was sending pupils to Cambridge by 1650: the school still exists and is the oldest preparatory school in England. It was already fashionable by the late seventeenth century. William Gilpin, senior, was headmaster of the school from 1750 or 1751 until 1778. He was a notable educational pioneer and during his time at Cheam introduced a new method of school government which experimented with student self-discipline. Boys were introduced to the world of business and commerce through the keeping of shops. In addition each boy cultivated a miniature garden, which he could will to another on leaving Cheam.[17]

Cheam and other unendowed classical boarding schools were administered by men who believed in the necessity of a classical education but opposed the methods of teaching used in the old grammar schools. On occasion, however, the teacher was not motivated by the desire to offer an alternative form of classical education. Isaac Milles, Rector of Highclere, Hampshire, began his school because he could not afford to send his three sons to a good classical grammar school and because some neighbouring gentlemen had asked him to prepare their sons for university. He attracted so many pupils that he could no longer accommodate them in the rectory and built boarding houses in 1794. Interestingly, his patron, Thomas Herbert, Earl of Pembroke, set his seal of approval on the school by sending Milles his three sons. So Highclere School became fashionable through the patronage of Herbert and sent many pupils to both universities.[18]

If large numbers still were convinced of the value of a traditional classical education for some at least of the nation's youth, few indeed shared the earlier view that a classical education provided the ideal preparation for all classes and the way through which the young would discover their various vocations. For Sir John Eardley Wilmot, Chief Justice of the Common Pleas in the eighteenth century, a humanist education was in no sense vocational.

Obedience is one of the capital benefits arising from a public education, for though I am very desirous of having young minds impregnated with classical knowledge, from the pleasure I have derived from it, as well as the utility of it in all stations of life, yet it is but a secondary benefit in my estimation of education; for to break the natural ferocity of human nature, to subdue the passions and to impress the principles of religion and morality, and give habits of obedience and subordination to paternal as well as political authority, is the first object to be attended to by all schoolmasters who know their duty.

Yet not all saw education chiefly as a vehicle of social control. As early as 1646 the *Moderate Intelligencer* had argued for a more directly vocational education even for state servants. It urged turning aside from ancient languages and concentration on 'maxims of state, skill in arms, . . . knowledge in the rational part of divinity and the laws of other countries, how to enrich their country, make great their prince, to discourse in public places of, and act as occasion, in these'. And John Dury had noted the need 'for furnishing each class with the form of education suited to its particular needs' and to oversee this attempt. The mid-century preoccupation with the uselessness of the classical curriculum culminated in the writings of John Locke in the late seventeenth century on the utility of learning. In effect, such suggestions tended to make more rigid the pre-existing social stratification of educational provision and to make social mobility more rather than less difficult to achieve. For the time being this tendency was obscured by the continuation of the six-teenth- and seventeenth-century practice of teaching all classes and all subjects under one roof in all but a few fashionable schools.[19]

The development of non-classical secondary schools

Unendowed academies which taught a mixed curriculum existed in all but name in the early seventeenth century. Because of the pau-city of early documentation it is impossible to say whether their num-bers rose dramatically after the Restoration or not. Increased con-centration on commerce and manufacture during this later period, however, suggests that an increase might be expected in schools cul-tivating commercial, mercantile and navigational skills. It is possible to describe the curricula of the eighteenth-century academies. Five types of curricula were offered: grammar; naval; military; commer-cial; and technical. For each of these curricula the clientele is easily identifiable: university entrants; naval and mercantile marine candidates; army hopefuls; business and law clerks; technical profes-sionals. In most cases this specific curriculum would be superim-posed upon a common core curriculum for all pupils at the academy. Some academies, such as the Tower Street Academy and Islington Academy in London, might offer all five curricula; others would offer a combination of three or more; still others would spe-cialise in only one course.

Once again, these unendowed schools openly criticised the teaching methods and curricula of the free grammar schools. They stressed the advantages of individualised learning, merit promotion, small numbers and direct methods. The majority of these academies were situated in or around London, although there were many academies in urban centres throughout the country. Most of them catered for a lower-middle-class clientele (teachers, artists, mer-chants, farmers) although there were a few élite academies in the direct tradition of Balthazar Gerbier's Academy – namely those at Hackney, Kensington, Bath and Ewell.

The contrast between the different types of unendowed academy is startling. Hackney Academy, for example, possessed large prem-ises, including a cricket field, and offered students excursions to study natural history and the opportunity to appear in theatrical per-

formances as well as an élite group of companions. In 1764 James
Elphinston's Plan of Education at the Academy at Kensington
advertised the school's extensive grounds, good library and garden
with allotments for each pupil as well as the wide range of subjects
available. Little Tower Street Academy, however, had a much more
comprehensive clientele. The school arose out of John Bland's tuition in commercial and vocational subjects: a classical curriculum
was added to please a wealthier clientele, which included one of the
sons of the Duke of Montrose, but the commercial/vocational subjects remained to attract boys from humbler circumstances. The
Soho Academy also catered for a commercial/business clientele
although it seems to have attracted future artists and actors (including Joseph Turner, 1775–1851) and to have fed their interests with
amateur dramatics. At Islington academy

Youth are generally boarded, tenderly treated, and expeditiously instructed
in the languages, writing, arithmetic, merchants' accounts, and mathematics, with dancing, drawing, music, fencing and every other accomplishment
requisite to form gentleman, scholar and the man of business upon the
most reasonable terms which may be known by applying as above: under
one general price, the whole expenses may be included for board, education
and necessaries, or otherwise a fixed price for board and education only . . .

Here the methods were geared to practical usage: for instance, boys
were taught double-entry book-keeping to a high level of competence. The Randall Academy at York offered, among other things,
to provide a boy with 'the necessary qualifications for the Navy and
Army' for a fee of five guineas (plus board and public schooling in
the common core). In Cheshunt, Hertfordshire, pupils were taught
French by the direct method from a native Frenchman. And then
there were the specialised technical academies, such as the Naval
Academy at Chelsea, which taught subjects relevant to a career in
the navy (mathematics, navigation, astronomy, geography, gunnery)
or the Military Academy of Little Chelsea, which concentrated on
military subjects. The masters of many of these schools, however,
did include an education in vernacular subjects for all students. Still
other academies specialised in commercial subjects: the City Commercial School and the Newcastle upon Tyne Mathematical School
are representative.[20]

Distinct from the academies were the activities of private masters, some of whom also ran academies, who gave tuition in particular subjects, often in the pupil's own home. Chiefly, such masters
tutored in writing, mathematics and foreign languages (especially
French) and were concentrated in the towns. It used to be thought
that the popularity of French dated from the years of the French
Revolution, after which may Frenchmen were exiled in Britain and
made a living through teaching. Derek Robson has shown, however,
that in Cheshire Frenchmen were teaching their language long be-

fore the Revolution. For instance the *Courant* of 5 November 1751 carried the following advertisement:

Monsieur Reillie, lately from Paris, begs leave to inform the public, that he intends to teach the French tongue, in a method the most concise and intelligent, that has hitherto been practised, with due accent as spoke by the nobility in Paris and Blois. Attendance will be given at the Widow Shereman's, stay-maker, in Bridge Street, Chester, from nine to eleven in the forenoon, and from two to four in the after; the other hours he reserves for the use of such gentlemen and ladies as choose to be taught in their own houses.

Monsieur de St Marie was offering French lessons in Eastgate Street, Chester, in 1755. By 1790 five private academies were employing Frenchmen to teach the language and Macclesfield Grammar School employed a native teacher of French. All this was in addition to the growing number of schools which offered French taught by Englishmen.[21]

Whereas by the later seventeenth century and certainly by the eighteenth century the concept of a continuous and graded school career had caught hold in the grammar schools, the academies still functioned on the older model. A youth might attend an academy for a couple of years and acquire given skills at his own pace. It seems that many pupils were of above conventional school age. Some of the academies and private teachers deliberately appealed to an adult clientele. For instance, Mr Sproston of Chester had taught writing, mathematics, merchants' accounts, mensuration, trigonometry and navigation between 7 p.m. and 9 p.m. in the 1780s. He was appealing to young men seeking better opportunities in trade and shipping. Some of the courses offered might be regarded less as vocational training and more as cultural enrichment. Into this bracket probably fall the science lectures and classes which seem to have become popular from the 1690s onwards in London and many provincial cities. For example, Dr John Theophilus Desaguliers (an Anglican clergyman and a leading Mason) lectured in London on mathematics and natural philosophy from 1712 to 1744. A course covering mechanics, hydrostatics, pneumatics and optics was delivered by him on Monday evenings during 1724 and 1725 at a cost of two and a half guineas. In 1774 Dr Bryan Higgins gave a three-month course in practical chemistry in Soho. Such courses also found popularity in the new industrial centres and in market towns and ports. James Jurin lectured on natural philosophy in Newcastle upon Tyne between 1709 and 1715. Lectures in mathematics were delivered in Manchester in 1719. Philosophical lectures took place in Birmingham in 1747 and 1750 and even Scarborough had its chemistry course in 1733. Such courses multiplied in the second half of the eighteenth century. The fees charged suggest a largely middle-class audience.[22]

The diary of Richard Kay, son of a Lancashire physician and surgeon, indicates the impact which such lecture courses might have upon the members of the middle class. Richard Kay began his diary in 1737 at the age of twenty-one when he was searching for his vocation. He was drawn to the dissenting ministry, although forced by circumstance to assist his father as local physician at Baldingstone. It was not until 1743 that Richard Kay decided instead to train to become a surgeon at Guy's Hospital, London. Kay was somewhat resentful at having had his own educational career cut off early by his father: in 1737 he noted that a schoolfellow of his had been sent to Glasgow university and 'for my part I cannot say but that it occasions something of an uneasiness in my thoughts, when I consider him as one but standing upon a level with myself, and now so far outstripping and excelling me through his education in many amiable and desirable accommodations and recommendations...'. Meanwhile he sought to acquaint himself the better with his father's 'business and calling of life'. He shows himself treating patients on a day-to-day basis, conferring with his father concerning remedies, and spending time in his father's closet 'to get better knowledge of his drugs'. He became aware of his need for a knowledge of anatomy in April 1741 when he had to treat a young man with a dislocated hip and in March 1742/3 he attended an anatomy lecture in Manchester, having had his expenses defrayed by a cousin. Already in June 1742, he had recorded attending operations by Dr Taylor 'from London, the famous occulist, as he advertises himself. Lord, may I be an instrument of much good in my day.' But Kay also attended several courses of lectures in subjects less directly connected with his future plans. In the summer of 1741 he subscribed to Mr Hamer's ten geographical lectures; in February 1742 he attended Hamer's trigonometry lecture in Manchester; and in the summer of 1743, after he had decided to spend a year at Guy's, he went to lectures delivered in Manchester by the Reverend Mr Rotheram from Kendal on the nature of matter, the attraction and repulsion of matter (for which he paid a guinea), electric attraction, mechanics, the laws of motion, motion 'as to projectiles and pendulums', dioptics, katoptics, the dissection of an eye, hydrostatics, optics, pneumatics and astronomy. Clearly such lecture courses found at least a part of their clientele among the youths whose formal educational careers had been cut short by family pressures and who were forced to find a less conventional route to satisfy their ambitions. This was, of course, only part of the story, for there is evidence that much of the audience was made up of women.[23]

This is not to say that there were not working-class scientific and mathematical societies operating in the eighteenth century. Weavers, in particular, demonstrated an interest in mathematics: in 1717 the Spitalfields Mathematical Society was founded and this had its provincial equivalents in the Manchester Mathematical Society and the Oldham Mathematical Society, which, again, were largely composed of weavers. Such societies sponsored courses of lectures for their memberships.

The best known of the societies were, however, designed for gentlemen. Most reflected that interest in applied science which accompanied the Industrial Revolution. The Lunar Society of Birmingham, which counted among its members Matthew Boulton, James Watt, Erasmus Darwin, R.L Edgeworth, Josiah Wedgwood and Joseph Priestley, is the most notable example and the precursor (in 1775) of many similar late eighteenth- and nineteeth-century societies, which were especially abundant in the industrial North and Midlands. The contemporary interest in science both fed and was nourished by the establishment of public museums and libraries. The earliest known provincial public library was that created by Richard Greene in Lichfield. In 1780 the Scottish Society of Antiquaries founded that museum which was later to be known as the National Museum of Antiquities. Most significant of all, however, was the foundation of the British Museum in 1753 and its opening to the public in 1759.[24]

Dissenting academies

Up to this point nothing has been said of the dissenting academies, which to many have seemed the most novel and distinctive feature of eighteenth-century education in England and Wales. The dissenting academies developed for a variety of reasons, chief among which were the creation of Protestant nonconformity in 1662 and the consequent closure of the universities to dissenting youth and, secondly, the interest demonstrated by many dissenters in the provision of a realist education such as that prescribed earlier by Samuel Hartlib, Hezekiah Woodward, William Petty and Comenius. This latter interest seems to echo the much earlier interest of radical Protestants in the writings of Ramus. It has been said, therefore, that 'The Dissenting academies gave not merely an education to Dissenters but a "dissenting" education – an education, that is, which was different from that in the other schools – an education which became much broader than that in the universities and in the schools established by the law and controlled by the church.' This statement seems to be justified amply by the evidence but it does neglect to set the dissenting academies within the context of the other academies set up during the period which also kept alive the spirit of Bacon, Petty, Woodward, Hartlib, Dury and Comenius. Undoubtedly what set the dissenting academies apart was their function, at least in part, as seminaries for dissenting ministers and schools for the sons of nonconformists.[25]

The standard work on the history of the dissenting academies sees their development in terms of three main stages.[26] At first such academies were founded by ejected clergymen. They were generally small, with only one teacher and perhaps thirty to forty students. They provided the equivalent of a grammar school education for boys intending a professional career in law, medicine or the dissenting ministry. Such academies included Charles Morton's well-known Newington Green Academy, short-lived academies at Islington and Wapping, Mill Hill Academy, Sheriffhales Academy, Shrewsbury Academy, and the famous Rathmell Academy at Settle, Yorkshire. These academies were founded between 1663 and 1690. While classics formed the core of their curricula, these subjects did tend to be taught at an advanced level, when compared with the average grammar school. For instance, the textbooks used were those normally used in the universities, with the exception of the addition of the writings of Ramus. Moreover, modern subjects were taught in the schools, usually through a private reading/tutorial system. But science had a formal place in the core curriculum. Daniel Defoe recorded that he mastered five languages, studied mathematics, natural philosophy, logic, geography and history and read 'politics as a science', at Newington Green. At Sheriffhales Academy there was a common core of logic, anatomy, mathematics, physics, ethics and rhetoric. Students could specialise in theology, law or medicine. The teaching methods emphasised practical skills: for instance, students were required to prepare model sermons, write English compositions, compose almanacs, dissect animals, make sundials and perform land surveys. Naturally enough, these academies did emphasise their differences from the grammar schools when advertising their existence, but this information as to their curricula and methodology appears reliable. While these early dissenting academies catered in part to the needs of intending nonconformist ministers they also appealed to a more secular clientele. We know, for example, that the sons of knights, gentlemen and nobility attended Newington Green. Samuel Wesley's description of it makes it sound remarkably like Hackney private academy: 'This academy was indeed the most considerable, having annexed a fine garden, bowling green, fish pond and within, a laboratory and some not inconsiderable rarities with air pump, thermometer and all sorts of mathematical instruments.' Whereas the early graduates of Rathmell were few, the school expanded enormously during the later seventeenth century: of fifteen pupils at the school between 1699 and 1673, six became dissenting ministers; of 142 students in 1688, one third entered the ministry.

These early dissenting academies, like the unendowed secular academies, were the property of individual teachers. The academies of the second period (1691–1750), on the other hand, were generally owned by a church, a society or a fund, such as the London Congregational Fund Board of 1695. As a rule they were larger, with several specialist tutors. In addition their curricula were less classical and more orientated towards modern subjects although several continued as theological colleges first and foremost. That at Attercliffe, for example, became the Rotherham College and was later absorbed into the Yorkshire United College, Bradford. A good example of the development of one of these second-period dissenting academies is that of the Northampton Academy. This was founded in 1715 by the Reverend John Jennings but on his death in 1723 no successor was appointed and the academy (then located at Hinckley) appeared to have collapsed. Then, in 1729, a group of local nonconforming ministers assembled and decided to open the academy again. In 1730 the Reverend Philip Doddridge, an ex-pupil of Jennings, reopened the Academy. At first it functioned entirely as a theological college for three students (1730–32) and scarcely warranted the name of Academy. But from 1733 it attracted some thirty to fifty pupils per annum, bent on a wide range of careers, although numbers fluctuated wildly. The Academy was attractive to parents because of the excellent supervision which it offered and because of the low fees charged. In 1743 Doddridge drew up a detailed curriculum for the Academy. Its timetable indicates that the teaching of languages was relatively neglected here, although Doddridge attempted to rectify this situation in 1750 when he arranged that each boy would receive individualised teaching of languages by the direct method. The influence of the school was most felt in the sphere of theological education. Doddridge organised a syllabus of 250 lectures in psychology, ethics and divinity, delivered entirely in English. This later became standard practice in other academies. Students were taught a modified form of Rich's shorthand to facilitate their study. When Doddridge left the Academy in 1751, it was removed to Daventry under the control of the trustees of Mr Coward. The new theology tutor was Mr Caleb Ashworth. Eventually, after several other removals, Coward College was established in Byng Place, London, in 1833: students took advantage of the arts course taught at University College while receiving only theological training at Coward.

By the early eighteenth century dissenting academies had taken on the distinctive character of dissenting seminaries. They were controlled by specific denominations. They sought, through their curricula, to gear themselves to the specific needs of their sponsor denominations. While the academies of this period have been compared to the universities, it is more accurate to describe them as functioning as theological colleges which also provided an advanced modern education.

The academies of the third period (1750 onwards) may be seen as providing professional training of all kinds and a good general practical education for youths entering the world of business. The academy at Warrington, for example, attracted 393 students between 1757 and 1783. We know what courses were pursued by 196 of these students: 22 went into law, 24 into medicine, 52 into divinity and 98 into commerce. When Joseph Priestley taught at the school between 1761 and 1767 he further revolutionised the curriculum by introducing the study of chemistry, anatomy, history, geography, languages and *belles lettres*. The academy at Exeter was specifically created as 'a seminary not for the ministry alone but also for other learned professions and for civil life' and it offered a broad modern curriculum similar to that at Warrington. Because this was the period of greatest expansion in the number of dissenting academies, this development is of particular significance. There is a real sense in which the dissenting academies were providing lay dissenters with the university education which was deliberately denied them in England and for which they had previously had to go to Scotland. In addition, this type of education tended to perpetuate the principal characteristics of English nonconformity – an interest in practical theology; a rationalist approach to learning; a tendency towards experimental, empirical study of science. While there is a danger of our overemphasising the distinction in these respects between dissenters and non-dissenters, there is also the danger that we will ignore the possibility that such characteristics were not what drew men towards nonconformity but what a few influential dissenters (clergy and educators) sought to cultivate in their disciples.

Conclusions

The changed educational scene in post-Restoration and eighteenth-century England and Wales is characterised by the altered character of the endowed grammar schools and the rise of alternative forms of schooling. There was, in society as a whole, a declining demand for classical education. Such demand as there was was now divided between the conforming and the nonconforming communities. When the dissenters began to provide themselves with a classical education and to withdraw in great numbers from the grammar schools (which their puritan forefathers had patronised) this in itself affected numbers in the endowed schools. The contracting opportunities within the Church, the financial condition of many of the endowed schools, and the tendency of the social élite to patronise either a few fashionable schools (which were later to be dubbed the nine great public schools) or, in the case of the bourgeoisie, the larger, better endowed urban grammar schools meant that fewer endowed grammar schools than previously were able to maintain an exclusively classical curriculum and survive. Many were flexible and adapted themselves to the demand for a vernacular curriculum among their existing clientele. As we have seen this had already been characteristic of some rural grammar schools in the early seventeenth century.

Some few died completely. One may be less convinced than W. L. Vincent that the unendowed academies offered no unwelcome, harmful competition to the endowed schools. Any competition was surely unfortunate at a time when the total demand for classical education was reduced. Nevertheless, competition was not a new thing in itself. Most detrimental for the grammar schools was the decreased demand for classical education and the commensurate rise in demand for 'realist' education, which poorly paid, poorly educated teachers, bound by antiquated statutes, were ill-equipped to satisfy. While the grammar schools may well have contained within them the seeds of their eventual decay in the early seventeenth century, it is at least debatable whether they would have received nourishment in the eighteenth century had not social and economic conditions and developments in that century prompted contemporaries to search for a different type of education than that advised by sixteenth-century humanists.

It is probable that schools offering a curriculum of modern subjects rose in number quite dramatically during the years after 1660. Nevertheless, it is not the absolute rise in their number which must interest us most but their relative growth in a society formally dominated by classical grammar schools and universities.

Unfortunately, that other major concern of educational historians – whether there was as much educational demand *per se* and as much educational provision *per se* for the middle and upper classes in the period 1660–1800 – is incapable of solution in the absence of comparable statistics. It is true that many of the unendowed schools established during the period were small indeed, while attendance at the endowed schools and the universities also fell, but the whole story is not told unless we take into account the numerical expansion of some of the grammar schools and the emergence of some large dissenting academies and unendowed academies. In addition, we may at least speculate whether a society involved in industrial and intellectual revolution could have been less interested in education than its pre-industrial predecessor.

Chapter 12

Education for Scottish society, 1450–1800

While it would be foolish to superimpose twentieth-century awareness of nationality upon Britons of the sixteenth and seventeenth centuries, at a time when we know that allegiances were often most deeply felt for the locality or the county, it remains true that for much of the period with which we are dealing Scotland and England were not part of a United Kingdom in any meaningful sense. It was only in 1603 that the two kingdoms came to be united under the same ruler, King James VI of Scotland and I of England, and it was not until 1707 under the Act of Union that the kingdoms themselves were unified under a common Parliament and Privy Council. One of the basic assumptions of this book is that every society produces an educational system tailored for its own needs. It would be meaningless, therefore, to speak of Scotland, of Ireland for that matter, in the same breath as England. On the other hand, western societies in general and Scotland and England in particular did have many features in common and educational developments were frequently similar in outline if not in detail. For this reason it would be unacceptable, especially in a book of this length, to present a detailed parallel account of the development of Scottish educational provision alongside our discussion of English education. Instead, this chapter attempts to outline the general features of Scottish educational history from the later fifteenth to the later seventeenth centuries, underlining their specific relationship to Scottish society of the time and contrasting them, where appropriate, with features of English theory and practice. Then the chapter concentrates upon the development of Scottish education immediately before and after the Union of 1707. A succeeding chapter examines both English and Scottish universities in the eighteenth century and their relationship with contemporary society.

The apparent revolution in Scottish education in the sixteenth century

When examining the educational history of Scotland in the early modern period one is struck first of all by the apparent revolution which occurred in the context of the control of the schools and colleges during the sixteenth century. In the later Middle Ages there existed in Scotland several types of monastic school, some of which were cloistral schools intended for the instruction of younger monks (such as those at Dunfermline, Melrose and Holyrood) or priory schools which eventually also offered fee-paying tuition to sons of gentry and free tuition to the poor, and some of which were extra-mural abbey schools which catered more directly to the requirements of the citizenry. Simultaneously, from the thirteenth century onwards, we know that parish priests were offering instruction in the ABC and the rudiments of religious education within some parishes. As in England, the foundation of sees was of great importance to the development of educational provision. The foundation of eleven such sees in late twelfth-century Scotland heralded the emergence of cathedral schools, many of which appeared almost immediately. Initially, the schools were controlled by the Cathedral Chancellor and the master was appointed by and responsible to that official. In the fourteenth century Scottish nobles founded collegiate churches which in some cases made provision for the support of song schools, in which could be taught such grammar and song as was necessary for the performance of the Church's liturgy. These schools paralleled developments in the South and in other European countries. Those abbeys, cathedrals and castles which dominated the lives of Scottish townsmen also provided Burgh schools for the nearby citizenry. These Burgh schools generally remained under Church control until the sixteenth century. One is faced, therefore, with a Scottish educational system controlled and dominated by the Catholic Church.

Most of the education offered was designed to produce servants of the Church – both secular and religious clergy as well as youths in minor orders to say the Church's services, tend the Church's property and sing masses. The Church also responded to the demands of townsmen for tuition in basic literacy and grammar but maintained control. As a result, by the later fifteenth century there was a grammar school in every burgh of any size (judged according to fifteenth-century standards) in Scotland and, we have reason to believe, in many others also. For instance, the Burgh records of both Kirkcudbright and Kirkcaldy mention a grammar school in their earliest minutes (late sixteenth century) suggesting that their grammar schools were of long-standing existence. Yet the curriculum of even the Burgh schools was still determined by the requirements of the Church service. In other words, reading, writing and *spoken* Latin were taught. Thus in 1531 at Edinburgh, 'Master Adam Mwre, master of the High School, oblist [sic] him to make the bairns perfect grammarians within three years'.[1]

The history of the Scottish universities suggests a similar pattern.

Although some teachers in the monastic schools were capable of teaching scholastic theology, it was common for pre-fifteenth-century Scots to go abroad for their higher education. The flow of Scottish students to England was well established in the thirteenth century when, in 1263, Sir John de Balliol made endowment for poor Scots youths to be educated in Oxford and when, in 1282, his widow founded Balliol College for that purpose. Even during the Anglo-Scottish War of 1357–93 some ninety Scots obtained passports to study at Oxford without molestation. Yet more marked was the tendency of Scots to attend continental universities, especially that of Paris. The names of 400 Scots who attended continental universities have been recovered. In the year 1365 alone 81 Scots were accorded safe transit through England to study at French universities. In the early fourteenth century Scottish students at Paris were sufficiently numerous to prompt the Bishop of Moray to make a bequest for the support of poor Scottish students therein (although the existence of such a bequest may also have made Scottish attendance more feasible) and this was probably the origin of the Scots College at Paris. When we examine the composition of the English Nation at Paris in the late fourteenth century it is significant that of twenty-one members, nine were Scots and that all of these nine eventually became Scottish bishops. The universities of the Middle Ages were international bodies serving an international Church. The wars of the period were essentially dynastic as opposed to national struggles and conflicted little at all with the desire to educate church leaders.

In the fifteenth century, due to a combination of circumstances, the Scottish universities saw their beginnings under strict ecclesiastical control. In 1411 the Bishop of the Diocese of St Andrews granted a charter to the small corporation of clerks (eight ex-graduates of the University of Paris, under the leadership of one of their number, Laurence of Lindorcs) who had in 1410 associated to discuss the *Sentences* of Peter Lombard and other works of scholasticism. In 1413 Pope Benedict XIII confirmed the position of St Andrews as a *Studium Generale*. In the mid fifteenth and early sixteenth centuries the university acquired, under episcopal and archiepiscopal patronage, its three colleges – St Salvator (1450); St Leonard's (1512); and St Mary's (1537). Somewhat later, in 1451, the University of Glasgow was founded, 'to the end that there the Catholic faith may be spread. As well in theology and canon and civil law as in arts.' It was not until the foundation of the University of Aberdeen in 1494/5 that provision was made for the education of laymen as well as clerics in a Scottish university's foundation. During the fifteenth century the establishment of native Scots universities gained considerable support for two reasons. It was now much more difficult for Scots to travel abroad for their education (owing to the Scots-French alliance in the Hundred Years War). In addition, the conditions during the Great Schism, during which the Scots supported Pope Clement VII's claims and the English those of Urban VI, brought home to the Scottish Church the urgent need for a native bulwark against heretical beliefs and made the common concern for the fate of a universal Church a little less believable. Yet, despite considerable efforts to improve the organisation of the three Scottish universities during the fifteenth and early sixteenth centuries, the discipline within them was so poor and the curriculum and learning facilities so attenuated and impoverished that they became little more than preparatory institutions for the Continental universities which they had sought to replace. Aberdeen, for example, had no library collection until after the Reformation, despite the existence of its library building. The curriculum at St Andrews was a shortened form of that offered at Paris and that at Glasgow represented a condensation even of the truncated St Andrews syllabus. While the terms of the various foundations emphasised the importance of theological and legal studies, in point of fact only arts faculties were well established before the Reformation, with theology fighting for survival as a distinct faculty.[2]

This picture of educational provision dictated by the needs of the Catholic Church and controlled by that Church in its own interests appears at first glance to be in sharp contrast with the situation in post-Reformation Scotland. By 1560 the universities were almost totally emasculated, with very few students, buildings in ruins and severely plundered funds. The grammar schools were all in the hands of the burgh councils. The New Kirk and the civil government demonstrated a new interest in the power of education to do more than prepare youths for a religious or secular vocation in the Church. The energies of both Church and State were directed towards achieving a more or less universal general instruction in the rudiments of learning and the elements of the Protestant faith as a bulwark against the re-emergence of Catholicism in their midst. The belief that attack was the best form of defence showed itself as much in this respect as it did in the energetic training of young men for the Protestant ministry. This change of emphasis in Scottish education from the specific instruction of the few for the Church's service to the general instruction of the many for the defence of Protestantism owed a good deal to the co-operation between kirk and burgh. The programme for Scottish educational development set out in John Knox's abortive *First Book of Discipline* allowed for, indeed depended upon, the emerging power and independence of the Scottish burghs and parishes. While many of the weaknesses of Knox's proposal lay in this very reliance upon local initiative for co-operation in the provision and support of schooling throughout Scotland, there can be no doubt that the proposal acknowledged the reality of the fragmentation of the unity of the Catholic Church and the emergence of power in the burghs. It was sufficiently farsighted to see that any attempt by the Church to ignore political reality and ride roughshod over the needs of the urban communities in the race towards the establishment of a truly reformed Church was doomed to failure. This sensitivity to the situation owed much to the fact that the leading Scottish reformers were close to the hub of urban affairs and to the fact of the urban leadership of the Reformation itself within Scotland.

Continuity with the pre-Reformation period

This sharp contrast between the Church-controlled and directed educational system of the fifteenth and early sixteenth centuries and the system of the post-Reformation period, dominated by the burghs and the new kirk, is in many ways more apparent than real. The most misleading suggestion made in implying such a contrast is that change in the Scottish educational scene occurred as a result of the Protestant Reformation, which came late to Scotland and may be dated from 1560.

The emerging power of the Scottish burghs may be seen well before the Reformation. By 1464 the town council of Peebles had established its right to appoint the schoolmaster. In 1502 Ayr Grammar School, which was in existence in 1233 as a cathedral school, became a Burgh school. Already in 1516 the Edinburgh High School was being mentioned in the minutes of the town council and in 1552 its new buildings were made a charge upon the council. Similarly, the town council of Aberdeen funded the rebuilding of its grammar school in 1527. There was indeed, in many other places, an even longer tradition of burgh responsibility for the provision of and maintenance of school buildings. In 1522/3 Robert Christisoun was appointed as master of Stirling Grammar School by the town council. In Edinburgh in 1499 it was the town council which sought to restrict private teaching in the city: 'it is forbidden that any schools be holden by any manner of persons, men or women, under the pain to the holder of banishing this town', and in 1519 this admonition was repeated to protect the business of the High School, when the town records forbade citizens to send their children to any other school 'for any teaching but the grace book, primer and plain donat' on pain of a ten-shilling fine which would go to the grammar school master. In 1521 the town council of Aberdeen and in 1555 the town council of Ayr made similar moves to protect their burgh grammar schools against private competition. In 1557 it is interesting to note that when permitting David Elles to work in the city, the town council of Stirling stipulated that he should not be allowed to teach anything but the 3 Rs to a child over six years of age without the specific licence of the grammar school master.

At the same time, the chancellors of the cathedrals were certainly loth to see the town councils assume control over the schools. In

1418 the town council of Aberdeen appointed a master to the school but, as much as a century later, the cathedral chancellor was claiming the right to depose a teacher on grounds of unsuitability. Yet in 1523, during this squabble, the town council finally did establish that it alone possessed the right of patronage to the school and the right to depose inadequate teachers when John Marschel, master of the grammar school, confessed that 'he had the school' of them and sought the pardon of the council. But the Church successfully clung to the patronage of several cathedral schools: for example, in 1494 the chancellor of Glasgow was accepted as the patron of the grammar school. It was not until well after the Reformation that the Church finally relinquished all say in the running of the grammar schools.

Church control over late medieval education in Scotland was also modified to some extent by the interest in educational provision displayed by the Crown. King James I (1406–37) had wanted to create a national university by transferring the foundation of St Andrews to Perth. Moreover, he had asked both the governors of grammar schools and of St Andrews to notify him of particularly able pupils so that he could promote them in the Scottish Church. Later James IV (1488–1513) tried to improve the educational level of the nobility and gentry in the interests of the state by ordering in 1496 that the heirs of barons and freeholders attend grammar school and university. It is clear that this Act of Parliament was little observed and that it was not enforced (there are no records of fines collected under the Act) but it did introduce the idea of compulsory education of laymen for lay purposes and marked the first intervention of the State (as opposed to the monarch as personal patron) in educational affairs. In 1507 James IV brought the printing press to Edinburgh under the control of Walter Chapman and Andrew Millar. Among his other activities, James IV patronised Aberdeen University, even endowing a medical lectureship therein. His activities mark him as one of the new monarchs of the late fifteenth and early sixteenth century, the nearest Scotland ever came to having a Renaissance Prince.

It is also simplistic to claim that the Protestants were the first to attempt to educate the populace in basic literacy and the rudiments of religion in an effort to defend the nation against heresy. There are signs that Scottish laymen and churchmen were demonstrating the same critical spirit as their southern neighbours in the later fifteenth and early sixteenth centuries with regard to the practice of the Catholic religion. Not only the foundation of the Scottish universities (which were designed chiefly with the clergy in mind) but also the fostering of Bible reading and instruction bear witness to this. In 1543 an Act of Parliament gave authority to all lieges to possess an English or a Scottish Bible and in 1549 the Church provided for the instruction of the laity in the Scriptures and the Early Fathers. In 1552 it was ordered that catechisms should be issued to all clergy and to their congregations. In 1559 a decision was made to send non-preaching clergy to school to fit them for their missionary task in the parishes.[3]

Of course, much of this activity was defensive. Yet the fact that both Crown and Church did too little too late to save the Catholic Church in Scotland from schism or to satisfy the demands of laymen for an appropriate education should not obscure the fact that many of the features of Scottish education after the Reformation had been clearly foreshadowed in the preceding period.

The significance of the Book of Discipline, 1560

The most interesting statement of the Reformers' educational position was contained in the Book of Discipline of May 1560, which contained chapters on both schools and universities. Predictably, given the opposition of the Reformers to the religious life of contemplation, the Book of Discipline envisaged the parish as the fount of education within the state. In rural parishes the minister or his assistant would teach the young; in larger, urban parishes a special schoolmaster would be provided. It was assumed that only the urban schools would teach Latin grammar to a higher level but provision was to be made for brighter boys in rural parishes to attend urban grammar schools after examination. Similarly, a further test would control entrance to the universities. The motivation behind this scheme was entirely religious. As John Knox wrote in 1556:

For the preservation of religion it is most expedient that schools be universally erected in all cities and chief towns, the oversight whereof to be committed to the magistrates and godly learned men of the said cities and towns.

While the system provided for the elementary education in reading and catechism for all 5/6- to 8-year-olds, this was essentially because by teaching all children the minister or schoolmaster could assess the potential of individual children for the ministry and ensure the instruction of all the young in the rudiments of the faith:

the children of the poor must be supported and sustained on the charge of the Church, till trial be taken, whether the spirit of docility be found in them or not.

There is nothing here of the *right* of very child to an elementary education. Everything is related to the needs of the Church or, to a more limited extent, of the State.

This attitude to the utility of universal education is reflected in the curriculum proposed:

A certain time must be appointed to reading and learning of the catechism; a certain time to the grammar and to the Latin tongue; a certain time to the arts, philosophy and to the tongues, and a certain time to that study in which they intend chiefly to travel for the profit of the commonwealth.

The most remarkable feature of this proposal was not that it contained a movement towards the principle of a universal right to education (which it certainly did not aver) but that it realised that, in order to harness the potential of the nation most efficiently to the Protestant cause, the system would have to be highly organised and controlled. Thus the system is divided into clearly defined levels: schools in both urban and rural areas which will teach the catechism and reading to 5-to 8-year-olds; urban schools which also offer the rudiments of Latin to that age-group and Latin to those up to 12 years of age; colleges and high schools in the more important towns which offer Greek, Hebrew and rhetoric to older boys; and universities which provide an eight-year course divided into a three-year training in the arts and a five-year course of professional education. A system of ten superintendents is to be created to ensure that the schools and colleges actually function in the way intended. A system of examinations will control the passage from one level to another. These examinations were, of course, on the sixteenth-century model – being a certificate of the youth's suitability from his minister and high school master, for example, when the boy wished to move from school to university – but they were proposed, none the less, as a mechanism of control. Similarly, the passage of a youth from the arts course to the five-year professional training period (in theology, law or medicine) was dictated not only by his ambition but also by examination results. At St Andrews, for instance, the three colleges were to assume the character of professional training colleges – St Salvator's for arts and medicine; St Leonard's for law, ethics and politics; St Mary's for divinity (Greek and Hebrew). Within this new context the system of one teacher, one class made little sense. The generalist regent, therefore, was to be replaced by the specialist subject teacher. Salaried Readerships in Hebrew, Greek, Divinity, Medicine and Laws were to be founded at Aberdeen. No longer would one teacher carry one group of students throughout their university career in all subjects. The demands of the new society were too sophisticated for that.

The educational proposals outlined in such detail in the *First Book of Discipline* were, of course, heavily influenced by the model of the Genevan Academy. The proposal was accepted by the General Assembly but was rejected in January 1561 by the Scottish Parliament. It was never adopted by the Privy Council or made part of Scottish law and, therefore, had little practical effect. Moreover, it was not available in printed form until much later. Yet it is impressive as an expression of the educational thought of the early Scottish reformers. No English ecclesiastic or group of ecclesiastics ever sat down and planned such a rigorous system of education to serve the needs of the new faith before the mid seventeenth century. English reformers elected, or were forced, to adapt existing educational provision to serve reformed goals. Because Scotland's was a religious as well as a political reformation, ecclesiastics were at least placed in the position of believing that they could *plan* their Church.[4]

Despite the importance of the Scottish document as a rational approach to education which reflected the ideas of Geneva, we must reiterate that it was not a democratic proposal in the sense in which many educational historians have understood it. The reformers cared little for the *rights* of either individuals or groups to any level of education. They planned their education utopia from the point of view of the Church's needs. The provision of bursaries for the poor to attend university and train for the ministry or other professions must not blind us to this fact (impressive as may seem the proposed 72 bursaries to St Andrews, 48 to Glasgow and 48 to Aberdeen).[5]

Most certainly the document reflected the belief that talent and suitability for the Church's or the State's service were not attributes of specific social classes, but it is questionable whether this attitude marked a sharp break from that of the pre-Reformation Catholic Church or whether it was any more than a parallel to the provision for limited social mobility present in the English endowed schools. Its significance lies then in its rational, planned form and its assumption that a centralised institution should have the power to impose upon society an educational system which would serve its own requirements.

The detailed proposals made in the *First Book of Discipline* were abortive and it is difficult to ascertain what were its indirect effects. The system of parish schools which it advocated was never fully achieved; the burgh schools which it saw as the cornerstone of the scheme were, in general, already in existence before the Reformation; the rationalisation of the organisation of the universities was very slow to come into being. In the latter context we note that the first entrance examination was introduced by Professor Ramsay of Glasgow University when admitting students to his Latin class in 1878. The Scottish universities were slow to change the system of regent teaching; Glasgow brought in specialist subject teachers in 1727, St Andrews in 1747 and Aberdeen in the late eighteenth century. Significantly enough, the one Scottish university to be founded in the sixteenth century, Edinburgh (1582), as a divinity school nevertheless retained the ancient system of regent teaching and was not to surrender it until 1708.[6]

Moreover, to say that the New Kirk and the Parliament often expressed views and tried to put into practice schemes which were reminiscent of those advocated in the *First Book of Discipline* is not to say that this was because of the influence of that document. The preachers of the time shared the same assumptions as its authors concerning the relevance of education to the predicament in which the Church and State found themselves and these were, in fact, the common assumptions of Europeans belonging to the reformed churches. A sermon such as that of David Ferguson:

Our youth ought also to be nourished and maintained at the schools, and there out of afterward might spring preachers, counsellors, physicians, and all other kinds of learned men that we have need of. For the schools are the seed of the kirk and the commonwealth and our children are the hope of the posterity, which being neglected, there can nothing be looked for but that barbarous ignorance shall overflow all.

sums up the attitude of the New Kirk, an attitude which the *First Book of Discipline* reflected as well as nourished, and an attitude which bears as many marks of humanist and reformed influences as did that of William Perkins and the like in England. It does not surprise us that the Tounis College, Edinburgh was founded as a result of the persistence of the Edinburgh ministers, who led the town council, and that its stated goal was that of carrying out 'the academic ideals of Calvin in the production of good Christians who would also be intelligent and responsible citizens' and a sizeable number of ministers.[7]

Education after 1560: provision and purpose

We are able, of course, to trace in outline the progress of this educational effort in Scotland after 1560. During the remainder of the sixteenth century relatively little attention was paid to the foundation of schools. In 1579 the Scottish Parliament passed an act in an attempt to arrest the decline of the song schools, a necessary measure given the still alarming shortage of parish schools, but this had little effect. Despite good intentions, the Kirk itself was too preoccupied with the need to establish reformed churches and ministers to make the planning of schools a priority. There were unsuccessful attempts to persuade the government to divert monies arising from the dissolution of religious houses to educational purposes. The General Assembly also intervened to set up commissions for founding new schools in Moray, Banff, Inverness and Ross in 1563 and 1571 and in Caithness and Sunderland in 1574. In 1565 Master John Row was sent out to visit all kirks and schools in Kyle, Carrick and Cunningham. He was instructed to remove or suspend inadequate teachers and ministers. Several petitions were received for permission to found new schools with the rents of the old Kirk. There were a few individual endowments of parish schools but, generally speaking, formal educational provision was neglected in late sixteenth-century Scotland.[8]

The seventeenth century, on the contrary, presents a picture of complaint concerning the lack of schools and of measures to correct this situation. These stemmed both from the Kirk and from the Parliament. In 1616 two Acts of Parliament were passed which expressed the anxiety of the state. The first Act provided for the establishment of a parish school and schoolmaster in every parish at the parishioners' expense. It also attacked the use of Gaelic and sought to enforce the use of English so that the 'irish language which is one of the chief, principal causes of the continuance of barbarity and incivility in the Highlands may be abolished and removed'. The second Act ordered compulsory education for children from the clans in lowland schools. No one was to be allowed to inherit property unless he were literate and well versed in spoken English. This reflected similar assumptions to those later expressed in the 1609 Statutes of Icolmkill which were drawn up by the chieftains of the Western Isles at the instigation of Bishop Andrew Knox and which stipulated that 'Every gentleman or yeoman within the said islands or any one having threescore kine shall put at least their eldest son, or, having no children male, their eldest daughter to the schools in the lowland and bring them up there until they may be found sufficiently to speak, read and write English.'[9]

Uppermost in the minds of both civil and ecclesiastical authorities was the need to unify the state of Scotland. This was not simply a conflict between the Protestant Lowlands, heavily influenced by English culture, and the Catholic Highlands, representing a native and untouched Scottish culture. It was, in a real sense, a continuance of the attempt by the medieval Church to impose Christian values upon a pagan society. In the views of many, Catholicism itself had become more paganised than Christianising. It had sought to convert pagans to Christianity by adapting and Christianising pagan customs and beliefs and had, in the process, become corrupted. The introduction of a new religion and a new political regime alarmed the Highlanders and Islanders and threatened the precarious balance which had been achieved over the centuries because neither was prepared to compromise with the old culture. Both Kirk and civil government were determined to bring the youth of the old culture into their schools and educate them out of the old ways into the new.[10]

Although there were certainly parallels to this situation in England, they were never so dramatic. While the government and the church hierarchy put more effort into peopling the North with staunchly Protestant ministers and encouraging endowed schools, the gap between North and South was never so sharply delineated as that between Highlands and Lowlands in Scotland. Strong as provincial and local cultures and ties were, and notwithstanding the difficulties which someone such as Samuel Ward had in making himself understood by his Cambridge contemporaries, by the later sixteenth century the English universities were already acting as a melting pot for diverging local cultures; some of the schools also exercised a wide geographical drawing power; and the court itself provided a not insignificant focus for aristocrats and gentlemen from all regions. Scotland, on the other hand, still retains an educational system which prides itself upon its localism: even today the majority of Scottish pupils live at home while they study. The task which faced the English, therefore, while similar to that facing the Scots, was, nevertheless, less intransigent and further advanced in its accomplishment.[11]

In 1627, the Commissioners for the Plantation of Kirks presented a report on the situation in 49 lowland parishes which suggests that the act of 1616 was slow to take effect. Of these parishes 29 had no school; 13 had one (although some were in danger of collapse) and 7 had two schools. When in 1633 a further act was passed to encourage the establishment of parish schools there was an effort to comply but the war and the accompanying religious troubles stymied expansion. In 1650, of 83 parishes in Aberdeenshire, only 28 had parish schools. It was clear that the local university had small chance of tapping the potential of the youthful population of its area when the provision of schools was so poor and geographically patchy.[12]

The Kirk as a whole and various of the presbyteries were concerned. In 1611 the Kirk expressed its dissatisfaction with the existing English school at Burntisland and ordered the foundation of a grammar school forthwith. When the burgh proved slow to act the Kirk resorted to legal action to enforce its order. In 1638 the Presbytery of Glasgow was urging that more schools be built. It petitioned Parliament in 1641 to the effect that schools should be ordered in all burghs and large villages. In 1643 the Presbytery of St Andrews analysed the situation thus:

that the woeful ignorance, rudeness, stubbornness, incapacity seen among the common people proceed from want of schools in lanward, and not putting bairns to school where they are – therefore it is ordained that all possible means be used, that there be a school in every congregation, and that where there is one already, everyone that hath children put them to school if past seven years old – if the parents be poor, that the kirk session take order for paying the schoolmaster either out of the poor's box or by quarterly collection – but if the parents be able, then let them be obliged . . . to send their bairns when the session gives order.

Certainly the Kirk made some endowments specifically for the better education of the poor, as at Stirling from the late 1620s and at Aberdeen from 1658.[13]

The municipalities also brought pressure to bear upon their inhabitants. In 1628, for example, the town council of Cupar ordered all parents to present their children at school early in the morning forthwith. In 1637 the council of Peebles threatened to fine parents who did not ensure their children's attendance.

In an age of change, Protestant leaders realised that it simply was not safe to leave the education of the young to the natural parents. Always one must recall that the ignorance and rudeness of which they spoke was essentially an ignorance of the Protestant faith and the cultural assumptions of Lowlanders. Between 1567 and 1707 statutes of the Parliament made it abundantly clear that the schools were there to inculcate true religion above all else. The Assembly Act of 1578 commanded parents to educate their children in Scotland and not at popish schools abroad. An earlier Act of 1567 had provided that the Church should license all teachers and an Act of 1609 stipulated that private tutors should be examined for orthodoxy. Throughout the seventeenth century the Church insisted upon its rights of examination and inspection of schools. In general, the burghs conceded this right, agreed to Church examination of the schoolteachers which they themselves elected and, on occasion, sought the advice of the Church when making an appointment. In 1690 the Parliament ordered all teachers to sign the confession of faith and in 1693 another Act gave the presbyteries power to try, judge and censure teachers accused of unsuitable qualifications or behaviour.[14]

It is indeed difficult to establish literacy rates in Scotland during the sixteenth and seventeenth centuries either on a national or a regional basis. We have a very few limited indications of the degree of illiteracy, which may be totally unrepresentative. In 1600 in Inverurie, 15 out of 16 burgesses who signed a contract did so 'by our hands at the pen led by the notary because we cannot write ourselves'. The 1627 Report of the Commissioners for the Plantation of Kirks, which covered 48 parishes, indicated that 33 out of 92 lay commissioners were unable to write even their own names. As these commissioners were representatives of the wealthier farming families this suggests that the rate of literacy in the rural community was not high. When in 1640 the Kirk Session of Dalmellington, Ayrshire, reported on the Solemn League and Covenant it maintained that 179 out of 222 signatories subscribed by proxy because they could not write. With such fragmentary and undifferentiated evidence it is difficult, not to say dangerous, to draw firm conclusions about levels of illiteracy in seventeenth-century Scotland. The most one can do is to draw attention to the *apparent* comparability of the 1627 figures for yeoman illiteracy with David Cressy's figures for yeoman illiteracy in England in the period 1580 – 1630. Clearly one should not allow one's prior knowledge of Scotland's relatively high levels of literacy in the late eighteenth and nineteenth centuries to colour one's impression of earlier literacy levels – proof is still needed. Moreover, given what we know about the provision of schools, we would expect that there would be a dramatic difference between levels of illiteracy in the towns and lowlands, on the one hand, and the highland areas, on the other.[15]

Late sixteenth and seventeenth century Scottish towns appear to have been well provided with grammar schools. Edinburgh, for example, had three, all with early sixteenth-century origins. Edinburgh High School is first mentioned in 1503, Canongate in 1529 and South Leith in 1521. Such schools varied in size. In 1587 Perth Grammar School had 300 pupils. The Royal High School, Edinburgh, was also large. Both Canongate and South Leith were considerably smaller. The curriculum offered was similar to that in English grammar schools. After 1560 first formers at Glasgow learned the Latin rudiments, syntax and moral sentences. In the second year they went on to learn from Despauter's grammar, Corderius's *Colloquies*, Cicero's *Epistles*, Erasmus, and Castalio's *Sacred Colloquies*. The third year saw more use of Despauter and Cicero and study of Terence's comedies, Ovid, Buchanan's psalms and the making of themes. In the fourth year boys studied Despauter on versification, Virgil, Ovid, Horace and Buchanan and learned to compose verse. During the fifth year Cassander, Cicero, Ovid, Sallust and Caesar were set works. The student learned to write themes in set styles. In this school he also learned the rudiments of Greek. There were, of course, differences between the curricula offered at various schools. At Aberdeen Grammar School boys were taught to converse in French. In 1574 French was offered at the Royal High School, Edinburgh, also. We know that Greek was taught at both Edinburgh and Glasgow and, from 1558, at Perth. In 1672 the Privy Council banned the teaching of Greek in schools and it was rarely taught until 1772 when the Royal High School won a struggle with the College at Edinburgh for the right to teach the subject. The use of Buchanan's psalms and other works distinguishes Scottish grammar school education from English but, generally speaking, both systems offered a humanistic classical curriculum with a strong emphasis on instruction in the Protestant faith. Scottish students spent as long hours in school as did their English counterparts. At Glasgow in 1595 pupils made a 5 a.m. start, although by the seventeenth century the day began at 6 a.m. and ended at 6 p.m. An hour apiece was allowed for breakfast and lunch. Pupils had a half day's work on Saturdays, with supervised play in the afternoon, and spent Sunday at school and kirk. The length of vacations varied: most schools (although not Aberdeen) allowed two or three weeks at Christmas plus a month for harvesting. Before 1600 half-holidays were few but they became more numerous in the seventeenth century. At Jedburgh, for example, school closed at 4 o'clock on Wednesdays and Thursdays and at 3 on Saturdays. As far as we can tell, discipline in Scottish schools was similar to that in the South. Some schoolmasters flogged boys. Others preferred to use positive methods of encouraging learning: by the late sixteenth century competitions were held at Glasgow Grammar School and the same was true of Edinburgh and Aberdeen by the seventeenth century.[16]

Before and after the Union of 1707: accommodating new realities

During the seventeenth century England was developing as a trading nation which challenged and eventually overwhelmed Dutch supremacy. Scotland, however, was excluded from this growing prosperity by the operation of the navigation laws and by the shortage of native capital. The leaders of Scottish society believed that Scotland had a historical destiny as a great nation and that this could be achieved by making Scotland self-sufficient and, moreover, by turning her into a trading nation on the model of England and Holland. In the later seventeenth century there were many attempts to foster new manufactures in Scotland through legislation and monopolies but this push for self-sufficiency was doomed for the most part by the lack of any expanding domestic market and by the shortage of internal capital. Scotland was unable to provide for her own needs and export manufactures. By the 1690s there was a realisation that the way to prosperity lay in a re-export trade; it was, therefore, absolutely necessary to reorder Scotland's relations with England. Through this realisation some members of Scotland's ruling oligarchy were led to support the idea of union with England and some to oppose it – but all appear to have agreed that Anglo-Scottish relations needed to be transformed to provide a framework in which Scotland could partake of the advantages accorded English merchants. In both cases it was acknowledged that Scotland's future prosperity depended upon her relationship with England, although some were uncertain that union would bring independence and prosperity in its train.[17]

The educational history of Scotland in the late seventeenth and eighteenth centuries reflects, not less than that of England, the need to accommodate new economic realities. Education, preoccupied before the 1640s with religious questions, was from 1660 onwards increasingly secular in emphasis. In this respect developments in Scotland closely paralleled those in England although often, as Donald Withrington and N. Phillipson have shown, in a distinctively Scottish fashion.[18]

There might be a temptation to assert that after the Union of 1707 Scottish education became secularised and came heavily under the influence of commercial needs. Certainly this would seem to be the case if one directly compared educational provision in, for example, Edinburgh in the eighteenth century with that in the same city in the early years of the seventeenth century. But the temptation to make this comparison is dangerous: as Donald Withrington has shown, an understanding of developments in the later seventeenth century is essential if we are to see Scottish educational change in its correct perspective.

In the late seventeenth century there was considerable dissatisfaction with the educational system as it stood. Preoccupation with proposals for more practically orientated education – especially for the poor – emerges as a feature of the Scottish as of the English scene. In 1633, for example, a spinning school was established in Peebles, although it was a failure. During the later seventeenth century it became common enough for the burgh councils to appoint, and on occasion pay salaries to, sewing mistresses – as at Glasgow in 1674. In 1641 the Scottish Parliament had proposed that each burgh should support from the rates a school of apprenticeship in the allied clothing trades. The proposal was again raised in 1645 but, as with so many other schemes, it was forgotten during the wars. When it was revived in 1661 it failed to take root. During the eighteenth century this tradition of industrial education was given practical manifestation in the work of the Scottish Society for the Propagation of Christian Knowledge, the Board of Trustees for Scottish Manufactures and the administration of the forfeited estates of Jacobites.[19]

Some provision was made also for education in mathematics and navigation. In 1680, for instance, the Trinity House of Leith appointed a Professor of Mathematics at a salary of £120 Scots per annum, to be paid from a levy of 5s per annum on shipmasters of Leith. In December 1695 Robert Whytingdale was employed by the town council of Glasgow as 'fit for teaching the art of navigation, book-keeping, arithmetic and writing'. He held this post until 1704. Glasgow again appointed a teacher for these subjects in 1710. In 1700 the Glasgow Synod's report on education in its constituent presbyteries indicated the precarious nature of the parish system, the poor quality of teaching in the schools, the irrelevance of the grammar school curriculum to the needs of the community at large, and the desire to place the emphasis squarely upon arithmetic, geometry, music and history as opposed to the classics. Even the rural presbytery of Hamilton favoured increased concentration on the vernacular in the schooling system.[20]

In the light of the evidence available, it is apparent that the practical and commercial bent of Scottish education in the eighteenth century was not a consequence of the Union as such but part of a continuing and intensifying tradition. Mid and late seventeenth century Scotsmen were subject to the same disillusionment with the classical curriculum as their English contemporaries. This disillusionment was fuelled further by a consciousness of Scotland's economic impoverishment.

Detailed studies of education in eighteenth-century Scotland are for the most part wanting but work on Edinburgh and more general information regarding the country as a whole permits us to sketch in the line of development after 1700. The burgh schools of the smaller towns were introducing modern subjects into their curricula during the first half of the century. Navigation and book-keeping were taught at Ayr and Dunbar in 1721, at Stirling in 1728 and at Perth in 1729; mathematics and geography also appeared on their curricula. Significantly, an assistant at Ayr in 1729 explained the need for instruments in mathematics and geography to the town council – they were 'highly necessary for forming the man of business'. 'As the world now goes' he argued, 'the mathematical part of learning is a principal part of a gentleman's education'. Doubtless these new subjects were added in order to maintain enrolments and, as a result, salaries. The larger and better established burgh schools, however, retained their exclusively classical curricula and offered additional subjects as *extras* if at all. In some of the larger burghs private enterprise offered opportunities for education in modern subjects both to pupils attending the burgh schools and to full-time private students. The real boom in such private education took place in the second half of the eighteenth century although there were considerable numbers of private establishments in the early century also.[21]

In Edinburgh the town council appears to have decided early that the high schools and the burgh-supported English schools could not satisfy the demand for education present in the town. A lenient attitude to private schools enabled them to flourish. One argument which has been put forward to explain the lack of an Academy in eighteenth-century Edinburgh has been that there was no need for an establishment on the model of the English dissenting academies given the enormous variety of private schools offering the same subjects and the same advanced methods of teaching. Between 1705–09 and 1775 the number of private masters teaching reading, writing and arithmetic in Edinburgh had risen from 5 to 44. There was also a wealth of private schools teaching elocution, classics, English according to the new method, modern languages (especially French), arithmetic, mathematics, book-keeping, writing, music, art and design. Some of this new provision has, of course, to be seen in the context of the boom in Edinburgh's population, which rose from 25,000 in 1700 to 100,000 in 1800, with the absolute rise being greatest in the later century. Nevertheless, it cannot be denied that the sort of education offered was geared to the needs of a society absorbed with commercial activity. The simple arithmetic taught in the English schools and Charity Schools of the seventeenth century had been replaced by both theoretical and practical mathematics, in the teaching of which the vocational and real applications were constantly stressed. In 1705 the town council appointed John Dickson, merchant and accountant, as master and professor of book-keeping in the city. In 1706 one Alexander Heriot, a professional accountant, advertised tuition in book-keeping according to the new method and attracted a clientele of businessmen and apprentices. In 1708 William Beatt was licensed by the town council to keep a public school for writing and arithmetic; in the next year there is record of Ralph Morton's school for writing, book-keeping and both vulgar and decimal arithmetic. William Smart, minister, was teaching mathematics, surveying, astronomy, navigation and the use of all globes in 1708. Simultaneously the retired professor of mathematics at St Andrews, Mr Sandars, was in the city teaching 'mathematical arts', navigation, fortification and gunnery and selling a textbook on geometry, logarithms and trigonometry. Other commercial subjects, such as shorthand, were being offered by private masters as early as 1716.[22]

In other Scottish burghs, however, the teaching of modern and commercial subjects did not advance to such an extent in the private sector. In some cases the town schools appear to have departmentalised. At Ayr burgh school in 1746 there were three quite distinct streams – arithmetic and commercial subjects; classics; vernacular. By 1796 this situation had altered: all boys at the school were instructed in classics and English before proceeding to a mathematics course which was seen as a substitute for the university and was called an 'academy'. The establishment of academies, properly speaking, began in Scotland in 1760 with the foundation of Perth Academy after a report made by the town council on the English dissenting academies. This school was separate from the burgh school initially and was aimed at a middle-class clientele involved in commercial expansion. The academy movement was closely connected with contemporary criticism of the universities, rather than of the grammar schools – as may be seen in William Thorn's *Letter to J—M—Esq. on the Defects of an University Education and its unsuitableness to a commercial people; with the expediency and necessity of erecting at Glasgow an Academy for the Instruction of Youth.* In their early days these academies were seen as alternative forms of higher education – Irene Parker believed that this was the case in England also as the dissenting academy was, in her view, providing university level education. But by the 1790s in Scotland the academies (of which sixteen were in a flourishing condition) were providing an intermediate stage between grammar school and university for many as well as offering a substitute for further education for the middle classes. Some of the later establishments, at Ayr 1796 and Dumfries 1802, for example, were simply amalgamations of preexisting grammar and English schools and had small pretensions to being advanced seminaries.[23]

The Scottish Enlightenment

While the adaptation of the Scottish educational system to the needs of a new commercial society provides the historian with one significant perspective from which to view educational developments, yet another valuable approach has been suggested by some of the historians currently working on the Scottish Enlightenment. N. T. Phillipson's study of Edinburgh in the eighteenth century argues that the Scots were faced at the Union with the need to fill a vacuum in society.[24] Between 1707 and 1727 Scottish society was faced with economic depression and political uncertainty as a result of the dislocation of trade by war and English competition and the removal of the seat of Scottish government from Edinburgh to London. The greater Scottish nobility moved south to London, leaving their great town houses in Canongate to degenerate into slums. Their place was taken by members of the lesser nobility, substantial gentry and their dependents who either lived within easy riding distance of the city, rented town homes during the 'season' or lived permanently in the city. The outward manifestations of aristocratic society continued – assemblies, balls, salons – but the aristocracy had no institutionalised function now that there was no Scots Parliament or Privy Council. N. T. Phillipson suggests that the aristocracy/upper class solved their identity crisis by a threefold process: the emergence of a tiny and distinctive new élite of *literati* in the years between 1707 and 1727; the organisation of the landed classes along new lines and their assimilation of the *literati* during the 1720s; and, finally, the leadership of the aristocracy by the *literati* during the 1750s. The *literati* of whom he speaks totalled only hundreds in a population of 25 to 30,000; for the most part they were young – students, ex-students, young lawyers, ministers and physicians. They were often trained at the College: in the immediate post-Union period they tended to be Jacobite but by the 1720s they tended to be loyalists, trying hard to define the values of the Union and preoccupied with metaphysics, Augustan ethics and neoclassical literature. Significantly, they institutionalised by forming literary clubs such as the Easy Club (1712–15) and the Rankenian Club (1716–64). Their professed values reflected the wider scale of values represented in English culture. As the University gained an international reputation and as the *literati* produced leaders, the nobility and gentry found themselves eager to associate with this group. Already the Society for Improvement in the Knowledge of Agriculture was providing the oligarchy with a new identity and the *literati* assumed leadership of this society. Ironically, the new town of Edinburgh, built during the 1750s, was designed to house a society which was already well on the way to withdrawing from Edinburgh and moving south to London. Yet for a brief while the oligarchy, led by the *literati*, made Edinburgh the Athens of the North. In 1754 the Select Society was founded by David Hume, Adam Smith and Allan Ramsay the younger to discuss social structure, social progress and social criticism rather than metaphysics. In 1754 the topic of the modernisation of society was debated and in 1755 a campaign was launched for the improvement of Scottish society. For example, in 1755 the Edinburgh Society for the Encouragement of Arts, Sciences, Manufactures and Agriculture, an offshoot of the Select Society, offered prizes to encourage projects; in 1755 there appeared the short-lived *Edinburgh Review*; and in 1761 was established the Select Society for Promoting the Reading and Speaking of the English Language in Scotland.[25]

Seen in this context certain features of educational change in Edinburgh seem more readily explicable. Although the old nobility had withdrawn from the capital, their place had been taken by a new aristocracy. This new aristocracy had no *raison d'être* in government itself and sought a new one in cultural leadership. What we see in Edinburgh, therefore, is not only the intensification of interest in commercial education but also the expansion of what may fairly be called institutions of polite learning – fashionable girls' and boys' boarding schools; private tutors of modern languages; a college and a high school newly designed to produce an élite. Noticeable also was the dedication to making Scotland part of the wider British society and culture. In part this involved an onslaught upon the use of Gaelic and the Scottish dialects. In 1748 Mr Davies, one of the managers of the new concert hall and an actor, gave lectures on the reading and speaking of English. Thomas Sheridan lectured on the correct pronunciation of English in 1761. In that year a society for the English language was created which gave classes in correct pronunciation to both groups and individuals. These classes were taught by out-of-work actors and actresses. There was a simultaneous obsession with the eradication of so-called Scotticisms from speech. Appended to David Hume's *Political Discourses* in 1752 was James Elphinstone's first list of Scotticisms; it was followed in 1764 by another list in the *Scots Magazine* by Elphinstone and in 1779 by James Beattie's collection. Also part of the cultural movement were the many lectures on taste and composition given by Adam Smith. In 1762 Hugh Blair was made the Regius Professor of Rhetoric at the College, which constituted the first chair in a Scottish university devoted to rhetoric and to English literature. Blair was already a pioneer in the teaching of *belles lettres* in the College. Great interest was also shown in the arts. The foundation of the Musical Society of Edinburgh (1728), the opening of the concert hall; the establishment of a theatre; the foundation of the Edinburgh School of St Luke in 1729 (which gave potential artists formal training); the opening of the Edinburgh Academy of Design in 1760 and the work of Edward Graham's private art academy in the 1790s and Robert Robinson's lectures on perspective in 1757 may seem like reflections of developments in English provincial capitals but, seen in the context of the search for a *raison d'être* among the new Edinburgh élite which would not deny but instead reinforce the values of the Union, they become much more than this.[26]

Conclusions

This brief study of Scottish educational developments shows the gradual adaptation of the education system to an increasingly secular society. In the fifteenth and early sixteenth centuries educational attitudes and provision were shaped essentially by the Church but already the burghs were seeking to control education within their bounds. The Reformation, which greatly increased the power of the burgh or town councils, represented a dramatic intensification of this trend. Moreover, the Reformers were interested not only in educating personnel to serve in the New Kirk but also in educating laymen for lay lives. Given the poverty of the evidence, it is difficult to decide whether the result was a more highly literate populace than that of England. Certainly some relatively small Scottish urban communities were extraordinarily well provided with grammar school places. There seems little reason to doubt, however, that there were significant differences in literacy rates between town and country, Highlands and Lowlands, just as there were between different areas in England.

Because the burgh councils intervened so much in education after the Reformation, they were in a position to mould the educational provision to an individual town's needs. The case study of Edinburgh education provided by Alexander Law well demonstrates the extent to which an individual burgh was able to do this. The provision of schooling in Scotland depended not so much on individual endowment as in England as upon the initiative of the burgh councils and the New Kirk working together. During the later seventeenth and eighteenth centuries Scotland underwent the same revulsion from a traditional classical education as did England. Education was regarded in secular utilitarian terms.

Viewing educational developments in this context of the commercialisation of Scottish society does not preclude us from acknowledging that other forces were at work on the educational scene. During the early eighteenth century Edinburgh became the intellectual and social centre of the country. Focused upon Edinburgh was a movement to make Scotland a part, and a superior part, of the wider British culture. To eminent *literati* the Union was to be a vehicle for the elevation and not the subjugation of Scotland.

Chapter 13

Education and the problem of poverty

Earlier in the book we have touched upon the issue of the education of the poor. This is an issue warranting more detailed consideration if only because it demonstrates the use of education as a social cement rather than as an agent for change.

The problem of poverty

Recent research into poverty in early modern England has made us aware that there was no homogeneous and permanent class of the poor. Broadly speaking, there were two types of pauper – the vagrant poor (mainly able-bodied men) who drifted from town to town in search of relief; and the domestic poor, men, women and children who moved in and out of poverty depending upon the availability of work, their health and the success of the harvest, and which included that section of the community which always depended upon alms – the aged and the infirm. It is probable that more strain was placed on an individual's economic resources at particular points in his life: childhood; when he or she was left responsible for a large family; and in old age. Families with large numbers of children were particularly susceptible to poverty. The problem of poverty was aggravated considerably in years of shortage and in years of plague. High mortality and malnutrition can be shown to have been linked. Mortality was highest in the poorest areas of a town, due to a combination of poor hygiene, overcrowding, malnutrition and sickness. Prices were highest during years of bad harvest and the resulting malnutrition had a direct effect upon death rates and upon rates of conception – suggesting that whatever measures urban governments took to alleviate the effects of bad harvest or to isolate cases of sickness and thus protect the healthy were insufficient to prevent a direct impact on the total population in poor urban parishes. It is known that a dramatic fall in calorific intake has an enormous effect upon the sexual activity of human beings, especially females – until food supplies improved birth rates were liable to remain low.

The severity of the problem of poverty was in part a consequence of the inflation of food prices and the fall in real wages during the sixteenth and early seventeenth centuries. Agriculture failed to meet the increased demand for food from a fast-growing population. This was especially serious as more and more of the people were living in towns and unable to subsist from their own produce. The period was characterised by recurrent commercial depressions, particularly in the cloth trade which was so important in many English towns. In fact, the problem of poverty may well have been the most severe in the 1620s, when it particularly hit cloth-making centres in recession.[1]

There is some indication of an abatement of the problem in the later seventeenth and eighteenth centuries when rates of mortality were falling, when overall the growth in population appears to have been slackening and when urban governments were perhaps in more control of the situation. Agricultural production was also relatively increased. London, however, continued to experience poverty as an acute social problem throughout the eighteenth century – perhaps because she continued to experience heavy immigration at the same time that death rates were falling within her domestic population. Moreover London tended to attract subsistence migrants (the truly vagrant poor) in far greater numbers than did smaller English towns.

When we wish to examine attitudes towards and provision for the education of the poor, it is important to grasp this fact of the shifting nature of the poor population and the relative newness of the problem. The armies of vagrants and the larger numbers of able-bodied poor within the towns were a comparatively new feature of the English landscape – contemporaries associated them with the evils of enclosure, engrossment and the general depopulation of the countryside. Certainly the study of urban communities in the sixteenth and seventeenth centuries suggests that while opportunities for work in rural society were contracting seriously, landless labourers felt that their salvation lay in the towns. Work on the emigration of indentured servants to the Americas in the seventeenth century suggest that young adult males, often orphans, were worst hit by the economic problems of the age, for they had no property and no capital behind them. And the English towns really did not offer permanent salvation. Poverty became an essentially urban problem in its most exaggerated forms because of the drift towards the towns of subsistence migrants and because large sections of the indigenous population were frequently pushed into poverty by lack of work. Betterment migrants from nearby villages might also become 'domestic poor' when the improved economic opportunities which had lured them from the villages disappeared overnight. The settlement laws (reinforced in the Act of 1662) tried to redress this problem by making each individual pauper the responsibility of his native parish.[2]

Town governments were traditionally concerned with the successful regulation of the town's economic life in the interests of the masters. Only slowly did urban governors assume responsibility for sanitation, social and educational facilities. In most cases such responsibilities were thrust upon them. Although it used to be thought that most provision was made for the poor through private charity – Professor Jordan suggesting that only 7 per cent of poor relief was provided through taxation – it can be shown that in some towns, at least, 50 per cent of the provision made for the poor arose from the poor rate.[3]

Why did urban governors step in to provide for the poor? Clearly they did not do so simply because of a feeling of Christian charity. The orders for the poor in Norwich (1572) specifically attacked 'foolish pity moving many to make provision at their doors'. Some historians have believed that the motivation behind relatively systematic poor relief by the community was the preservation of social order. But poor relief was more customarily extended to those groups of the poor who were not associated with threats to the public order. It went to orphans, widows, widowers with large families, old and infirm men and women. Poverty itself was not a threat to order – riots and rebellions depended upon the leadership of apprentices and journeymen. It was these groups which the town governments had to satisfy and pacify. So, while the urban governments of early modern England regarded the treatment of the poor as part of a programme of social control, this was not necessarily because they feared or expected rebellion from that quarter. Early modern men were, as we have observed, obsessed with a view of society as hierarchical and delicately balanced – a society which was shaped by God and in which every man, woman and child had a rightful place. Within this perfectly balanced community there was no room for idleness, excess or rejection. The able-bodied poor should be encouraged to take up their rightful place in the *working* population; the unfortunate should be helped until they too could do this; the vagrant was to be reformed and, if he had no place in this community, provision for his rehabilitation should be taken care of in the parish where he was born.

Provision for the poor, therefore, was but part of a rounded programme of social control which concerned itself also with the position of the upper and middle classes in the ideal society. This society was in no sense a thing of the future, to be worked towards and achieved. Most contemporaries looked to a traditional vision.

The Elizabethan Poor Laws (1572, 1598 and 1601) were, broadly speaking, more concerned with the problem of controlling or reforming the army of sturdy beggars who migrated from town to town than with the plight of the underemployed, industrious urban poor or the sick and aged domestic poor. Sixteenth-century laws provided for the whipping of vagrants and their return to parish of birth. In 1662 the Act of Settlement formalised this system by insisting that non-vagrant migrants carry a certificate: potentially the town authorities would be able to distinguish between different categories of migrant when deciding whom to dismiss from the town's limits. In 1697 the system was modified further to allow for the positive channelling of migrant labour into areas in actual need of labour supply. Such legislation never deterred vagrancy and may have aggravated the problem considerably by forcing armies of honest subsistence migrants to keep on the move because of the reluctance of the towns through which they passed to accept any responsibility.[4]

The towns themselves were more concerned with the plight of their domestic poor. Underemployment as opposed to unemployment was often the problem faced by the able-bodied domestic poor. From 1547 onwards many towns had compulsory poor rates, although such rates were not introduced into some English towns until the early seventeenth century. Dole payments were made from the rates and from private charity. The sums awarded were not extravagant, being equivalent perhaps to the wages of a boy labourer, and they often supplemented existing wages rather than acted as a substitute for wages. These doles were made to only a fraction of the poor population. Amounts spent on such outdoor relief rose between 1600 and 1700 and more than kept pace with inflation and growth of population. Institutionalised charity was also offered to a percentage of the domestic poor – normally the aged and infirm and the orphans. For this small percentage the community became a substitute family. Revolving loan funds were set up in some towns and provided an important source of credit for town dwellers but their services were normally extended to apprentices and young merchants rather than to the true poor.

Communal responsibility for the education of the children of the poor

The community also acknowledged some responsibility for the provision of facilities which would prepare each individual to fill his or her preordained station in life. The concept of levelling or of offering impoverished children the opportunity for social mobility played little or no part in the thinking of contemporaries on the education of the poor – domestic or vagrant.

Projects for the education of the poor fall into two broad categories: proposals for academic education and proposals for practical industrial training. While one or other of these types might be dominant at any one point in time between 1500 and 1780, the co-

existence of these two ideas is at all times notable. Above all contemporaries seem to have seen the children of the poor as one group
– vagrant and domestic poor alike. The reason for this lay in the fact
that it was dangerously easy for any child reared in unfavourable circumstances to become a vagrant in later life. While this danger was
most apparent among the children of vagrants, it was none the less
present even in the poorer quarters of the town. Poverty was
thought of as a disease caught through surrender to idleness. Thomas Starkey commented in his *Dialogue* (1533–36) on the enormous number of beggars at large in England: 'As touching the multitude of beggars it argueth not poverty, but rather much idleness,
and ill policy; for it is their own cause and negligence that they do
beg; there is sufficient enough here in our country of all things to
maintain them without begging.[5]

Many early sixteenth-century thinkers felt that poverty was self-
inflicted. The tendency of the poor to idleness could perhaps be cor-
rected through the education of the young. Vives' work *On the Relief of the Poor* was written to benefit the people of Bruges but his
views were probably being discussed at the court of Henry VIII.
Vives' conviction was that the problem of poverty could be
approached via the careful education of the children. The young
children of the poor were presently villainously brought up in the
ways of beggary and prostitution. All refused honest work because
these two occupations were certainly more profitable. If beggary
were banned, orphans placed in hospitals and other children made
apprentices the alternatives to honest labour would be removed and
the work of moral improvement could proceed. Here is Vives' proposal for care of the destitute:[6]

let there be a hospital where abandoned children may be nurtured, to
whome appointed women shall act as mothers; these shall nurture them until the sixth year: then let them be moved on to the public school, where
they shall receive education and training, together with maintenance . . . . In
selecting teachers of a suitable kind let the magistrates spare not expense.
They will secure for the city over which they rule a great boon at small cost
. . . . I would say the same about the girls' school in which the first rudiments
of letters are taught. If any girl show herself inclined for and capable of
learning, she should be allowed to go further with it.

The belief that the educator might and should act *in loco parentis*
for the good of the state or the community was, of course, a persistent one in Tudor and Stuart England. Puritans such as William Perkins later disagreed with the traditional arrangement whereby children either followed their father's career or the path chosen for
them by their parents regardless of aptitude or preference. Education was in his eyes a process through which each individual could
discover his god-given vocation. Another puritan writer, Richard
Greenham, was aware of the sensitivity of the child to his or her en-

vironment. Both home and school could have a good or bad effect upon the child. In order to control the development of the child a deliberate policy had to be pursued – the child would be inevitably moulded by its environment and experience and, therefore, no education would be a corrupt education. Education outside the home was conceived of as a force for good, able to counter the evil influences of the poor home and to mould the child's character acccording to Christian precepts. Schools, as we observed earlier, were seen as socialising agencies with respect to all social classes. This function was seen as of equal importance to their academic function: indeed, in one sense, the academic programme may be seen to have assisted with this socialising aim rather than *vice versa*. This type of moral improvement was seen to be necessary in all sections of the community which deviated from the ideal – Roman Catholics as much as idle paupers. One thinks of the optimistic and strenuous attempts made by Jacobean and Caroline bishops to convert Roman Catholics within their dioceses. One recalls the insistence that all teachers should be of conformable religious opinions and unblameable life.

Some of the best examples of such a policy in practice are undoubtedly continental. While Lutheran reformers did not believe that man's nature was perfectable they were convinced that his mind was malleable and that education could be used to make a necessary impression upon it. Parish vernacular schools in Hamburg, for example, were used to indoctrinate both girls and boys in Lutheran beliefs, to teach them basic literacy, and to inculcate good habits. The radical evangelical Protestant community of the Hutterites, on the other hand, assumed total responsibility for the children of their members. Small children were removed from their parents and placed in communal schools where they were cared for by a few adults. Once the child was weaned, the community became his or her family. This community responsibility extended to the power of the community to remove a child from the care of parents who had been banned from the congregation. Some contemporaries found the Hutterite denial of the natural family offensive. For instance, Lutherans charged that:

The way of communal life in Moravia is an immoral one, and it is particularly cruel that they take away the young children from the parents and that they should be brought up alike in a common school, and that many children die because of hunger and other neglect. Summa, such a devilish communism is an impossible thing against all nature and law.

Certainly the training programme was rigorously prescribed and designed to fit the children for adult life in the Hutterite community. Instruction was provided in the three Rs and religion. Elementary education was extended to all children, whatever their station, but the ends of this education were narrowly religious. The physical and spiritual care offered was good and the attitude towards the children kindly. The Hutterite community was severely conservative and anti-individualistic. The child had to be taught to bend its individual will to the communal will. The Hutterite boarding school is an institutionalisation of the community.[7]

Sixteenth century Europeans possessed ambivalent attitudes towards the rights of the natural family and the responsibility of the community for the bringing up of the young. In 1525 the town of Ypres inaugurated an experiment in poor relief which relied heavily upon Vives' model. In 1535 William Marshall, a convert to these ideas, printed an English version of the Ypres regulations and in the same year drafted a poor law which made similar provision for vagrant as well as orphan children. Marshall's poor law emphasised the misfortune of the children of vagrants and the need to counter evil influences immediately, before the vagrant bred more vagrants. Significantly, the 1536 Act appears to have been based on Marshall's draft, even down to the wording. The parish authorities were now empowered to take vagrant children between the ages of 5 and 14 and apprentice them to husbandry and crafts. Adolescent beggars who refused to work might be beaten into submission. Unfortunately, this Act did not produce the desired results because householders were very loth to take in beggar apprentices. After a period of riots and unsettled conditions, the state proceeded to infringe yet more upon the parental authority of beggars. In 1547 it was enacted that children of 5 to 14 years should be removed into the care of the parish until they came of age – 20 in the case of females; 24 in the case of males. Any vagrant child who ran away might be chained and enslaved until the end of the term stipulated. Although the harsher aspects of this legislation were removed in the 1549 amending act, the state retained parental rights over the children of beggars. Later poor laws demonstrated the same feature. The revised Elizabethan Poor Law of 1601, for instance, authorised the churchwardens and the overseers of the poor to set to work and apprentice not only the children of vagrants and the destitute but also any children whose parents were deemed to be unfit to care for them. Of course, early moderns were accustomed to the idea of a child being separated from the family home at an early age and placed under the authority of another family. The experience would not be as traumatic as it might be today. Yet there was a distinction: generally speaking, sending one's child into service or apprenticeship was a voluntary act – for the beggar it was involuntary and unwelcome. Above all it leads us to speculate on the strength of the concept of community as against individual family in that time. Historians are accustomed to think of the poor laws as expressions of state control and state intervention. This is perhaps unwise. The Tudor legislation strengthened the arm of the parish community not of the State.[8]

The need for such intervention in defiance of parental rights seemed abundantly clear to most contemporaries throughout the sixteenth and seventeenth centuries. In the metropolis in particular, beggars, vagabonds, prostitutes and thieves banded together for common profit and protection. They formed a distinct community with special jargon and customs. The liberty of Southwark, outside the City jurisdiction, was a haven for the vagabond community, from which the beggars and prostitutes would sally forth into the City daily. In this environment a new generation of thieves and prostitutes was trained. Well known is the letter from Fleetwood to Burghley in 1585 which described Alehouse keeper Wotton's school for cutpurses:[9]

There was a school house set up [within the alehouse] to learn young boys to cut purses. There was hung up two devices: the one was a pocket, the other was a purse. The pocket had in it certain counters and was hung about with hawks' bells, and over the top did hang a little sacring bell; and that could take a counter without any noise was allowed to be a 'Public Foister'; and he that could take a piece of silver out of the purse without the noise of any bells, he was adjudged a 'Judicial Nipper'.

The outer suburbs of London, with their high concentration of poor, were known for their street gangs of children, who held travellers in fear of their lives and property. Contemporaries, justifiably or not, made a connection between crime and juvenile poverty.

A comprehensive approach to the treatment of the poor which acted as a model for official urban programmes elsewhere was that effected in London in 1552. The City took over the management of the four old monastic hospitals. St Bartholemew's and St Thomas's were to house the sick and the aged poor; Grey Friars (Christ's Hospital) was to care for the children of the poor, and Bridewell was to rehabilitate the vagrant and thriftless poor, young and old alike. In a statement to the Privy Council in 1552 the citizens of London declared:

And first, we thought to begin with the poor child, that he might be harboured, clothed, fed, taught and virtuously trained up

so that

neither the child in his infancy shall want the virtuous education and bringing up, neither when the same shall grow into full age shall lack matter whereon the same may virtuously occupy himself in good occupation or science profitable to the common weal.

Within this scheme Christ's Hospital would take fatherless children and children whose parents were not deemed suitable to care for them from the streets of the City, while Bridewell would offer both relief and technical education for older children with no academic bent.[10]

To finance the system the Committee of Thirty set up to manage the four royal hospitals relied upon personal subscriptions and upon an energetically pursued public campaign for funds. The Lord Mayor himself spoke at St Paul's; individual committee members approached ministers and churchwardens and asked them to elicit subscriptions from their parishioners; the message was reinforced by a printed pamphlet appealing for funds; householders were circulated with slips of paper on which to pledge their regular contributions.

When Christ's Hospital opened its doors in the autumn of 1552 it offered generous provision to some 380 children. The attitude towards the education of the poor orphans appears to have been influenced by the views of Vives, at least indirectly. All children would receive a basic education in the three Rs and a decision regarding their further educational course would be taken on the basis of their demonstrated capabilities. Boys 'very apt to learning' would remain in the grammar school 'in the hope of preferment to the university; where they may be virtuously educated, and in time become learned and good members in the common weal'. By contemporary standards the number of teachers was extremely generous. In addition to providing an elementary and a classical education, the hospital offered craft education for those destined for apprenticeship and some children attended Bridewell daily for vocational training while remaining in lodging at Christ's Hospital.

There can be no doubt that Christ's Hospital did much good but it could scarcely scratch the surface of the problem of child poverty in the capital. In 1557 it was forced to bar illegitimate children from its doors and later to limit its services to the children of citizens and freemen of London. In 1556 it ordered that numbers be limited to 150 infants and 250 school-age children. Effectively it became an institution caring for the dometic, responsible poor rather than the vagrant child.[11]

Bridewell acted as a training institution for the young. Its object was 'to train up the beggar's child in virtuous exercise, that of him should spring up no more beggars'. On Sundays the Beadle of Christ's Hospital combed the streets of the city and rounded up vagrant children for Bridewell. Many of these vagrants had been attracted to London by abundant work in good years, only to be left on the streets when the economy contracted, while others were the sons and daughters of vagrants. In addition, Bridewell taught some of the children of poor freemen and supplemented the resources of Christ's Hospital either by taking children from Christ's (four or five a year) as day pupils or by offering orphans from the hospital board and lodging in addition to training courses.[12]

The early London experiment was important and it was mimicked in several English towns. Bristol, Exeter, Plymouth and Norwich founded small orphanages and Bridewell training schools were attached to Christ's Hospital, Ipswich (1569), Reading Hospital (1578), St John's Hospital, Nottingham, and St Thomas's Hospital, York. As we shall note, hospitals again became important as a way of protecting poor orphans from the evil environment in Scotland in the late seventeenth and eighteenth centuries. They always had the character of havens from the cruel reality of destitution – hospices in the medieval sense of the word. As such they are representative of the early modern conception of the community as surrogate family, eager to substitute communal ideals for individual when a natural family deviated from the norm accepted by society.

It is true that a rather less institutionalised approach was also important. In 1570 the city of Norwich conducted a census of the poor which led to important orders for the poor in 1572 which projected an organised form of outdoor relief and education. While a compulsory rate maintained a few children and women in the Hospital of St Giles, where the young were taught their letters and work was provided for women and older children, the emphasis of the orders was on the provision in each ward of *select women* to supervise up to twelve women and children each in the domestic cloth industry at a salary of up to 20s. per annum. The children concerned were to be taught their letters as well as to work. The disciplinary control exercised by the select women was to be carefully regulated and supervised and only the totally recalcitrant were to be removed to Bridewell. When a child reached the appropriate age he or she was to be set to work or apprenticed. Another important part of the Norwich scheme was the absence of a test for eligibility for relief. The deacons paid out the dole at their discretion and they were empowered to help adults overly burdened with large families, families with sick children and so forth. It is debatable whether contemporaries doubted the desirability of institutionalisation of the poor child: probably the outdoor relief scheme was inspired as much by a realisation that the city simply could not afford to place all poor children in hospitals as by a belief that it was better to preserve the family unit. However, it is true that the Norwich orders were intended to tackle the social problems consequent upon a slump in the cloth industry and a desire to revive it and to help the domestic poor who had been hardest hit by recession. The poor children placed in the care of the select women, like the women, belonged to what one might term the respectable poor among which deliberate deviation from the community ideal was not necessarily suspected. Urban schemes such as those of Norwich do represent a growing awareness that the idleness and poverty of the poor were not always self-inflicted. Unfortunately for the success of outdoor relief and training schemes, the situation in individual towns was often aggravated rather than relieved, as extensive programmes of poor relief attracted migrant poor to the city concerned.[13]

Nevertheless, the national government in its legislation of 1572

ordered similar censuses of the poor in all cities and the inaugura-
tion of a compulsory poor rate. Late Tudor poor relief legislation
built upon existing ideas. Little that was new was introduced and the
legislation itself floundered upon the inability of Tudor or Stuart officials to operate it efficiently. Before 1629 the Privy Council made
no attempt to enforce the poor law as a whole, merely intervening
in specific instances or in especially hard years. In the early Stuart
period, 1605–29, there appears to be evidence that the administration of the poor law sank to a new low, with parish overseers in
town and country failing to apprentice poor children. It is suggested
that the Privy Council attempted to improve the application of the
Elizabethan poor law during the personal rule of Charles I, but that
the Civil Wars spelt serious disruption in both the administration of
the poor law and in private giving. For instance, the number of children at Christ's Hospital fell from 900 in 1641 to 682 in 1647. Dor-
chester Hospital was forced to close down sometime between 1643
and 1646 because of lack of finance. Vagrant begging is said to
have been on the increase in London.[14]

In the later seventeenth and eighteenth centuries the answer to
the problems associated with poverty among young and old alike was
again seen in the institutionalisation of the poor away from reinforcing influences. John Locke's *Report to the Board of Trade* of 1697
recommended the foundation of workhouse schools for children
aged three to fourteen. Locke was struck both by the rise in the
number of over-large poor families and also by the idle habits incul-
cated in the children of such households. As has been observed,
many of the proponents of the workhouse as a panacea for all evils
were swayed excessively by the desire to remove the burden of poor
relief from the rates. Many also believed that this was the best way
to make poverty appear as undesirable to the poor as it did to the
rich. Humanitarian desire to help the poor in the best way possible
was often a secondary concern. But some thinkers, such as Samuel
Hartlib and Sir Matthew Hale, were still strongly of the opinion that
poverty equalled idleness. As such, poverty could be conquered by
the substitution of the work ethic for sloth and the replacement of
bad environmental influences by good.[15]

In this context it is well worth noting the features of the Clerken-
well Workhouse, which was the only workhouse founded specifically
under the Act of Settlement of 1662. While originally intended to
house 600 able-bodied and 100 impotent poor, by 1687 a half of it
had been given over to the care of parish orphans under the gov-
ernorship and inspiration of one of the Middlesex Justices, Sir Thomas Rowe. Rowe and the Middlesex JPs tried to persuade London
parishes to send a quota of poor children to the College or Nursery
of Infants in the interests of 'making them capable of getting an
honest livelihood by their labour' but for some parishes the alternative to outdoor relief was too expensive. The Nursery constituted a

humanitarian experiment, inspired by the same goals as that of Christ's Hospital and often resembling it in form, but it was too small and, moreover, often extended a helping hand to those whose parents were in a peripatetic line of work (sailors, for example) who were not technically poor in preference to the true poor. As we observed in earlier chapters dealing with the establishing of grammar schools, one of the common features apparent in Tudor and Stuart institutions is the tendency of the upper and middle classes to take over facilities intended for their social inferiors for their own use. The same was to happen to Christ's Hospital, Charterhouse and the Blue Coat Schools. The S.S.P.C.K. and S.P.C.K. English schools in Scotland and England suffered a similar upgrading. Historians of the nineteenth century likewise observe the tendency of the semi-skilled and skilled artisan classes to take over schools intended to provide basic literacy and religious instruction for the very poor and to demand more advanced syllabuses and mechanisms of improvement.[16]

In 1698 a new London Corporation of the Poor set up a workhouse which seems to epitomise the attitude of the better sort of workhouse to the plight of the poor child and the appropriate rehabilitative environment. It is impossible to determine how typical this enlightened attitude was of workhouses in general in the later seventeenth and eighteenth centuries. There are certainly horror stories enough of workhouses run on far different principles, which were corruptions of the original intent. Originally the Corporation of the Poor conceived of a work centre which would give 6-week-long training courses in spinning to 1,000 of the able-bodied poor to prepare them for work, giving them warm shelter and food meanwhile. The scheme envisaged a rapid turnover. It collapsed when it became clear that the poor, having been taught to work, could not find employment. A residential workhouse in Bishopsgate, therefore, concentrated on the plight of the poor child as being the original cause of adult poverty. The initiators of the scheme blamed neither the economy nor the attitude of society as a whole but the environmental influences on the poor from childhood onwards. Vagrant and poor children of seven years and upwards were taken in, educated in basic literacy and numeracy, taught a skill and encouraged to support themselves by making their own clothing and shoes. Physically the children were well provided for: staff who engaged in indiscriminate whipping were dismissed; the children were housed separately from the adults and lame children were sent to a house in Bunhill fields where they might benefit from the country air and undertake relatively light work.[17]

There are countless other examples of workhouses, supported by a mixture of private charity and public rates, which approached the education of poor children in a relatively compassionate if traditionalist manner. Most thought that academic education was, except in a few cases of demonstrated ability, a waste of time and actually conducive to habits of idleness.

In other workhouses the emphasis was not upon reform and re-habilitation – for the situation was deemed irreversible – but upon low-cost provision for the poor. The Governor of St Giles' Work-house, Bloomsbury, for instance, was instructed in 1722 to 'maintain the poor as cheap as may consist with reason': as a consequence perhaps, the regime of this particular workhouse was marked by a monotonous diet, punitive and humiliating if not inhuman discipline and isolation from the total community. And we know that some workhouses were far worse – producing children who were inade-quately fed, clothed and housed and who were certainly not re-moved from the evil influences within the workhouse which earlier reformers were convinced were the origin of their species. Critics of the workhouses were convinced that it was the institutions them-selves which 'harden them to vice'.[18]

In general the workhouses boarded out infants. A foster mother was awarded a lump sum payment, although it was often made dif-ficult for her to collect. Because high turnover was actually profit-able, neglect of infants boarded out was common. Moreover, many workhouses did not exercise close supervision over the selection of nurses or their performance. Jonas Hanaway once called St Giles' Workhouse the 'greatest sink of mortality in these kingdoms'. He observed that 122 children under the age of 3 had been admitted to St Giles in 1765 and that 40 per cent of these had died within a month. At St George's, Middlesex, 19 children under 3 were admit-ted and 12 of these had died within fifty days and a further 4 in less than nine months. Spurred on by these revelations Hanaway and Thomas Coram became the founders of The Foundling Hospital, which achieved lower rates of mortality by improved hygiene. Han-away also recommended intense supervision of the parochial board-ing-out system. He wanted to provide incentives for nurses to pro-tect the health of their charges. Under this influence, the poor relief system of St James's Westminster (1763) allocated payments to nurses if children in their care survived beyond the first birthday or recovered from illness; dismissed nurses who had had two infant fatalities within a year; and made payments for teaching children to read and write. Children under seven were to continue in the coun-try before being brought in to the workhouse proper.[19]

The investigations of the mid eighteenth century both exposed the iniquities of the boarding-out system of child care and education and influenced legislators. A Parliamentary Commission discovered that only 7 in 100 poor children admitted to a workhouse survived a two-year period. The Commission underlined Hanaway's propos-als and in 1767 an Act was put on the statute book which was cred-ited with cutting infant mortality considerably. Unfortunately, this Act had no enforcing mechanism and, therefore, its effects were in fact much less than might have been anticipated. By the 1770s some reformers were trying to exclude children from the workhouses altogether or to make special provision for them compulsory. In 1774 a cottage home plan was put forward in Sheffield and in 1781 St James's Westminster founded a school of industry designed to separate treatment of the juvenile poor from that of the adult. Reformers were becoming acutely aware of the abuses of the system of educating the poor child in an institution away from his natural parents. This awareness did not, it seems, force them into the position of disagreeing with the basic premiss behind the system itself – that poverty was a fault of the family environment, with no deeper roots in society itself.[20]

The Scottish approach to the education of poor children

Scottish provision for the poor was in many ways similar to the English. It appears that experiments in vocational education there were closely linked to a more conscious desire to deal with economic under-development, perhaps because problems of extreme urban poverty came later to Scotland. Schools of industry were especially popular. These took various forms. A craft school for boys, for example, was endowed in Dundee by Bailie William Rodger (1658). There were abortive attempts by mid seventeenth-century local and national governments to establish burgh schools of industry and parish apprenticeship systems. In the 1720s the Board of Trustees for Scottish Manufactures set up three schools of spinning and employed four teachers in the Highlands. In 1747 and 1752 the forfeited estates of Jacobites were used by Parliament to finance schools which taught the three Rs, agriculture and manufacturing skills. Ten schools of spinning and seventeen classes were supported in this way and their continuance was guaranteed by the Scottish Society for the Preservation of Christian Knowledge in 1788. While the eighteenth century saw unemployment in the Highlands, it witnessed considerable population drift into the larger Scottish burghs, which suffered as a result. Some employers experimented with worker education while employees in a few cases were eager to finance elementary teaching by subscription.[21]

The burghs had a long tradition of the supervision of education for the poor. The town councils appear to have exercised control over the operation of charity schools, sometimes even managing funds bequeathed for the purpose. There was an awareness that poverty was a result of 'hard times' at least among the domestic poor. Day Schools for the poor, which parallel the large number of such schools set up in London in the latter years of the seventeenth century, were aimed at the domestic and not the vagrant poor. As with all other forms of education made free or at low cost to the domestic poor, abuses crept in and the lower middle classes sought to take them over. McLurg's Charity School in Edinburgh offers an example of this: the school bequest was made in 1718; by 1794 it was necessary to insist that entrants have their poverty certified by the magistrates before admission, that the numbers be limited to forty and that scholars be allowed to remain there for only five years. In some cases the S.S.P.C.K. stepped in and supported the activities of these pre-existing charity free schools with donations of school books.[22]

Scottish towns also encountered a problem of vagrancy. The Edinburgh workhouses, dating from the 1740s, were comparatively well run with low mortality rates by the standards of the time. Boys and girls were housed separately from adults within them. The S.S.P.C.K. supported the Charity Workhouse of Edinburgh (1743) and the Paul's Work Foundation there laid heavy emphasis upon the religious, vernacular and technical training of the children. The Canongate and West Kirk workhouses set up in 1761 each had a teacher: that at Canongate taught vocational subjects and catechism; that at West Kirk offered the three Rs and church music in addition. In 1733 the orphan hospital was founded in Edinburgh by public subscription, although this also was later contributed to by the S.S.P.C.K. Fifty-four orphans received religious instruction and industrial training and were introduced to reading, writing, arithmetic and church music. The number housed in the hospital reached 130 in 1784. The S.S.P.C.K. founded three working schools in Edinburgh in 1758: these taught primarily spinning, stocking knitting, the three Rs and church music. These three charity working schools formed one part of an agreement with the Edinburgh town council whereby the town council supported four English schools with a schoolmaster and curriculum approved by the presbytery. The high fees asked by English schools in the city were blamed for the low literacy levels among the poor of Edinburgh.[23]

The significance of the Charity Schools

Since the publication of M. G. Jones's *The Charity School Movement: A Study of Eighteenth Century Puritanism in Action*, it has been usual to attribute to the S.P.C.K. the foundation of large numbers of charity schools in early eighteenth-century England. More detailed analysis of education in particular counties indicates that this may well have been true only in the metropolis. Joan Simon argues convincingly that the S.P.C.K. had only a slight and temporary influence on the provision of elementary schooling in Leicestershire. Her work indicates that the S.P.C.K. succeeded in mobilising the high church parochial clergy in some parishes in Leicestershire to open catechetical schools rather than communities to establish schools by subscription. On the other hand, Derek Robson indicates rather less success among the clergy of Cheshire. Moreover, it appears that the catechetical schools actually inspired by S.P.C.K. activity tended to be established in small parishes where the problem of poverty was not acute. Because they often depended upon the enthusiasm of one man for the cause, they frequently closed their doors for good when the incumbent died or moved. In a few cases, as at Hallaton, the school appears to have changed its character, by coming under clerical control and catering for the education of poor children in religion. Hallaton was a market town which had hit bad times and had an increasingly acute poverty problem. But in Leicestershire parish schools, with a number of free places for poor inhabitants and fee-paying places for others, continued as a living tradition. For instance, a school was founded in the township of Barrow-on-Soar with an endowment from the parson and subscriptions. It was designed to teach Latin but became an English school on popular demand. It served the whole community and was in no sense a charity school. (We are certainly well advised to avoid classifying all English schools as charity schools. In 1759 Edinburgh already had twenty-four English schools: of these only two were charity schools properly speaking and of the twenty-two remaining, four or five charged fees of 10s. 6d. per quarter plus coal money; twelve charged 5s. per quarter; four 4s. and one 3s. The town council of Edinburgh at that time advocated fees of 2s. per quarter to bring vernacular schooling within reach of the domestic poor.) The only school founded by subscription in Leicestershire during the period of S.P.C.K. activity was in point of fact a charity school, with no marks of the S.P.C.K.'s programme.[24]

Charity schools were, correctly speaking, founded to deal with the specific problem of urban poverty by replacing a deficient physical and moral environment with a satisfactory one. Such motivation was non-sectarian although Christian. In London in the late seventeenth century some charity schools had an anti-Catholic motivation but they were generally non-catechetical in approach. Thomas Tryon's appeal to the common council and citizens of London in 1691 to set up twenty free schools for the education of poor children seems to have generated a considerable amount of activity. Day schools were supported by subscription for the education of the children of the domestic poor. Some of these day charity schools also had a permanent endowment. In many respects these schools mimicked the blue-coat schools for orphans – such as Christ's Hospital or the Reading Blue Coat School, which was first founded in 1646 and renewed in 1719. But these schools were day foundations and, moreover, they were open to all poor children and not just to orphans. They were very clearly differentiated from parish schools which served the entire community. The S.P.C.K., then, did not initiate the subscription school movement in London – rather it turned the charitable initiative of others to its own ends. It used its sermons and its propaganda to encourage the foundation of subscription schools and the adaptation of existing schools 'for the education of poor children in the knowledge and practice of the Christian Religion, as professed and taught in the Church of England . . . . and for teaching them such other things as are most suitable to their condition'. The S.P.C.K. was only incidentally concerned with the relief of poverty. Its priorities were different from those of the founders of the Blue Coat Charity schools and subscription schools. Its members bewailed the decline of religion among the poor. It was this decline which they wished to arrest. Academic learning was peripheral in their scheme.[25]

Cheshire, for example, had a number of Blue Coat or Blue Cap schools. These were endowed foundations, springing from the local desire to help the poor. The Blue Coat School at Chester; the Blue Cap School at Nantwich; the Blue Cap School at Holmes Chapel; the Charity School, Wybunbury; the Darnall Blue Coat School; and Little Budworth School all combined a basic English education with the provision of uniform and, in some cases, industrial training. For instance, shoemaking, a local industry, was taught the boys of the Blue Cap School, Nantwich. In some towns the S.P.C.K. co-operated with other bodies to found Blue Coat Charity Schools. A notable example is that of York where the S.P.C.K., the archbishop, dean and chapter and the lord mayor and corporation joined to establish two subscription charity schools in 1705 – a Blue Coat School for forty boys and a Grey Coat school for twenty girls. The children at these schools were to be the orphans or dependent children of poor freemen burdened with large families. The school provided a uniform, diet, education in the vernacular and preparation for apprenticeship at the age of fourteen (boys) and twelve (girls). More common still was the practice of extending support to existing charity schools and workhouses by the free donation of books. The S.S.P.C.K., for instance, donated 200 copies of the first page of Kerr's Spelling Book to John Wightman's Charity School in Edinburgh. It also provided books for the Orphan Hospital of Edinburgh.[26]

While there is clearly a need for more detailed examination of elementary school provision in individual countries, it is difficult to disagree with the contention that there was no charity school movement as such in eighteenth-century England and that the S.P.C.K. neither engineered nor controlled such a movement. Elementary schools were set up with a multitude of different motivations. While almost all elementary schools were charity schools in a legal sense, only a few were run by the relatively rich for the education of the very poor. Such existed before the S.P.C.K. was founded. For example, the S.P.C.K. subscription school at Alderley, Cheshire, was founded in 1628 and was, moreover, an endowment rather than a subscription. Several other schools in Cheshire which were claimed as S.P.C.K. subscription schools appear to have had a longer history. Some of these schools were undoubtedly *adopted* by the S.P.C.K. But, as Joan Simon observed, the S.P.C.K., during the years 1700–24, had a different purpose from charity in mind. Its intention was to counter nonconformist influence in elementary education, to support high church doctrinal positions and to play the game of high church politics. The name of the society spelt out its intent. Its attempts to influence pre-existing institutions and to stimulate the creation of catechetical schools in London should not be permitted to disguise the fact that the foundation of schools specifically to deal with the problems of urban poverty owed little to the society.[27]

The Sunday schools and the poor child

The Sunday school movement has sometimes been seen as a progeny of the so-called Charity School Movement. It has been customary to see the Sunday schools as the creation of individuals such as Hannah More, Sarah Trimmer and Robert Raikes. It is true that Raikes, for example, founded four small Sunday schools in Gloucestershire in 1781. But no single person can be credited with the beginnings of the movement, for it was rooted, somewhat obscurely, in the past. According to ecclesiastical law, the curate was responsible for the catechising of the youth of the parish on Sundays. Even before the Civil Wars lay people had been involved in the work of Sunday schools – for instance, the Ferrar sisters taught at Little Gidding – and in the 1690s Sunday school charities were established at both Walsall and Bristol. This interest quickened in the 1750s and 60s when both laity and clergy of the Church of England founded or worked in Sunday schools. By the later 1780s, however, the Sunday schools had become a much more frequent recipient of middle-class benefactions.

The Sunday school movement to which most historians allude, however, represents but one aspect of a much wider movement. In the later eighteenth century the Church of England was very active in founding new Sunday schools. Evangelically minded bishops of the Church lent their support. An interdenominational but predominantly Anglican Sunday School Society was set up in 1785. This spread information about Sunday schools, donated spelling books, Testaments and Bibles, and occasionally made grants to individual schools. Anglican clergymen urged the expansion of the movement because they saw in children the future of the Church. Occasionally their views were heavily influenced by Lockeian views of the child as *tabula rasa*. Not infrequently supporters of Sunday schools saw their classes as a necessary substitute for the neglected responsibilities of the family. It was desirable that the father and mother should teach the young child to read the Scriptures but many were unable and many were unwilling so to do. Laity were often deeply involved in this work.[28]

It may be argued that Hannah More viewed the movement as associated only with the education of the poor in true religion.

When I settled in this country thirteen years ago, I found the poor in many of the villages in a deplorable state of ignorance and vice. There were, I think, no Sunday schools in the whole district, except one in my own parish, which had been established by our respectable Rector, and another in the adjoining parish of Churchill. This drew me to the more neglected villages. . . . My plan of instruction is extremely simple and limited. They learn on week days, such coarse works as may fit them for servants. I allow of no writing for the poor. My object is not to make fanatics but to train up the lower classes in habits of industry and piety. I knew no way of teaching morals but by teaching principles; or of inculcating Christian principles without imparting a knowledge of Scripture.

The books from which she taught were 'safe books' – approved catechisms, prayers and tracts. The child was never taught to think critically, and was not encouraged to become actively literate.[29]

Hannah More and others who founded Sunday schools in the later eighteenth century saw the schools as a way to giving poor children or children from immoral homes what middle-class and wealthy children were obtaining from their home or school life. They did not see the Sunday schools in terms of social control but of religious revival. Hannah More reacted in horror when it was suggested that her 'safe books', particularly the Scriptures, might lead directly to Jacobinism. The schools were neither an educational nor a social charity by intent.

According to recent work on the Sunday schools, however, those of the late eighteenth century did not cater exclusively for members of the working classes, let alone the pauper classes. Some eighteenth-century Sunday schools did have a largely working-class clientele, although from a wide spectrum within that class. Others drew pupils from the lower middle class also. It was in the nineteenth century that the Sunday school movement exclusively belonged to working-class culture. From an early date the schools proved popular in the large industrial cities of the North and Midlands. In 1784 the interdenominational Sunday school in Manchester already had 1,800 pupils; the number trebled by 1788. Yet the schools were not essentially an urban phenomenon: they were also strong in many rural communities. Only the capital did not prove receptive to the movement. It has been estimated that, by the 1820s, nearly every working-class child had attended a Sunday school at some time. Average attendance was four years. They studied reading, spelling and religion for between four and six hours every Sunday. In the schools children were largely taught by working-class teachers.[30]

The nature of their contribution to the problem of poverty is debatable. The schools increasingly were operated by members of the working classes themselves. Their purpose was not that of social control or charity but of religious revitalisation. Nevertheless, many schools were founded upon clerical or middle-class initiative and were the recipients of middle-class benefactions. Moreover, it was frequently the case that Sunday schools provided other amenities to the working-class community – loans, contributions towards medical bills and funerals, or donations of food and clothing. And the Sunday school movement reached out to adults as well as children. The age of pupils ranged from five to thirty. Hannah More, for example, was anxious to reach the parents of the children whom she taught. Her complaint was a familiar one: 'what the children learned at school, they commonly lost at home by the profaneness and ignorance of their parents...'.[31]

It seems more proper to describe the Church Sunday School movement of the 1780s and 90s as a movement of middle-class philanthropy than it is to describe the nineteenth-century Sunday school movement in such terms. And even in this we should be cautious. Those who founded and supported Sunday schools in the later eighteenth century were evangelists, not philanthropists. Their prime aim was to revive religion – not, perhaps, enthusiasm but a sound knowledge of religion and moral principles which would humanise and civilise the poor and the not so poor. Charity was a by-product of this movement. Rehabilitation was seen in religious and not secular terms. The work of the schools was significant for the history of approaches to the problem of poverty through education not because they concentrated on that problem but because they concentated on the religious education of the entire working class.

Certain assumptions were shared by evangelists and others alike. For example, it was considered necessary to remove the child from the evil influences of the home if true religion were to be implanted in that child. It was believed possible to educate the child and thus ensure that the Word of God do its own work. According to Hannah More, reading the Bible could not lead to radicalism. In other words it was thought possible to control the amount of education given to each child and the thoughts and habits of mind which this stimulated.

The evangelists did bring a more positive view to their work of the value of the individual child than was often the case. The Reverend Daniel Turner described children as 'the heritage of the Lord and the fruit of the womb in His reward' in a sermon favouring Sunday schools of 1794. Because children were malleable, the salvation of mankind lay in their proper instruction. It is significant that the Sunday school movement relied heavily upon the hymns of Isaac Watts and the Wesley brothers. These hymns espoused a positive vision of childhood. Many of Watts' hymns (which went into 125 British editions between 1715 and 1800) countered teaching on original sin with an emphasis on the idea of the child as totally innocent. They encouraged cheerful piety among the young. Wesley's hymns also stressed the innocence of the child. This assumption that the child had a positive value acted as an antidote to the popular view that the poor child possessed the characteristics of his or her parents. The latter was a view which informed much of the thinking on children in workhouses and workhouse schools.[32]

It is impossible to assess with confidence the degree of impact which the late eighteenth-century Sunday schools made upon mass illiteracy. By the year 1800 some 200,000 children (not all of working-class origin) attended such schools. Some of these might, under normal circumstances, have learned to read in any case. More by far would not have learned to read had it not been for the revival of the Sunday schools. But in the late eighteenth century such schools were not widely distributed by later standards. It was not until Sunday schools spread into almost all communities of any size that a great impression could be made upon the entire working class.

Conclusions

An examination of schemes for the education of the poor in Britain between 1500 and *circa* 1780 may confirm our initial assumption that education was used as a social cement rather than as an agent of change. Even the more advanced social thinkers were not democrats or communists (with the exception of Gerard Winstanley) and, when they saw the implications of universal education, advocated only a limited social mobility for the very able. Others shied away entirely from the idea of any such mobility via education. Nevertheless, there were differing attitudes to the problem of poverty and its eradication or amelioration. In the sixteenth and early seventeenth centuries it was most common to see poverty as a moral problem – the result of wanton idleness – although there was a fast-growing realisation that poverty among the unsettled domestic poor was often beyond the power of the afflicted themselves to cure. Better training was suggested as the answer to this economic problem. In both cases, removal of the poor child from his or her environment was thoroughly recommended. While educationalists in the years of the Interregnum were more concerned with the education of the whole nation as opposed to simply the gentry and the urban middle classes, their diagnosis of the problem of poverty was not significantly different from that of their forbears. However, they did work out in some detail the theoretical advantages of workhouse and industrial schools, no doubt preparing their successors to lay increasing emphasis upon the workhouse approach to lifting poor children from poverty.

Although it is common to stress the abuses of the workhouse system, it seems that one must divorce the laudable aims of social reformers such as Thomas Rowe and Thomas Coram from the attempts of others to fulfil resented social obligations at the least possible cost to the community at large. It may also be impossible to determine the balance between these two attitudes in society at any one time. The more positive view of the value of all children within the Christian commonwealth held by the religious revivalists of the late eighteenth century certainly helped to offset the much harsher view adopted by many of those who operated the workhouses. Yet the bias in the eighteenth century as a whole appears to have been against academic education for the poor and towards industrial and 'useful' training. Even the evangelists did not counsel full-time education for the working-class child. The impetus towards even limited social mobility appears to have been depleted rather than increased. It is characteristic of British society that a more positive view of the value of each individual could be accepted much more readily and much earlier in the religious realm than in the material world.

Chapter 14

Traditional educational institutions and society, 1640–1800

During the late seventeenth and eighteenth centuries England, and later Britain as a whole, became a major commercial power in the world. Within the life of the nation the role of the merchant and business community was more complicated. Although the commercial community's aggregate share of the country's wealth rose during the eighteenth century and that held by landlords and farmers fell (from a half in 1700 to one third in 1800), political and social status did not follow suit. It was not until the later eighteenth century that there was a sharp rise in the number of merchants and lawyers in the House of Commons. The peers occupied high offices within the kingdom, including the Lord Lieutenancies; the gentry filled the House of Commons, served as justices of the peace and performed other leading local roles; within the parishes farmers served as churchwardens, overseers and surveyors. During a period of agricultural expansion many landlords profited considerably. Prosperous farmers were particularly numerous in the home counties, Sussex, Hampshire, Somerset, Gloucestershire, East Anglia and the North Riding of Yorkshire. The great estates prospered because of the expansion of the London market. Meanwhile lesser landowners were able to enclose and consolidate their estates. It was more difficult than ever for the well-to-do commercial man to penetrate this world of the landed gentry. Between the 1730s and 1800 there was a slower inflow of new families into the gentry than there had been in the previous two hundred years. This slow-down is attributable, at least in part, to the widening cultural gulf between the landed and business communities. In the years before 1660 the whole community relied upon the grammar schools and the ancient universities for education. Although, as we have argued earlier, the role of the grammar school or university as a vehicle of social mobility can be exaggerated, it is true that the town grammar schools offered to the prosperous artisan in search of improvement the same basic classical education which it offered to the sons of the local gentry. After 1660 the religious rift between members of the Church of England and the dissenters; impatience with the premises upon which classical education rested; and the increasing cost of a university education brought about a change. No longer did the commercial classes normally attend the same educational institutions as the landed gentry and the clergy. The value systems of the communities had diverged and this divergence tended to be confirmed through the medium of education. Whereas the gentry were groomed for leadership in the state at national or at local level, the son of the shopkeeper was groomed to make his own living.[1]

The tradition of education among the commercial classes

The growth of an alternative system of education for the business community had a history, of course. In the seventeenth century there was considerable debate concerning the curriculum and methodology employed at the ancient universities of Oxford and Cambridge. The realistic approach of Pierre de la Ramée was contrasted with the scholastic approach of the humanists. Whereas one concerned itself with matter, the other, older tradition concerned itself with words. According to the latest studies, Ramism was all but defeated even in Cambridge by the early seventeenth century. The works of Francis Bacon, however, kept alive a strong current of interest in realist, utilitarian education. His writings had a considerable influence upon products of the universities in both a direct and an indirect fashion. During the 1620s and 30s his Utopian proposals and suggestions that learning should be advanced in the interests of the common weal appealed to many of the more radical Protestants.

Charles Webster has shown how the millennial eschatology of puritans such as Joseph Mead, John Stoughton, Richard Holdsworth, Benjamin Whichcote and John White made them critical of social institutions and optimistic about the power of the human intellect to overcome problems. A common viewpoint on such issues as social reform was achieved because of the personal connections between these men, who clustered in just a few colleges (especially Emmanuel, Christ's and St John's, Cambridge, Magdalen Hall, Oxford, and Trinity College, Dublin) and who had further connections with educational theorists from abroad (Samuel Hartlib, John Dury and John Amos Comenius) and prominent London preachers. Bacon's writings provided a general philosophical framework for the Utopian and practical proposals of men like Hartlib and Petty, while more detailed suggestions were made by Comenius.

These men intended to put their plans into practice. Hartlib, for example, founded an academy in Chichester in 1630, on Baconian principles. Not a few puritans found the idea of settling in America and establishing Utopias of their own attractive. At least in intent, Gresham College, London, was founded to provide a utilitarian education in scientifically orientated subjects, although the practice fell far short of the ideal. The Laudian persecution forced intellectuals of a Baconian frame of mind to look outside the established channels if they were to put their ideas into effect. With the advent of the Civil War the climate of intellectual life changed considerably. It seems that new ideas were actually encouraged by interregnum governments. Dury, Hartlib and other social reformers put forward detailed proposals for educational reform and received some practical encouragement for their schemes. At the same time the extra-curricular atmosphere of Oxford and Cambridge prompted scientists and philosophers to engage in new fields of activity, although it is demonstrable that the curriculum for undergraduates changed little if at all.[2]

The new science

Some scholars believe that the new science established itself at both Oxford and Cambridge well before the Civil War. The foundation of the Savilian Chairs of Geometry and Astronomy at Oxford (1619), the Sedleian Lectureship in Natural Philosophy at Oxford (1619) and the Tomlins Anatomy Lecture, also at Oxford, in 1624 are cited as evidence. In addition some individual tutors were enthusiastic practitioners and advocates of modern studies – for instance, William Oughtred (mathematician) at King's College, Cambridge; Thomas Allen (mathematician and astrologer) at Gloucester Hall, Oxford; Samuel Ward at Sidney Sussex College, Cambridge, and John Crowther at Magdalen Hall, Oxford, who taught both astronomy and geography. Against this school of thought may be cited the insignificance of the new foundations from the point of view of the undergraduate studying at either university. Although Francis Bacon's will provided for two lectureships at Cambridge (one in the natural sciences), his insolvency meant that neither was founded. And those chairs and lectureships established at Oxford affected the graduate and not the undergraduate. It was difficult for even an interested undergraduate to obtain tuition in certain subjects in the university before the Civil War. John Wallis obtained his knowledge of mathematics at Felsted School and later claimed that of 200 students at his Cambridge College only two possessed reasonable mathematical competence. When Seth Ward sought mathematical tuition at Sidney Sussex, he could find no one able to help him with mathematics books from his own college library.[3]

Christopher Hill has argued that it was not the universities but intellectuals and practitioners working in London who acted as the pacemakers for scientific change. He notes the interest in mathematics at Gresham, in medicine at the Royal College of Physicians, in the Barber Surgeons Company and the Society of Apothecaries and suggests that from them both personnel and new techniques and ideas entered the ancient strongholds of learning. For example, in

1619 Henry Briggs moved from Gresham to Oxford as first Savilian Professor of Geometry, accompanied by John Bainbridge as first Savilian Professor of Astronomy. As a result the influence of the new science even at Oxford, where there had been some break-throughs in institutional terms, was channelled essentially through personal courses.[4]

In the 1640s and 50s there is every indication that this same pattern pertained. Although the state endowed no new lectureships or chairs in scientific and mathematical studies, many members of the group of 1645 (who met in London to discuss a wide range of scientific and mathematical subjects and new discoveries at a variety of locations) were eventually given university preferments after 1648. John Wilkins, John Wallis and Jonathan Goddard were all preferred within Oxford and Francis Glisson, Harvey's most celebrated pupil, was already at Cambridge. During the interregnum there was certainly much interest in scientific inquiry at the universities. The Oxford Experimental Philosophy Club met at Wadham College on a weekly basis on the model of the London meetings of 1645. Prominent members were John Wilkins, Warden of Wadham; Jonathan Goddard, Warden of Merton; John Wallis, Savilian Professor of Geometry; Joshua Crosse, Sedleian Lecturer; William Petty, assistant to the Professor of Physic; and Seth Ward, Savilian Professor of Astronomy. In the 1650s Robert Boyle and Robert Hooke joined the group. Charles Webster has noted that with the removal of Wilkins to Cambridge, the emphasis of their enquiries shifted rather to medicine, although the activities of the Club over the whole period were marked by their catholicity, their utilitarian slant, their use of collaborative enterprise and their concentration on new theories and discoveries. The members of the Club were interested in the improvement of husbandry, for example. Wilkins invented an improved plough; Petty produced a mechanical sower. A number of useful if minor devices resulted from the work of Wilkins, Petty and Christopher Wren. A glass beehive was set up in Wilkins' college garden: the concept was introduced to the wider public in Hartlib's *Reformed Commonwealth of Bees*. The Club members built up a chemistry laboratory, established an observatory and worked in the areas of optics, physics and medicine.[5]

In Cambridge the chief scientific activity focused upon the Cambridge Platonists. This group was not Baconian in its emphasis: its members were more interested in the metaphysical problems of science than in experimental methodology. None the less, their desire to demonstrate the wisdom of God in his creation led many Cambridge Platonists into a careful study of natural history. As a consequence there was a very active naturalist group, centred on John Ray, Henry Power and Francis Willoughby. Meanwhile, Francis Glisson's notebooks reveal the vitality of the study of medicine within Cambridge during the parliamentary period. Dissection was taken seriously at Cambridge at this time, although it was not practised systematically at either university during the seventeenth century. Glisson had two very able students from Yorkshire – Matthew Robinson and Henry Power, who were enthusiastic students of botany, chemistry and physiology. Interest was shown in Harvey's later work in embryology. Examination of the medical faculty at Oxford during the period 1651–60 led Charles Webster to conclude that there had been a deep and swift permeation of new ideas from the world of practical and experimental medicine. Disputation topics reflect an interest in the new physiology, showing that the medical disputations were an excellent forum for debate of novel theories and that they encouraged a generally critical approach to existing theories and methodology.[6]

On almost every scientific and mathematical front there is evidence of enthusiasm and experimentation at Oxford but the university as an institution did little to initiate this state of affairs. It depended upon the personal interests of scholars preferred to university posts during the interregnum, not upon the foundation of new chairs or lectureships. And it touched the undergraduate little if at all. The liberal arts curriculum remained exceedingly conservative, with scholastic texts in use even at Wadham, centre of the new experimental science. Gifts of contemporary books on science, mathematics and philosophy were made to the college libraries and some tutors guided their students to a wider range of interests than the university curriculum required, but the new science played no formal, institutionalised role in interregnum undergraduate studies.

In fact, some of the scholars most interested personally in the new science (for example Seth Ward) were keen to preserve the existing university discipline and the role of the liberal arts curriculum as necessary to the preparation of clergy and of noble and gentle youths. The new science would be useless for them. The universities certainly did not wish to turn away their chief clientele. 'Their [the gentry's] removal is from hence commonly in two or three years, to the Inns of Court, and the desire of their friends is not, that they be engaged in those experimental things, but that their reason, and fancy, and carriage, be improved by lighter institutions and exercises that they may become rational and graceful speakers, and be of an acceptable behaviour in their countries'.[7]

The proposals of the social reformers for special colleges, which would recruit poor but able boys for the church's ministry and train them along non-scholastic lines and introduce a realist approach to the education of all, were set outside the existing universities because of the hostility of these venerable institutions to any such change. While the political regime and the existence of a number of leading intellectuals at the universities provided an atmosphere congenial to the growth of the new philosophy and science within the universities, the radical criticism levelled at the curriculum by those seeking a social revolution in the educational world actually prevented the emergence of new statutes and a new *raison d'être* for the universities. For most university academics too much was coming too fast. Although Dell, Master of Caius, agitated for reform of the undergraduate curriculum in a utilitarian fashion, most of the radical critics of the universities worked from without. John Hall, in his *Humble Motion . . . Concerning the Advancement of Learning and the Reformation of the Universities* (1649), and Noah Biggs, in his *Mataeotechnia Medicinae,* saw education as the handmaid of a social reformation to prepare England for the coming of the new Jerusalem. Only a little support was gathered for such a view within the universities – for instance, William Sprigg of Lincoln College, Oxford (later on the faculty of Durham College), and Henry Langley, Master of Pembroke College, Oxford, shared this Baconian vision.[8]

Mid seventeenth century blueprints for reform

With the patronage of the state the social reformers might have succeeded in radically altering the type of higher education on offer. Blueprints for change certainly abounded. John Dury's *The Reformed School* (1650) envisaged universities which would produce socially useful graduates. Hugh Peter wanted to see a university with sixteen colleges – eight to train ministers according to the new spiritual guidelines and eight to provide education in other spheres for intending professionals. John Webster's *Academiarum Examen* wanted to make the new science a part of the formal curriculum of Oxford and Cambridge and to replace speculative with utilitarian subjects. As we have noted earlier, in 1653 Samuel Hartlib and John Dury presented the Committee for the Advancement of Learning with a proposal for a new educational system. For all of these men the reformation of the existing system was important but so also was the creation of new institutions. Hugh Peter, for example, wanted the creation of a system of local colleges to provide a utilitarian education for youths from Yorkshire, Cornwall, Wales and so forth. Dell echoes this with a proposal for the foundation of urban colleges. He thought that decentralisation would lower costs for poorer parents and, significantly, counter harmful influences met at the universities with closer parental supervision. Dell's scheme was designed to combine intellectual with practical training for the young. Some of the proposals were designed to suit the needs of one class – Sprigg's *A Modest Plea* (1659), for instance, envisaged a college for the education of the gentry in scientific and gentlemanly pursuits. Such a college would have been in the direct tradition of the polite academies established by Kinnersley and Gerbier.[9]

And, in fact, there were some tentative ventures in the direction of putting these ideas into execution. The Westminster Assembly put its weight behind a plan for a University of London specifically created to train ministers. Hartlib and Petty's projected university based on Gresham and containing eleven colleges with very specific educational goals met with some practical support. Hartlib wanted his college to be a state regulated institution, which would provide a utilitarian education and also stimulate state supported research for practical ends. This federated university never came into being but Hartlib was made Agent for Universal Learning at a salary of £100 per annum. Ideas for a Welsh college came from various quarters but met with no success. The proposals for an Irish college to supplement or replace the more or less defunct Trinity College, Dublin, however, did receive some official and influential support. In 1651 the Committee to order Irish Schools was set up and, significantly, was dominated by Hartlib's associates, Petty, Worsley, Anthony Morgan and Henry Jones. During the early 1650s they put forward a scheme for secondary and higher education based upon Trinity College, Dublin. At the same time Samuel Winter began to revive the fortunes of Trinity itself (aided by John Stearne's work in the Trinity Medical School). The proposals made by the Committee made but slow progress because they were not sponsored actively by the central government. A more effective initiative came from Henry Cromwell, the Protector's son. His patronage in 1656 resulted in the purchase of Archbishop Ussher's library for a new college, in the selection of a site for such a college and in the foundation of a grammar school designed to prepare boys for this institution and for Trinity. In December 1657 Cromwell presented carefully thought out proposals for a new university at Dublin, incorporating Trinity and a new college, a library, free school and a staff of public professors to the Trustees. The blueprint envisaged the teaching of both medicine and natural philosophy as part of the formal curriculum. Unfortunately this project never came to anything. Because the constitution was so unspecific, tutors at Trinity were able to continue teaching in the traditional manner and of the new professors only Miles Symner was an enthusiastic practitioner of the new experimental science. The visible result of Henry Cromwell's patronage was the deposit of Ussher's library at Trinity.[10]

Cromwellian patronage, in this case that of Oliver, was more fruitful with respect to Durham College. In 1650 the citizens of Durham petitioned Parliament for the appropriation of the Dean and Chapter's sequestered buildings for the purposes of higher education, saying that they wished to establish 'some college or school of literature or academy's to serve the population thereabouts. Immediately the proposal caught Cromwell's eye but nothing came of it until the mid 1650s when both John Lambert and Sir Arthur Heselrig supported the agitation for a grant of Letters Patent. Under the Letters Patent Durham College was to be housed in both Castle and Cathedral buildings. It was to take over the library and the mathematical apparatus of the bishops and to be allowed a printing press. The Provost was to be Philip Hunton (a man interested in the new medicine among other things); there were to be two senior fellows and preachers and twelve other fellows. The college was established in 1657 and a number of the staff immediately came into residence, including William Sprigg, Ezerel Tong, Thomas Vaughan and Philip Hunton. Apparently the whole faculty was recruited from among the disgruntled reforming academics of Oxford. As such the college was likely to develop a utilitarian emphasis. Hartlib's comments on Tong and Sprigg suggest that modern subjects were taught: 'One Sprigg is a fellow of Durham College excellent for drawing and painting and very optical also'; [Tong] proposed the 'foundation of a mechanical school and acquainted me [Hartlib] with the whole design of founding a college of sciences with several schools and a library [and] a workhouse in Durham'. In his 1659 work, *A Modest Plea*, Sprigg seems to indicate that he saw Durham College not as a seminary but as a training place for 'the youth of the gentry in learning and good manners' according to the new utilitarian principles. As such, it is not surprising that Sprigg's covert attempts to secure full university status for the college annoyed the ancient universities and resulted in hostility to the new experimental venture, efforts to win Richard Cromwell's support notwithstanding.[11]

Middle-class nonconformist enterprise, 1660 – 1800

If interregnum governments and, particularly, that of Cromwell conceded that state intervention in the world of education in the cause of reform was desirable, they were in general frightened of revolutionary change and anxious not to alienate the educational establishment. During the years 1642 to 1660 there was certainly more receptivity to new educational ideas and more freedom for private enterprise both within and without the universities, but little of the support offered by the state took on an institutionalised form. It is not surprising that at the Restoration the impetus to create a more utilitarian type of education was deflected into middle class, nonconformist enterprises for the most part. It may well be that some historians have overstressed the unique contribution of the dissenting academies to realist, modern education after the Restoration, as we observed in chapter 10. There is a case for arguing that at least some of the grammar schools broadened their curricula in order to meet new demands. There were a number of academies, not specifically nonconformist in origin, which catered to the specific needs of particular groups, in addition to myriad small boarding schools which espoused modern methods of teaching traditional subjects and, in some cases, new subjects under schoolmasters loyal to the established Church. Nevertheless, some of the more spectacular experiments in modern education after the Restoration were controlled by puritan spirits active in the Durham College project – Tong, for instance, established the renowned Islington Academy for Girls, Richard Frankland the Rathmell Academy and others, and Robert Wood became mathematics master at Christ's Hospital. The caucus of Hartlib sympathisers in interregnum Oxford – Henry Langley, Thomas Cole and Henry Cornish – appear to have taken tutoring positions in the vicinity after 1660.[12]

Despite a greater freedom during the interregnum for new educational ideas to develop, despite the sympathetic ear of the government and despite the establishment of a firm tradition of experimental methodology among some scholars, the educational system was not brought under state control and made to serve the needs of the middle classes as opposed to the landed classes. If a youth wished to enter trade and to learn more relevant subjects (such as modern languages and mathematics) he could do so only by ignoring the traditional universities and looking elsewhere for instruction, whether in a school or in the home.

The function of Oxford and Cambridge, 1670 – 1809

The universities began to lose their clientele in the later seventeenth century. A numerical depression such as was experienced between 1670 and 1809 signified the withdrawal of the universities from the life of the nation. Total numbers were reduced in all social categories while, as we have noted, the plebeian classes were most depleted proportionately. The universities continued to train men for the ministry. They made no attempt to cater for the needs of members of the new professional groups. Nonconformists were barred from taking degrees at Cambridge until 1858, even later at Oxford. They were not allowed to attend the University of Oxford and were only admitted to Cambridge under extraordinary circumstances. Although 'closed' scholarships did permit some 'poor' students (i.e. students with only moderate means) to obtain a university education, these scholarships were tied to particular schools, counties and families and were often held by boys from clerical or gentle families. Those students (perhaps over one sixth of the total undergraduate body) who acted as servitors (Oxford) or sizars (Cambridge) were treated contemptuously and made to feel distinctly inferior by their adoption of separate uniform and rigid codes of behaviour. The lowly status of the servitor was felt especially at Oxford. The difficulties facing the middle and lower classes in attending the universities (in terms of cost) and the deficiencies of the curriculum for those desiring a more modern education guaranteed the decline of the ancient universities as centres of scientific and modern scholarship. They also ceased to be socially heterogeneous.[13]

An examination of the student body between 1752 and 1886 confirms this impression.[14] The two universities drew four-fifths of their clientele from three social groups – the gentry, the clergy and the military. The proportions of these classes differed considerably as between Oxford and Cambridge. For example, 39 per cent of fathers at Oxford were in the military whereas only 6 per cent of fathers of Cambridge students were military. Cambridge took significant proportions of its students from medical and legal backgrounds (11 per cent as against 3 per cent at Oxford), business, (9 per cent : 1 per cent) and academia (3.3 per cent: 0 per cent). The total percentages of business, professional and plebeian students at Cambridge was 29 per cent whereas Oxford supported only 6 per cent from these origins. Clearly, Oxford had a much more socially homogeneous student body than did Cambridge. And Oxford became increasingly military in complexion over the period 1762 to 1829 – the percentage rose from 25 per cent of entrants to 50 per cent.

Yet more significantly, neither university sent these students into the new professions or business in large numbers. Fully three-quarters of the alumni of the universities were listed as clerics although only one-quarter had had fathers in the clergy. The new clerics were drawn from military and gentry families. Similarly, a larger number of students went into legal and academic life than might have been anticipated from the number originating in legal or academic families. When we note that only one-half of the sons of plebeians later listed themselves as plebeians, we may surmise that a university education had brought them some social and occupational mobility. But the alumni records indicate that they were attracted by careers in the law, academia, Church and government, not business.

The universities in the eighteenth century were even more disproportionately used as seminaries than they had been in the seventeenth century. The Church took between 57 and 72 per cent of Oxford students in the period cited and between 38 and 76 per cent of Cambridge students, although there was a sharp drop after 1830 at Cambridge and a gradual decline over the period as a whole at Oxford.

An analysis of the pattern of degree-taking at Oxford and Cambridge suggests that most students at Cambridge took the degree because they had specific vocational plans, whereas at Oxford there were some groups in which degree-taking was the usual pattern and others where it was not. Intending military officers at both universities more often than not neglected to take the degree. At Oxford, where such students were more plentiful, 47 per cent took the degree. On the other hand, a full 90 per cent of Oxford students entering the Church, law, medicine and academia took the degree.

It was much more common for university-educated sons of clergymen to enter the Church than it was for student sons of lawyers, doctors, businessmen and civil servants to follow in their fathers' footsteps. This was undoubtedly because the university formed the normal channel of recruitment into the Church whereas it was far from the accepted avenue to the other careers. Although a large number of sons of clergy did enter orders, the Church drew its recruits from a wide diversity of backgrounds, but almost always through the universities.

Education of business recruits, 1660–1800

The above discussion suggests that the universities continued to be recruiting grounds for the Church, first and foremost, contributing but little to the search for well-educated businessmen. Where, if anywhere, did business recruits obtain their higher education? The majority of Leeds merchants down to 1780, both wealthy and less wealthy, sent their sons to the Free Grammar School until the age of fifteen. Their classical education was supplemented by private tuition in writing, book-keeping, mathematics and languages on an occasional basis. After 1780 it was much more common for merchants' sons to attend one of the dissenting academies or one of the Anglican private academies prior to apprenticeship. Benjamin and John Gott, for example, sons of a wealthy Anglican merchant, were sent to Heath Academy and then to Canon Tate's school in Richmond for two years, before transferring to a school in Dumfries. They attended two sessions of lectures at the University of Edinburgh from 1809 to 1811. This was lavish education: more typical was entry to apprenticeship at the age of fifteen. Before 1750 this apprenticeship often included a year in Holland visiting foreign correspondents and picking up languages which would be useful in the Leeds export trade. The popularity of the dissenting academies as preparatory schools for merchants is also attested to by Gordon Jackson in his study of eighteenth-century Hull. Once again, he notes that such academies (Mercantile Academy, Bond Street Academy, Brigham's Academy and Hull Academy) achieved this popularity not before the last quarter of the century. Presumably Hull's merchant community was content to use the grammar school before this date.[15]

We do know that some merchants' sons chose to attend one of the Scottish universities, which catered to a much larger extent than the English for the sons of business and professional men. Yet one should be careful not to exaggerate the Scottish connection. W. M. Matthew's study of the University of Glasgow indicates that while foreign students made up a surprisingly high proportion of the student body (25.4 per cent in 1740) a large number of these students were Irish, not English. And we have the greatest evidence for the attendance of both English and Irish students in medical faculties both at Glasgow and at Edinburgh, not the arts faculties. Studies of the English business community (such as those of Bristol by R. I. James, Hull by Gordon Jackson and Leeds by R. G. Wilson) suggest that British businessmen were not very interested in higher education. When they were interested in providing a university education for their sons it was intended almost exclusively to channel them into another calling. Thus it seems to have been reasonably common for second and third sons to be sent either to a university or to an Inn of Court to prepare for a gentle calling. Most sons of merchants who attended Hull grammar school and went on the Cambridge, took up careers in the Church although a few made more unorthodox choices, such as a diplomatic or military career. We are on relatively safe ground if we conclude that the business community did not bypass the English universities in order to train sons destined for a business career at one of the Scottish universities. Neither did they recruit many members from among the graduates of either Scottish or English universities.[16]

Modernisation of the English universities' curriculum

If we accept that the English universities continued to be preoccupied with the requirements of the English Church, it is nonetheless possible to argue that the curriculum was modernised in the interests of society. When Nicholas Hans examined the careers of 494 outstanding eighteenth-century scientists he discovered that no fewer than 34 per cent had received an education at either Oxford or Cambridge. The percentage was even higher among non-medical and non-technological celebrities. This alone cannot prove that the universities formally provided an atmosphere conducive to scientific advance. Nevertheless, there were institutional innovations at the ancient universities which suggest some attempt to acknowledge the natural place of the sciences in an academic syllabus.[17]

Such innovations appear to have occurred largely in the early eighteenth century. For instance, a Readership in Chemistry was established at Oxford in 1704 and the appointee John Freind lectured to large audiences in the Ashmolean Museum, publishing them in 1709. In the late 1730s the Dutch trained chemist Nathaniel Alcock lectured privately at Jesus, Oxford. His popularity prompted the university to provide formal lectures in his subjects, chemistry and anatomy. When Alcock continued to capture the student audience, he was made Praelector in Chemistry at the university. He continued to lecture enthusiastically until 1759 when he left Oxford.

John Keill, lecturer in natural philosophy at Hart Hall, introduced experimental methods into his comparatively well-attended lectures and continued to give these lectures from the time of his appointment as Savilian Professor of Astronomy in 1712 until his death in 1721. At this time a course of lectures in astronomy was established. James Bradley, who was his successor as Savilian Professor from 1721 to 1729, was from 1729 to 1760 Whiteside Lecturer in experimental philosophy. In this capacity he offered two courses of lectures per annum, which commanded an average attendance of fifty-seven students despite the levy of an extra fee. The study of botany, which had been popular in the mid seventeenth century universities (with the foundation of the only English botanical garden) was now further entrenched by the establishment of the Sherardian Chair of Botany in 1728 and its occupancy from 1734 until 1747 by John Dillenius, a prominent Swedish botanist.

At Cambridge also the study of astronomy and of mathematics was furthered by the preferment of able individual scholars to university positions. The newly established Plumian Chair of Astronomy (1704) was held between 1705 and 1716 by Roger Cotes, who was a pioneer of experimental methodology. In 1707 Cotes and the Professor of Mathematics, William Whiston, offered a course in hydrostatics and pneumatics at the Trinity College Observatory. Whiston's successor, the blind mathematician Nicholas Sanderson, was the leading mathematician of the period. John Colson, who succeeded him in 1739 and held the position until 1760, lectured regularly. Similarly, Cotes had an able and conscientious successor. The chair of chemistry was founded in 1703 and at least two of its three early holders, John Hickleburg and John Hadley, held regular lecture courses. Chairs of anatomy (1707), botany (1724) and geology (1728) were created although the last two appear to have been held as sinecures.[18]

The signs are that a decent scientific education was available to a few students in the early eighteenth-century universities. Hans argued that the rot set in during the later eighteenth century, when chairs were used as rewards and the real work was allocated to resentful assistant lecturers. Nevertheless, he urged that the constant flood of scientific publications from the Cambridge University Press indicates that the University itself was still concerned to maintain and improve its scientific reputation.[19]

Quite clearly the universities did not totally neglect scientific studies. Not only the dissenting academies offered a scientific education. Nevertheless, only a fraction of the student population would have partaken of the university offering, which was extended for the most part to students with the bachelor's degree. As residence requirements were not enforced for the MA degree it was inevitable that lecture courses would be poorly attended. In 1728 only twenty-eight chemistry students attended Hickleburg's lectures.[20]

The education of physicians and surgeons

The rising number of physicians and surgeons in late seventeenth-
and eighteenth-century England were certainly not the products of
the ancient universities of England. Many, like Richard Kay, received their education in school and then through a combination of
'extra-mural' courses in urban centres and apprenticeship, and took
their training in one of the London teaching hospitals. Kay was
made a pupil of the House Apothecary of Guy's Hospital for one
year. His experience was practical: he worked in the wards and
attended lectures and demonstrations but never commented upon
his reading. The only mention of books in his diary for this period is
made when he packs up his belongings for the return home. The
training resembled that of the apprentice rather than that of the student. It is interesting to note that he attended a course in midwifery
(practical as well as theoretical) in Ferrard Street along with his
master, another apothecary and a young physician from St Thomas's
hospital. Perhaps this means that the personnel of the London hospitals took advantage of private enterprise extra-mural courses in
medical specialties.[21]

Other physicians had attended a continental or a Scottish university medical school. But until the eighteenth century even Scottish medical students studied abroad, usually at Leyden. It is true
that King's College, Aberdeen, had a Mediciner even before the
Reformation, that Glasgow had a chair of medicine in 1637 and that
Edinburgh possessed three chairs of medicine in 1685 but the
teaching of medicine in the Scottish universities during the seventeenth century was theoretical and often perfunctory. Medicine
established itself in the Scottish universities in the eighteenth century. Edinburgh added a chair of anatomy in 1705, a chair of midwifery in 1739 and series of lectures in clinical medicine at the Royal
Infirmary in 1746. The chair of medicine at Glasgow was made
permanent in 1714; the Chandos Chair was established at St
Andrews in 1730 and a new chair of medicine was founded at Marischal College, Aberdeen, in 1700. The practical aspects of medical
teaching, so neglected in the seventeenth century, were given their
rightful attention with the creation of hospitals in the university
towns. The Royal College of Physicians helped build Edinburgh's
first hospital in 1729 (a larger one was built in 1741); Aberdeen Infirmary was erected in 1741; in 1794 Glasgow's Royal Infirmary was
built.[22]

The growing importance of medical education in certain of the
Scottish universities can be attested to by the expansion of numbers
at the universities during the eighteenth century and the proportion
of this expansion which was accounted for by the growth of medical
studies. In the seventeenth century Edinburgh was chiefly a seminary with fewer than two hundred students. By 1700 there were 300

students and 8 faculty. By the end of the eighteenth century the figures were 1,279 students and 21 faculty: 660 of the students were studying medicine. Glasgow expanded from a mere 100 students in 1600 to 400 in 1700. By the third decade of the nineteenth century over a third of enrolments were in the medical faculty. Neither Aberdeen nor St Andrews shared in this boom and St Andrews offered no course in medicine despite the existence of an MD degree there. The number of MD degrees granted by Edinburgh, the leading producer of doctors for most of the eighteenth century, itself rose only gradually, mounting to a crescendo in the second decade of the nineteenth century (Table 14.1).

Table 14.1 Average number of M.D.s granted by the University of Edinburgh per annum.

1727–50	6
1750s	12
1776	18
1786	32
1796	31
1806	37
1816	76
1826	118

In the eighteenth century it was far from uncommon for the country physician to have avoided totally so-called institutions of higher education in the interests of more practical training.[23]

Neither must we rush to assume that the medical education offered in Scotland was good, or even adequate, nor to believe that all who possessed an MD from a Scottish university had actually studied there. We know for instance that Andrew Bell obtained an MD degree from St Andrews in 1786 although he had never studied medicine there. The Royal Commission which inquired into the state of the Scottish universities in 1826 commented adversely on the sale of medical degrees. St Andrews, for example, had been selling an average of twenty MDs per annum *in absentia*. The Senatus banned this only in 1826. The Commission exonerated Edinburgh alone from blame. It is known that Tobias Smollett purchased the degree of MD from Marischal for £28 Scots and a certificate from two friends after he had practised medicine for a while. In 1722 James Clegg failed to obtain a degree *in absentia* from Edinburgh but was awarded a 'diploma medicum' from King's College, Aberdeen, in 1729 on the recommendation of three medical practitioners. It was common for colonial, and perhaps English, students to spend one or two years at a London teaching hospital prior to taking a medical degree at a Scottish university after a year or less of study. In 1767 the University of Edinburgh tried to tighten up on this practice by introducing to its statute book a requirement that all students take a three-year curriculum of medical study, which included at least one year in residence at Edinburgh, before being permitted to take the MD degree.[24]

There has been some controversy regarding the state of the English universities in the eighteenth century. Some studies convey an impression of communities of students of ample means dedicated to a life of idleness, indulging in extravagant liberality and venting their boredom in violence and frivolity, on the one hand, and groups of hard-working, poor servitors and sizars concentrating on their work and currying favour with the well-connected, on the other. According to this view, the professors used their chairs as sinecures; the dons were relatively well paid and negligent. An opposing view, put forward by Dame Lucy Sutherland in the James Bryce Memorial Lecture of 1972, urges that this picture is excessively reliant upon the impressions of Gibbon, who criticised the standards of college teaching in the early 1750s. Gibbon, she observed, was a fellow-commoner and, therefore, not intended to be a 'serious student'. Other evidence suggests that commoners were in regular and frequent contact both with their tutors and with their lecturers. In fact, Dame Lucy argued, the students' study was too regimented, if anything, and the burden of classes too heavy rather than too light. There were frequent complaints that college teaching was both 'lifeless and mechanical' but little suggestion that it was negligently performed. It was difficult to persuade fellows to become college tutors and lecturers – the majority were non-resident and not marked by intellectual distinction. Those who did undertake tutorial teaching were conscientious. At the same time, early eighteenth century Oxford was characterised by much extra-curricular cultural activity. Students took private lessons in music, arts and modern languages and formed their own discussion and study groups. The university itself offered courses in poetry, common law and science. There seems to have been considerable intellectual activity in the area of Anglo-Saxon, classical, theological and scientific studies in the first half of the century, which was followed by relative stagnation but not by complete 'intellectual inertia' in the mid century.[25] Does either caricature fit the Scottish universities equally well?

The Scottish universities

While it is true that the English universities had defined catchment areas, the Scottish universities were much more closely connected to their surrounding hinterlands. Glasgow, for example, expanded considerably during the later eighteenth century because of a notable population explosion in the West Central counties of Ayr, Renfrew and Lanark upon which she drew. In 1755 these three counties accounted for 16 per cent of the Scottish population; by 1831 they held 25 per cent of the total population. This was the most rapidly industrialising part of Scotland and the social origins of Glasgow students reflected the changing class structure of the locality. Whereas in 1740–49 26 per cent of the students came from an industrial or commercial background and 31.9 per cent from a noble or landed background, by 1790–99, 49.9 per cent of the students originated in the industrial and commercial classes and only 6.7 per cent in the noble or landed classes. By the late eighteenth century the Scottish rural upper classes were tending to educate their offspring in England. Over the same period the proportion of working class youths (from skilled artisan and master craftsman backgrounds) also rose dramatically – from 1.9 per cent in 1740–49 to 47.9 per cent in 1790 –91. According to W. M. Matthew this rise was due to the fact that these classes were profiting from the general expansion of wealth and commerce in the area. The percentage of working-class students fell in the nineteenth century (although the total number rose) when the Scots weaving industry was hit by mechanisation.[26]

These figures should not mislead us into thinking that the University of Glasgow was feeding highly educated men back into commercial and industrial communities, either at the middle or lower levels of society. The indications are that higher education represented a way out of these communities for all but a small percentage of students. For instance, the Presbyterian ministry took the majority of Scottish working-class students. Training for the ministry was extremely cheap: in the mid eighteenth century it was possible to obtain a university education for about £5 a year (as against £100 or £50 at Oxford or Cambridge) and no fees were charged for divinity students. The outlay needed had risen only to £20 by 1820. Only 12 per cent of matriculands entered business careers: even this is significant when we compare it with the 3 per cent of Cambridge alumni entering business late in the nineteenth century but it indicates, nevertheless, that great numbers of Glasgow students from business families were determinedly moving away from their background. The contention that large numbers of students in the Arts faculty eventually entered medicine is difficult to test in the absence of adequate documentation. Certainly medicine attracted 38.7 per cent of enrolments in the period 1831–36.[27]

In the late seventeenth century Edinburgh College was extremely poor, unable to attract a distinguished faculty and offering an unspecialised, unthought out curriculum. From 1703 William Carstairs, the new Principal, reorganised the College on the lines of the Dutch universities in an attempt to attract both local and foreign students. The College was no longer just a Presbyterian seminary but also a professional school with modern faculties of law and medicine. Until 1708 the College had adopted a teaching system of rotating regents which did not favour the growth of either advanced or specialised study. Each class would remain with the same regent master for the four years of the undergraduate course and be taught by him in all subjects. Only in 1708 were specialist chairs of humanity, Greek, logic and metaphysics, natural and moral philosophy founded. Shortly thereafter three specialist legal chairs were created as was the Chair of Universal Civil History, and Greek and Roman Antiquities. The eighteenth century witnessed the establishment of many more specialist chairs in the medical faculty and the sciences. Despite these innovations, the education offered was still traditional in tone. For example, much of the teaching in the arts faculty was done in Latin down to the middle of the century. But standards did improve and the number of students rose. In 1704 65 men graduated and in 1705 104. The medical faculty began to draw men from both England and Ireland. Within the College as a whole there existed a deep gulf between the well-to-do foreign students and the poor local boys.

By the 1720s the University had gained an international reputation and, because many alumni, faculty members and students belonged to the clubs of the new *literati* (even, in the case of the Professor of Mathematics, Colin McLaurin, providing leadership), the University itself became involved in the movement to lead Edinburgh society and permeate Scottish culture with its ideology. McLaurin demonstrated his conviction that science was an agent of social progress through his lectures on Newtonian science. Moreover, he deliberately sought to include non-academics in the membership of the university medical society and to open his lectures to polite Edinburgh society as well as to university students in an attempt to show the utility of learning.[28]

Such a course brought problems in its train. In the later eighteenth century the College almost ceased to be a degree granting institution. Students attended classes but neglected to graduate. In the eighteenth century the Senatus did attempt to make graduation from the arts faculty compulsory for new divinity students (*c.* 1738) but this measure had no permanent effect, probably because the Church's General Assembly never made graduation compulsory for new ordinands although it did insist that candidates had attended classes. Although estimates of the numbers of graduates per annum vary, it is clear that graduation was sorely neglected. And this was common to all the Scottish universities except Aberdeen.[29]

Yet student numbers at all the Scottish universities taken together increased from 1,000 in 1700 to 2,700 in 1800. This pattern is in marked contrast to that in England where graduation was less common among 'gentlemen' but was regarded as more or less obligatory for intending ordinands. The example of Walter Scott who attended courses of lectures in the Edinburgh arts faculty but who did not take his MA prior to studying law was less peculiar to Scotland than the example of the prospective ordinand who also neglected to take the MA. Edinburgh College appears to have been a dilettante community in which foreign students with a good deal of money spent their days attending extra-curricular lectures, for which they paid extra fees, and searching for universal knowledge rather than narrow scholarship or defined expertise. Yet our awareness of the fact that ordinands had to attend classes in the college before entering the divinity faculty should remind us that there may well have been many serious students also. When graduation ceased to be the norm, the curriculum ceased to have any meaning. Poorly paid university teachers neglected their regular classes and concentrated on fee-paying classes in an effort to make ends meet. In the earlier eighteenth century even the professors at Scottish universities earned only between £15 and £30 per annum. The average had been raised to only £50 by the century's end and it was by offering private classes that the more successful earned fees which raised their total income to approximately £150 a year. Contemporary critics of the universities blamed the poverty of the regular student body for this state of affairs: had the universities been able to ask realistic fees from the serious student there would have been no need to offer additional fee-paying courses, the professorate would have been adequately compensated and it would have performed its services conscientiously.[30]

Donald Withrington has argued that both Glasgow and Edinburgh responded to complaints about poor salaries and an antiquated curriculum by offering extra courses at an additional charge. In neither was this avenue closed by the existence of private academies. Both St Andrews and Aberdeen found it more difficult to solve the problem of poor salaries in such a way. Both universities were set in areas of less population and less wealth. After 1760 academies offered more satisfactory curricula. Moreover, in both cases separate institutions within the university were competing with one another for students. In 1747, after almost a decade of negotiations, two of St Andrews' colleges (St Leonard and St Salvator) were united. At Aberdeen attempts to unite the depressed Marischal and King's Colleges began in the 1640s but failed on several occasions because of disputes regarding the eventual location of the united college.[31]

Of particular interest to us is the fact that both colleges in Aberdeen demonstrated a keen awareness of the need to reorganise their respective curricula along more utilitarian and 'modern' lines. In 1753 the regent system was ended at Marischal and specialist professors were appointed to teach a curriculum which included a first year of Latin and Greek; a second year in which mathematics, natural history, geography and civil history were taught; a third year of essentially scientific studies (natural philosophy, mechanics, hydrostatics, pneumatics, optics, astronomy, magnetism, electricity);

and a final year of abstract philosophy. It was hoped 'that following this natural order will tend to render the study of the sciences [i.e. all learning] more advantageous in life than it is generally thought to be, and will remove the prejudices some have entertained against University Education as useless'. Apparently as a direct consequence of this reorganisation, numbers rose from 1755 onwards. King's College also revised its curriculum in 1753 along similar lines, extended the teaching year and provided larger bursaries to attract poorer, able students. Aberdeen was clearly adapting itself to suit the needs of students who were not necessarily bent on careers in the learned professions. In the absence of an analysis of the origins and eventual careers of Aberdeen graduates it is impossible to contrast the complexion of that university with, for example, Glasgow. Nevertheless, it is evident that the curriculum offered at Aberdeen was significantly more modern and utilitarian than that offered the undergraduate at other Scottish universities (as part of the set syllabus) or either English university.[32]

Conclusions

An examination of the British universities in the seventeenth and eighteenth centuries indicates that little attempt was made to adapt the traditional undergraduate education to the needs of the young man involved in commercial, industrial or scientific enterprise. After 1660 there is little evidence that the business community used the ancient universities of Oxford and Cambridge either as a recruiting ground or as a desirable way of preparing its own children for merchant life. More surprisingly, the Scottish universities, while more heavily patronised by the business and industrial classes, channelled a relatively small proportion of their intake into commerce and industry. It is true that this conclusion might be modified if we knew something of the eventual careers of Aberdeen and St Andrews' undergraduates after 1750 (although the numbers involved there were small in comparison) but the conclusion would still hold true for the larger universities of Edinburgh and Glasgow. Scottish students from lower- and middle-class backgrounds used the universities as a way to social mobility or, at the least, occupational mobility when the parent could not guarantee a livelihood. By the later eighteenth century, with some exceptions, intending businessmen, and many prospective professionals, were turning away from the burgh schools (in Scotland) and the grammar schools (in England) to the alternative of the dissenting academies or the Anglican academies for a preparatory education. This preliminary education was followed not by university but by a period of apprenticeship. The grammar schools and the universities continued to educate the landed classes and young men eyeing a career in the Church, although the Scottish universities lost their landed clientele to the South. Young men with other careers in mind were no longer satisfied that higher education offered anything relevant to their needs.

Conclusion

Writing the history of education is a more complicated business than many would concede. One cannot safely assume that this history can be written in terms of monolithic change. All sixteenth-century men did not worship at the shrine of a classical education. The sixteenth and early seventeenth-century universities did not deny their traditional role absolutely and perform an entirely new one – that of educating the gentry for civic service. The first degree did not become all important. The first literate laymen did not emerge during the days of the Tudors. In the eighteenth century the grammar schools did not disappear in the face of competition from the dissenting or other 'private' academies.

Of course, all the arguments which seek to pinpoint particular and important changes during the period contain some truth. My contention here has been to demonstrate that it is all too easy to exaggerate the pace and extent of change. Rarely, for example, did all groups within society or, even, members of one social class subscribe to an identical educational philosophy. Theory was seldom translated into practice without some local modification. While it is important to bring meaning out of history and to resist the temptation to dismiss the past as a mere tangle of inextricable events, ideas and attitudes, it is equally important that we should resist the temptation of bringing too much order out of chaos. The forces of conservatism and of change were both at work in early modern British society.

It is in this respect that a general monograph can best prove useful. For it is in the context of a long time-span that an attempt may best be made to assess the balance of various forces, to place detailed arguments in perspective and to arrive at a broad estimate of the contribution of that age to long-term educational development in Britain.

Notes and references

Chapter 1: Children and childhood

1. Philippe Aries, *Centuriès of Childhood*, Penguin, 1973.
2. William Perkins, 'A Treatise of the Vocations or Callings of Men' in *Works*, 1612 edition, vol. I, pp. 47–79; cf. Richard Baxter, *A Christian Directory*, 2nd edn, 1678, p. 110b; Richard M. Douglas, 'Talent and Vocation in Humanist and Protestant Thought' in T. K. Rabb and J. F. Seigel (eds), *Action and Conviction in Early Modern Europe*, Princeton University Press, 1969; Thomas Powell, *Tom of All Trades*, 1631 edn.
3. Peter Clark and Paul Slack, *English Towns in Transition*, Opus, 1976; Open University Course A322, *English Urban History, 1500–1780*, Milton Keynes, 1977; and A203, *Seventeenth-Century England: A Changing Culture, 1618–1689*, Milton Keynes, 1981, contains information on changes in domestic architecture.
4. Lawrence Stone, *The Family, Sex and Marriage in England, 1500–1800*, Weidenfeld & Nicolson, 1977, pp. 29–30, 132–5.
5. Margaret Spufford, 'First Steps in Literacy', *Journal of Social History*, 1980, *passim*.
6. John Marshall, *Diary of William Stout of Lancaster*, Chetham Society, 1967, p. 70.
7. Steven R. Smith, 'The London Apprentices as Seventeenth-Century Adolescents' in *P. & P.*, 1973; and 'Religion and the Conception of Youth in the Seventeenth Century', *History of Childhood Quarterly*, 1975; Anne Yarborough, 'Apprentices as Adolescents in Sixteenth Century Bristol', *Journal of Social History*, 1979.
8. K. J. Allison, 'An Elizabethan Village "Census"', *B.I.H.R.*, 1963; cited in Alan Macfarlane, *The Family Life of Ralph Josselin*, Cambridge University Press, 1970, p. 209.
9. *Family, Sex and Marriage, passim*; Lloyd De Mause, 'The Evolution of Childhood', *History of Childhood*, 1974.
10. Magdalen King-Hall, *The Story of the Nursery*, Routledge & Kegan Paul, 1958, pp. 46; Keith Thomas, 'The Changing Family', *Times Literary Supplement*, 21 October 1977.
11. Perkins, op. cit., vol. III, p. 759.
12. Richard Parkinson, *Life of Adam Martindale*, Chetham Society, 1845, p. 24–5; *Diary of William Stout*, pp. 70–1; Charles Jackson, *Yorkshire Diaries* Life of John Shaw, p. 123.

13. 'First Steps in Literacy', pp. 415, 417–18.
14. *Diary of William Stout*, p. 110.

Chapter 2: Literacy

1. Peter Heath, *English Parish Clergy on the Eve of the Reformation*, Routledge & Kegan Paul, 1969, pp. 13–26.
2. Entering orders provided an escape from serfdom for many villeins. Villeins were forbidden to attend school (because this implied eventual entry to orders) without permission from the lord, but many obtained this permission. Sometimes this was on condition that they would re-enter serfdom should they renounce orders. Nicholas Orme, *English Schools in the Middle Ages*, Methuen, 1973, p. 51; R. B. Dobson, *The Peasants' Revolt of 1381*, Macmillan, 1970, p. 346; S. R., II, 1816, pp. 157–8: according to the statute of Labourers, 1405/6, serfs no longer had to pay fines for schooling; Jo Ann Moran, 'Educational Development and Social Change in York Diocese from the Fourteenth Century to 1548', unpublished PhD thesis, Brandeis University, 1975, pp. 191–202; Robin L. Storey, 'Recruitment of English Clergy in the Period of the Conciliar Movement', *Annuarium Historiae Conciliorum*, 7, 1975.
3. *English Schools in the Middle Ages*, pp. 27–9, 32.
4. Ibid., pp. 11–56; Basil Cottle, *The Triumph of English, 1350–1400*, Blandford, 1969; Sylvia Thrupp, *The Merchant Class of Medieval London, 1300–1500*, University of Chicago Press, 1948; Helen Suggett, 'The Use of French in England in the Later Middle Ages' in R. W. Southern (ed.), *Essays in Medieval History*, Royal Historical Society, 1968.
5. Margaret Aston, 'Lollardy and Literacy', *History*, 62, 1977.
6. For a discussion of the impact of printing on the mind of man see Elizabeth Eisenstein, *The Printing Press as an Agent of Change*, Cambridge University Press, 1979, vol. I, pp. 43–159 *et passim*; for searching criticisms see Anthony T. Grafton, 'The Importance of Being Printed', *Journal of Interdisciplinary History*, 1980, pp. 265–85.
7. Some assume that because a vernacular Bible was adopted so enthusiastically by Reformers, there was already a substantial public who could read, ready and waiting for it. It is more probable that there was a nucleus of literate persons whom the Reformers wished to reach.
8. Thomas More, *Works*, 1557, p. 850; R. DuBoulay, *An Age of Ambition*, Nelson, 1970, p. 118; *Merchant Class*, pp. 156–8.
9. Jo Ann Moran, 'Literacy and Education in Northern England, 1350–1550', shortly to appear in *Northern History*. I thank Dr Moran for permission to read and to quote from her unpublished paper. See Nicholas Orme, *Education in the West of England*, University of Exeter Press, 1976, who agrees with Dr Moran that the number of schools had been seriously underestimated in his earlier work.
10. Imogen Luxton, 'The Reformation and Popular Culture' in F. Heal and R. O'Day (eds), *Church and Society in England, Henry VIII to James I*, Macmillan, 1977, pp. 67–8.
11. Charlotte A. Sneyd (ed.), *Italian Relation of England*, Camden Society, 1847, p. 23; David Cressy, *Literacy and the Social Order*, Cam-

bridge University Press, 1980, pp. 48–52; Keith Thomas, *Religion and the Decline of Magic*, Weidenfeld and Nicolson, 1971, pp. 45, 241, 494.

12. Leona C. Gabel, *Benefit of Clergy in England in the Later Middle Ages*, Smith College Studies in History, Massachusetts, 1928.

13. Patricia Took, 'The Government and the Printing Trade, 1540–1560', unpublished University of London Ph.D. thesis, 1979, *passim*.

14. Moran, *thesis cit.*, ch. 8, esp. pp. 311, 312, 340; 'The Reformation and Popular Culture', *passim* and esp. pp. 63–4.; Charles Phythian Adams, 'Ceremony and the Citizen : The Communal Year at Coventry, 1450–1550' in P. Clark and P. Slack (eds), *Crisis and Order in English Towns, 1500–1700*, Routledge & Kegan Paul, 1972, pp. 57–85; W. K Jordan, *The Charities of Rural England, 1480–1660*, Allen & Unwin, 1961; and *Philanthropy in England, 1480–1660*, Allen & Unwin, 1959; for a critique see L. Stone, 'The Educational Revolution in England, 1560–1640', *P. & P.*, 1964, pp. 44–7.

15. *Literacy and the Social Order*, p. 47.

16. 'The Educational Revolution' *passim*; Mark Curtis, *Oxford and Cambridge in Transition*, Oxford University Press, 1959.

17. David Cressy, 'Levels of Illiteracy in England, 1530–1730', *H. J.*, 1977, pp. 1–23; and 'Occupations, Migration and Literacy in East London, 1580–1640', *Local Population Studies*, 1970.

18. *Literacy and the Social Order*, pp. 118–41.

19. L. Stone, 'Literacy and Education in England, 1640–1900', *P. & P.*, 1969, pp. 99–101.

20. *Literacy and the Social Order*, pp. 62–103.

21. David Cressy, 'Educational Opportunity in Tudor and Stuart England', *History of Education Quarterly*, 16, 1976.

22. Ibid., p. 317.

23. *Literacy and the Social Order*, pp. 72–5.

24. Ibid., p. 65.

25. Ibid., p. 16.

26. Statute XLII, Merchant Taylors' School, London, 24 September 1561, instructed new poor scholars of the foundation to be placed on probation for one month : 'being found not apt and meet to learn, as aforesaid, that then this our admission of him to stand as void. . .'.

Chapter 3: A schooled society?

1. Joan Simon, *Education and Society in Tudor England*, Cambridge University Press, 1967, pp. 59–101; Kenneth Charlton, *Education in Renaissance England*, Routledge & Kegan Paul, 1965, pp. 89–130; see pp. 83, 86, 396, 405–6.

2. Charles Webster, *The Great Instauration*, Duckworth, 1975, *passim*.

3. The following paragraphs are based on Rosemary O'Day, 'Church Records and the History of Education in Early Modern England, 1642: A Problem in Methodology', *History of Education*, 1973, pp. 115–32.

4. Joan Simon, 'Town Estates and Schools in the Sixteenth and Early Seventeenth Centuries' in Brian Simon (ed.), *Education in Leicestershire: A Regional Study, 1540–1940*, Leicester University Press, 1968.

5. J. F. A. Mason, *The Borough of Bridgnorth, 1175–1957*, Bridgnorth, 1957; J. O. Halliwell (ed.), *The Autobiography and Correspondence of Sir Simonds D'Ewes*, 2 vols, London, 1845, I, p. 30; W. S. L., HM 308/ 40, Commonplace Book of James Whitehall, Rector of Checkley, Staffordshire; F. P. and M. M. Verney (comp.), *Memoirs of the Verney Family during the Seventeenth Century*, 2 vols, New York, 1907, i, pp. 433–4; J. D. Marshall (ed.), *The Diary of William Stout of Lancaster, 1665–1752*, Chetham Society, 1967, p. 72; J. C. Hodgson, 'Extracts from The Diary of Timothy Whittingham of Holmside', *Archaeologia Aeliana*, 3rd Ser., vol. XXI, 1924, pp. 206, 209.

6. P. Locatelli, 'L'enseignement primaire et les maitres d'école à la fin du xvii siècle dans la diocese d' Auxerre', *Revue d'Histoire de l'Eglise de France*, 1972, pp. 96–106.

7. Margaret Spufford, 'The Schooling of the Peasantry in Cambridgeshire, 1575–1700', *Agr. H. Rev.*, 1970, supplement, *passim*; W. G. Hoskins cited in B. Simon, 'Leicestershire Schools, 1625–1640', *B.J.E.S.*, 1954, pp. 56–7; A. F. Leach, *English Schools at the Reformation*, 1896, II, *passim*.

8. L.J.R.O., B/V/1/31; B/V/1/45; Alan Smith, 'Private Schools and Schoolmasters in the Diocese of Lichfield and Coventry in the Seventeenth Century', *History of Education*, 1976, p. 121.

9. Lawrence Stone, 'The Educational Revolution in England, 1560–1640', *P. & P.*, 1964, pp. 46–7; 'Private Schools and Schoolmasters', p. 121.

10. Edward Calvert (ed.), *Shrewsbury School Register, 1562–1635*, Shrewsbury, 1892; J. B. Oldham, *The History of Shrewsbury School*, Blackwell, 1952; G. W. Fisher, *Annals of Shrewsbury School*, Methuen, 1899. Alec Macdonald, *A Short History of Repton*, Benn, 1929; Bernard Thomas (ed.), *Repton, 1557–1957*, Batsford, 1957; Mrs G. Stephen, *Repton School Register, 1557–1910*, Lawrence, Repton, 1910.

11. Alec Macdonald, *A Short History of Repton*, Benn, 1929; Bernard Thomas (ed.), *Repton, 1557–1957*, Batsford, 1957; Mrs G. Stephen, *Repton School Register, 1557–1910*, Lawrence, Repton, 1910.

12. David Cressy, 'Educational Opportunity in Tudor and Stuart England', *History of Education Quarterly*, 1976, p. 310.

13. Ibid., pp. 310–11.

14. *V. C. H. Cambridge*, vol. II, p. 325.

15. 'Leicestershire Schools, 1625–1640', p. 50.

16. Ibid., p. 50.

17. G. P. Mander, *History of Wolverhampton Grammar School*, Wolverhampton, 1913, pp. 373–5; 280–1.

18. W. A. L. Vincent, *The State and School Education in England and Wales, 1640–1660*, Church Historical Society, S.P.C.K., 1950, pp. 20, 52–5, 96–7, 106, 111; T. Richards, *A History of the Puritan Movement in Wales*, National Eisteddford Association, 1920, pp. 226–31.

19. See pp. 81–8; Nicholas Orme, *English Schools in the Middle Ages*, Methuen, 1973; *Education in the West of England, 1066–1548*, University of Exeter, 1976; Jo Ann Moran, 'Literacy and Education in Northern England, 1350–1550', read before publication in *Northern History* by kind permission of Professor Moran.

20. A. J. Fletcher, 'The Expansion of Education in Berkshire and Oxford-shire, 1500–1670', *B.J.E.S.*, 1967, pp. 51–9.
21. 'Literacy and Education in Northern England', pp. 19ff. and accompanying table.

Chapter 4: Curriculum and method in schools, *c.* 1550–1650

1. John Byddell, *A Primer in English, with certain prayers and godly meditations, very necessary for all people that understand not the Latin tongue*, 1535.
2. Thomas Cromwell, *Injunctions given by the authority of the King's Highness, 1536.*
3. Thomas Cromwell, *Injunctions given by the authority of the King's Highness*, 1538.
4. *The Primer set forth by the Kinges maieste and his clergie . . .*, 1545.
5. See W. T. Costello, *The Scholastic Curriculum at Early Seventeenth Century Cambridge*, Harvard University Press, 1958, pp. 7–35 for a good discussion of the habits of mind encouraged by early seventeenth-century teaching and learning methods.
6. Margaret Aston 'Lollardy and Literacy', *History*, 62, 1977, pp. 348–50, 353–60.
7. John Foxe, *Acts and Monuments*, S. R. Cattley and G. Townsend (eds), London, 1837–1841, vol. IV, pp. 235–9; see also J. A. F. Thompson, *The Later Lollards*, Oxford University Press, 1965, pp. 90, 93.
8. See Frank Davies, *The Teaching of Reading in Early England*, Pitman, 1973, pp. 105–7 for a discussion of different catechisms in use: W. H. Rylands, 'Booksellers and Stationers in Warrington'.
9. Immanuel Bourne, *A Light from Christ Leading unto Christ*, London, 1646; Richard Baddiley, *Life of Thomas Morton*, York, 1669.
10. John Stalham, *Catechism*, 1644, cited in K. Wrightson and D. Levine, *Poverty and Piety in an English Village, Terling, 1525–1700*, Academic Press, 1979, p. 153; Charles Jackson (ed.), *Autobiography of Mrs Alice Thornton*, Surtees Society, 1875, p. 7.
11. Margaret Spufford, 'First Steps in Literacy: the reading and writing experiences of the humblest seventeenth-century spiritual autobiographers', *Journal of Social History*, 1979, especially pp. 411–15.
12. I. H. Chester Heralt [John Hart], *An Orthography containing the due order and reason, how to write or paint the image of man's voice, most like to the life or nature*, 1569; John Hart, *A Method or comfortable beginning for all unlearned whereby they may be taught to read*, 1570; Roger Ascham, *The Scholemaster*, 1570; see pp. 166–7.
13. Edmund Coote, *The English Schoolmaster*, 1596.
14. John Brinsley, *Ludus Literarius or the Grammar School*, 1612.
15. Ibid., p. 9.
16. Ibid., p. 10.
17. Ibid., p. 9.
18. Ibid., p. 10.
19. Ibid., p. 15.
20. Ibid., p. 16.

21. Ibid., p. 16.
22. Ibid., p. 17.
23. *The English Schoolmaster.*
24. *Ludus Literarius*, pp. 21–4; cf. the older tradition of moral education as cited in F. Furnivall (ed.), *The Babees Book*, E.E.T.S., 1868, pp. 1–9, 13–15.
25. *Ludus Literarius*, pp. 254–61.
26. For examples see *Ludus Literarius*, pp. 48–50.
27. John Stow, *Survey of London, 1598*, Everyman edition, 1912, p. 68. It is interesting to note that Colet had specifically forbidden the scholars of St Paul's to participate in these disputations, dismissing them as 'foolish babbling and loss of time', Joan Simon, *Education and Society in Tudor England*, Cambridge University Press, 1967, p. 95.
28. See Richard Mulcaster, *Positions*, 1581, pp. 279, 284, 288; and *Elementary*, pp. 22–3; Richard Parkinson, *Life of Adam Martindale*, Chetham Society, 1845, p. 13. J. Gailhard, in his *The Compleat Gentleman: or Directions for the Education of Youth as to their Breeding at Home and Travelling Abroad. In 2 treatises*, 1678, p. 17, maintained that teachers were accused by parents 'at one time of too much severity, another of neglect, and another time for giving too hard tasks'.
29. Useful discussions of the patronage system are contained in Guy Fitch Lytle, 'Patronage Patterns and Oxford Colleges, c.1300–c.1530' in L. Stone (ed.), *The University in Society*, Princeton University Press, 1974, vol. I, pp. 111–49; Rosemary O'Day, *The English Clergy, 1560–1640*, Leicester University Press, 1979, *passim*; and Rosemary O'Day, 'Ecclesiastical Patronage: who controlled the Church?' in F. Heal and R. O'Day (eds), *Church and Society in England, Henry VIII to James I*, Macmillan, 1977, *passim*.
30. Richard Mulcaster, *Elementary*, pp. 55–6, 'I will be as careful that the matter which he shall read may be so fit for his years and so plain to his wit, as when he is at school he may desire to go forward in so comfortable an argument, and when he comes home he may take great pleasure to be telling of his parents what pretty petty things he doth find in his book, and that the parents also may have no less delight to hear their little ones speak.'
31. *Ludus Literarius*, pp. 14–17.
32. Ibid., p. 23.
33. F. A. Specht, *History of Education in Germany from the earliest times to the middle of the thirteenth century*, Stuttgart, 1885, cited in *The Teaching of Reading*, p. 124.
34. *The Teaching of Reading*, p. 124.
35. Ibid., p. 124.
36. Ibid., pp. 124–6.
37. Tobias Ellis, *The English School*, 16.
38. Thomas Morley, *A Plain and Easy Introduction to Practical Music*, 1608, cited in *The Teaching of Reading*, p. 133.
39. John Buno, *Newly Set Out ABC and Reading Book*, 1650, cited in *The Teaching of Reading*, p. 133.
40. Foster Watson, *Vives, On Education, a Translation*, Cambridge University Press, 1913.

41. *The Teaching of Reading*, pp. 137–40; Sir Hugh Plat, *Jewel House of Art and Nature*, 1635, gives an illustration of an ABC Dice Game with rules; Charles Hoole, *A New Discovery of the Old Art of Teaching School*, 1660, describes several reading games; Thomas Tryon, *Some Memoirs of the Life of Mr Tho: Tryon, late of London, merchant: written by himself*, 1705, pp. 13–15 shows Tom himself learning to read the hard way at the age of 13 but he advocated much earlier instruction for others, using the equivalent of flash cards, pp. 122–3.
42. *Life of Adam Martindale*, p. 5.
43. Alan Macfarlane (ed.), *The Diary of Ralph Josselin*, British Academy, 1976, p. 423.
44. Ibid., p. 62.
45. Ibid., p. 75.
46. Ibid., p. 183.
47. Ibid., p. 191.
48. J. O. Halliwell (ed.), *Autobiography of Sir Simonds D'Ewes*, I, p. 30.
49. *Ludus Literarius*, p. 9, supports this contention.
50. For example, Philippe Ariès, *Centuries of Childhood*, Penguin, 1973, p. 226, shows that in the fifth class at Chalon in 1618 no single age-group accounted for more than 20 per cent of the class; and, p. 215, he illustrates the precocity of Grosley, who completed his studies at the Oratory of Troyes after two years in the logic class. At Wolverhampton Grammar School in 1609 the age-range of the accidence class was six to ten, with one pupil aged thirteen; form II contained fifteen boys between eight and eleven; form III had fifteen boys aged from nine to thirteen; division one of form IV contained eight boys in the age-range eleven to thirteen; division two possessed a nine-year-old, two seventeen-year-olds who had just come to the school, and eight boys ranging from twelve to fourteen years of age; in form V were seven boys aged from fourteen to seventeen; form VI contained two boys only, aged seventeen and eighteen. G. P. Mander, *A History of Wolverhampton School*, Wolverhampton, 1913, pp. 280–1, 373–5.
51. *Life of Adam Martindale*, p. 11.
52. W. S. L. Stafford, HM 308/40. Commonplace Book of James Whitehall, Rector of Checkley, Staffordshire; *Autobiography of Sir Simonds D'Ewes*, I, *passim*; J. and S. C. Venn, *Admissions to Gonville and Caius College, Cambridge . . . 1558–1579*, London, 1887, shows just how short a period many youths had spent at their last school prior to admission.
53. *Life of Adam Martindale*, p. 12.
54. Ibid., pp. 12–13.
55. Ibid., pp. 13–14.
56. Ibid., pp. 14–15; 24–5.
57. Ibid., pp. 25–8.
58. Cf. Richard Baxter, *Reliquiae Baxterianae*, 1696, p. 12.
59. Elizabethan Schoolroom Woodcut, 1592, from Radio Times Hulton Picture Library.
60. See pp. 54–5; William Perkins, *Works*, Cambridge, 1611 edition, *passim*; Robert Recorde, *Ground of Arts*, 1551.
61. *Ludus Literarius*, pp. 38–9; for examples of writing in school see W. A. L. Vincent, *The Grammar Schools: their continuing tradition*,

1660–1714, John Murray, 1969, p. 73, where he notes that the statutes of Clare (post 1660), Deptford (1672) and Kingsbury (1686) stipulated the ability of the master to teach writing as well as grammar, and observes that both Durham and Camberwell offered writing prizes. Presumably the practice grew more common in the second half of the seventeenth century.

62. *Autobiography of Sir Simonds D'Ewes*, I, pp. 95, 104.
63. *Ludus Literarius*, pp. 27–38.
64. Robert Recorde, *Ground of Arts*, 1551; discussed in Foster Watson, *The Beginning of the Teaching of Modern Subjects in England*, 1909.
65. See p. 174; cf. Richard Billingsley, *An Idea of Arithmetic*, 1655, prepared for pupils of Thurlow Free Grammar School, Suffolk; *Life of Adam Martindale*, pp. 36, 175–8; *The Grammar Schools*, p. 99.
66. Will of Gervase Sleigh, P.R.O., PCC. 1624.
67. *The Grammar Schools*, p. 22 et passim.
68. *The Grammar Schools*, p. 69; Will of Gervase Sleigh cited; also see discussion in Kenneth Charlton, *Education in Renaissance England*, Routledge & Kegan Paul, 1965.
69. Joan Simon, 'Private Classical Schools in Eighteenth Century England: a critique of Hans', *History of Education*, 1979, pp. 179–91, has drawn attention to the inappropriate use of the term 'private school' in the early modern period.
70. See David Cressy, 'Educational Opportunity in Tudor and Stuart England', *History of Education Quarterly*, 16, 1976, *passim*, but especially pp. 302, 316.
71. *Education in Renaissance England*, p. 105.
72. John Brinsley, *A Consolation for Our Grammar Schools*, 1622.
73. For example Christ's Hospital; see, *Education and Society in Tudor England*, pp. 240, 284; *History of Wolverhampton Grammar School*, pp. 373–5, gives a good example of this hierarchy of subjects.
74. Mulcaster, *Positions . . . The Training up of Children*, 1581, pp. 235–7.
75. *Education in Renaissance England*, pp. 109–11; *Autobiography of Sir Simonds D'Ewes*, I, pp. 95, 104; R. P. Sorlien, *The Diary of John Manningham*, University of Rhode Island Press, 1976, *passim*.
76. John Holte, *Lac Puerorum or Mylke for Children*, 1479; both *Education in Renaissance England* and *Education and Society in Tudor England* contain excellent discussions of Tudor textbooks.
77. *The Grammar Schools*, pp. 80–1.
78. *Life of Adam Martindale*, pp. 14–15, 22.
79. Ibid., pp. 26–8, describes the teaching methods and subjects of a master for whom he had a greater respect and who taught Adam Greek for three years.
80. John Baret, *Alvearie or Triple Dictionarie*, 1573, preface; see J. H. Sledd, 'Baret's "Alvearie", an Elizabethan reference book', S. P., 43, 1946, pp. 147–63; D. T. Starnes, 'An Elizabethan "Dictionarie for Yonge Beginners"', *Studies in English*, 29, 1950, pp. 51–6.
81. Elizabeth Eisenstein, *The Printing Press as an Agent of Change*, Cambridge University Press, 1979, especially pp. 86–106 for comments on the impact of techniques developed by printers on the world of scholarship.
82. *The Grammar Schools*, p. 82; *Education in Renaissance England*, pp.

51–2, 116; Sir Thomas Elyot, *Bibliotheca Eliotae: Eliot's Librarie*, 1538; revised edition 1542; enlarged editions by Thomas Cooper, Master of Magdalen School, 1548, 1552, 1559.

83. For a discussion of misrule see K. V. Thomas, 'Rule and Misrule in the Schools of Early Modern England', The Stenton Lecture, 1975, University of Reading, 1976, *passim; Ludus Literarius*, pp. 37, 51, 68, 268.

84. *The Grammar Schools*, p. 62, suggests the following timetable:

6 or 7 a.m. – 8 or 8.30 a.m.	lessons
half or three-quarters of hour	breakfast
9–11 a.m.	morning school
11–1 p.m.	lunch break
1–5 or 6 p.m.	afternoon school

Half Day
Tuesday or Thursday.
Holidays
5–8 weeks, distributed between Christmas, Easter and Whitsun.
The timetable varied between seasons and between school and school, however.

85. 'Rule and Misrule', p. 7, quoting from John Wilmot, *Memoirs of the Life of Sir John Eardley Wilmot*, 1811, p. 178.

Chapter 5: The role of the ancient universities to 1640

1. This interpretation of the development of Oxford and Cambridge in the later Middle Ages is based on a reading of A. B. Cobban, *The Medieval Universities, their Development and Organization*, Methuen, 1975, especially pp. 96–109; 110–15; Mark Curtis, *Oxford and Cambridge in Transition*, Oxford University Press, 1959, pp. 16–24; Hastings Rashdall, *The Universities of Europe in the Middle Ages*, F. M. Powicke and A. B. Emden (eds), Oxford University Press, 1936, 3-volume 2nd edn, vol. III.

2. Claire Cross, *The Royal Supremacy in the Elizabethan Church*, Allen & Unwin, 1969; also see Claire Cross, 'Churchmen and the Royal Supremacy' in F. Heal and R. O'Day (eds), *Church and Society in England, Henry VIII to James I*, Macmillan, 1977.

3. S. R., 13 Eliz. I, c. 29; cf. *Oxford and Cambridge in Transition*, p. 29.

4. I am currently preparing a detailed study of church government in the context of the professionalisation of the clergy.

5. *Statuta Reginae Elizabethae*, 'An. XIImo Edita', c. 41; George Dyer (ed.), *The Privileges of the University of Cambridge*, London, 1824, pp. 189–91; John Griffiths, *The Laudian Code of Statutes* (with an introduction by C. L. Shadwell), Oxford, 1888, title xvii, sec. 4, art. i; title xiii.

6. See *Oxford and Cambridge in Transition, passim*; Lawrence Stone, 'The Educational Revolution in England, 1560–1640', *P. & P.*, 1964, *passim*. Almost all later literature takes this assumption as read, even including Hugh Kearney's, *Scholars and Gentlemen: Universities and Society*, Faber & Faber, 1970, *passim*.

7. Elizabeth Russell, 'The Influx of Commoners into the University of Oxford before 1581: an optical illusion?', in *E.H.R.*, 92, 1977, pp. 721–45. T. H. Aston, G. D. Duncan and T. A. R. Evans are more ambivalent about the relationship between their own findings and Stone's in 'The Medieval Alumni of the University of Cambridge', *P. & P.*, 1980.
8. G.F. Lytle, 'Oxford Students and English Society, c.1300–1530', Unpublished PhD thesis, Princeton University, 1974, pp. 68 seq.; T. H. Aston, 'Oxford's Medieval Alumni', *P. & P.*, 1977, pp. 17–18; 19; 'The Medieval Alumni of ... . Cambridge', p. 52.
9. 'The Medieval Alumni of ... Cambridge', pp. 13–18; 52; 'Oxford's Medieval Alumni', pp. 19, 53.
10. A. B. Emden, *A Biographical Register of the University of Oxford to A. D. 1500*, 3 vols, Oxford University Press, 1957–9, pp. 500–11; 'Oxford's Medieval Alumni', pp. 10–11.
11. 'The Medieval Alumni of ... Cambridge', pp. 26–8; see pp. 108–12.
12. *Medieval Universities*, pp. 134–5; Clara P. McMahon, *Education in Fifteenth Century England*, Johns Hopkins University Press, 1968, pp. 26–30.
13. 'Oxford Students and English Society', p. 31.
14. See G. F. Lytle, 'Patronage Patterns and Oxford Colleges' in Lawrence Stone (ed.), *The University in Society*, Princeton University Press, 1974, vol. I, *passim*; 'Oxford Students and English Society', pp. 51–6; F. Pegues, 'Royal Support of Students in the Thirteenth Century', *Speculum*, 1956, pp. 454–62.
15. *Medieval Universities*, p. 139; 'Oxford Students and English Society', p. 31.
16. *Medieval Universities*, pp. 139–40. Cobban makes it clear that this was a gradual decline. Even in 1550, 8 halls accommodated 200 students, compared with 450 in 13 colleges. This probably was true even in the 1580s after the first wave of the great expansion: cf. Lawrence Stone, 'The Size and Social Composition of the Oxford Student Body, 1580–1910', in L. Stone (ed.), *The University in Society*, vol. I, p. 34.
17. 'The Influx of Commoners ...', pp. 735–6.
18. *Medieval Universities*, pp. 142–4; Kenneth Charlton, *Education in Renaissance England*, Routledge & Kegan Paul, 1965, pp. 132–4: God's House was an undergraduate college from the start. 'Size and Social Composition', p. 25, gives the date of the introduction of the formal tutorial system as at Exeter (1564), Balliol (1574), Brasenose (1576) and University (1583); 'Influx of Commoners', pp. 725–6.
19. 'Influx of Commoners', pp. 732, 734–5, 741, 743–4.
20. 'Medieval Alumni of ... Cambridge', pp. 12–13, 26; *V. C. H. Cambridge*, vol. III, pp. 160, 162; *The Historical Register of the University of Cambridge*, 1917, p. 987.
21. *Scholars and Gentlemen*, p. 22.
22. Joel T. Rosenthal, *The Purchase of Paradise*, Routledge & Kegan Paul, 1972, *passim*; 'Oxford Students and English Society', p. 131; R. W. Chambers, *Thomas More*, Cape, 1935, p. 66; J. H. Hexter, 'The Education of the Aristocracy in the Renaissance', in *Reappraisals in History*, Longman, 1963; K. B. Macfarlane, *The Nobility of Later Medieval England*, Clarendon Press, 1973, *passim*; 'Medieval Alumni of ... Cambridge', pp. 48–51, 84–6.

23. 'Education of the Aristocracy . . .', *passim*; *V. C. H. Cambridge*, vol. III, pp. 176–7.
24. R. M. Fisher, 'Thomas Cromwell, Humanism and Educational Reform, 1530–1540', *passim. B.I.H.R.*, 1977.
25. See More's attack on the role of the aristocracy in political life in E. Surtz, S. J. and J. H. Hexter (eds), Thomas More, *Utopia*, Yale University Press, 1965, pp. li–liv; and Thomas Elyot on the civic role of the gentleman serving the king in S. E. Lehmberg (ed.), Thomas Elyot, *The Book Named the Governor*, Everyman, 1962, *passim*; 'The Educational Revolution', p. 60.
26. 'The Educational Revolution', p. 60; F. J. Furnivall (ed.), *William Harrison's Description of England, 1577*, New Shakespeare Society, Ser. IV, pt. i, 1877, pp. 77–8.
27. Henry Peacham, *The Compleat Gentleman*, 1622, pp. 39–40.
28. Simonds D'Ewes, B.L. Harl. MS 379, fo. 65, cited in Richard Tyler, 'The Children of Disobedience'; 'the social composition of Emmanuel College, Cambridge, 1596–1645', unpublished PhD thesis. University of California, Berkeley, 1976, p. 100.
29. 'Children of Disobedience', p. 100.
30. Ibid.
31. Cf. James McConica, 'Scholars and Commoners in Renaissance Oxford', in L. Stone (ed.), *The University in Society*, vol. I, p. 175; Lord Burghley to the Vice Chancellor, 30 June 1587, B.L. Lansd. 54, fo. 27r; Bodleian MS Rawlinson, C. 936, 1, 5, dated 5 April; J. R. Bloxam, *Register of Magdalen*, Oxford, 1853, vol. IV, pp. 194 seq.
32. 'Children of Disobedience', p. 101; 'Scholars and Commoners', pp. 160, 161, 165, 169, 170.
33. 'Children of Disobedience', pp. 101–2.
34. Folger Library, Bagot MSS La 56; *Education in Renaissance England*, p. 149.
35. *Oxford and Cambridge in Transition*, pp. 60–1; Joan Simon, 'The Social Origins of Cambridge Students, 1603–1640', *P & P.*, 1963, pp. 58–67.
36. 'Children of Disobedience', pp. 147–52; 'Scholars and Commoners', *passim*.
37. 'Children of Disobedience', p. 109.
38. Ibid., p. 110.
39. J. and S. C. Venn, *Admissions to Gonville and Caius College, Cambridge . . . 1558–1579*, London, 1887, s. n. Nicholas Cobbe, 1564.
40. Bodleian Tanner MS 50, fo. 53; Lawrence Stone, 'Communication: The Alienated Intellectuals', *P. & P.*, 1962.
41. Wilfrid Prest, *The Inns of Court*, Longman, 1972, pp. 30–2; 'The Educational Revolution', p. 59. Although the social status of members of the Inns was falling over the late sixteenth and early seventeenth centuries, this was because of a rise in the number of sons of lawyers entering, themselves an ambiguous category.
42. 'Children of Disobedience', pp. 47, 49, 54.
43. 'Children of Disobedience', p. 53; 'Size and Social Composition', p. 10; *Education in Renaissance England*, p. 140; 'Scholars and Commoners', *passim*.

44. 'The Educational Revolution', p. 63.
45. J. H. Gleason, *The Justices of the Peace in England, 1558–1640*, Oxford University Press, 1969.
46. 'Education of the Aristocracy', p. 55.
47. T. G. Barnes, *Somerset, 1625–40*, Oxford University Press, 1961, p. 31; 'Size and Social Composition', pp. 28–9.
48. 'Size and Social Composition', p. 27.
49. See p. 133; for a discussion on the same lines relevant to the Inns of Court see *The Inns of Court*, p. 39 concerning Alan Harding, *A Social History of English Law*, Penguin, 1966, p. 250; Also see L. A. Knafla, 'The Matriculation Revolution and Education at the Inns of Court in Renaissance England', in A. J. Slavin (ed.), *Tudor Men and Institutions*, Louisiana State University Press, 1972, pp. 243–4. This demonstrates also the continuity of college connections at the Inns (p. 243 and Table VII).
50. Victor Morgan, 'Cambridge University and the "Country"', in L. Stone (ed.) *The University in Society*, vol. I, pp. 183–245.
51. G.L.M.S. 9535/2; see discussion of the role of the universities in the geographical mobility of the clergy in Rosemary O'Day, *The English Clergy, 1560–1640*, Leicester University Press, 1979, pp. 4–8, 137–9.
52. *The English Clergy*, pp. 6–7; 'Scholars and Commoners', p. 175. Emmanuel drew upon Essex, Kent, Suffolk, Norfolk, Northants, and Sussex; St John's, Jesus and King's on Essex, Kent, Lincs, Yorks and Wales.
53. See pp. 106–12; 115.
54. 'Size and Social Composition', p. 39; 'Children of Disobedience', pp. 47, 163, 175–6.
55. 'Children of Disobedience', p. 114.
56. Ibid., pp. 153, 171.
57. J. G. Milne, *The Early History of Corpus Christi College, Oxford*, Basil Blackwell, Oxford, 1946; *V. C. H. Oxon*, III, 1954; 'Size and Social Composition', p. 38; H. C. Porter, *Puritanism in Tudor England*, Macmillan, 1971, pp. 182–194 reprints an extract from the statutes of Emmanuel, 1585; 'Children of Disobedience', p. 69, citing Benjamin Whichcote to Anthony Tuckney in Benjamin Whichcote, *Moral and Religious Aphorisms*, 1753; 'Children of Disobedience', pp. 40–2, 68, 75, 91; the number of students who followed their migrating tutors is well illustrated in *Admissions to Gonville and Caius, passim*.
58. 'Size and Social Composition', p. 36; 'Children of Disobedience', pp. 157–8; see pp. 94–5; Folger Library, Bagot MSS La. 176, 177, 61, 62, 55, 58, 59, 286.
59. See pp. 132–50.
60. David Cressy, 'Educational Opportunity in Tudor and Stuart England', *History of Education Quarterly*, 16, 1976, p. 312; Margaret Spufford, 'The Schooling of the Peasantry in Cambridgeshire, 1575–1700', *Agr. H. Rev.*, 1970, Supplement, pp. 115, 118; Margaret Spufford, 'First Steps in Literacy', *Journal of Social History*, 1979, *passim*.
61. 'Children of Disobedience', pp. 148–9, 110; *The English Clergy*, p. 161.
62. 'Educational Opportunity', p. 312.

Chapter 6: Teaching and learning in the Tudor and Stuart Universities

1. Mark Curtis, *Oxford and Cambridge in Transition*, Oxford University Press, Oxford, 1959, pp. 85–92; *Statuta Reginae Elizabethae*, c. vi; George Dyer, *The Privileges of the University of Cambridge*, 1824, i, p. 164; 'Nova Statuta of 1564/5' in Strickland Gibson (ed.), *Statuta Antiqua Universitatis Oxoniensis*, Oxford University Press, 1931, pp. 389–90.
2. *Statuta Reginae Elizabethae*, c. iv; *Privileges*, i, pp. 161–2.
3. Lawrence Stone, 'Size and Social Composition of the Oxford Student Body', in L. Stone (ed.), *The University in Society*, 2 vols, Princeton University Press, 1974, vol. I, pp. 29–33; Kenneth Charlton, 'Ages of admission to educational institutions in Tudor and Stuart England: a comment', *History of Education*, 1976, pp. 221–6; Richard L. DeMolen, 'Ages of Admission to Educational Institutions in Tudor and Stuart England', *History of Education*, 1976, pp. 207–19; David Cressy, 'School and College Admission Ages in Seventeenth Century England', *History of Education*, 1979.
4. *Statuta Antiqua*, section i, p. 530; *Oxford and Cambridge in Transition*, p. 88; John Griffiths (ed.), *Statutes of the University of Oxford codified under the authority of Archbishop Laud*, Oxford, 1888, title iv, sec. i, chapters 2, 3, 4, 5, 6, 12.
5. *Oxford and Cambridge in Transition*, *passim*, and especially p. 123.
6. Ibid., pp. 98–9.
7. Emmanuel College Library, Cambridge, MS. 48 (Pressmark 1, 2, 27), 30 fos, cited in Hugh Kearney, *Scholars and Gentlemen*, Faber & Faber, 1970, pp. 103–4; *Oxford and Cambridge in Transition*, p. 99, discusses authorship in appendix also; Hugh Aveling and W. A. Pantin (eds), *The Letter Book of Robert Joseph* 1530–1533, Oxford Historical Society, 19, 1967, pp. 269–85.
8. Rosemary O'Day, 'The Ecclesiastical Patronage of the Lord Keeper, 1558–1642', T.R.H.S., 1973, pp. 89–109; John Pruett, *The Parish Clergy under the Later Stuarts*, University of Illinois Press, 1978, pp. 41–2, 49–50, 54–5; *Oxford and Cambridge in Transition*, pp. 150–1.
9. See pp. 196–216; 260–81.
10. Cf. Wilfrid Prest, *The Inns of Court*, Longman, 1972, pp. 137–42, 153–66.
11. J. Bass Mullinger, *The University of Cambridge*, 3 vols, Cambridge, 1873–1911, II, pp. 96–7; Andrew Clark, *Register of the University of Oxford*, 2 vols in 5 parts, Oxford Historical Society, 1885–9, I, part i, pp. 67, 70; H. Stuart Jones, 'The Foundation and History of the Camden Chair', in *Oxoniensia*, 1943–4.
12. Christopher Hill, *The Intellectual Origins of the English Revolution*, Oxford University Press, 1965, pp. 54–5.
13. *Oxford and Cambridge in Transition*, pp. 89–90; W. T. Costello, *The Scholastic Curriculum at Early Seventeenth Century Cambridge*, Harvard University Press, 1958, pp. 14–31, and especially p. 15, John Day's MA notebook, Oriel College, Oxford, Bodleian MS Rawlinson,

D274; Richard Parkinson (ed.), *Life of Adam Martindale*, Chetham Society, 1845, p. 53.

14. *V.C.H. Cambridge*, III, p. 190.
15. James Heywood (compiler and translater), 'statutes of King Edward VI in his *Cambridge University and College Statutes in the English Language*, London, 1855, II, p. 171; Folger Library, Bagot MSS La. 56, 179.
16. Godfrey Davies (ed.), *Autobiography of Thomas Raymond and Memoirs of the Family of Guise of Elmore, Gloucs.*, Camden Society, 1917, p. 116; Bodleian MS Gr. Misc., D. 2, fo. 48; Samuel Clarke, *A Collection of the Lives of Ten Eminent Divines...*, 1662, pp. 86, 129, 57; E. J. L. Scott (ed.), *Letter-book of Gabriel Harvey, 1573–1580*, Camden Society, 1884, pp. 52–4; James Duport, 'Undergraduate Life under the Protectorate' (ed.), G. M. Trevelyan in *Cambridge Review*, 1943, pp. 328–30; P. Bliss (ed.), Anthony Wood, *Athenae Oxonienses*, 2 vols, London, 1813, ii, pp. 561–2; J. O. Halliwell (ed.) *Autobiography and correspondence of Sir Simonds D'Ewes*, I, pp. 107, 122, 128, 147–8; Folger Library, Bagot MSS La. 859, 177.
17. *Autobiography and correspondence of Sir Simonds D'Ewes*, I, pp. 120–2: Jefferson Loomey, 'Undergraduate Education at Early Stuart Cambridge', *History of Education*, 1981, p. 14.
18. Daniel Featley's notebook, *c.* 1604–5, Bodleian MS Rawlinson, D47, fos 55r–56r, 57r.
19. Thomas Newman's notebook, Bodleian MS Top. Oxon, fo. 39, fos 18r, 19r.
20. See especially Bodleian MS CCC 254, fo. 23, cited in *Oxford and Cambridge in Transition*, pp, 120–1.
21. Notebook of John Gandy, Bodleian MS Rawlinson, D947.
22. Folger Library, Bagot MSS La. 53.
23. E. Bourcier (ed.), *Diary*, p. 136.
24. R. B. McDowell and D. A. Webb, 'Courses and Teaching at Trinity College, Dublin during the first 200 years', *Hermathena*, 1947, pp. 9–10.
25. *V. C. H. Oxon*, III, p. 124; John F. Fuggles, 'A History of the Library of St John's College, Oxford from the Foundation of the College to 1660', unpublished BLitt thesis, University of Oxford, 1975, p. 3; F. M. Powicke, *The Medieval Books of Merton College, Oxford*, Clarendon Press, 1931, pp. 11, 196–7; R. W. Hunt, 'The Medieval Library', in John Buxton and Henry Williams (eds), *New College, Oxford, 1379–1979*, Warden and Fellows of New College Oxford, 1979, pp. 321–2; Vivian Green, *The Commonwealth of Lincoln College, 1427–1977*, Oxford University Press, 1979, pp. 25, 49.
26. *Lincoln College*, pp. 34–5, 36, 49–51; N. R. Ker, 'Oxford College Libraries in the Sixteenth Century', *Bodleian Library Record*, 1957–61, p. 482; *et passim*.
27. E. F. Jacob (ed.), Sir Edmund Craster, *The History of All Souls College Library*, Faber & Faber, 1971, pp. 20, 37–40.
28. *All Souls*, pp. 41; 'Library of St John's College', pp. 8, 35, 57–9, 65–6, 96.

29. *Merton*, p. 8; *All Souls*, pp. 13, 14, 16, 20, 29, 33; 'The Medieval Library', pp. 318, 328–36; 'Library of St John's College', p. 100.
30. 'The Medieval Library', p. 337; 'Library of St John's College', pp. 8, 40, 135; 'The Medieval Library', pp. 317–18; 'Oxford College Libraries', 1959, VI, pp. 470–2, 507–8; *All Souls*, pp. 49–50.
31. 'The Medieval Library', pp. 336 *seq.*; *All Souls*, pp. 59–60.
32. *V. C. H. Oxon*, III, pp. 15, 22–3; *Merton*, p. 255; *Lincoln*, p. 225.
33. *Merton*, p. 248; *Lincoln*, pp. 148–50.
34. *V. C. H. Oxon*, III, pp. 22–3.
35. C. E. Mallett, *A History of the University of Oxford*, 2 vols, Methuen, 1924, p. 220.; *V. C. H. Cambridge*, III, p. 312, indicates that by a statute of 1471/2, access to the University Library was restricted to graduates; this rule was relaxed to allow monks to use the library in 1550. In 1533/4 the doors were ordered to be locked and only graduates and 'gremiats' were given a key.
36. 'Undergraduate Education', *passim*; *Lincoln*, pp. 226–7, suggests the type of 'luxury' book buying which a wealthy undergraduate might indulge in.
37. B. L. Harl. 3783, fo. 43r.
38. Bodleian MS. Tanner, fos 29–30v, copy letter from Earl of Essex to Sir Fulke Greville; *Letter-book of Gabriel Harvey*, p. 168; S. R. Maitland, 'Original Papers Relating to Whitgift', *The British Magazine*, 1847, 1848; Whitgift's contribution is discussed in Hugh Kearney, *Scholars and Gentlemen*, pp. 37–8; Kearney discusses the 'country humanist' tradition, in which he claims both clergy and gentry were educated, on p. 44 and cites the example of the Carnsew brothers, P.R.O. SP46/15.
39. *Oxford and Cambridge in Transition*, pp. 93–4.
40. Ibid., pp. 94–5.
41. *Scholars and Gentlemen*, pp. 46–70; D. Fenner, *Arte of Logike*, 1584; R. MacIlmaine, *The Logike*, 1574.
42. *Scholars and Gentlemen*, p. 47; *Letter-book of Gabriel Harvey*, p. 167.
43. *Scholars and Gentlemen*, pp. 51–2.
44. Webster implies that Mead was anti-Aristotelian in approach: Charles Webster, *The Great Instauration*, Duckworth, 1975; *Scholars and Gentlemen*, pp. 84–5; Kenneth Charlton, *Education in Renaissance England*, Routledge & Kegan Paul, 1965, pp. 146–8.
45. William Perkins, 'On Callings', in *Works*, 3 vols, 1612.
46. *Scholars and Gentlemen*, pp. 51–2.
47. James McConica, 'Humanism and Aristotle in Tudor Oxford', *E. H. R.*, 1979, pp. 291–317, maintains the continued vitality of academic Aristotelianism in the sixteenth century. His study of the teaching of Aristotle is extremely detailed but his point does not contradict that of *Scholars and Gentlemen* (which accepts that Ramism had little direct influence at Oxford) so much as that of *Oxford and Cambridge in Transition*, p. 253.
48. *Letter-book of Gabriel Harvey*, pp. 78–9, 167; *Oxford and Cambridge in Transition*, pp. 136–7.
49. *Oxford and Cambridge in Transition*, p. 185; *Ten Eminent Divines*, p. 275; *Statuta Antiqua*, p. 309 (in 1579 all Oxford colleges were instructed to engage a catechist).

Chapter 7: Educating clergymen

1. For general background works see section in the bibliography 'Clergy of the Church of England'.
2. Rosemary O'Day, *The English Clergy, 1560–1640*, Leicester University Press, 1979, pp. 24–32; 126–43.
3. See Peter Heath, *English Parish Clergy on the Eve of the Reformation*, Routledge & Kegan Paul, 1969, pp. 187–90.
4. *English Parish Clergy*, p. 16; H. S. Bennett, 'Medieval Ordination Lists in English Episcopal Registers', in J. Conway Davies (ed.), *Studies Presented to Sir Hilary Jenkinson*, Oxford University Press, 1957.
5. For a detailed discussion of these attempts see *The English Clergy*, pp. 33–85, 126–43.
6. F. D. Price, 'Gloucester Diocese under Bishop Hooper', *T.B.G.A.S.*, 1939, pp. 51–151.
7. *The English Clergy*, p. 25.
8. Ibid., pp. 128–31.
9. N.L.W. MS 4919D, The Letter Book of Bishop Thomas Bentham of Coventry and Lichfield, fos 49, 65, 81; G.L.M.S. 9535/1.
10. J. Bruce (ed.), *Correspondence of Matthew Parker*, Parker Society, Cambridge, 1853, pp. 120–1.
11. *The English Clergy*, pp. 49–65; C.U.L.E.D.R. A5/1; see also C. W. Foster (ed.), *Lincoln Episcopal Records in the time of Thomas Cooper*, Lincoln Record Society Publications, II, 1912, p. 138.
12. *Matthew Parker*, pp. 120–1.
13. *The English Clergy*, p. 50.
14. H. G. Owen, 'The London Parish Clergy in the Reign of Elizabeth I', unpublished PhD thesis, University of London, 1957, pp. 122–37; *The English Clergy*, pp. 66–74.
15. R. W. Henderson, *The Teaching Office*, Edinburgh University Press, 1962, p. 233; R. Donaldson, 'Patronage and the Church: A Study in the Social Structure of the Secular Clergy in the Diocese of Durham, 1311–1540', unpublished PhD thesis, University of Edinburgh, 1955, has interesting information on the numbers of non-resident graduate clergy.
16. See pp. 88–97.
17. John Griffiths (ed.), *Statutes of the University of Oxford codified under the authority of Archbishop Laud*, Oxford, 1888.
18. Richard Baxter, *Reliquiae Baxterianae*, 1696, p.12; *The English Clergy*, pp. 126–43; Richard Parkinson (ed.), *Life of Adam Martindale*, pp. 48–9; Lawrence Stone, 'The Size and Social Composition of the Oxford Student Body', in L. Stone (ed.), *The University in Society*, 2 vols, Princeton University Press, 1974, I, p. 27.
19. *The English Clergy*, pp. 135–6, citing G.L.M.S. 9535/2; G.C.L, G.D.R. Bishops' Act Books; L.J.R.O. B/A/4A/17, 18; Bodleian Library ODP, c264 vol. II; e9, e12, e13; N.R.O. Ordination Books of the Diocese of Peterborough, 1570–1642.
20. For an extreme position see Mark Curtis, 'The Alienated Intellectuals of Early Stuart England', reprinted in Trevor Aston (ed.), *Crisis in Europe*, Past and Present, 1965, pp. 295–316; for discussion see *The English Clergy*, pp. 17–23.

21. *The English Clergy*, pp. 126–43; Hugh Kearney, *Scholars and Gentlemen*, p. 31.
22. *Scholars and Gentlemen*, pp. 34–45.
23. Taken from the extracts printed in H. C. Porter, *Puritanism in Tudor England*, Macmillan, 1971, pp. 182–94.
24. Richard Baddeley, *Life of Thomas Morton*, 1669, p. 96; L.J.R.O., B/A/4A/18; W. Scott and J. Bliss (eds), *Works of William Laud, 1847–1860*, 7 vols, Oxford, vol. V, p. 363.
25. For details of the anti-ministry lobby see Christopher Hill, *Change and Continuity in Seventeenth Century England*, Weidenfeld & Nicolson, 1974, pp. 127–48; R. L. Greaves, *The Puritan Revolution and Educational Thought*, Rutgers University Press, 1969, *passim*.
26. *The English Clergy*, pp. 159–71; Alan Macfarlane (ed.), *The Diary of Ralph Josselin*, British Academy, 1976, *passim*.
27. P. Collinson, 'Lectures by Combination', *B.I.H.R.*, 48, 1975, *passim*.
28. *The English Clergy*, pp. 167–70.
29. John Morgan, 'Godly Learning', unpublished PhD thesis, University of Cambridge, 1977, pp. 337–49.
30. *Puritan Revolution*, pp. 9, 15–25; verse taken from *Rump: or an exact collection of the choicest poems and songs relating to the late times*, 1662, pt i, p. 15 (cited *Puritan Revolution*, p. 20).
31. John Pruett, *The Parish Clergy under the Later Stuarts*, University of Illinois Press, 1978, pp. 38–9; 'Size and Social Composition', pp. 35–38.
32. A good short account is given in F. W. B. Bullock, *A History of Training for the Ministry*, St Leonards on Sea, 1955, upon which this section is based; see also T. Wilson, *Short Account of Dr Sherlock*, in the reprint of Thomas Wilson, *Works*, Oxford 1863, vol. vii, p. 277; *D.N.B.* Sherlock; J. Keble, *Life of Thomas Wilson*, Oxford, 1863, pt i., p. 34; *D.N.B.* Whitby (for Burnet); G. Burnet, *A Discourse of the Pastoral Care*, 1692, Ch. 7.
33. C. Cruttwell, *Life of Thomas Wilson*, Bath, 1781, vol, i, p. xxiv; S. L. Ollard, G. Crosse and M. Bond, *A Dictionary of Church History*, articles 'Theological Colleges' and 'Wilson'.
34. *Training for the Ministry*, pp. 94–5.

Chapter 8: Legal change and the education of lawyers before the
Civil Wars

1. Thomas Powell, *Tom of All Trades*, 1631 edn.
2. Lewis Abbott, *Law Reporting in England, 1485–1585*, Athlone 1973, pp. 15, 23.
3. *Law Reporting*, pp. 227–39. This discussion is particularly good. J. H. Baker (ed.), *The Reports of Sir John Spelman*, vol. 2, Selden Society, 94, 1978, also deals with the way in which the common law met 'the new range of potentially lucrative problems'.
4. *Law Reporting*, pp. 219, 223, 226–7.
5. Although many prominent lawyers did spend time at an Inn of Chancery; for example from autumn 1560 until autumn 1561 Thomas Egerton was a member of Furnivall's Inn, administered by Lincoln's Inn.

(D. S. Bland (ed.), *Early Records of Furnivall's Inn*, Newcastle upon Tyne, 1957, p. 93.)
6. Wilfrid Prest, *The Inns of Court*, Longman, 1972, p. 141.
7. Ibid., pp. 119–30.
8. E. Bourcier (ed.), *Diary*, pp. 103–5, 132, 153, 159, 191; R. P. Sorlien, *The Diary of John Manningham*, University of Rhode Island Press, 1976, p. 73. One of the most thorough and illuminating discussions of the education of an individual lawyer is contained in Louis Knafla, *Law and Politics in Jacobean England*, Cambridge University Press, 1977, pp. 39–64; and 'The Law Studies of an Elizabethan Student', *H.L.Q.*, 1969, pp. 221–40.
9. *Inns of Court*, pp. 119–20.
10. William Holdsworth, *A History of English Law*, 3rd edn, Methuen, 1945, vol. 5, pp. 340–55; 393–6; Kenneth Charlton, *Education in Renaissance England*, Routledge & Kegan Paul, 1965, pp. 174–87; Michael Birks, *Gentlemen of the Law*, Stevens & Sons, 1960, pp. 103–6; *Inns of Court*, pp. 119–30.
11. *Law Reporting*, pp. 104–13, especially p. 105.
12. *Law and Politics*, pp. 50–1.
13. H. S. Bennett, *English Books and Readers, 1475–1557*, 2nd edn, Cambridge University Press, 1969, pp. 76–81; and *English Books and Readers, 1558–1603*, Cambridge University Press, 1965, pp. 156–66; *Inns of Court*, pp. 132, 143–9.
14. L. A. Knafla, 'The Matriculation Revolution and Education at the Inns of Court in Renaissance England', in A. J. Slavin (ed.), *Tudor Men and Institutions*, Louisiana State University Press, 1972, p. 242: the percentage of university students enrolling at the Inns between 1561 and 1581 rose more than threefold – from 13 per cent to 42 per cent of the annual admissions. By 1601 49 per cent of admissions were to university students. It is not possible from these figures to ascertain whether more sons of lawyers attended university before the Inns of Court than other types of entrant.
15. J. F. Mozley, *John Foxe and His Book*, S.P.C.K., 1940, p. 5.
16. *Diary*, pp. 139–40.
17. Although it was not described in so many words by Fortescue. It had first been described thus by Sir George Buc in 'The Third Universitie' according to *Inns of Court*, p. 115n.
18. *Tom of All Trades*, pp. 23–4.
19. Ibid., p. 24 (this page is mispaginated: it should be p. 25).
20. Ibid.
21. Huntington Library, Ellesmere MSS 482; 5647–5713; 5810–5892; as cited in *Law and Politics*.

Chapter 9: Was there a teaching profession?

1. Kenneth Charlton, 'The Professions in Sixteenth Century England', *U.B.H.J.*, 1967; Patrick Orpen, 'Schoolmastering as a Profession in the Seventeenth Century: the career patterns of the grammar schoolmaster', *History of Education*, 1977; Richard L. DeMolen, 'Richard Mulcaster and the Profession of Teaching in Sixteenth Century England',

J.H.I., 1974; Kenneth Charlton, 'The Teaching Profession in Sixteenth and Seventeenth Century England', in P. Nash (ed.), *History and Education*, Random House, 1970; Alan Smith, 'Private Schools and Schoolmasters in the Diocese of Lichfield and Coventry in the Seventeenth Century', in *History of Education*, 1976; W. R. Fayerharm, 'The Status of the Schoolmaster and the Continuity of Education in Elizabethan East Anglia', in *History of Education*, 1976; David Cressy, 'Education and Literacy in London and East Anglia, 1580-1700', unpublished PhD thesis, University of Cambridge, 1973.

2. Nicholas Orme, *English Schools in the Middle Ages*, Methuen, 1973, pp. 151-5.
3. Ibid., pp. 156-60.
4. Roger Ascham, *The Scholemaster*, 1570, title page.
5. Richard Mulcaster, *Positions*, 1581, pp. 269, 251.
6. William Perkins, 'Of the Calling of the Ministerie', in *Works*, 1612, vol. III, p. 433.
7. 'Schoolmastering as a Profession', pp. 185, 189, 190.
8. Taken from my own survey of Salop archdeaconry using L.J.R.O. records; Lawrence Stone, 'The Educational Revolution in England, 1560-1640', in *P. & P.*, 1964, pp. 46-7.
9. L.J.R.O. B/A/4A/17, 18 (subscriptions); B/V/1/32, 37, 57, 62; B/V/1/38 -46, 48-50, 53-6, 58-61, 63-6 under relevant parish name.
10. L.J.R.O. B/V/1/31, 33; 45; 34; 51-2; 33; S.R.O. Q.S.R. Epiphany 1634/5, 29.
11. *Letter-book of Gabriel Harvey*, p. 181.
12. 'Schoolmastering as a Profession', p. 186; Richard L. DeMolen, 'Richard Mulcaster, An Elizabethan Savant', unpublished PhD thesis, University of Michigan, 1970, pp. 20, 25, 30-6, 40, 42.
13. W. A. L. Vincent, *The Grammar Schools: their continuing tradition, 1660-1714*, John Murray, 1969, pp. 161-3, 166.
14. *Grammar Schools*, p. 113; L.J.R.O. B/A/11B, Nominations of Schoolteachers by parish, incomplete.
15. Richard Parkinson (ed.), *Life of Adam Martindale*, Chetham Society, 1845, *passim*.
16. L.J.R.O. B/A/11B, under parish.
17. Ibid.
18. Nicholas Hans, *New Trends in Education in the Eighteenth Century*, Routledge & Kegan Paul, 1951. pp. 63-135.

Chapter 10: The education of girls and women in society, 1500-1800

I owe a good deal to discussions with Professor Hilda Smith of the University of Maryland, College Park. I am indebted to her for permitting me to read and to cite from her forthcoming monograph, *Reason's Disciples*, to be published by University of Illinois Press.

1. For the working life of women see: Alice Clark, *Working Life of Women in the Seventeenth Century*, 1919; Mildred Campbell, *The English Yeoman*, Merlin Press, 1942.

2. John Marshall (ed.), *The Diary of William Stout of Lancaster*, Chetham Society, 1967, pp. 68, 74, 75.
3. Roger Thompson, *Women in Stuart England and America*, Routledge & Kegan Paul, 1974, *passim*; but see K. Wrightson and D. Levine, *Poverty and Piety in an English Village, Terling 1525–1700*, Academic Press, 1979, p.47, which does suggest that the age of women at marriage was not universally high. Richard Parkinson (ed.), *Life of Adam Martindale*, pp. 6–7.
4. Lawrence Stone, *Family and Fortune*, Clarendon Press, 1973, pp. 108–9; John Barrett, *Spa Towns*, in Open University Course A322, *English Urban History, 1500–1780*, Milton Keynes, 1977.
5. Folger Library, Bagot MSS La.598, 599, 486: the last of these demonstrates that even in gentry families in the sixteenth century daughters were sometimes allowed a veto on their marriage partner. This was certainly true in middle-class families such as that of Ralph Josselin in the later seventeenth century. *Diary of William Stout*, p. 159. H. J. Morehouse (ed.) 'Dyurnall of Adam Eyre', *passim*.
6. Dorothy Gardiner, *English Girlhood at School*, Oxford University Press, 1929, pp. 197–201, 126, 121–2, 125, 232; I. Pinchbeck and M. Hewitt, *Children in English Society*, Routledge & Kegan Paul, vol. I, 1969, pp. 27–33. See also D. M. Meads (ed.), *Diary of Lady Margaret Hoby, 1599–1605*, Routledge & Sons, 1930, *passim*. in the introduction.
7. J. L. Vives, *Instruction of a Christian Woman*, translated by Richard Hyrd and reprinted in Foster Watson (ed.), *Vives and the Renaissance Education of Women*, London, 1912.
8. Richard Mulcaster, *Positions*, 1581, pp. 180–1, 173–4; also see *English Girlhood*, p. 151, for the attitude towards the education of Beatrice of Naples.
9. *Positions*, pp. 166–83; W. A. L. Vincent, *The Grammar Schools: their continuing tradition*, John Murray, 1969, pp. 46–7, 106–7; Norma McMullen, 'The Education of English Gentlewomen, 1540–1640', in *History of Education*, 1977, p. 88, claims that Polesworth, Warwickshire, with a divided schoolroom in March 1654/5, was the first school specifically for both sexes.
10. Eileen Power, *Medieval English Nunneries*, Cambridge University Press, 1922, pp. 268–9; Thomas Becon, *Catechism*, in John Ayre (ed.), *Works of Thomas Becon*, Parker Society, Cambridge, 1844, II, pp. 370, 377; *English Girlhood*, pp. 195, 209–11, 217.
11. Folger Library, Tamworth MSS, Ph MS 28688 Folder: I used this manuscript shortly before the collection was sorted and catalogued by the Folger Library. This is the old class mark. I wish to thank Professor Esther Cope for drawing my attention to its existence and Dr Laetitia Yeandle, Archivist of the Folger, for her assistance in dating the document.
12. Samuel Pepys, *Diary*, 1825 edn, p. 44; Alan Macfarlane (ed.), *The Diary of Ralph Josselin*, pp. 367, 540, 574, 585; *English Girlhood*, pp. 214–17.
13. *English Girlhood*, pp. 217–19.
14. Mary Astell, *A Serious Proposal to the Ladies for the Advancement of their True and Greatest Interest*, 1697, pp. 42–52; Samuel Tuke, *Education in the Society of Friends*, 1871, pt i, p. 10.

15. Bathsua Makin, *An Essay to Revive the Antient Education of Gentle-women*, 1673, p. 42.
16. J. Axtell (ed.), *The Educational Writings of John Locke*, Cambridge University Press, 1968, especially pp. 354–5; Daniel Defoe, *An Essay upon Projects*, 1697, p. 302.
17. Nicholas Hans, *New Trends in Education in the Eighteenth Century*, Routledge & Kegan Paul, 1951, pp. 198–9, 203–5; Lawrence Stone, *The Family, Sex and Marriage in England, 1500–1800*, Weidenfeld & Nicolson, 1977, pp. 343–60, gives numerous examples of eighteenth-century girls' schools.
18. Derek Robson, *Some Aspects of Education in Cheshire in the Eighteenth Century*, Chetham Society, 1966, pp. 78–9; in Edinburgh James Blundell's aristocratic Latin school took 94 girl pupils (as against 567 boys) in the eighteenth century.
19. David Cressy, 'Levels of Illiteracy in England, 1530–1730', *H. J.*, 1977; especially p. 8; and his *Literacy and the Social Order*, Cambridge University Press, 1980, pp. 145, 147.
20. Alan Macfarlane, *The Family Life of Ralph Josselin*, Cambridge University Press, 1970, pp. 44–51, 91–98.
21. *Diary of John Evelyn*, 1819 edn., II, p. 300.
22. Patrick Collinson, 'The Role of Women in the English Reformation . . .', in G. J. Cuming (ed.) *Studies in Church History*, II, pp. 258–72; K. V. Thomas, *Women and the Civil War Sects'*, *P. & P.*, 1958, pp. 44–57; Patricia Higgins, 'The Reactions of Women' in B. Manning, (ed.), *Politics, Religion and the English Civil War*, Manchester University Press, 1973.
23. *English Girlhood*, p. 235.
24. Information taken from Hilda Smith, *Reason's Disciples*, University of Illinois Press, forthcoming; Alexander Law, *Education in Edinburgh in the Eighteenth Century*, Athlone, 1965, pp. 157–70.
25. *Diary of William Stout*, pp. 68, 90, 91, 103, 105, 74, 81, 135, 112, 119, 151.

Chapter 11: The educational scene, 1660–1800: an overview

1. Figures are taken from Lawrence Stone, 'The Size and Social Composition of the Oxford Student Body, 1580–1910', in L. Stone (ed.), *The University in Society*, 2 vols, Princeton University Press, 1974, I, passim.
2. Richard Parkinson (ed.), *Life of Adam Martindale*, Chetham Society, 1845, p. 24; John Eachard, *The Grounds and Occasions of the Contempt of the Clergy and Religion*, 1671, p. 143; John Pruett, *The Parish Clergy under the Later Stuarts*, University of Illinois Press, 1978, p. 53.
3. 'Size and Social Composition', p. 43.
4. The two preceding paragraphs are based on material contained in W. A. L. Vincent, *The Grammar Schools: their continuing tradition, 1660–1714*, John Murray, 1969, pp. 3–9, 36ff.
5. A. F. Leach, 'Schools', in *V. C. H. Derbyshire*, II, pp. 221, 242; *V. C. H. Sussex*, II, p. 423; *Grammar Schools*, p. 5; Nicholas Hans, *New Trends in Education in the Eighteenth Century*, Routledge &

Kegan Paul, 1951, *passim*; Joan Simon, 'Private Classical Schools in Eighteenth Century England', *History of Education*, 1979, pp. 179–91; Richard S. Tompson, *Classics or Charity?* Manchester University Press, 1971, *passim*.

6. R. Pemberton, *Solihull and its Church*, Exeter, 1905, p. 152; *Grammar Schools*, pp. 50, 52, 55, 56; *V. C. H. Gloucs.*, II, p. 395.

7. Anon, *The Children's Petition*, 1669; *Grammar Schools*, p. 65, quoting *The Spectator*, no. 157 (30 Aug. 1711); and no. 168 (12 Sept. 1711), pp. 151, 160, 211, 212.

8. *Grammar Schools*, pp. 102–3; A. A. Mumford, *The Manchester Grammar School, 1515–1915*, Manchester, 1919, pp. 192–7, 232.

9. L.J.R.O., B/A/11B Nominations of Schoolmasters and Mistresses, incomplete, by parish.

10. *Grammar Schools*, p. 106; Nicholas Carlisle, *A Concise Description of the Endowed Grammar Schools in England and Wales*, 2 vols, London, 1818, II, pp. 209, 278; *V. C. H. Essex*, II, p. 545; *Grammar Schools*, p. 99, citing Schools Inquiry Commission, vol. I, appendix iv, p. 73.

11. *Grammar Schools*, p. 105, citing Wase MSS, CCC Oxon, 390/2 fo. 203; M. McDonnell, *A History of St Paul's School*, London, 1909, p. 403.

12. *Grammar Schools*, p. 102, citing W. H. D. Rouse, *A History of Rugby School*, 1898, pp. 120, 130–4, 137–9, 156.

13. *New Trends*, p. 20; M. V. Wallbank, 'Eighteenth Century Public Schools and the Education of the Governing Elite', *History of Education*, 1978, pp. 1–19 *passim*.

14. *Parish Clergy under the Later Stuarts*, pp. 41–2, 49–50, 54–5; *New Trends*.

15. Daniel Hirschberg, 'A Social History of the Anglican Episcopate, 1660–1760', unpublished PhD thesis, University of Michigan, 1976, citing William Cowper, *Letters*.

16. *New Trends*, however defective as an interpretation, remains the standard general source for the *types* of education available in eighteenth-century England.

17. *New Trends*, pp. 121–4; K. V. Thomas, 'Rule and Misrule in the Schools of Early Modern England', The Stenton Lecture, 1975, University of Reading, 1976, p. 12.

18. *New Trends*, pp. 117–35, *passim*.

19. 'Rule and Misrule', p. 7, citing John Wilmot, *Memoirs of the Life of . . . Sir John Eardley Wilmot*, 1871, p. 178; *The Moderate Intelligencer*, 5–12 Feb. 1645/6; John Dury in B. L. Sloane MSS 649, fos 52–3, also cited *Grammar Schools*, p. 95; John Locke, *Some Thoughts Concerning Education*, 16, pp. 138–9, 170–1, 174–5.

20. *New Trends*, pp. 63–116, *passim*; Derek Robson, *Some Aspects of. Education in Cheshire in the Eighteenth Century*, Chetham Society, 1966, pp. 76–7; *Poetical Blossoms*, 1766, contains this advertisement which is cited in *New Trends*, p. 92.

21. *Education in Cheshire*, pp. 80–1.

22. Ibid., p. 83; Thomas Kelly, *A History of Adult Education in Great Britain*, University of Liverpool Press, 1970, pp. 99–100.

23. W. Brockbank and F. Kenworthy (eds), *The Diary of Richard Kay, 1716–1751*, Chetham Society, 1968, pp. 58, 14, 42, 52, 61, 63.

24. *Adult Education*, pp. 103, 105–7, 109–11.

25. Irene Parker, *Dissenting Academies in England*, New York, 1969 edn. Charles Webster, *The Great Instauration*, Duckworth, 1975, *passim*.
26. This section is based upon the structure given in *Dissenting Academies*, *passim*.

Chapter 12: Education for Scottish society, 1450–1800

1. James Scotland, *The History of Scottish Education*, 2 vols, 1969, I, pp. 11–15, 17.
2. Alexander Morgan, *Scottish University Studies*, Oxford University Press, 1933, pp. 157–60; William Watt, 'Scottish Masters and Students at Paris in the Fourteenth Century', *A.U.R.*, 1955, p. 170; *Scottish Education*, pp. 24–36; 'Scottish Masters and Students', pp. 172–3; Robert Rait, 'The Place of Aberdeen in Scottish Academic History', *A.U.R.*, 1933, p. 107; James Grant, *The Burgh Schools of Scotland*, Glasgow, 1896, pp. 14–17.
3. John Stuart (ed.), *Extracts from the Council Register of the Burgh of Aberdeen, 1643–1747*, Scottish Burgh Records Society, 1830, I, p. 107; J. D. Marwick (ed.), *Charters of the City of Glasgow, 1175–1649*, Edinburgh, 1894, p. 89, cited in *Scottish Education*, p. 14; *Burgh Schools*, p. 33; *Scottish Education*, pp. 43–4, 45, 48, 37–9.
4. G. Donaldson, *The Scottish Reformation*, Cambridge University Press, 1960; J. L. Ainslie, *The Doctrines of the Ministerial Order in the Reformed Churches of the Sixteenth and Seventeenth Centuries*, Edinburgh University Press, 1940, *passim*; William Croft Dickinson (ed.), John Knox's *History of the Reformation in Scotland*, 2 vols, 1849, Appendix 8, pp. 296–7; David Laing (ed.), *The Works of John Knox*, 6 vols., Edinburgh, 1846–64, IV, pp. 1555–8; John Knox, *Brief Declaration to England*, 1556; Alexander Law, *Education in Edinburgh in the Eighteenth Century*, Athlone, 1965, pp. 1–15.
5. *Scottish Education*, pp. 44–8, exaggerates its democratic properties; *History of the Reformation in Scotland*, p. 296.
6. *Scottish Education*, pp. 46–8.
7. Ibid., p. 48.
8. Ibid., pp. 49, 51.
9. Ibid., pp. 49–52.
10. A. D. Wright 'The People of Catholic Europe and the People of Anglican England', *H. J.*, 1975, *passim*.
11. See pp. 97–9; *Scottish Education*, pp. 47–8; *Scottish University Studies*, *passim*.
12. *Scottish Education*, pp. 52–3; Ian J. Simpson, *Education in Aberdeenshire before 1872*, University of London Press, 1947, pp. 16–21; *Reports on the State of Certain Parishes in Scotland made to H. M. Commissioners in 1627*, Edinburgh, 1835, pp. 2, 10, 54–5, 76, 84, 106.
13. *Burgh Schools*, p. 79; *The New Statistical Account of Scotland, by the Ministers of the Respective Parishes*, 15 vols, Edinburgh, 1845, IX, Dunino; *Scottish Education*, pp. 49, 50, 53; *Education in Edinburgh*, p. 15.
14. *Burgh Schools*, pp. 308–9.
15. *Scottish Education*, p. 49.

16. Ibid., pp. 76–80.
17. N. T. Phillipson, 'Culture and Society in the Eighteenth Century Province: The Case of Edinburgh and the Scottish Enlightenment', in L. Stone (ed.), *The University in Society*, 2 vols, Princeton University Press, 1974, II, pp. 408–9, 412–20.
18. Ibid.; Donald J. Withrington, 'Education and Society in the Eighteenth Century', in N. T. Phillipson and Rosalind Mitchison (eds), *Scotland in the Age of Improvement*, Edinburgh University Press, 1970.
19. *Scottish Education*, pp. 102–3.
20. 'Education and Society', p. 169; *Education in Edinburgh*, pp. 167 seq.
21. 'Education and Society', pp. 169–70; *Education in Edinburgh*, pp. 144; *Scottish Education*, pp. 103–6.
22. *Education in Edinburgh*, p. 144 seq.
23. 'Education and Society', p. 187; *Scottish Education*, p. 106.
24. 'Culture and Society', *passim*.
25. *Education in Edinburgh*,
26. Ibid., pp. 157 seq.

Chapter 13: Education and the problem of poverty

1. For a good discussion of the problem of poverty in Early Modern England see Paul Slack, *Social Problems and Social Policies*, Open University Course, A322, *English Urban History, 1500–1780*, Milton Keynes, 1977.
2. Anthony Salerno, 'The Social Background of Seventeenth Century Emigrants to America', *J. B. S*, 1979, *passim*.
3. W. K. Jordan, *Philanthropy in England, 1480–1660*, Allen & Unwin, 1959, p. 140; W. T. MacCaffrey, *Exeter, 1540–1640*, Harvard University Press, 1975, Chapter 4, part iii, analysed in *Social Problems and Policies*.
4. *S. R.*, 14 Eliz. I, c. 5; 39 Eliz. I, c. 3; 43 Eliz. I, c. 2; I. Pinchbeck and M. Hewitt, *Children in English Society*, Routledge & Kegan Paul, 1969, I, pp. 97–8; P. Styles, 'The Evolution of the Law of Settlement', *U.B.H.J.*, 1963, pp. 33–63, *passim*.
5. Thomas Starkey, *Dialogue*, 1533–36, ed. K. M. Burton, London, 1948, p. 89.
6. J. L. Vives, *On the Relief of the Poor*, 1524, printed in F. Salter (ed.), *Some Early Tracts on Poor Relief*, Methuen, 1926, p. 32.
7. Gerald Strauss, *Luther's House of Learning*, Johns Hopkins University Press, 1978, p. 13.
8. *Children in English Society*, pp. 94 ff.; *S. R.*, 22 Henry VIII, c. 12; 27 Henry VIII, c. 25; 1 Edward VI, c. 3; 3 & 4 Edward VI, c. 16; 43 Eliz. I, c. 2.
9. Fleetwood to Burghley, 1585, in B. L. Lansd. MSS no. 44, pt 38; R. H. Tawney and Eileen Power, *Tudor Economic Documents*, Longman, Green & Co., 1951, II, pp. 337–8; *Children in English Society*, p. 102.
10. *Children in English Society*, pp. 127–9.
11. E. H. Pearce, *Annals of Christ's Hospital*, London, 1908, pp. 20–1; C. L. Kingsford (ed.), John Stowe's *Survey of London*, 2 vols, 1908, I, p. 319; *Children in English Society*, p. 129.

12. *Christ's Hospital*, pp. 35–8; *Children in English Society*, pp. 131–3.
13. W. Hudson and J. C. Tingey (eds), *The Records of the City of Norwich*, 2 vols, 1910, II, pp. 344–7, 352–6; also cited in *Children in English Society*, pp. 133–5.
14. *S. R.*, 14 Eliz. I, c. 5; *Children in English Society*, pp. 143–4; E. M. Leonard, *The Early History of English Poor Relief*, Cambridge University Press, 1900, pp. 242–4.
15. *Children in English Society*, pp. 147–8; John Locke, *Report to the Board of Trade*, 1697.
16. *Children in English Society*, pp. 149–53, discussing *An Account of the General Nursery, or Colledge of Infants, set up by the J. P.s of the County of Middlesex*, 1686.
17. *Children in English Society*, pp. 153–60.
18. *Children in English Society*, p. 168; see also *Rules and Orders to be Observed by the Officers and Servants in St Giles Workhouse and by the poor therein*, 1726, pp. 7–11.
19. Jonas Hanaway, *Serious Considerations on the Salutary Design of the Act of Parliament for a regular, uniform Register of the Parish Poor in all the parishes within the Bills of Mortality*, 1762, p. 10; and *An Earnest Appeal for Mercy to the Children of the Poor*, 1766, pp. 41–3.
20. *Journal of the House of Commons*, 31, 1767, p. 248; *S. R.*, 7 George III, c. 39; examples taken from *Children in English Society*, pp. 193–4.
21. James Scotland, *The History of Scottish Education*, 2 vols, University of London Press, 1969, pp. 102–3, 97–102; Irene F. M. Dean, *Scottish Spinning Schools*, 1930, pp. 118–19, 43.
22. Alexander Law, *Education in Edinburgh in the Eighteenth Century*, Athlone, 1965, pp. 36–7; S. S. P. C. K., 30 Nov. 1758, cited in above, p. 37.
23. Ibid., pp. 41–7; 54–7.
24. M. G. Jones, *The Charity School Movement: A Study of Eighteenth-Century Puritanism in Action*, Cambridge University Press, 1938; Joan Simon, 'Was there a Charity School Movement?' in Brian Simon (ed.), *Education in Leicestershire: A Regional Study*, Leicester University Press, 1968, pp. 55–100; Derek Robson, *Some Aspects of Education in Cheshire in the Eighteenth Century*, Chetham Society, 1966, pp. 17–43; *Education in Edinburgh*, pp. 47–54.
25. *Children in English Society*, pp. 288–91.
26. *Education in Cheshire*, pp. 24–5; *Education in Edinburgh*, p. 37.
27. *Education in Cheshire*, pp. 20–1; 'Was there a Charity School movement?', pp. 56–9.
28. T. W. Laqueur, *Religion and Respectability: Sunday Schools and Working Class Culture, 1780–1850*, Yale University Press, 1976, pp. 24, 25, 21, 10, 6, 30–2.
29. E. A. Smith and A. Aspinall (eds), *English Historical Documents, 1783–1832*, Eyre & Spottiswoode, 1959, pp. 706–7, Document 469, Hannah More to the Bishop of Bath and Wells, 1801.
30. *Religion and Respectability*, pp. 86–7, 53, 42, 61, xi.
31. Ibid., pp. 24–5; *English Historical Documents*, pp. 706–7.
32. Rev. Daniel Turner, *Hints on Religious Education, Being Two Sermons in Favour of Sunday Schools*, 1794, pp. 9–10; *Religion and Respectability*, pp. 11–17.

Chapter 14: Traditional educational institutions and society, 1640–1800

1. G. Mingay, *English Landed Society in the Eighteenth Century*, Routledge & Kegan Paul, 1963, *passim*.
2. This section is based upon Charles Webster, *The Great Instauration*, Duckworth, 1975, pp. 19–27, 32–44, 44–7; R. L. Greaves, *The Puritan Revolution and Educational Thought*, Rutgers University Press, 1969, pp. 26–47; I. R. Adamson, 'The Administration of Gresham College and its Fluctuating Fortunes as a Scientific Institution in the Seventeenth Century', *History of Education*, 1980, pp. 13–25.
3. Mark Curtis, *Oxford and Cambridge in Transition*, Oxford University Press, 1959, pp. 227–60; Barbara Shapiro, 'The Universities and Science in Seventeenth Century England', in *J.B.S.*, 1971, pp. 47–82; *Great Instauration*, pp. 122–9; C. J. Scriba, 'The Autobiography of John Wallis', *Notes and Records of the Royal Society*, 1970, also cited *Great Instauration*, p. 120; Walter Pope, *The Life of the Right Reverend Father of God, Seth, Lord Bishop of Salisbury*, 1697; P. Allen, 'Scientific Studies in the English Universities of the Seventeenth Century', *J.H.I.*, 1949, pp. 219–53.
4. Christopher Hill, *Intellectual Origins of the English Revolution*, Oxford University Press, 1965, pp. 14–84.
5. *Great Instauration*, pp. 153–78, 144–53.
6. Ibid.
7. *Puritan Revolution*, pp. 63–92; Seth Ward, *Vindiciae Academiarum*, Oxford, 1654, p. 50; *Great Instauration*, pp. 183–4; with the exception of Dell, see following paragraph.
8. *Great Instauration*, pp. 190–1, 193; John Hall, *An Humble Motion to the Parliament of England Concerning the Advancement of Learning and the Reformation of the Universities*, 1649; Noah Biggs, *Mataeotechnia Medicinae Praxeos. The Variety of the Craft of Physick. Or, a New Dispensatory*.
9. *Great Instauration*, pp. 210–42.
10. *Puritan Revolution*, p. 56; *Great Instauration*, pp. 225–31; J. P. Mahaffy, *An Epoch in Irish History, Trinity College Dublin*, Dublin, 1903, pp. 293–324; An Act for the Better Advancement of the Gospel and Learning in Ireland, *Firth & Rait*, II, pp. 355–7.
11. *Great Instauration*, pp. 232–42, gives a detailed account of the founding of Durham College. See also G. H. Turnbull, 'Oliver Cromwell's College at Durham', *Durham Research Review*, 1952, pp. 1–7; C. D. R. Ransom, *Oliver Cromwell's College at Durham*, Durham, 1913 C.J. vi, pp. 389, 410, 489–90; *Ephemerides*, 1655, 1656, 1657.
12. *Great Instauration*, pp. 242–5.
13. See pp. 196–8; Lawrence Stone, '"The Size and Social Composition of the Oxford Student Body', in L. Stone (ed.), *The University in Society*, 2 vols., Princeton University Press, 1974, pp. 42–3.
14. The following analysis is based upon C. Arnold Anderson and Miriam Schaper, *School and Society in England: Social Backgrounds of Oxford and Cambridge Students*, Annals of American Research, Public Affairs Press, Washington D. C., 1952.
15. R. G. Wilson, *Gentlemen Merchants*, Manchester University Press,

308   *Education and Society 1500–1800*

1971: Gordon Jackson, *Hull in the Eighteenth Century*, Oxford University Press with University of Hull Press.
16. W. M. Matthew, 'The Origins and Occupations of Glasgow Students, 1740–1839', *P. & P.*, 1966, p. 76; Nicholas Hans, *New Trends in Education in the Eighteenth Century*, Routledge & Kegan Paul, 1951, p. 24; R. I. James, 'Bristol Society in the Eighteenth Century', in C. M. MacInnes and W. F. Whittard (eds), *Bristol and Its Adjoining Counties*, Bristol, 1955.
17. *New Trends*, p. 53.
18. Ibid., pp. 47–53.
19. Ibid., p. 53.
20. Ibid., p. 50.
21. W. Brockbank and F. Kenworthy (eds), *The Diary of Richard Kay, 1716–1751*, Chetham Society, 1968, pp. 26, 42, 61–2, 63, 66, 83, 89.
22. James Scotland, *A History of Scottish Education*, 2 vols, 1969, I.
23. James Coutts, *History of the University of Glasgow, 1451–1909*, Glasgow, 1909, p. 173; John Durkan and James Kirk, *The University of Glasgow, 1451–1577*, University of Glasgow Press, 1977, pp. 328–30, describes the difficulties which Glasgow and St Andrew's experienced in setting up faculties of medicine; Alexander Morgan, *Scottish University Studies*, Oxford University Press, 1933, p. 117.
24. *Scottish University Studies*, pp. 118–19, citing *The Report of the Royal Commission of 1826*, p. 412; also p. 116; John Duffy, *The Healers*, Illini Books, 1976, p. 92; Vanessa S. Doe (ed.), *The Diary of James Clegg of Chapel en le Frith, 1708–1755*, Derbyshire Record Society, 1978, pp. 46, 55, 71, 73.
25. Sheldon Rothblatt, 'The Student Sub-culture and the Examination System in Early Nineteenth Century Oxbridge' in L. Stone (ed.), *The University in Society*, 2 vols, Princeton University Press, 1974, II. Dame Lucy Sutherland, 'The University of Oxford in the Eighteenth Century', James Bryce Memorial Lecture, Oxford, 1973, *passim*.
26. 'Glasgow Students', pp. 77, 80–1.
27. Ibid., pp. 83, 87, Matthew gives 0% going into business from Cambridge; Anderson and Schaper give 3%, p. 85.
28. Alexander Law, *Education in Edinburgh in the Eighteenth Century*, Athlone, 1965, pp. 22–5; I. Kenrick, 'The University of Edinburgh, 1660–1715. A Study of the Transformation of Teaching Methods and Curriculum', unpublished PhD thesis, Bryn Mawr, 1956; N. T. Phillipson, 'Culture and Society in the Eighteenth Century Province: The Case of Edinburgh and the Scottish Enlightenment', in L. Stone (ed.), *The University in Society*, 2 vols, Princeton University Press, 1974, II, pp. 426–9.
29. Morgan, *Scottish University Studies*, pp. 76–7.
30. *Scottish University Studies*, pp. 76–7; 'Culture and Society', p. 440; *Education in Edinburgh*, pp. 25, 165; Donald J. Withrington, 'Education and Society in the Eighteenth Century', in N. T. Phillipson and Rosalind Mitchison (eds), *Scotland in the Age of Improvement*, Edinburgh University Press, 1970, p. 187; *Scottish Education, passim*.
31. 'Education and Society', pp. 185–6.
32. Ibid.

Select bibliography for further reading

Child and family (For Girls see separate section)

Philippe Ariès, *Centuries of Childhood*, Penguin, 1973.
Walter Arnstein, 'Reflections on the History of Childhood', in Selma K. Richardson (ed.), *Research about Nineteenth Century Children and Books*, University of Illinois Graduate School of Library Science, Monograph 17, 1980.
B. M. Berry, 'The First English Pediatricians and Tudor Attitudes towards Childhood', J. H. I. 1974.
Lloyd De Mause, 'The Evolution of Childhood', in *The History of Childhood*, Psychology Press, 1974.
M. King-Hall, *The Story of the Nursery*, Routledge & Kegan Paul, 1958.
Alan Macfarlane, *The Family Life of Ralph Josselin*, Cambridge University Press, 1970.
Alan Macfarlane, Review article, *History and Theory*, 1979.
Ivy Pinchbeck and Margaret Hewitt, *Children in English Society*, Routledge & Kegan Paul, vol.I, 1969; vol.II, 1973.
Lawrence Stone, *The Family, Sex and Marriage in England, 1500–1800*, Weidenfeld & Nicolson, 1977. See this also for girls' discipline, independence.
Keith Thomas, 'The Changing Family', *Times Literary Supplement*, 21 October 1977.
M. J. Tucker, 'The Child as Beginning and End', in *The History of Childhood*, Psychology Press, 1974.

Adolescence and youth

J. R. Gillis *Youth and History: Tradition and Change in European Relations, 1770–Present*, Academic Press, 1974.
Steven R. Smith, 'The London Apprentices as Seventeenth-Century Adolescents', *P. & P.*, 1973.
Steven R. Smith, 'Religion and the Conception of Youth in the Seventeenth Century', H. C. Q., 1975.
Ann Yarborough, 'Apprentices as Adolescents in Sixteenth-Century Bristol', *Journal of Social History*, 1979.

Literacy and books

J. W. Adamson, *The Illiterate Anglo-Saxon*, Cambridge University Press, 1946.

Margaret Aston, 'Lollardy and Literacy', *History* **62**, 1977.

H. S. Bennett, *English Books and Readers*, 3 vols, Cambridge University Press, 1969, 1965, 1970.

Carlo M. Cipolla, *Literacy and Development in the West*, Penguin, 1969.

Peter Clark, 'The Ownership of Books in England, 1560–1640' in **L. Stone** (ed.), *Schooling and Society*, Johns Hopkins University Press, 1976.

David Cressy, *Literacy and the Social Order*, Cambridge University Press, 1980.

David Cressy, 'Educational Opportunity in Tudor and Stuart England', *History of Education Quarterly*, **16**, 1976.

David Cressy, 'Levels of Illiteracy in England, 1530–1730', *H. J.*, 1977.

David Cressy, 'Occupations, Migration and Literacy in East London, 1580–1640', *Local Population Studies*, 1970.

Elizabeth L. Eisenstein, *The Printing Press as an Agent of Change*, Cambridge University Press, 1979.

Thomas Laqueur, 'The cultural origins of popular literacy in England, 1500–1850', *Oxford Review of Education*, 1976.

Victor E. Neuburg, *Popular Literature, a history and guide*, *Penguin, 1977*.

R. S. Schofield, 'The measurement of literacy in pre-industrial England' in Jack Goody (ed.), *Literacy in Traditional Societies*, Cambridge University Press, 1968.

Herbert C. Schulz, 'The Teaching of Handwriting in Tudor and Stuart Times', *Huntington Library Quarterly*, 1943.

Margaret Spufford, 'First Steps in Literacy: the reading and writing experiences of the humblest seventeenth-century spiritual autobiographers', *Journal of Social History*, 1979. Also useful for schooling and attitudes to children.

Richard T. Vann, 'Literacy in Seventeenth Century England: some hearth tax evidence', *Journal of Interdisciplinary History*, 1974.

Formal schooling

N. Carlisle, *Endowed Grammar Schools in England and Wales*, London, 1818.

Kenneth Charlton, *Education in Renaissance England*, Routledge & Kegan Paul, 1965. Useful also for textbooks and curricula.

A. J. Fletcher, 'The Expansion of Education in Berkshire and Oxfordshire' 1500–1670 B. J. E. S., 1967.

Nicholas Hans, *New Trends in Education in the Eighteenth Century*, Routledge & Kegan Paul, 1951. Also useful for girls' education and for the place of science in education.

Rosemary O'Day, 'Church Records and the History of Education, in Early Modern England, 1558–1642: A Problem in Methodology, *History of Education*, 1973.

Nicholas Orme, *English Schools in the Middle Ages*, Methuen, 1973.

Irene Parker, *Dissenting Academies in England*, New York, 1969.

Brian Simon, 'Leicestershire Schools, 1625–1640', *B. J. E. S.*, 1954.

Joan Simon, *Education and Society in Tudor England*, Cambridge University Press, 1967.

Joan Simon, 'Town Estates and Schools in the Sixteenth and Early Seventeenth Centuries' in Brian Simon (ed.), *Education in Leicestershire: A Regional Study, 1540–1940*, Leicester University Press, 1968.

Joan Simon, 'Private Classical Schools in Eighteenth Century England: a critique of Hans', *History of Education*, 1979.

Alan Smith, 'Endowed Schools in the Diocese of Lichfield and Coventry, 1660–1699', *History of Education*, 1975.

Alan Smith, 'Private Schools and Schoolmasters in the Diocese of Lichfield and Coventry in the Seventeenth Century', *History of Education*, 1976.

Margaret Spufford, 'The Schooling of the Peasantry in Cambridgeshire, 1575–1700', *Agr. H. Rev.*, 1970, Supplement.

Lawrence Stone, 'Literacy and Education in England, 1640–1900', *P. & P.*, 1969.

K. V. Thomas, 'Rule and Misrule in the Schools of Early Modern England', The Stenton Lecture, 1975, *University of Reading*, 1976.

Richard Tompson, *Classics or Charity?*, Manchester University Press, 1971.

W. A. L. Vincent, *The State and School Education in England and Wales, 1640–1660*, Church Historical Society, S.P.C.K., 1950.

W. A. L. Vincent, *The Grammar Schools: their continuing tradition, 1660–1714*, John Murray, 1969.

M. V. Wallbank, 'Eighteenth Century Public Schools and the Education of the Governing Elite', *History of Education*, 1978.

Curriculum and method

Frank Davies *The Teaching of Reading in Early England*, Pitman, 1973.

Foster Watson, *The Beginning of the Teaching of Modern Subjects in England*, reprinted S.R. Publishers, 1971. First published Pitmans 1909.

Foster Watson, 'The Curriculum and textbooks of English schools in

312   *Education and Society 1500–1800*

the first half of the seventeenth century', *Transactions of the Bib-liographical Society*, VI, 1901.

Theory

G. H. Bantock, *Studies in the History of Educational Theory, Vol. I, 1350–1765*, Allen & Unwin, 1980.

Adult education

Thomas Kelly, *A History of Adult Education in Great Britain*, University of Liverpool Press, 1970.

University education

C. Arnold Anderson and Miriam Schaper, *School and Society in England: Social Backgrounds of Oxford and Cambridge students* Annals of American Research, Public Affairs Press, Washington D.C. 1952.

T. H. Aston, 'Oxford's Medieval Alumni', *P. & P., 1977*.

T. H. Aston, G. O. Duncan and **T. A. R. Evans**, 'The Medieval Alumni of the University of Cambridge', *P. & P.*, 1980.

A. B. Cobban, *The Medieval Universities, their Development and Organization*, Methuen, 1975.

W. T. Costello, *The Scholastic Curriculum at Early Seventeenth Century Cambridge*, Harvard University Press, 1958.

Mark H. Curtis, *Oxford and Cambridge in Transition*, Oxford University Press, 1959.

Mark H. Curtis, 'The Alienated Intellectuals of Early Stuart England', in Trevor Aston (ed.), *Crisis in Europe, P. & P.*, 1965.

R. L. Greaves, *The Puritan Revolution and Educational Thought*, Rutgers University Press, 1969.

Vivian Green, *The Commonwealth of Lincoln College, 1427–1977*, Oxford University Press, 1979.

Hugh Kearney, *Scholars and Gentlemen: Universities and Society*, Faber & Faber, 1970.

J. H. Hexter, 'The Education of the Aristocracy in the Renaissance', in *Reappraisals in History*, Longman, 1963.

N. R. Ker, 'Oxford College Libraries in the Sixteenth Century', *Bodleian Library Record*, 1957–61.

James McConica, 'Humanism and Aristotle in Tudor Oxford', *E.H.R.*, 1979.

James McConica, 'Scholars and Commoners in Renaissance Oxford', in L. Stone (ed.), *The University in Society*, vol.I, Princeton University Press, 1974.

R. B. McDowell and D. A. Webb, 'Courses and Teaching at Trinity College, Dublin during the first 200 years', *Hermathena*, 1947.

Clara P. McMahon, *Education in Fifteenth Century England*, Johns Hopkins University Press, 1968. Also useful for schooling.

C. E. Mallett, *A History of the University of Oxford*, 2 vols, Methuen, 1924.

W. M. Matthew, 'The Origins and Occupations of Glasgow Students, 1740–1839', *P. & P.*, 1966.

Alexander Morgan, *Scottish University Studies*, Oxford University Press, 1933.

Victor Morgan, 'Cambridge University and the "Country"' in L. Stone (ed.), *The University in Society*, vol. I, Princeton University Press, 1974.

J. B. Mullinger, *The University of Cambridge*, 3 vols, 1873–1911.

N. T. Phillipson, 'Culture and Society in the Eighteenth-Century Province. The Case of Edinburgh and the Scottish Enlightenment' in L. Stone (ed.), *The University in Society*, vol. II, Princeton University Press, 1974.

H. C. Porter, *Puritanism in Tudor England*, Macmillan, 1971.

Sheldon Rothblatt, 'The Student Sub-culture and the Examination System in Early Nineteenth-Century Oxbridge' in L. Stone (ed.), *The University in Society*, vol. II, Princeton University Press, 1974.

Elizabeth Russell, 'The Influx of Commoners into the University of Oxford before 1581, an optical illusion', *E.H.R.*, **92**, 1977.

Joan Simon, 'The Social Origins of Cambridge Students, 1603–1640', *P. & P.*, 1963.

Lawrence Stone, 'The Educational Revolution in England, 1560–1640', *P. & P.*, 1964.

Lawrence Stone, 'The Size and Social Composition of the Oxford Student Body, 1580–1910' in L. Stone (ed.), in *The University in Society*, vol. I, Princeton University Press, 1974.

Dame Lucy Sutherland, 'The University of Oxford in the Eighteenth Century', *James Bryce Memorial Lecture*, published Oxford, 1973.

Scotland

James Grant, *The Burgh Schools of Scotland*, Glasgow, 1896.

Alexander Law, *Education in Edinburgh in the Eighteenth Century*, Athlone, 1965.

James Scotland, *The History of Scottish Education*, 2 vols, University of London Press, 1969.

Donald J. Withrington, 'Education and Society in the Eighteenth Century' in N.T. Phillipson and R. Mitchison (eds), *Scotland in the Age of Improvement*, Edinburgh University Press 1971.

Girls (see under 'Child and family')

Dorothy Gardiner, *English Girlhood at School*, Oxford University Press, 1929.
Derek Robson, *Some Aspects of Education in Cheshire in the Eighteenth Century*, Chetham Society, 1966.
Hilda Smith, *Reason's Disciples*, forthcoming from University of Illinois Press.

The Poor

M. G. Jones, *The Charity School Movement: A Study of Eighteenth-Century Puritanism in Action*, Cambridge University Press, 1938.
W. K. Jordan, *Philanthropy in England, 1480–1660*, Allen & Unwin, 1959.
W. K. Jordan, *The Charities of Rural England*, Allen & Unwin, 1961.
T. W. Laqueur, *Religion and Respectability: Sunday Schools and Working Class Culture, 1780–1850*, Yale University Press, 1976.
Joan Simon, 'Was there a Charity School Movement?' in Brian Simon (ed.), *Education in Leicestershire: A Regional Study, 1540 1974*. Leicester University Press, 1968.

The clergy of the Church of England

Rosemary O'Day, *The English Clergy, 1560–1640*, Leicester University Press, 1979.
John Pruett, *The Parish Clergy under the Later Stuarts*, University of Illinois Press, 1978.

The barrister

Lewis Abbott, *Law Reporting in England, 1485–1585*, Athlone, 1973.
R. M. Fisher, 'Thomas Cromwell, Humanism and Educational Reform', *B.I.H.R.*, 1977.
Louis Knafla, 'The Law Studies of an Elizabethan Student', *H.I.Q.*, 1969.
Wilfrid Prest, *The Inns of Court*, Longman, 1972.

Attorneys

C. W. Brooks, 'The Common Lawyers in England, c.1558–1642' in Wilfrid Prest (ed.), *Lawyers in Early Modern Europe and America*, Croom Helm, 1981.

Teachers

Kenneth Charlton, 'The Professions in Sixteenth Century England', *U.B.H.J.*, 1967.
Kenneth Charlton, 'The Teaching Profession in Sixteenth and Seventeenth Century England' in P. Nash (ed.), *History and Education*, Random House, 1970.
Richard L. DeMolen, 'Richard Mulcaster and the Profession of Teaching in Sixteenth Century England', *J.H.I.*, 1974.
Patrick Orpen, 'Schoolmastering as a Profession in the Seventeenth Century: the career patterns of the grammar schoolmaster, *History of Education*, 1977.

Short list of useful printed sources

Roger Ascham, *The Scholemaster*, 1570.
Hugh Aveling and W. A. Pantin (eds), *The Letter Book of Robert Joseph, 1530–1533*, Oxford Historical Society, NS **19** 1967 (for 1964).
Richard Baxter, *Reliquiae Baxterianae*, 1696.
Elisabeth Bourcier, *The Diary of Sir Simonds D'Ewes, 1622–24*.
John Brinsley, *Ludus Literarius or the Grammar School*, 1612.
W. Brockbank and F. Kenworthy (eds), *The Diary of Richard Kay, 1716–1751*, Chetham Society, 1968.
J. P. Cooper (ed.), *Wentworth Papers, 1597–1628*, Camden Series, 1973.
Vanessa S. Doe (ed.), *The Diary of James Clegg of Chapel en le Frith, 1708–1755*, Derbyshire Record Society, 1978.
Levi Fox (ed.), *Correspondence of the Reverend Joseph Greene, Parson, Schoolmaster and Antiquary, 1712–1790*, Dugdale Society and Historical Manuscripts Commission Joint Publication, 1965.
E. Gibbon, *Autobiography of the Life of Edward Gibbon...*, 1900.
J. O. Halliwell (ed.), *The Autobiography and Correspondence of Sir Simonds D'Ewes*, 2 vols, London, 1845.
Thomas Heywood (ed.), *The Diary of Henry Newcome, 1661–1663*, Chetham Society, 1849.
Charles Jackson (ed.), *Autobiography of Mrs Alice Thornton*, Surtees Society, 1875.

Charles Jackson (ed.), Life of John Shaw in *Yorkshire Diaries*, Surtees Society, 1877 (for 1875).
S. Lee (ed.), *Autobiography of Lord Herbert of Cherbury*, 1907.
Alan Macfarlane (ed.), *The Diary of Ralph Josselin*, British Academy, 1976.
John Marshall (ed.), *The Diary of William Stout of Lancaster*, Chetham Society, 1967.
H. J. Morehouse (ed.), A Dyurnall, or catalogue of all my accions and expences from the 1st of January 1646–7 (Adam Eyre), in *Yorkshire Diaries*, Surtees Society, 1877 (for 1875).
Richard Mulcaster, *Positions, . . . The Training up of Children*, 1581.
Richard Mulcaster, *The First Part of the Elementarie*, 1582.
Richard Parkinson (ed.), *Life of Adam Martindale*, Chetham Society, 1845.
Edward J. L. Scott (ed.), *Letter-book of Gabriel Harvey, 1573–1580*, Camden Society, 1884.
R. P. Sorlien, *The Diary of John Manningham of the Middle Temple, 1602–1603*, University of Rhode Island Press, 1976.

Bibliographies

There is no full-scale bibliography of the history of education in Great Britain, 1500–1800. The following lists are useful for old school histories:
W. E. Tate, 'Sources for the Histories of the English Grammar School', *B.J.E.S.*, 1953–54.
P. J. Wallis, 'Histories of Old Schools: A Preliminary List for England and Wales', *B.J.E.S.*, 1965, 1966.
The best critical bibliography, unfortunately covering the Tudor period only, appears in **Joan Simon**, *Education and Society in Tudor England*, Cambridge University Press, 1967.
Good bibliographies of printed sources and secondary materials appear in the two volumes of **Ivy Pinchbeck and Margaret Hewitt**, *Children in English Society*, Routledge & Kegan Paul, 1969, 1973.

Index